DAVID BUSCH'S
SONY® α a7R III
GUIDE TO DIGITAL PHOTOGRAPHY

David D. Busch

rockynook

David Busch's Sony® α a7R III
Guide to Digital Photography

Project Manager: Jenny Davidson
Series Technical Editor: Michael D. Sullivan
Layout: Bill Hartman
Cover Design: Mike Tanamachi
Indexer: Valerie Haynes Perry
Proofreader: Mike Beady

ISBN: 978-1-68198-379-0
1st Edition (2nd printing, February 2021)

Rocky Nook, Inc.
1010 B Street, Suite 350
San Rafael, CA 94901
USA
www.rockynook.com

Distributed in the UK and Europe by Publishers Group UK
Distributed in the U.S. and all other territories by Ingram Publisher Services

Library of Congress Control Number: 2017959869

For Cathy

Acknowledgments

Thanks to everyone at Rocky Nook, including Scott Cowlin, managing director and publisher, for the freedom to let me explore the amazing capabilities of the Sony a7R III in depth. I couldn't do it without my veteran production team, including project manager, Jenny Davidson and series technical editor, Mike Sullivan. Also, thanks to Bill Hartman, layout; Valerie Hayes Perry, indexing; Mike Beady, proofreading; Mike Tanamachi, cover design; and my agent, Carole Jelen, who has the amazing ability to keep both publishers and authors happy.

About the Author

With more than 2.5 million books in print, **David D. Busch** is the world's #1 bestselling camera guide author, and the originator of popular series like *David Busch's Pro Secrets, David Busch's Compact Field Guides,* and *David Busch's Quick Snap Guides.* He has written more than 50 hugely successful guidebooks for Sony and other digital SLR models, including the all-time #1 bestsellers for several different cameras, as well as many popular books devoted to photography, including *Mastering Mirrorless Photography.* As a roving photojournalist for more than 20 years, he illustrated his books, magazine articles, and newspaper reports with award-winning images. He's operated his own commercial studio, suffocated in formal dress while shooting weddings, and shot sports for a daily newspaper and an upstate New York college. His photos and articles have appeared in *Popular Photography, Rangefinder, Professional Photographer*, and hundreds of other publications. He's also reviewed dozens of digital cameras for CNet and other CBS publications.

When About.com named its top five books on Beginning Digital Photography, debuting at the #1 and #2 slots were Busch's *Digital Photography All-In-One Desk Reference for Dummies* and *Mastering Digital Photography.* He has had as many as 18 books listed in the Top 100 of Amazon.com's Digital Photography Bestseller list—simultaneously! Busch's 250-plus other books published since 1983 include bestsellers like *Digital SLR Cameras and Photography for Dummies.*

Busch is a member of the Cleveland Photographic Society (www.clevelandphoto.org), which has operated continuously since 1887. Visit his website at http://www.sonyguides.com.

Contents

Chapter 3
Camera Settings I Menu 51

Chapter 4
Camera Settings II Menu

Chapter 5
Network and Playback Menus   155

Chapter 6
Setup and My Menus   179

Chapter 7
Nailing the Optimum Exposure   205

Chapter 8
Mastering Autofocus Options   249

Chapter 9
Advanced Techniques 273

Chapter 10
Movie-Making Basics 293

Chapter 11
Advanced Video Features   317

Chapter 12
Choosing and Using Lenses   329

Chapter 13
Working with Flash   365

Chapter 14
Troubleshooting and Prevention   395

Index   413

Preface

The Sony a7R III, the latest edition of the company's high-resolution full-frame camera, is the most versatile E-mount mirrorless model the company has ever offered. Its 42 megapixels offer enough resolution to satisfy the most discerning landscape, commercial, or portrait photographer's needs, and it can fire off continuous bursts at a 10-frames-per-second rate that make it a sports photographer's dream. With advanced autofocus, five-axis anti-shake image stabilization built into the camera body, and 4K video capabilities, the a7R III comes close to being a "do-everything" model that is a jack of all trades—and master of them, as well.

In a few short years, Sony has gone from being a Nikon and Canon competitor that offered warmed-over Konica Minolta digital camera technology, to an acknowledged innovator with a lineup of cameras that are smaller, lighter, faster to focus, and loaded with cutting-edge features that many of us have been dreaming about. So, it's no wonder you're excited about your new Sony a7R III. With all these features at your disposal, you don't expect to take good pictures with such a camera—you demand and anticipate *outstanding* photos.

Unfortunately, your gateway to pixel proficiency is dragged down by the limited instructions provided by Sony. Over the years, Sony has reduced the amount of useful information included in its printed guidebooks, often to a scant 100 pages or so, and relegated more detailed instructions to online HTML-based guides and PDF versions that are difficult to navigate. And, sad to say, not everything you need to know is included.

What you really need is a guide that explains the purpose and function of the cameras' basic controls, how you should use them, and *why*. That's what I am giving you in this book. If you want a quick introduction to focus controls, flash synchronization options, how to choose lenses, or which exposure modes are best, this book is for you. If you can't decide on what basic settings to use with your camera because you can't figure out how changing ISO or white balance or focus defaults will affect your pictures, you need this guide.

Introduction

With the a7R III, Sony has packaged up the most alluring features of advanced digital SLRs and stuffed them into a compact, fully featured body, which boasts at least a few capabilities you won't find in cameras from other vendors. They include a new Pixel Shift capability, which captures four different images, each displaced from the last by a single pixel, and which are then combined in the free Imaging Edge software to provide the detail you'd expect to find in a sensor with a whopping 168 megapixels. Many of the a7R III's other features are significant upgrades from previous models and include facilities introduced in Sony's flagship mirrorless camera, the a9.

Of course, once you've confirmed that you made a wise purchase, the question comes up, *how do I use this thing?* All those cool features can be mind-numbing to learn, if all you have as a guide is the mediocre manual furnished with the camera. Basic functions and options are explained, but there's really very little about *why* you should use particular settings or features, and the organization may make it difficult to find what you need. Multiple cross-references may send you flipping back and forth between two or three sections of the book to find what you want to know. The basic manual is also hobbled by black-and-white line drawings and tiny pictures that aren't very good examples of what you can do.

Help is on the way. I sincerely believe that this book is your best bet for learning how to use your new camera, and for learning how to use it well. I've tried to make *David Busch's Sony Alpha a7R III Guide to Digital Photography* comprehensive, but easy to comprehend. The roadmap sections use large, color pictures to show you where all the buttons and dials are, and the explanations of what they do are longer and more detailed. I've tried to avoid overly general advice, including the checklists and recipes you'll find in other manuals on how to take a "sports picture" or a "portrait picture" or a "travel picture." If you want to know where you should stand to take a picture of a quarterback dropping back to unleash a pass, there are plenty of books that will tell you that. This one concentrates on teaching you how to select the best autofocus mode, shutter speed, f/stop, or flash capability to take, say, a great sports picture under any conditions.

What You'll Learn

This book is aimed at Sony veterans as well as newcomers to digital photography. Both groups can be overwhelmed by the options the a7 III series offers, while underwhelmed by the explanations they receive in their user's manual, which some suspect was written by a Sony employee who last threw together instructions on how to operate a camcorder or DVD player.

Although this book's main focus is *still* photography, I *will* devote a lot of space to helping you get up to speed on using the a7R III's video capabilities. After all, the a7R III is capable of shooting awesome, professional-level movies, but extensive discussions about choosing between Internal UHD 4K30 and 1080p/120 fps recording, or technical information about S-Log3 gamma and display assist functions are beyond the scope of this book. Given that I expect that only a relatively small—albeit important—segment of the readers of this book want or require such information, I'm going with Vulcan philosopher Spock Prime's observation early in *The Wrath of Khan* that "Logic clearly dictates that the needs of the many outweigh the needs of the few."

Who Am I?

After spending many years as the world's most successful unknown author, I've become slightly less obscure in the past few years, thanks to a horde of camera guidebooks and other photographically oriented tomes. You may have seen my photography articles in the late, lamented *Popular Photography, Rangefinder, Professional Photographer*, and dozens of other photographic publications. But, first, and foremost, I'm a photojournalist and made my living in the field until I began devoting most of my time to writing books. Although I love writing, I'm happiest when I'm out taking pictures, which is why I spend many winters ensconced in the Florida Keys, dividing my time between writing books and taking photographs. You'll find images of many of these visual treats within the pages of this guide.

Like all my digital photography books, this one was written by someone with an incurable photography bug. I've worked as a sports photographer for an Ohio newspaper and for an upstate New York college. I've operated my own commercial studio and photo lab, cranking out product shots on demand and then printing a few hundred glossy 8 × 10s on a tight deadline for a press kit. I've served as a photo-posing instructor for a modeling agency. People have actually paid me to shoot their weddings and immortalize them with portraits. I even prepared press kits and articles on photography as a PR consultant for a formerly dominant (and now vestigial) Rochester, NY company. My trials and travails with imaging and computer technology have made their way into print in book form an alarming number of times, including hundreds of volumes on photographic topics.

Like you, I love photography for its own merits, and I view technology as just another tool to help me get the images I see in my mind's eye. But, also like you, I had to master this technology before I could apply it to my work. This book is the result of what I've learned, and I hope it will help you master your Sony a7R III.

I'd like to ask a special favor: let me know what you think of this book. If you have any recommendations about how I can make it better, visit my website at www.sonyguides.com, click on the E-Mail Me tab, and send your comments, suggestions on topics that should be explained in more detail, or, especially, any typos. (The latter will be compiled on the Errata page you'll also find on my website.) I really value your ideas and appreciate it when you take the time to tell me what you think! Some of the content of the book you hold in your hands came from suggestions I received from readers like yourself. If you found this book especially useful, tell others about it. Visit http://www.amazon.com/dp/1681983796 and leave a positive review. Your feedback is what spurs me to make each one of these books better than the last, and if enough of you like what I've done, Rocky Nook may be moved to ask me to follow up with a new book the next time Sony introduces one of its photographic innovations. Thanks!

Meet Your
Sony Alpha a7R III

I wrote this "Meet and Greet" chapter to satisfy the needs of both semi-experienced E-mount users as well as newcomers to the Sony world (which would include the hordes who jumped to the Sony mirrorless world from the Nikon or Canon realms). Whether you're an advanced shooter looking to improve your comfort level with the features of this well-designed (yet complex) camera or are looking forward to starting from scratch, you'll find that the advice I'm about to offer useful. You can zip right through the basics, and then dive into learning a few things you probably didn't know about your a7R III. Veterans might want to skim through the material in this chapter and move on. I promise I didn't charge you extra for it; even in the days of digital publishing it's not possible to provide *only* the material a particular reader needs, and nothing else. You'll find that stuff you already know well may be unfamiliar to other owners of a camera, even one as advanced as the a7R III.

Fortunately, the a7R III can be incredibly easy to use, right out of the box. As ridiculous as it may seem, the a7R III *can* be used as a point-and-shoot camera. Charge the battery, mount a lens, and insert a formatted memory card. (If you are using just one card instead of two, it must be loaded into Slot 1, the slot closest to the bottom of the camera.) Then, just flick the power switch to On; it's concentric with the shutter release button on top of the camera. Press the mode dial lock release button in the center of the mode dial (which is located just southwest of the shutter release) and rotate the dial to select the Program (P) label or green Intelligent Auto icon. (See Figure 1.1.) Your current shooting mode (including Intelligent Scene modes described in the sidebar that follows) is displayed in the upper-left corner of the frame. Compose your image on the monitor (the rear LCD screen) or by looking through the viewfinder. Press the shutter release button when you're ready to take your first shot.

Power switch

Mode dial

Figure 1.1
Select Program or
Auto and take a
picture.

HIDDEN SCENES

The a7R III does not have a Scene position on the mode dial but does resort to Scene-style settings when you use Intelligent Auto. Although you can't specify most settings on your own in Intelligent Auto mode, the a7R III will evaluate your scene and switch to Portrait, Infant, Night Portrait, Night Scene, Backlight Portrait, Backlight, Landscape, Macro, Spotlight, Low Light, and Night Scene (Tripod) modes. (If you've disabled Face Detection, as described in Chapter 3, Portrait, Infant, Night Portrait, and Backlight Portrait scene modes are not available.)

In practice, though, it's not a bad idea, once you've taken a few orientation pictures with your camera, to go back and review the basic operations of the a7R III from the beginning, if only to see if you've missed something. This chapter is my opportunity to introduce new owners to the camera and review the setup procedures for those among you who are already veteran users, and to help ease the more timid (even those few who have never before worked with an interchangeable-lens camera) into the basic pre-flight checklist that needs to be completed before you really spread your wings and take off. For the uninitiated, as easy as it is to use initially, your Sony a7R III *does* have some dials, buttons, and menu items that might not make sense at first but will surely become second nature after you've had a chance to review the instructions in this book.

But don't fret about wading through a manual to find out what you must know to take those first few tentative snaps. I'm going to help you hit the ground running with this chapter (or keep on running if you've already jumped right in). If you *haven't* had the opportunity to use your a7R III yet, I'll help you set up your camera and begin shooting in minutes. You won't find a lot of operational detail in this chapter. Indeed, I'm going to tell you just what you absolutely *must* understand, accompanied by some interesting tidbits that will help you become acclimated. I'll go into more depth and even repeat some of what I explain here in later chapters, so you don't have to memorize everything you see. Just relax, follow a few easy steps, and then go out and begin taking your best shots—ever.

LENS NOMENCLATURE

In the discussion of lenses in the section that follows, you're going to find me describing certain E-mount lenses using their full, formal product names, which can be rather unwieldy. However, for the most part in this book, I'll use shorter, more compact nomenclature when there is little chance of confusion. For example, Sony offers four full-frame prime lenses in the 50-55mm focal length range. So, to be clear, I may need to refer to the Sony FE 50mm f/1.8, Sony Planar T* FE 50mm f/1.4 ZA, Sony Sonnar T* FE 55mm f/1.8 ZA, or Sony FE 50mm f/2.8 macro lens, as appropriate. Most of the time, a shorter version of the lens' name will do.

Your Out-of-Box Experience

Your Sony a7R III comes in an attractive box filled with stuff, including a multi-purpose USB/charging cable, basic instructions, some pamphlets, and a few other items. The most important components are the camera and lens, battery/charger, and, if you're the nervous type, the neck strap. You'll also need a Secure Digital or Memory Stick card, as one is not included.

The first thing to do is to carefully unpack the camera and double-check the contents with the checklist on one side of the box. While this level of setup detail may seem as superfluous as the instructions on a bottle of shampoo, checking the contents *first* is always a good idea. It's better to know *now* that something is missing so you can seek redress immediately, rather than discover a few days later that the box didn't contain the cable protector—which keeps an accessory cable securely attached to the camera.

So, check the box at your earliest convenience, and make sure you have (at least) the following:

- **Sony a7R III body.** This is hard to miss. The camera is the main reason you laid out the big bucks, and it is tucked away inside a nifty protective envelope you should save for re-use in case the camera needs to be sent in for repair. It almost goes without saying that you should check out the camera immediately, making sure the color LCD on the back isn't scratched or cracked; the battery compartment, memory card door, and connection port doors open properly; and, when a charged battery is inserted, and lens mounted, the camera powers up and reports for duty. Out-of-the-box defects in these areas are rare, but they can happen. It's probably more common that your dealer played with the camera or, perhaps, it was a customer return. That's why it's best to buy your camera from a retailer you trust to supply a factory-fresh camera.

- **Lens.** At its introduction, the Sony a7R III was in very high demand, and was available in a limited number of configurations, often the body alone, or packaged in several different kits that included accessories such as the VG-C3EM Vertical Grip and NPA-MQZ1K Multi-Battery Adapter Kit. It was also available with the new Sony FE 24-105mm f/4 G OSS lens ($1,300), Sony FE 28-70mm f/3.5-5.6 OSS (about $500), the Zeiss Vario-Tessar T* FE 24-70mm f/4 ZA OSS (about $1,200), or even the premium Sony FE 24-70mm f/2.8 GM (G Master) ($2,200).

My recommendation: I already owned the Zeiss Vario-Tessar 24-70mm f/4, so I bought my a7R III with the 24-105mm zoom. *You probably do not need both lenses* because the newer lens completely overlaps the range of the three 24/28-70mm optics. You might make an exception for the 24-70mm f/2.8 G Master if you do a *lot* of shooting in the shorter focal length neighborhood and want a super-sharp lens with a fast f/2.8 maximum aperture.

As the owner of a 42MP camera, you probably won't be satisfied with the low-cost 28-70mm f/3.5-5.6 OSS lens, as it's not the sharpest lens in the drawer. The Zeiss 24-70mm version is a bit better, and its constant maximum aperture gives you f/4 (rather than f/5.6) at the 70mm setting. Of course, you may not use this particular focal length range at all. Many shooters tend to "see" images as "wide-angle/perspective distortion/maximum depth-of-field" shots or, conversely, as "longer lens/selective focus" photos. If you are in either camp, eschewing all these lenses and putting the money toward a different lens is a good option. I use my Sony Vario-Tessar T* FE 16-35mm f/4 ZA OSS lens quite often and have been relying on the 24-105mm zoom more frequently as a "walk-around" lens.

- **Info-Lithium NP-FZ100 battery.** This is the power source for your Sony camera. Charge yours as soon as possible (as described next).

My recommendation: Although the a7R III's 2280 mAh battery is more than twice as powerful than the one furnished with the a7/a7R II–series cameras, it's smart, nay, *essential* to have more than one battery pack. Although tiny in size, this camera gulps power, and, even with the generous standards Sony cites in its literature, each is likely to last for no more than 530 to 650 still shots or roughly 190 minutes of non-stop video capture. (The figures given vary depending on whether you are using the electronic viewfinder or LCD monitor screen to frame your image, plus other factors.) Buy *more*, and stick to Sony-brand products—even if third-party batteries eventually become available. Off-brand packs have been known to fail quickly, sometimes in potentially destructive ways.

- **Sony BC-QZ1 external charger.** This handy device (see Figure 1.2) allows you to recharge one battery while another is ensconced in your camera as you continue shooting.

My recommendation: I strongly prefer the faster external charger to the alternative cable charging method, accomplished by plugging a USB cable into a computer or USB charger. However, an even better choice than the BC-QZ1 is the $400 NPA-MQZ1K Multi Battery Adapter Kit, described shortly.

Figure 1.2 The Sony BC-QZ1 charger allows rejuvenating your battery outside the camera, so you can keep shooting with a spare battery.

■ **Micro Type-C cable.** Use this USB cable (and included cable protector) to link your Sony to a computer when you need to transfer pictures but don't have an optional card reader accessory handy. While the camera is connected with the cable, the battery inside the body will also be charging. The USB cable can also be connected to an optional AC adapter (which can be the Sony AC-UUD12 adapter, or virtually any 5V/2A smart device power cube) if you want to charge the battery using household power. (See Figure 1.3.)

My recommendation: An AC adapter is especially useful while traveling, as it eliminates the need to have a computer or laptop powered up to charge the battery. Note that you can use the Type-C cable plugged into the a7R III's Type-C port, or a Micro B USB 2.0 cable inserted in the camera's Multi/Micro USB terminal. I'll list these other options in an upcoming section titled "Charging the Battery."

Figure 1.3
An optional AC adapter takes several hours to provide a normal charge to a battery pack that was completely depleted.

■ **Shoulder strap.** Sony provides a suitable neck or shoulder strap, with the Sony logo subtly worked into the design.

My recommendation: While I am justifiably proud of owning a fine Sony camera, I never attach the factory strap to my camera, and instead opt for a more serviceable strap from UPstrap (www.upstrap-pro.com). If you carry your camera over one shoulder, as many do, I particularly recommend UPstrap (shown in Figure 1.4). It has a patented non-slip pad that offers reassuring traction and eliminates the contortions we sometimes go through to keep the camera from slipping off. I know several photographers who refuse to use anything else. If you do purchase an UPstrap, be sure to tell photographer-inventor Al Stegmeyer that I sent you hence.

■ **Multi Interface Shoe cap.** This plastic piece slides into the camera's multi interface shoe on top (what we used to call a "hot shoe") and protects the contacts from dirt, moisture, and damage when you don't have an electronic flash, microphone, or other accessory attached.

My recommendation: If you are *very* careful about how you insert an external flash or microphone into the multi interface shoe, and avoid drenching moisture, you can remove this piece and leave it off for the rest of your life. I *have* lost shots while fumbling with protective covers and manage to lose the shoe cap with alarming frequency. If you misplace yours, USA shooters can get a cheap replacement from www.laserfairepress.com for a few bucks.

Figure 1.4
Third-party neck
straps, like this
UPstrap model, are
often preferable to
the Sony-supplied
strap.

- **FDA-EP18 eyepiece cup.** This rubber accessory is already installed on the electronic view-finder eyepiece when you receive the camera; if you want to remove it, slide it up. It's not easily lost, but this cup fits a variety of Sony cameras, including the Sony a99 II and other Sony full-frame mirrorless cameras, so you can pick up a replacement for about $11.

- **Application software.** Sony no longer includes a software CD in the package. The first time you power up the camera, it will display the current URL for your country where you can download imaging software for the a7R III. Be sure to get the new, free Imaging Edge software. It's a great RAW processor and editor and has a Remote application for tethered shooting (with your a7R III connected to a laptop or other computer). It's also an essential tool for the camera's Pixel Shift feature, combining four individual photos to create a single ersatz 168-megapixel final image.

- **Printed instruction manual.** The camera comes with a skimpy 100-page basic instruction manual. A 650-page Help Guide to the camera's operation can be accessed online in HTML format or downloaded as a more useful PDF file from Sony's esupport.sony.com website. The box will also contain warranty and registration information, and assorted pamphlets listing available accessories, including a free copy of the Sony-specific Capture One Express from Phase One. You can upgrade that software to the full version for a modest fee.

- **Body cap.** This accessory will probably already be attached to the camera body if you purchase your a7R III without a lens.

  My recommendation: Purchase an extra body cap. With mirrorless cameras like the a7R III series, it is especially important not to leave the sensor unprotected. If you lose your body cap, mount a lens as a "body cap" until you purchase spares. A body cap is essential when packing your camera for compact travel. Owners in the USA will find cheap body and rear lens caps at www.laserfairepress.com, too. (Nobody gets rich selling these items for a few dollars, but these are provided as a service because a key previous source for them has gone out of business.)

Initial Setup

The initial setup of your Sony is fast and easy. You just need to charge the battery, attach a lens (if that hasn't already been done), and insert a memory card. I'll address each of these steps separately, but if you already feel you can manage these setup tasks without further instructions, feel free to skip this section entirely. You should probably at least skim its contents, however, because I'm going to list a few options that you might not be aware of.

Battery Included

Your Sony a7R III is a sophisticated hunk of machinery and electronics, but it needs a charged battery to function, so rejuvenating the NP-FZ100 lithium-ion battery pack should be your first step. A fully charged power source should theoretically be good for 530 shots (when using the power-hungry viewfinder) or 650 shots (when working with the more juice-frugal LCD monitor screen). Expect 100 minutes of typical video capture, which includes standby time, zooming, and turning the camera on or off from time to time. When shooting continuously (for up to the limit of 29 minutes per single clip), you may be able to stretch a single battery for as much as 190 minutes of continual video capture. Theoretically. I frequently (always) deplete my batteries more quickly than that. Sony's estimates are based on standard tests defined by the Camera & Imaging Products Association (CIPA). If you often use the camera's Wi-Fi feature (discussed later), you can expect to take even fewer shots before it's time for a recharge. This is an Info-Lithium battery, so the camera can display the approximate power remaining with a graphic indicator.

Remember that all rechargeable batteries undergo some degree of self-discharge just sitting idle in the camera or in the original packaging. Lithium-ion power packs of this type typically lose a small amount of their charge every day, even when the camera isn't turned on. Li-ion cells lose their power through a chemical reaction that continues when the camera is switched off. So, it's very likely that the battery purchased with your camera, even if charged at the factory, has begun to poop out after the long sea voyage on a banana boat (or, more likely, a trip by jet plane followed by a sojourn in a warehouse), so you'll want to revive it before going out for some serious shooting.

My recommendation: At roughly $400, the NPA-MQZ1K Multi Battery Adapter Kit sounds pricey (it is!). However, it comes with two NP-FZ100 batteries (normally about $80 each), which means that, effectively, you're paying "only" $240 for the charger itself. The charger is extremely versatile: it can charge up to four NP-FZ100 batteries simultaneously but can be converted to a compact two-battery charger for use while traveling.

Even better, the charger can serve as a power pack when outfitted with fully-charged batteries. A dummy battery plugs into the battery compartment of the a7R III (or, with a supplied adapter, into any E-mount camera that uses the puny NP-FW50 batteries). Two USB ports allow rejuvenating other devices that use USB cable charging (including your smartphone!). It has six standard 1/4"-20 mounting sockets so it can be mounted to support systems (like the cages videographers use to attach external viewfinders and other accessories).

I own four NP-FZ100 batteries (so far) and keep one in the camera at all times. Nevertheless, I always check battery status before I go out to shoot, as some juice may have been siphoned off while the camera sat idle. I go to the Network 1 menu and turn Airplane Mode on (as described in Chapter 5) when I don't need Wi-Fi features.

Charging the Battery

While the included Sony BC-QC1 external charger or optional NPA-MQZ1K Multi Battery Adapter Kit should be your first choices, you have multiple other options, including charging the battery while it's still in the camera (best done when the camera is idle and not needed for shooting). You probably already own a suitable AC adapter/charger, in the form of any charging device you use for your smartphone, tablet, Kindle, or other electronic product. Their typical 5V/2A output will work fine. I also use a 20,000 mAh lithium-ion power "brick," which also can recharge my phone, my tablet, and, in a pinch (using an included cable) jump start a car. The brick comes with its own 12V DC charger, so I can keep it topped up using my vehicle's accessory outlet (what we used to call a "cigarette lighter" socket). I also have a more compact 5,000 mAh pack, about the size of a roll of quarters, that I keep in my camera bag.

When you're ready to charge the battery internally, turn the camera Off. Then, plug one end of the USB cable (with the smaller connector) into one of the two bottom ports on the left end of the a7R III. A standard USB 2.0 Micro B cable can be plugged into the lower of the two, or a USB 3.0 Type C cable into the one above it. (See Figure 1.5.) Plug the other end of either cable (with the familiar USB connector) into a computer's USB port, AC adapter, or battery-powered recharging device. Turn the camera On and you'll see a note on the LCD screen, USB Mode; this confirms that the connection has been made.

Whether you charge from a computer's USB port or household power, a Charge light next to the camera's USB/charging ports glows yellow, without flashing. It continues to glow until the battery completes the charge and the lamp turns off. In truth, the full charge is complete about one hour *after* the charging lamp turns off, so if your battery was really dead, don't stop charging until the additional time has elapsed. Be sure to plan for charging time before your shooting sessions, because it takes several hours in a warm environment to fully restore a completely depleted battery.

If the charging lamp flashes after you insert an externally charged battery into the camera, that indicates an error condition. Remove it and re-insert it. To insert/remove it, slide the latch on the bottom of the camera, open the battery door, and press a blue lever in the battery compartment that prevents the pack from slipping out when the door is opened; then, ease the battery out. To insert it, do so with the contact openings facing down into the compartment (see Figure 1.6).

Fast flashing that can't be stopped by re-inserting the battery indicates a problem with the battery. Slow flashing (about 1.5 seconds between flashes) means the ambient temperature is too high or low for charging to take place.

Charge indicator LED

Micro USB Type C terminal

Multi/Micro USB terminal

Figure 1.5 The charging cable is inserted into the Micro USB Type C Terminal or Multi/Micro USB Terminal.

Figure 1.6 Install the battery in the camera; it only fits one way.

Charging the battery with the supplied BC-QC1 external charger is even easier; just slide the battery in, connect to AC power, and the charger's yellow status light will begin to glow, accompanied by three green LEDs that illuminate progressively as charging proceeds, to let you know when the battery is fully charged. The yellow LED will extinguish when the cycle is over.

Final Steps

Your Sony a7R III is almost ready to fire up and shoot. You'll need to select and mount a lens (if not previously done) and insert a memory card. Each of these steps is easy, and if you've used any similar camera in the past, such as a Sony or other model, you already know exactly what to do. I'm going to provide a little extra detail for those of you who are new to the Sony or interchangeable-lens camera worlds.

Mounting the Lens

My recommended lens mounting procedure emphasizes protecting your equipment from accidental damage and minimizing the intrusion of dust. Select the lens you want to use and loosen (but do not remove) the rear lens cap. I generally place the lens I am planning to mount vertically in a slot in my camera bag, where it's protected from mishaps but ready to pick up quickly. By loosening the rear lens cap, you'll be able to lift it off the back of the lens at the last instant, so the rear element of the lens is covered until then.

After that, remove the body cap that protects the camera's exposed sensor by rotating the cap toward the shutter release button. You should always mount the body cap when there is no lens on the camera, because it helps keep dust out of the interior of the camera. Unlike traditional dSLRs, these cameras have no mirror or closed shutter to protect the sensor.

Figure 1.7
Match the raised white dot on the lens with the white dot on the camera mount to properly align the lens with the bayonet mount.

Once the body cap has been removed, remove the rear lens cap from the lens, set the cap aside, and then mount the lens on the camera by matching the raised white alignment indicator on the lens barrel with the white dot on the camera's lens mount (see Figure 1.7). Rotate the lens away from the shutter release side of the camera until it seats securely and clicks into place. (Don't press the lens release button during mounting.) Some lenses ship with a hood. If that accessory is included, and if it's bayoneted on the lens in the reversed position (which makes the lens/hood combination more compact for transport), twist it off and remount with the rim facing outward (see Figure 1.8). A lens hood protects the front of the lens from accidental bumps, and reduces flare caused by extraneous light arriving at the front element of the lens from outside the picture area.

Figure 1.8 A hood protects the lens from extraneous light and from accidental bumps, but not all lenses include this accessory.

Turn on the Power

Locate the On/Off switch that is wrapped around the shutter release button and rotate it to the On position. The LCD display will be illuminated. If you bring the viewfinder up to your eye, a sensor will detect that action and switch the display to the built-in electronic viewfinder instead. (You can disable this automatic switching in the FINDER/MONITOR setting within the Camera Settings II-6 (Display/Auto Review 1) menu, as I'll describe in Chapter 4.) After one minute of idling (the default), the a7R III goes into standby mode to save battery power. Just tap the shutter release button to bring it back to life. (You can select a longer time using the Power Save Start Time option in the Setup 2 menu, as I discuss in Chapter 5.)

When the camera first powers up, you may be asked to set the date and time. The procedure is self-explanatory (although I'll explain it in detail in Chapter 5). You can use the left/right directional buttons to navigate among the date, year, time, date format, and daylight savings time indicator, and use the up/down buttons to enter the correct settings. When finished, *press the control wheel center button* to confirm the settings and return to the menu system. Veteran users will know how to do this; if you're totally new to the E-mount system, I'll explain the control dials, wheels, and buttons in detail in Chapter 2.

Once the Sony a7R III is satisfied that it knows what time it is, you will be viewing a live view of the scene in front of the lens—on the LCD screen or in the viewfinder when that is held up to your eye—whenever you turn the camera on. The view is superimposed with many items of data over the display; these provide a quick method for checking many current camera settings, including current shutter speed and aperture (f/stop), shooting mode, ISO sensitivity, and other parameters.

Adjusting the Diopter Setting

The a7R III is equipped with a built-in electronic viewfinder or EVF, a small high-resolution (almost 4 million pixels) OLED (organic light-emitting diode) screen that can be used instead of the LCD screen for framing your photos or movies. A sensor detects your eye at the viewfinder and shuts off power to the LCD when you are using the EVF.

Usually, when you're learning to use the camera's many features, you'll rely on the LCD screen's display, but when you're actually taking photos, you'll sometimes want to use the EVF instead. You can also use it to review your photos or video clips and navigate menu selections.

Eye sensor   *Diopter adjustment dial*

If you wear glasses and want to use the EVF without them, or if you find the viewfinder needs a bit of correction, rotate the diopter adjustment dial located to the right of the viewfinder window (and shown in Figure 1.9). Adjust the dial while looking through the viewfinder until the image appears sharpest.

Figure 1.9 Diopter adjustment dial.

Inserting a Memory Card

You can't take actual photos without at least one memory card inserted in your Sony camera, although if you have the Release without Card entry in the Camera Settings II-4 (Shutter/Steadyshot) menu set to Enable, you can pretend to shoot. In that case, if you don't have a card installed, the camera will sound as if it's taking a photo (when using the mechanical shutter, of course), and it will display that "photo." However, the image is only in temporary memory and not actually stored; you'll get a reminder about that with a flashing orange NO CARD warning at the upper left of the LCD. If you go back later and try to view that image, it will not be there. So, be sure you have inserted a compatible card with adequate capacity before you start shooting stills or videos.

The memory card slots are located beneath a door on the right side of the camera. Press the door release switch upward, and the door will open, revealing two slots (see Figure 1.10). If you use only one memory card, you must insert it in the lower slot (seen at right in the figure). This slot has the fastest read/write speed, as I'll show you in Chapter 2, so you should put your fastest memory card here.

Both slots accept Secure Digital (SD), Secure Digital High Capacity (SDHC), Secure Digital Extra Capacity (SDXC), and Sony Memory Stick Pro Duo (or Memory Stick Pro-HG Duo) cards. The newest type of SD card, the super-high-capacity (and super-fast) SDXC type, at this writing, is available in capacities as high as 512GB.

Figure 1.10 The memory cards are inserted in the slots on the side of the camera.

Given the fast continuous shooting speeds available with the a7R III, you'll want to consider the speediest cards available, which, as I write this, are the Sony SF-G Series UHS-II U3 Class 10 SDXC memory cards, available in 128GB, 64GB, and 32GB capacities. They have a maximum 299 MB/second write speed (essential in order to transfer images from the a7R III's built-in memory buffer to the card quickly). Poky write speeds can be infuriating when a "Processing" warning appears on your screen and you're unable to continue shooting or review the images you've already taken until the buffer has emptied. (This was a huge problem for me when I owned this camera's predecessor, the a7R II.)

The Sony SF-G Series cards have a maximum read speed of 300MB/second, too. The latter spec is useful when it comes time to transfer your images from the memory card to your computer. Vendors typically tout their cards' read speed and downplay the write speed, which can be typically half as fast. With Sony's SF-G series, the card is wicked fast in both directions. (I suspect the 299/300 MB difference between write and read speeds is a marketing ploy to make sure consumers realize that both speeds are being shown.)

Unfortunately, only Slot 1 provides the fastest transfer speeds with UHS-II cards. Slot 2 provides only UHS-I speeds, regardless of which type card you're using, so you'll want to relegate it to your backup media. I'll explain the options in Chapter 2. However, Slot 2 can accept Sony Memory Stick Pro cards, if you have some.

You should remove the memory card only when the camera is switched off. Insert an SD card with the label facing toward the front of the camera (as shown in Figure 1.10), or toward the back if inserting any type of Memory Stick Pro card. In either case, the metal contacts go into the slot first; the card simply will not fit into the slot if it is incorrectly oriented.

Close the door, and your pre-flight checklist is done! (I'm going to assume you'll remember to remove the lens cap when you're ready to take a picture!) When you want to remove the memory card later, just press down on the card edge that protrudes from the slot, and the card will pop right out.

My recommendation: Size matters—when you're using a camera with a 42MP sensor. If you're buying new, rather than re-using old cards, I suggest eschewing 32GB cards and purchasing fast 64GB cards. With a 64GB card you can capture about 850 images in dual RAW/JPEG formats (recommended for reasons I'll outline in Chapter 2), which is not an unreasonable amount for a day or two of intense shooting. Even though the a7R III has two slots and can hold two cards, with smaller cards you still might find yourself swapping cards at inopportune times. And purchasing a more expensive 128GB memory card might tempt you to save a little with slower media. I do own both 128GB and 256GB memory cards, but they are, indeed, slower, so I load them in the less speedy Slot 2 for backup purposes. I put nothing but Sony SF-G cards in Slot 1. (Full disclosure: Sony's black media are difficult to photograph, so I used another brand for Figure 1.10.) **Note:** Later in this book I'll show you how to store images on cards in both slots simultaneously. In these modes, the a7R III decelerates to the speed of the slowest memory card.

There are three ways to create a blank memory card for your Sony a7R III, and two of them are at least partially wrong. Here are your options, both correct and incorrect:

- **Transfer (move) files to your computer.** You'll sometimes decide to transfer (rather than copy) all the image files to your computer from the memory card (either using a direct cable transfer or with a card reader and appropriate software, as described later in this chapter). When you do so, the image files on the card can be erased leaving the card blank. Theoretically. This method does *not* remove files that you've labeled as Protected (by choosing Protect from the Playback menu during review), nor does it identify and lock out parts of your card that have become corrupted or unusable since the last time you formatted the card. Therefore, I recommend always formatting the card, rather than simply moving the image files. The only exception is when you *want* to leave the protected/unerased images on the card for a while longer, say, to share with friends, family, and colleagues.

- **(Don't) Format in your computer.** With the memory card inserted in a card reader or card slot in your computer, you can use Windows or Mac OS to reformat the memory card. Don't even think of doing this! The operating system won't necessarily arrange the structure of the card the way the camera likes to see it (in computer terms, an incorrect *file system* may be installed). In particular, cards larger than 32GB must be initialized using the exFAT format, and while your computer may offer exFAT as an option, it may default to a different scheme. The only way to ensure that the card has been properly formatted for your camera is to perform the format *in the camera itself.* The only exception to this rule is when you have a seriously corrupted memory card that your camera refuses to format. Sometimes it is possible to revive such a corrupted card by allowing the operating system to reformat it first, then trying again in the camera to restore the proper exFAT system.

- **Setup menu format.** Use the recommended method to format a memory card in the camera, as described next.

To format a memory card, just follow these steps. I'm going to suggest some basic navigation controls for those who are new to E-mount cameras. However, Sony gives you multiple ways to move around with its screens, and I'll show you how to do that in Chapter 2, where I'll also explain how to use the touch screen to specify a focus area. (Veteran users can use the method of their choice, including the rear joystick.) For now, we'll just use the front and rear control dials to navigate.

1. **Press MENU.** When you press the MENU button, a menu screen will appear on the LCD monitor or electronic viewfinder. If you've previously selected a menu entry, the a7R III will remember that and return to *that menu screen* with the most recently used item highlighted with an orange bar, as seen in Figure 1.11. However, in most cases the most recent menu may not be the one you want to use to format a memory card. To quickly move from one main menu tab to the next, rotate the *front* dial (just fore of the shutter release) to the left to move the highlight upward until only the tab at top is highlighted—if necessary. You can then rotate the *rear* dial to jump among the available tabs. (I'll explain these controls in more detail in Chapter 3.)

2. **Navigate to the Setup tab.** Rotate the *rear* dial until the Setup tab (a yellow toolbox icon) is highlighted. Then use the *front* dial to move the orange highlighting down into the Setup menus.

3. **Navigate to the Setup 5 menu.** Use the rear dial to jump among the Setup tabs' menus until you arrive at the Setup 5 screen shown in the figure. Highlight Format, if necessary, and press the center of the control wheel to access the menu entry. (The relevant controls are shown in Figure 1.12.)

4. **Choose slot.** Rotate the front or rear dials (it doesn't matter), or use the directional buttons or joystick, to highlight the slot containing the card you want to format. Press the control wheel center button.

5. **Format.** A display will appear asking if you want to delete all data. If you're sure you want to do so, press up/down to choose OK, and press the center button to confirm your choice. This will begin the formatting process.

Figure 1.11
The Setup 5 menu.

Figure 1.12 Navigation controls.

Selecting a Shooting Mode

When it comes time to select the shooting mode and other settings on the a7R III camera, you may start to fully experience the "feel" of the user interface. Thanks to the mode dial shown earlier in Figure 1.1, it's simple and quick to set a shooting mode. Just press the mode dial lock release button in the center of the dial, and rotate it to the position you want, such as P (Program Auto).

There is a fully automatic shooting mode, Intelligent Auto. In that mode, the camera makes most of the decisions for you (except when to press the shutter). As I mentioned earlier, the a7R III will evaluate your scene and switch to an appropriate scene-type mode from among Portrait, Infant, Night Portrait, Night Scene, Backlight Portrait, Backlight, Landscape, Macro, Spotlight, Low Light, and Night Scene (Tripod) modes. Again, when Face Detection is disabled, Portrait, Infant, Night Portrait, and Backlight Portrait modes are not available. Scene detection may be incorrect if you're using the a7R III's digital zoom feature, discussed in Chapter 4. The scene modes selected by the camera are as follows:

■ **Portrait.** With the Portrait setting, the camera uses settings to blur the background and sharpen the view of the subject, while using soft skin tones. External flash will fire in low light if you have attached it and powered it up.

■ **Infant.** Optimizes settings for photographing small children, using bright, vivid colors.

■ **Night Portrait.** Choose this mode when you want to illuminate a subject in the foreground with flash, but still allow the background to be exposed properly by the available light. Be prepared to use a tripod or to rely on the SteadyShot feature to reduce the effects of camera shake. If there is no foreground subject that needs to be illuminated by the flash, you may do better by using the Night Scene mode, discussed next. Remember that you must attach and power up the external flash before taking a shot if you want the flash to fire.

- **Night Scene.** This mode uses slower shutter speeds to provide a useful exposure, but without using flash. You should use a tripod to avoid the effects of camera shake that can be problematic with a slow shutter speed.
- **Backlight Portrait.** This is like the Portrait setting but compensates exposure for lighting coming from the rear.
- **Backlight.** Provides exposure compensation for backlight for subjects that are not portraits.
- **Landscape.** Select this scene mode when you want a maximum range of sharpness (instead of a blurred background) as well as vivid colors of distant scenes. External flash will never fire in this mode.
- **Macro.** This mode is helpful when you are shooting close-up pictures of a subject such as a flower, insect, or other small object. External flash will fire in low light if you have popped it into the up position, but the flash may be too bright for a subject that's very close to the camera.
- **Spotlight.** This setting compensates for subjects that are illuminated by a small, direct light source, as in stage performances and concerts.
- **Low Light.** This special mode is designed for use in low light. The camera will set a high ISO (sensitivity) level to enable it to use a fast shutter speed to minimize the risk of blurring caused by camera shake.
- **Night Scene (Tripod).** This mode also uses slower shutter speeds, including those long enough to make use of a tripod mandatory.

The mode dial also includes a Movie position, three semi-automatic modes, (Program, Aperture Priority, and Shutter Priority), which allow you to provide more input over the exposure and settings the camera uses, and a fully Manual mode. I'll provide tips on using these in Chapter 7. The other positions include S & Q (for slow-motion and quick-motion shooting), and three Memory Recall settings "slots" to register frequently used settings. I'll explain how to use the Memory settings in Chapter 3. The mode dial options include:

- **P (Program auto).** This mode allows the a7R III to make the basic exposure settings, but you can still override the camera's settings to fine-tune your image.
- **A (Aperture Priority).** Choose this mode when you want to use a particular lens opening (called an aperture or f/stop), especially to control how much of your image is in focus. The camera will set the appropriate shutter speed after you have set your desired aperture using the rear dial that's around the mode selector dial.
- **S (Shutter Priority).** This mode is useful when you want to use a particular shutter speed to stop action or produce creative blur effects. You dial in your chosen shutter speed with the rear dial, and the camera will set the appropriate aperture (f/stop) for you.

- **M (Manual).** Select this mode when you want full control over the shutter speed and the aperture (lens opening), either for creative effects or because you are using a studio flash or another flash unit not compatible with the camera's automatic flash metering. You also need to use this mode if you want to use the Bulb setting for a long exposure, as explained in Chapter 6. You select both the aperture (with the front dial) and the shutter speed aperture (with the rear dial on the camera back). There's more about this mode, and the others, in Chapter 6.

- **Movie.** Allows shooting movie clips. You can capture video in other exposure modes, just by pressing the red Movie button located to the right of the electronic viewfinder. While you can shoot movies with the camera set to P/A/S/M modes, this dial position gives you more options over your movie settings.

- **1/2/3 (Memory Recall).** These three positions on the mode dial, simply marked 1, 2, or 3, aren't actually exposure modes. Instead, they correspond to either of two different groups of settings that you've previously stored in an internal memory storage "slot" (register) numbered 1, 2, and 3. You can use the memory registers to set up the a7R III for specific types of shooting scenes, and then retrieve those settings from the mode dial.

- **S & Q.** You can capture slow-motion and quick-motion video clips by moving the mode dial to this position and pressing the red Movie button. In the Camera Settings II-1 (Movie 1) menu's S & Q Settings entry, you can select Record Setting (60p, 30p, 24p) and frame rates in the S & Q Settings entry. If the a7R III's 10 frames-per-second continuous shooting isn't fast enough for you, you can shoot video at up to 120 fps, which slows down motion by a 5X factor. Quick-motion rates of up to 60X normal speed can also be selected. I'll show you how to use these in Chapter 4.

Choosing a Metering Mode

You might want to select a particular exposure metering mode for your first shots, although the default high-tech Multi (short for multi-zone or multi-segment) metering is probably the best choice while getting to know your camera. If you want to select a different metering pattern, you must not be using Intelligent Auto; in that mode, the camera uses Multi metering and that cannot be changed. To change the metering mode, press the MENU button and navigate to the Camera Settings I menu (the tab in the upper-left corner in Figure 1.11), and thence to the Camera Settings I-9 menu to the Metering Mode entry. Press the center button, then scroll up/down with the directional buttons to reach Multi, Center (for center weighted), Spot, Entire Screen Averaging, and Highlight selections. Press the center button to confirm your choice and return the camera to shooting mode. The metering options are as follows:

- **Multi metering.** In this standard metering mode, the camera attempts to intelligently classify your image and choose the best exposure based on readings from 1,200 different zones or segments of the scene. You can read about this so-called "evaluative" metering concept, as well as the other two options, in Chapter 7.

- **Center metering.** The camera meters the entire scene but gives the most emphasis (or weighting) to the central area of the frame.

- **Spot metering.** The camera considers only the brightness in a very small central spot, so the exposure is calculated only based on that area. You can set the size of the metering circle to Standard or Large, and either link the spot to a focusing point or fix it to the center position, as I'll explain in Chapter 7.

- **Entire Screen Averaging.** This mode sets exposure based on the mean value (in the arithmetic, rather than vengeful sense) of all the tones in the frame, which means the exposure will remain constant even if your subject moves around within the frame.

- **Highlight metering.** Emphasizes preserving tones in the highlights of an image to avoid overexposure, possibly at the expense of shadow detail. I'll show you how to balance exposures for lighter and darker images in Chapter 7.

OPTION OPTIONS

You'll soon find that your a7R III gives you multiple ways to make adjustments. In this Quick Start chapter, I may show you just one way of selecting options. For example, you can select a metering mode using the Camera Settings I-9 menu, as described, or you can press the Fn button on the right side of the back of the camera and specify the metering method from the 12-item Function menu that pops up. (See Figure 1.13, left.) Alternatively, when the "Quick Navi" screen is shown on the LCD monitor, you can press the Fn button to change the metering mode as well as most of the other shooting settings. (See Figure 1.13, right.) I'll show you how to use the other optional methods in Chapter 2.

Figure 1.13 Function menu (left); Quick Navi screen (right).

Choosing a Focus Mode

The focus mode can be selected using the Camera Settings I-5 menu entry or the Fn menu's Focus Mode (located second from the right in the top row of the Fn menu), or the Quick Navi screen. Focus mode is easy to understand; it determines *when* focus is established. The choices that are available when using P, A, S, or M mode are as follows:

- **Single-shot AF (AF-S).** This mode, sometimes called *single autofocus*, sets focus after you touch the shutter release button and the camera beeps to confirm focus (unless you've turned the beeps off). The active focus point(s) are shown in green on the screen and a green dot appears in the bottom-left corner of the display. The focus will remain locked as long as you maintain contact with the shutter release button, or until you take the picture. If the autofocus system is unable to achieve sharp focus (because the subject is too close to the camera, for example), the focus confirmation circle will blink. This mode is best when your subject is relatively motionless as when you're taking a portrait or landscape photo.

- **Continuous AF (AF-C).** This mode, sometimes called continuous servo or continuous tracking focus by photographers, sets focus when you partially depress the shutter button, but continues to monitor the frame and refocuses if the distance between the camera and the subject changes. (This allows it to continuously focus on a person walking toward you, for example.) No beep sound is provided. A green dot surrounded by two brackets (curved lines) appears to indicate that the camera is not having a problem achieving and maintaining focus. The brackets disappear when focus is achieved, leaving only the green dot. If the camera should fail to acquire focus, the green dot disappears, and the brackets remain. Continuous AF is a useful mode for photographing moving subjects.

- **Automatic AF (AF-A).** When using AF-A the a7R III will switch between AF-S and AF-C to account for a subject that is moving intermittently. When shooting continuously, even if AF-A is set the camera will automatically shift into AF-C mode *after* the first exposure in the series.

- **DMF (Direct Manual Focus).** Allows you to manually adjust focus after autofocus has been confirmed, using the focus ring on the lens.

- **Manual Focus.** Focus by rotating the focus ring on the lens. The a7R III offers magnification and Focus Peaking as aids to manual focus. I'll describe their use in Chapter 8.

Selecting a Focus Area

The Sony a7R III is equipped with an advanced hybrid autofocus system using both phase detection and contrast detection. I'll explain what those are and how they work in detail in Chapter 8. In Intelligent Auto mode, the focus area that will set focus is selected automatically by the camera; in other words, the AF system decides which part of the scene will be in sharpest focus. In the semi-automatic P, A, and S mode, and in the manual M exposure modes, you can allow the camera to select the focus point automatically, or you can specify which focus point should be used with the Focus Area feature.

Set the camera to one of the four modes mentioned above and select Focus Area from the Camera Settings I-4 (AF1) menu. Focus Area can also be selected using the Function and Quick Navi menus. By default, it will be set to Wide (multi-point autofocus). Scroll up/down until you reach the option you want to use (see Figure 1.14) and press the center button to confirm your selection. (The button is located in the middle of the control wheel that resides to the immediate right of the LCD screen.) There are six autofocus area options, described in Chapter 8. Here's a brief overview of the options.

- **Wide.** The a7R III automatically chooses the appropriate focus area or areas; often, several subjects will be the same distance from the camera as the primary subject. The active AF area or areas are then displayed in green on the LCD monitor or in the viewfinder, depending on which display you're using.

- **Zone.** In this mode, a frame that encompasses nine focus areas appears on the LCD while you're shooting. You can move this grid around the frame with the joystick controller shown in Figure 1.12 (*not* the directional buttons), and the camera will select which of the focus areas to use to focus within the zone you specify.

- **Center.** The camera *always* uses the focus area in the center of the frame, so it will focus on the subject that's closest to the center in your composition.

- **Flexible Spot.** After you select this option from Focus Area, you can use the joystick or left/right directional buttons to specify Small, Medium, or Large focus areas. Then, while viewing your subject, you can move the focus frame (rectangle) around the screen to your desired location, using the joystick. (But *not* the directional buttons. Those who have worked with previous Sony cameras that lack a joystick may need to get used to not using the directional buttons to move the AF area.)

Adjust the focus frame so it covers the most important subject in the scene; I'll discuss this topic in more detail in Chapter 8, where I'll cover many aspects of autofocus (as well as manual focus), including some not covered in this Quick Start chapter.

Figure 1.14
Choose Focus Area from this scrolling list.

- **Expand Flexible Spot.** Like standard Flexible Spot, in this mode, if the camera is unable to lock in focus using the selected focus point, it will also use the eight adjacent points to try to achieve focus.

- **Lock-On AF.** In this mode, the camera locks focus onto the subject area that is under the selected focus spot when the shutter button is depressed halfway. Then, if the subject moves (or you change the framing in the camera), the camera will continue to refocus *on that subject*. You can select this mode *only* when the focus mode is set to Continuous AF (AF-C). You can activate it for any of the five focus area options described above. That is, once you've highlighted Lock-On AF on the selection screen, you can then press the left-right directional button and choose Wide, Zone, Center, Flexible Spot, or Expand Flexible Spot.

SWITCHING AF AREAS/POINTS

You can set separate AF points and AF areas for horizontal and two different vertical orientations (horizontal upside-down is not supported) using the Camera Settings I-5 (AF1) menu, and I'll show you how to do use the Switch Vertical/Horizontal AF Area option in Chapter 8.

Other Settings

There are a few other settings you can make if you're feeling ambitious, but don't feel bad if you postpone using these features until you've racked up a little more experience with your Sony a7R III. By default, these camera features will be at Auto, so the camera will make a suitable setting.

Adjusting White Balance and ISO

If you like, you can custom-tailor your white balance (overall color balance) and the ISO level (sensitivity) as long as you're not using Intelligent Auto. To start out, it's best to leave the white balance (WB) at Auto, and to set the ISO to ISO 200 for daylight photos or to ISO 400 for pictures on a dark, overcast day or indoors when you'll be shooting with an external flash. You can adjust white balance with the White Balance entry in the Camera Settings I-12 (Color/WB/Img. Processing) menu; the ISO can be set either from the Camera Settings I-9 (Exposure 1) menu, after pressing the ISO section of the control wheel (the right directional button), or from the Function and Quick Navi menus. (So many optional options!)

After accessing either feature, navigate (scroll) to make the desired setting with the directional buttons, joystick, or by rotating the control wheel. The control wheel and several of the most important buttons are shown in Figure 1.15.

Figure 1.15
The control wheel and some key buttons.

Fn button

Control wheel

Drive mode button

ISO button

Center button

Using the Self-Timer

If you want to have time to get into the photo before the tripod-mounted camera takes the actual shot, the self-timer is what you need. You can select the self-timer using the Drive Mode button (the left directional button on the control wheel). Hold the Drive Mode button and rotate the control wheel to highlight either Self-Timer choice (described next). The dial also includes Single Shot; High-, Medium-, and Low-speed continuous; and various Bracketing options.

When the Drive Mode screen is visible, scroll up/down through the various options until you reach either the Self-timer (Single) or Self-timer CS (continuous) options. When the former is highlighted, press the directional buttons or joystick to choose 2-, 5-, or 10-second durations. With the Self-timer CS choice, you can also specify either 3 or 5 images to be taken after the timer elapses. Press the center button to confirm your choice and a self-timer icon will appear on the LCD monitor. Press the shutter release to lock focus and exposure and to start the timer. The self-timer lamp will blink, and the beeper will sound (unless you've silenced it in the menu) until the final two seconds when the lamp remains lit.

The multiple image option is handy if you are taking family group pictures with a few known inveterate blinkers to be pictured. Note that the self-timer setting is "sticky" and will still be in effect for multiple shots, even if you turn the camera off and power up again. When you're done using the self-timer, reset the camera to one of the other Drive Mode options.

Quick Start to Movie Making

I'm going to talk in more detail about your movie-making options with the a7R III in Chapters 10 and 11. For now, though, I'll give you enough information to get started, in case a cinematic subject wanders into your field of view before you get to that chapter. The overrides you have set for certain aspects while shooting still photos will apply to the video clip that you'll record; these include exposure compensation, the White Balance, any Creative Style, Metering Mode, Face Detection,

D-Range Optimizer, and Lens Compensation. You'll even retain your aperture setting if the camera is in A mode or the shutter speed if it's in S mode. You also get access to the settings for the movie file formats (AVCHD, XAVC S HD, and XAVC S 4K modes we'll explore later in this book) and the resolution in the Record Setting item of the Camera Settings II section of the menu.

After you start recording, you can change the aperture or the shutter speed; either step will make your movie brighter or darker as you'll notice while viewing on the EVF or LCD while making the adjustments. However, you can also set plus or minus exposure compensation for that purpose while filming. The a7R III provides an effective Continuous Autofocus in Movie mode and sound is recorded in stereo with the built-in mics located on the viewfinder housing on top of the camera.

Let's save the discussion of those aspects for Chapters 10 and 11. For the moment, let's just make a basic movie. With the camera turned on, aim at your subject and locate the red Movie record button located to the immediate right of the viewfinder. You don't have to switch to Movie mode using the mode dial; the Movie mode position simply gives you access to more movie-shooting controls, including the ability to adjust shutter speed and aperture.

Compose as you wish and press that button once to start the recording, and again to stop it; don't hold the button down. You can record for up to about 29 minutes consecutively if you have sufficient storage space on your memory card and charge in your battery. The camera will adjust the focus and exposure automatically, and you can zoom while recording, if you have a zoom lens attached to the camera.

After you finish recording a video clip, you can view it by pressing the Playback button at the lower right of the LCD screen. While a movie is being played back, press the down button to access an operation panel with playback controls. (See Figure 1.16.) Highlight the control you want to use with the joystick or directional buttons. I'll explain the use of these buttons in more detail in Chapter 10. From left to right at the bottom of the figure, they are: Previous Movie File, Fast-Rewind, Pause/Resume, Fast-Forward, Next Movie File, Photo Capture, Sound Volume Adjustment, and Close Operation Panel.

Figure 1.16 Movie playback options.

Reviewing the Images You've Taken

The Sony a7R III has a broad range of playback and image review options. I'll cover them in more detail in Chapter 2. Initially, you'll want to learn just the basics for viewing still photos, so I'll assume you have taken only such images. Note that, as always, you have several options—the left/right edges of the control wheel, the joystick, and rear control dial can all be used to view the previous or next image. I'll stick to just one method in the list that follows. After shooting some video or JPEG and/or RAW photos, here's how to view them, using controls shown in Figure 1.17.

Figure 1.17
Review your images using the pertinent camera controls.

Previous/Next image

Zoom

View thumbnails/ Calendar view

Rotate to Zoom in/out

Change amount of information displayed

Move zoomed area

Playback

Delete current image

- **Display the most recently taken image.** Press the Playback button. (It's the small button with a > symbol located to the lower right of the LCD monitor screen.) If you have shot both still photos as well as movie clips, the a7R III will show both in playback mode. Just press the control wheel's center button to play the movie.

- **View a previous image.** Rotate the rear dial to the left.

- **View the next image.** Rotate the rear dial to the right.

- **Change information displayed.** While viewing a photo, press the DISP button (top directional button) repeatedly to cycle among the available displays: views that have no recording data, full recording data (f/stop, shutter speed, image quality/size, etc.), and a thumbnail image with histogram display. (I'll explain all these in Chapter 2.)

- **Delete current image.** Press the lower-right button, marked with a C4 (Custom 4) label and trash can icon, to delete the currently displayed image.

- **Rotate image.** While the image is displayed, press the MENU button and from the Playback 3 menu, select Rotate, followed by pressing the center button, to rotate the image on the screen 90 degrees. Successive presses of the center button rotate the image 90 degrees each time. (You won't likely need this feature unless you have disabled automatic rotation, which causes the camera to display your vertically oriented pictures already rotated. I'll explain how to activate/ deactivate automatic rotation in Chapter 5.)

- **Zoom in.** Press the AF-ON/Zoom button located to the right of the viewfinder window to zoom into the image. Rotating the control wheel on the back of the camera allows you to zoom in and out. You can also scroll around inside the image using the directional buttons. To exit this screen and return to normal view, press the MENU button.

■ **Access thumbnail/calendar view.** While in Playback mode, press the AEL/Index button to display an index screen showing either 9 or 25 thumbnail images (select the number using the Image Index option in the Playback 3 menu). Keep scrolling downward to view the thumbnails of the next images (assuming you have shot lots of photos). Scroll to the thumbnail of the photo you want to view and press the center button; the photo will then fill the screen. In default Date View mode, the a7R III arranges index images by date shot, and includes a calendar view you can use to look for pictures taken on a specific date. (See Figure 1.18.) (When the left bar of the playback screen is highlighted, press the center button to toggle between Calendar and Date View modes.) You can also choose to play back images using Folder View, or display only specific video file formats. I'll explain those options in more detail in Chapter 6.

Figure 1.18 Viewing thumbnails (left) and calendar view (right).

VIEWING BURSTS

Capturing bursts of shots in continuous shooting modes produces a lot of separate images—up to 10 frames per second. Sony lets you speed up picture review by optionally "nesting" each burst sequence into a single "stack," which is represented by a single image overlaid on a "pile" icon. If you decide you do want to look at each image in the burst, press the center button to drill down into the stack, then press the left/right controls to view the images. Press center again to return to normal view. Enable the Display Continuous Shooting Group in the Playback 3 menu to activate the stacking feature.

Transferring Files to Your Computer

The final step in your picture-taking session will be to transfer the photos and/or movies you've taken to your computer for printing, further review, or editing. (You can also take your memory card to a retailer for printing if you don't want to go the do-it-yourself route.) Your a7R III allows you to print directly to PictBridge-compatible printers, without downloading the photos to a computer and to create print orders right in the camera. It also offers an option for selecting which images to transfer to your computer.

For now, you'll probably want to transfer your images by either using the USB cable from the camera to the computer or by removing the memory card from the a7R III and transferring the images with a card reader. The latter option is ordinarily the best, because it's usually much faster and doesn't deplete the camera's battery. However, you might need to use a cable transfer when you have the cable and a computer but no card reader. (You might be using the computer at a friend's home or the one at an Internet café, for example.)

Here's how to transfer images from a memory card to the computer using a card reader:

1. Turn off the camera.
2. Slide open the memory card compartment door and press on the card in Slot 1 or Slot 2, which causes it to pop up, so it can be removed from the slot. (You can see memory cards being removed in Figure 1.10.)
3. Insert the memory card into a memory card reader accessory that is plugged into your computer. Your installed software detects the files on the card and offers to transfer them. The card can also appear as a mass storage device on your desktop; in that case, you can open that and then drag and drop the files to your computer.

To transfer images from the camera to a Mac or PC computer using the USB cable:

1. Turn off the camera.
2. Open the lower port door on the left side of the camera (the upper door, marked with the candelabra-like USB symbol) and plug the USB cable furnished with the camera into the USB port inside that door. (See Figure 1.5, shown earlier in this chapter.)
3. Connect the other end of the USB cable to a USB port on your computer.
4. Turn on the camera. From this point on, the method is the same as in entry 3 in the card reader list above.

Wireless File Transfer

Your a7R III is also equipped with built-in Wi-Fi, which provides many options, including a method for wireless transfer of image files to a Mac or Windows computer when connected to a wireless network. This is a multi-faceted topic, so I won't begin to discuss it here; instead, you'll find full coverage in Chapter 5.

The camera is also compatible with the Eye-Fi-brand memory card that allows for wireless transfer of files to a computer. (It can also be used for wireless transfer to a smart device running a free app.) This card looks and acts exactly like an ordinary SD card, but with a big difference. Once you have the card set up with your local Wi-Fi (wireless) network, whenever you take a picture or record a movie with this card in the camera, the card wirelessly connects to your computer over that network and transmits the file to any location you have specified.

Since the a7R III already offers a wealth of Wi-Fi features, there's really no need to buy an Eye-Fi card. If you already own one for use with another camera however, it will work well with your Sony, too. This will initially preclude the need to learn how to use the camera's own Wi-Fi features, which can seem more complicated because of the sheer number of available options.

2

Your Camera Roadmap

The Sony a7R III has the same electronic viewfinder (EVF) as the Sony a9, with the Quad-VGA OLED (organic LED) EVF sporting a resolution of approximately 3,686k dots, and utilizing a Zeiss T* Coating to reduce reflections. On top of this, the a7R III supports a customizable frame rate for the EVF, with options of either 60 fps or 120 fps, again matching the 120 fps offered by the A9.

Sony calls the official manual for the a7R III a "Help Guide," which many take to mean that the average user needs a lot of help to use it. It's 650 pages long and includes pages of tiny black-and-white drawings impaled with dozens of callouts. Six pages are devoted just to labeling the 258 individual icons that can appear in the viewfinder and LCD screen. Seeking information about a specific feature is a lot like being presented with a world globe when what you really want is to locate the capital of Brazil.

I'll take a somewhat different approach in this book, particularly in this "roadmap" chapter. Rather than provide you with a satellite view, I'll give you a street-level map that includes close-up, full-color photos of the camera from several angles, with a smaller number of labels clearly pointing to each individual feature. And, I don't force you to flip back and forth among dozens of pages to find out what a component does. Each photo is accompanied by a brief description that summarizes the control, so you can begin using it right away. *Only when a feature deserves a lengthy explanation do I direct you to a more detailed write-up later in the book.*

Unfortunately, it's not possible to explain everything there is to know about every button and control with anything less than a mammoth 100-page chapter. But it is possible to tell you what you absolutely *must* know to get started. So, if you're wondering what the right directional button on the control wheel does (it summons the ISO adjustment screen), I'll tell you up front, rather than have you flip to several pages. This book is not a scavenger hunt. But after I explain how to use the drive mode dial to select continuous shooting, I *will* provide a cross-reference to a longer explanation later in the book that clarifies the use of the various drive modes, the self-timer, and exposure bracketing. Some readers write and complain about even my minimized cross-reference approach; they'd like to open the book to one page and read *everything* there is to know about bracketing, for example. Unfortunately, it's impossible to understand some features without having a background in what related features do.

So, my strategy is to provide you with introductions in the earlier chapters, covering simple features completely, and relegating some of the in-depth explanations to later chapters. I think this kind of organization works best for a camera as sophisticated as the Sony a7R III. However, by the time you finish this chapter, you'll have a good understanding of every control and of the various roles each can take on. I'll provide a lot more information about items in the menus and submenus in Chapters 3, 4, 5, and 6, but the following descriptions should certainly satisfy the button pusher and dial twirler in you.

Front View

When thinking about any given camera, we always imagine the front view. That's the view that your subjects see as you snap away, and the aspect that's shown in product publicity and on the box. The frontal angle is, essentially, the "face" of a camera like the Sony a7R III. But, not surprisingly, most of the "business" of operating the camera happens *behind* it, where the photographer resides. The front of the camera has very few controls and features to worry about. These few controls are most obvious in Figure 2.1:

- **AF illuminator/Self-timer lamp.** This bright LED flashes while your camera counts down the 2-second or 10-second self-timer. In 10-second mode, the lamp blinks at a measured pace off and on at first, then switches to a constant glow in the final moments of the countdown. When the self-timer is set to 2 seconds, the lamp stays lit throughout the countdown. Stop the self-timer, once initiated, by pressing the shutter release a second time. This lamp also serves as the AF (autofocus) Illuminator, emitting its orange-red glow in dark conditions to help the camera's autofocus system achieve sharp focus. You can enable/disable the AF illuminator in the Camera Settings I-6 (AF2) menu.

- **Front dial.** Adjusts various settings. It's often used in conjunction with the rear dial to control pairs of adjustments, such as shutter speed and aperture.

- **Remote sensor.** Detects infrared signals from the RMT-DSLR1 or RMT-DSLR2 Wireless Remote Commanders to take still pictures and (with the RMT-DSLR2 model only) to start/stop movie recording. Make sure the Remote Control entry in the Setup 3 menu is set to On. I'll show you how to adjust the various remote control options in Chapter 6.

- **Lens release button.** Press and hold this button to unlock the lens so you can rotate it to remove the lens from the camera.

- **Lens release pin.** Retracts when the release button is pressed, to allow removing the lens.

- **Mounting index.** Match this recessed, white index button with a similar white indicator on the camera's lens mount to line the two up for attaching the lens to the a7R III.

Figure 2.1

AF illuminator/
Self-timer lamp

Front dial

Remote sensor

Lens release pin

Lens release button

Internal Wi-Fi
receiver

Mounting index

Image sensor

Lens bayonet
mount

Electrical
contacts

- **Lens bayonet mount.** Grips the matching mount on the rear of the lens to secure the lens to the camera body. While some early E-mount cameras had relatively weak lens mounts, later models and the a7R III have a sturdy mount fully capable of supporting many longer lenses. However, it's always a good idea to hold one hand under a very long lens and, if using a tripod or monopod, attach the support to the tripod socket of the lens (if available), rather than the one on the bottom of the a7R III body.

- **Electrical contacts.** These metal contact points match up with a similar set of points on the lens, allowing for communication with the camera about matters such as focus and aperture.

- **Image sensor.** This fairly ordinary-looking little rectangle is the heart and soul of your digital camera. On the Sony camera, this EXMOR sensor is a CMOS (complementary metal-oxide semiconductor) device, approximately 36mm × 24.0mm in size, with 42 megapixels of resolution.

- **Internal Wi-Fi receiver.** You can't access the Wi-Fi/Bluetooth antenna built into the hand-grip of the a7R III, but it's good to know where it is, so you don't accidentally wrap it in tin foil or something.

On the right side of the a7R III (as seen when you're holding the camera to shoot) are several important components, shown in Figure 2.2:

- **Memory card door.** Slide open to insert one or two SD cards or one SD card in Slot 1, and a memory stick in Slot 2. The two slots are shown in the figure in x-ray view. Ordinarily you have to open the door to actually see them.

- **Memory card door switch.** Slide this switch toward the bottom of the camera to reveal the memory cards.

Figure 2.2

Memory card door switch

Slot 2: UHS-I/
Memory Stick or SD cards

Slot 1: UHS-I/
UHS-II SD cards

Memory card door

NFC indicator

- **NFC indicator.** This isn't a control per se; the label emblazoned on the side of the camera indicates the touch point for connecting the a7R III with an NFC (Near Field Communication) device, such as an Android smartphone. When linked, the two devices can communicate directly using short-range wireless technology, as I'll describe in Chapter 5.

- **Slot 1:** This memory card slot can be used with both UHS-I and the faster UHS-II SD, SDHC, and SDXC memory cards. I explained the advantages of UHS-II-compatible media, which are capable of transfer speeds of up to 312 MB/second, in Chapter 1. For continuous shooting or video, you'll want to put your fastest memory card in this slot and use it as the primary destination for your images and movies. Use the Select Media entry in the Camera Settings I-3 (Shoot Mode/Drive 1) menu tab.

- **Slot 2:** This slot accepts Sony Memory Sticks (if you happen to own some) as well as SD, SDHC, and SDXC media (henceforth referred to as *SD* cards). Transfer speeds for such cards top out at the UHS-I version's maximum of 104 MB/second. I use Slot 2 for overflow so the a7R III switches from Slot 1 to Slot 2 automatically when my primary card is full. In Chapter 6 I'll explain some other behaviors you can assign to your memory card slots, such as specifying one card for JPEG and the other for RAW files, or to save movies and still photos on different cards.

In Figure 2.3, left, you can see one of the port covers that provide a modicum of protection from dust and moisture for the six internal connectors. The other two ports are open and the cable protector, which holds any or all of three different cables firmly connected, as I'll describe shortly. At right in the figure you can see the six terminals:

- **Port cover.** Fold back this cover to reveal the six ports, and a charge lamp, described next.

- **Microphone jack.** Allows connecting an external stereo microphone to provide better audio recording than the a7R III's built-in mics.

■ **Custom 3/Protect button.** This button's dual features are not complicated. When shooting images, the C3 button changes Focus Mode (AF-S, AF-A, AF-C, Direct Manual Focus, and Manual Focus). In Playback mode, the button Protects or un-Protects the image being viewed, so it can/cannot be deleted. (Using the Format command overrides protection, however.) Both behaviors can be set to some other function using the Custom Key entry in the Camera Settings II-8 menu.

Tip

As you'll learn, the control wheel and many buttons, including C1 and C2 (located on the top surface of the camera) as well as C3 and C4 (on the back panel), can be redefined to some other action, allowing you to tailor the camera's operation so it best suits your needs using the Camera Settings II-8 menu. However, keep in mind that customizing your camera's behavior can lead to confusion—both for you and for others you may allow to use the camera.

■ **Function/Send to Smartphone button.** In Shooting mode, press the Fn button to produce a screen with shooting setting options, as seen in Figure 2.5. By default, the 12 functions shown are displayed. However, as I'll describe in Chapter 4, you can choose exactly which functions you'd like to display; you aren't locked into 12. If you prefer, you can define a single row of six favorite functions or include some other number/combinations of choices.

Figure 2.5
Up to 12 user-selectable choices are available in the Function menu. This is the default layout.

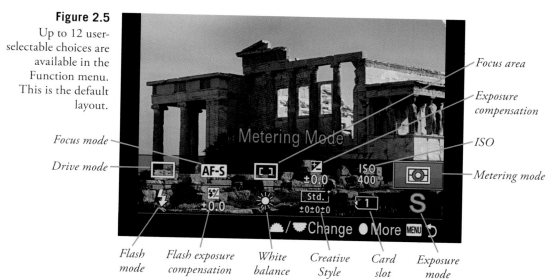

Focus mode

Drive mode

Focus area

Exposure compensation

ISO

Metering mode

Flash mode

Flash exposure compensation

White balance

Creative Style

Card slot

Exposure mode

To adjust any of the functions, just follow these steps.

1. Press the Fn button and use the directional keys to highlight one of the options. **Note:** Exposure Compensation is available from the Function menu *only* when the Exposure Compensation dial on top of the camera (described later in this chapter) is set to zero.

2. When your setting is highlighted:

   - **Press the center button** to produce an adjustment screen with all the choices shown. You might need to do this as you are learning to use your camera and would like to see all your options arrayed in a vertical column. Then use the directional buttons to select the one you want. If a choice has multiple options, it will be accompanied by a right-pointing or left-pointing arrow. For example, if you choose the self-timer, you can press the left/right buttons to select timer durations of either 5 or 10 seconds.

   - **Optionally, you can rotate the control wheel *or* the front dial** to cycle among the available choices, which will appear one by one as you spin. Some of the choices have multiple options in this mode as well, which will appear on the screen below the main selections. Rotate the *rear* dial to select one of these.

3. Press the center button to confirm your choice. You'll be returned to the Function menu (press MENU to exit) or will exit the settings entirely.

■ **LCD monitor screen.** This swiveling screen can be used to preview images and to view them afterward, and to display/navigate menus. The LCD monitor has 3:2 proportions, which is perfect for previewing/shooting/reviewing stills. When you're shooting movies or using the 16:9 aspect ratio for stills, black bars appear at the top and bottom of the screen.

You can set the LCD monitor brightness with an item in the Setup menu, to be discussed in Chapter 6; there's a special feature that provides a super-bright display, useful on bright days when the screen would otherwise be difficult to view. The monitor swivels upward or downward to provide a waist-level view (see Figure 2.6) or, by flipping the camera upside down, shoot images in "periscope" mode with the camera held overhead. The screen has limited touch functions, which I'll explain in the section that follows.

Figure 2.6
Tilting LCD.

■ **Playback button.** Displays the last picture taken. Thereafter, you can move back and forth among the available images by pressing the left/right directional buttons or spinning the control wheel (on the back of the camera) or front dial (on front of the camera) to advance or reverse one image at a time. To quit playback, press this button again. The a7R III also exits Playback mode automatically when you press the shutter release button halfway (so you'll never be prevented from taking a picture on the spur of the moment because you happened to be viewing an image).

■ **Multi-selector.** This joystick-like control serves as an all-purpose directional tool when navigating among menus, specifying a focus area within the frame when capturing images, and adjusting the zoomed area during playback. It can be pressed in the left/right/up/down directions and also diagonally.

- **Menu mode.** Navigate among menu tabs and screens using the directional function. In menus, it serves as an Enter/OK button when you press down on it (as if it were a button).

- **Shooting mode.** Use the directional function to position focus point (when available) and press down to move the focus point/area to the center of the frame.

- **Playback mode.** Directional functions move the zoomed area around with the frame. Press down to exit zoomed view.

■ **Control wheel.** This ridged dial, which surrounds the large center button, also has multiple functions, depending on the camera's mode. In both Shooting and Playback modes it can be useful for navigating menu screens to get to the item or option you want to use.

The control wheel performs several important functions and is the only control on the camera that can be activated in two different ways: you can rotate the ridged part of the wheel to perform certain actions (such as navigation or setting exposure controls), and you can press on the various edges at top, bottom, left, and right. In that mode the edges serve as directional buttons for navigating through menu screens, for example. I'll explain the use of the "button" component of the control wheel in the entry that follows this one. The functions of the wheel itself include:

- **Shooting mode.** By default, no function is assigned to the control wheel when shooting still photographs. However, you can redefine it to perform several optional functions if you like. Using the Custom Key entry of the Camera Settings II-8 menu, you can define the control wheel to move the AF point left/right or up/down, change the aperture, shutter speed, or ISO, or set white balance, Creative Style, or Picture Effect. Note that all these can be readily adjusted using their default controls, but you can assign these functions to the control wheel if you prefer.

- **Playback mode.** When reviewing images during playback, the control wheel always moves forward to the next image (when rotated clockwise) or to the previous image (when rotated counterclockwise). The rear dial and left/right buttons can also be used for that function. You cannot redefine the control wheel to do something else during playback.

YOUR CHOICE

Throughout this book, I'll be using the terms directional buttons, directional controls, left/right button/control or similar navigational descriptions. In most cases, you can use either the multi-selector joystick or the directional buttons for navigation, and I will generally refer to them as directional controls rather than explicitly say *multi-selector joystick* or *left/right/up/down buttons*. Choose the method that works best for you.

■ **Control wheel buttons (Playback mode).** During image review, the buttons along the edge of the control wheel are used for navigating. Keep in mind that many of the directional buttons' functions are also available using the multi-selector joystick. When an image is magnified in Playback mode, all four buttons and their diagonal counterparts can be used to move the viewing area around within the magnified image and within the index screens during playback. When the image is not magnified, the left/right buttons move to the previous/next image on your memory card in Playback mode.

■ **Control wheel buttons (Shooting mode).** The center, left, and right directional buttons (but not the down button) also have a default specific purpose that activates when pressed, and that function is labeled on the area outside the wheel itself. You can also redefine any of these keys (including Down) using the Custom Keys entry in the Camera Settings II-8 menu, as described in Chapter 4. Here's a summary of their default definitions:

• **Up key/DISP button.** The up key is labeled as DISP, for Display Contents, and it provides display-oriented functions, which vary depending on your Shooting/Playback mode:

◆ **Shooting mode.** When the camera is in Shooting mode, press the DISP button repeatedly to cycle among the three screens that display data in the electronic viewfinder display or the six screens that display information about current settings on the LCD screen.

The default display for the LCD is called Display All Info. This provides a full information display with a great deal of data overlaid over the live preview to show the settings in effect. The data provided when the camera is in a SCN mode or either Auto mode is quite limited; use P, A, S, or M mode to view all the available data in each display option. Not all the information shown in the figure will be displayed at all times.

When you keep pressing the DISP button, the camera LCD cycles through other viewing modes, including No Display Info, which provides a few bits of data, a Graphic Display that shows the shutter speed and aperture on two related scales along with some recording information, and a basic display with a histogram in the bottom right of the screen. There is also a For Viewfinder/Quick Navi text information screen that omits the thumbnail and shows only shooting information. When you press the Fn button when the For Viewfinder screen is visible, you can then select and change settings, as I'll describe shortly. You can enable/disable each of these information displays using the DISP entry within the Camera Settings II-6 menu, as I'll explain in Chapter 4.

    ◆ **Playback mode.** In Playback mode, the DISP button offers different display options, as you would expect. When viewing still images during playback, press the DISP button to cycle among the three available playback screens: full recording data, histogram with recording data, and no recording data. When displaying a movie on the screen, the DISP button produces only two screens: with or without recording information. There is no histogram display available.

● **Down button.** By default, the down key has no special function, but you can define one of your choices using the Custom Keys entry in the Camera Settings II-8 menu, as described in Chapter 4.

● **Left button/Drive mode button.** One press of this button in a compatible Shooting mode leads to a series of options that let you set the self-timer, enable the camera to shoot one frame at a time or continuously at a fast or very fast rate, or set up exposure bracketing. The latter causes the camera to automatically take a series of shots, varying the exposure for each to ensure you get the best exposure possible.

When you scroll to the Self-timer or Bracket item, you can press the right key to adjust options for those drive modes, as discussed in Chapter 5.

● **Right button/ISO button.** When not helping you navigate to the right through menus and other screens, this button lets you activate the ISO screen in a compatible Shooting mode. You can then scroll up/down among the options by rotating the camera's rear dial or control wheel or by pressing the wheel's directional buttons.

■ **Center button.** In shooting mode, the center button activates Eye AF, which tells the a7R III to look for human eyes and focus on them. (You'll find more on autofocus in Chapter 8.) In Playback mode, it exits the zoom function, while when using menus, it serves as an OK/Enter button. You can redefine the center button's behavior during still shooting and movie modes, as I'll explain in Chapter 4.

■ **Custom 4/Trash button.** This button enables/disables the touch screen when in Shooting mode (although you can specify another function using the Custom Keys feature). In Playback mode, the button serves as a delete key.

■ **Memory card access lamp.** Flashes red while the memory card is being written to. It is located on the back of the camera, to the right of the C4/Trash button.

Introducing the Touch Screen/Pad

Sony has added a touch screen/pad to the a7R III's arsenal of tools. The dual screen/pad nomenclature is applied because the touch feature can be used in two different ways: as a touch screen when you are using the LCD monitor to compose your photos and as a touch pad that you can tap when the camera is raised to your eye and you're using the electronic viewfinder. This section explains both modes and the options available once you've set up touch operations using the step-by-step instructions in Chapter 4.

Before you wax ecstatic, you'll want to know that the touch features are limited to the ability to specify a focus point when shooting stills and videos. You can't select menu entries, type in text, scroll through playback views, or pinch/expand with your fingertips to zoom in and out during image review. However, the touch focus feature is quite useful, especially when shooting movies, as it allows selecting a focus area with a gentle tap. Here are the two modes:

- **Touch screen.** When active and you're using the LCD monitor to compose, you can select a focus point or zone anywhere that the a7R III is able to achieve autofocus (that is, most of the frame other than the edges). You can tap the screen or hold down your finger and slide the focus area around. A "Focus Cancel" message appears; press the center button to cancel your focus selection. A quick tap may not register; this function requires a firm press. I'll explain the various AF-area modes in Chapter 8.

- **Touch pad.** When touch pad mode is active and you're using the electronic viewfinder to compose, you can touch the LCD monitor screen to specify the focus area. You don't have to tap the exact area (actually, that's impossible, because you're not actually looking at the LCD). Instead, when you touch the pad, a focus point appears in the viewfinder *relative to the location on the LCD.* That is, if you tap the center of the sensitive area, the focus point appears in the center; tap to the right or left, and the focus area appears to the right or left side. As I'll explain shortly, that mode is needed because you can change the size of the sensitive area of the LCD screen. Once the focus area is displayed, keep your finger on the screen and slide it around to the position you want, using your view through the EVF as your reference.

Touch Options

Three touch options are available from the Setup 2 and 3 menus. I'm not going to explain how to navigate menus in this Quick Start. You can learn exactly how to enter touch screen options in Chapter 6. Here, I'll just quickly describe the adjustments you can make, and why.

- **Touch operation.** Here you can turn touch operation on or off. If you don't want to use the touch screen you can disable it to avoid moving your focus point when you accidentally touch it.

- **Touch panel/Pad.** You can define whether the LCD-oriented Touch Panel or EVF-oriented Touch Pad, or *both* are active. Select Touch Panel Only, and the touch features operate only when you are composing using the LCD monitor; when you bring the camera up to your eye, the touch panel is disabled. Select Touch Pad Only, and touch features are disabled until you bring the camera up to your eye.

- **Touch pad settings.** This entry has three adjustments:

  - **Operation in vertical orientation.** You can specify whether touch controls are available when the camera is oriented in the vertical position (On), or only when the camera is held in horizontal orientation (Off). The touch feature can be a little awkward to use when rotated vertically, so some prefer to disable touch control for that mode.

  - **Touch position mode.** Specify whether touch functions operate using the *absolute* position on your screen (tap an exact position on the screen to move the focus point to the equivalent position on the sensor) or a *relative* position (tap the screen anywhere in the sensitive area, and then slide your finger to move the focus point in that direction from its current position).

  - **Operation area.** By default, the entire touch pad is sensitive when using the EVF, and that works well for most people. However, if your left eye is dominant (i.e., you're "left-eyed"), your nose will touch the screen, and the a7R III registers that as a finger press. To fix that or to adjust for your personal preferences, you can limit sensitivity of the touch *pad* to the right *or* left 1/2 or 1/4 areas of the screen; or the upper-right, lower-right, upper-left, or lower-left corners. The "relative" orientation remains the same but is limited to that reduced area.

LCD Panel Data Displays

The Sony a7R III provides a tilting and expansive 3-inch color LCD with high resolution to display everything you need to see, from images to a collection of informational data displays. Some of the data is shown only when you are viewing the Display All Info screen, but even then, not every item of data will be available all the time. (See Figure 2.7.) As discussed earlier, the electronic viewfinder display options provide much less data to avoid cluttering the live preview with numerals and icons during serious photography. **Note:** when you tilt the LCD monitor away from the camera body, the viewfinder is disabled, because the camera assumes you will be composing your image and performing other functions only with the LCD.

While it is not possible to describe all the dozens and dozens of icons available for the LCD screen; you'll find them shown on Pages 38 to 43 of the Sony Help Guide. The following is a description of the most important information that the camera can display in the LCD in Display All Info when it's set for P, A, S, or M mode; less data is available in other display modes and when other Shooting modes are being used. The For Viewfinder/Quick Navi text-only displays (shown only on the LCD monitor and not in the viewfinder) are pictured in Figures 2.8 and 2.9.

Figure 2.7
The Display All Info screen on the LCD.

Figure 2.8
The For Viewfinder information screen is available only for the LCD monitor and is not shown in the viewfinder.

Figure 2.9
The Quick-Navi screen on the LCD.

- **Shooting mode.** Shows whether you're using Program Auto, Aperture Priority, Shutter Priority, Manual, one of the scene modes, or one of the two Auto modes.

- **Memory card/Uploading status.** Indicates whether a memory card is in the camera. (If you remove the card, a blinking NO CARD indicator will appear instead.) If the camera is connected using Wi-Fi, the indicator will display icons representing the upload status.

- **Exposures remaining.** Shows the approximate number of shots available to be taken on the memory card, assuming current conditions, such as image size and quality. When shooting a movie, the recordable time remaining is shown instead.

- **Aspect ratio/Image size.** Shows whether the camera is set for the 3:2 aspect ratio or widescreen 16:9 aspect ratio (the image size icon changes to a "stretched" version when the aspect ratio is set to 16:9) and whether you're shooting Large, Medium, or Small resolution images. When the camera is set to the 16:9 aspect ratio, the display has black bands at the top and the bottom, as you would expect with the longer/narrower format vs. the 3:2 aspect ratio which is closer to square in shape.

- **Image quality.** Your image quality setting (JPEG Extra Fine, JPEG Fine, JPEG Standard, RAW, or RAW & JPEG) is displayed.

- **Frame rate/Movie recording settings.** These icons show what movie settings are in use such as 60i FH (full HD video at 60i). I'll discuss your movie-making options, including file formats and size, in Chapter 10.

- **NFC active indicator.** Shows when your a7R III is linked to another device using Near Field Communications.

- **Battery status.** The remaining battery life (in percent) is indicated by this icon.

- **Metering mode.** The icons represent Multi, Center, or Spot metering. (See Chapter 9 for more detail.)

- **Flash exposure compensation.** This icon is shown whenever an external flash is active to indicate the level of flash exposure compensation, if any, that you have set.

- **White balance.** Shows current white balance setting. The choices are Auto White Balance, Daylight, Shade, Cloudy, Incandescent, Fluorescent, Flash, Color Temperature, and Custom. I'll discuss white balance settings and adjustments in Chapter 4.

- **Dynamic Range Optimizer/HDR.** Indicates the type of dynamic range optimization (highlight/shadow detail enhancement) in use: Off, Auto DRO, levels 1–5 of DRO, or the special Auto HDR feature, all described in Chapter 9.

- **Creative style.** Indicates which of the six Creative Style settings (Standard, Vivid, Portrait, Landscape, Sunset, or Black-and-White) is being applied.

- **Picture effect.** Shows which of the special effects, such as Toy Camera, Pop Color, or Posterization, is being applied. I'll explain these options in Chapter 3.

- **SteadyShot indicator.** Provides information as to whether the image stabilizer is On or Off if you're using a lens with the SteadyShot mechanism and warns you that the shutter speed will be too long for the stabilizer to fully compensate for camera shake.

- **Flash charge in progress.** This lightning bolt icon appears on the screen when the flash unit is active; a solid orange dot beside it indicates the flash has recycled (charged) and is ready to fire.

- **AF Illuminator status.** This icon appears when conditions are dark enough that the AF Illuminator will be needed to light up the area so that the autofocus system can operate properly.

- **Flash mode.** Provides flash mode information when an external flash is active. The possible choices are Flash Off, Autoflash, Fill Flash, Slow Sync, Rear Curtain, and Wireless. Not all these choices are available at all times. I'll discuss flash options in more detail in Chapter 13.

- **Drive mode.** Shows whether the camera is set for Single-shot, Continuous shooting, Speed Priority Continuous shooting, Self-timer, Self-timer with continuous shooting, or Exposure bracketing. There is one additional option available: Remote Commander, which sets up the camera to be controlled by an infrared remote control.

- **AE Lock.** Appears when autoexposure has been locked at the current setting.

- **ISO setting.** Indicates the sensor ISO sensitivity currently set, either Auto ISO or a numerical value. I'll discuss this camera feature in Chapter 9.

- **Exposure compensation.** This indicator shows the amount of exposure compensation, if any, currently set.

- **Aperture.** Displays the current f/stop set by the camera or, in Manual or Aperture Priority mode, as set by the user. If you're viewing the Graphic display, icons indicate that wider apertures produce less depth-of-field (a "blurry" background) while smaller apertures provide a greater range of acceptable sharpness (increasing the odds of a more distinct background).

- **Shutter speed.** Shows the current shutter speed, either as set by the camera's autoexposure system or, in Manual or Shutter Priority mode, as set by the user. If the camera's Graphic display is used, the screen illustrates that faster shutter speeds are better for action and slower speeds are fine for scenes with less movement.

- **Focus indicator.** Flashes while focus is underway, and turns a solid green when focus is confirmed.

- **Focus mode.** Shows the currently selected focus mode, such as AF-S, AF-C, DMF (Direct Manual Focus), or MF (Manual Focus), as explained in Chapter 9.

- **Focus area mode.** Displays the active focus area mode, such as Wide, Zone, Center, or Flexible Spot, as explained in Chapter 9.

- **Face Priority mode.** Shows status of Face Detection mode (on/off). When the feature is activated, the camera attempts to detect faces in the scene before it, and, if it does, it adjusts autofocus, exposure, and white balance accordingly. When the Face Registration feature is also in use, the camera can detect a face that you have registered as a favorite. The camera can also use Eye AF to locate and focus on human eyes found within the frame, as long as you're using Single Autofocus (AF-S). Autofocus options are discussed in more detail in Chapter 8.

- **Picture Profile.** If you've specified a picture profile image customization setting in Camera Setting I-12, your choice (from PP1 to PP10) is indicated here. I discuss picture profiles in Chapter 3.

- **Zoom.** Shows when digital zoom modes are active.

- **Setting Effect.** Indicates whether the LCD shows the effects of any adjustments, including exposure, white balance, or Picture Effects in Shooting mode.

- **Database indicator.** This warning appears when your memory card's image database is full or has errors.

- **Audio recording.** Shows whether sound recording is enabled/disabled for movie shooting.

- **Airplane mode.** This icon appears when Airplane mode has disabled Wi-Fi and NFC communications.

Using the Quick Navi Function Menu

If you select the For Viewfinder screen by pressing the DISP button until it appears, the LCD monitor shows the For Viewfinder display, with only the data and no live view of the scene, as you can see in Figure 2.8. Press the Fn button to switch to the Quick Navi screen (see Figure 2.9). You can then use the multi-selector joystick or the left/right/up/down directional buttons to highlight any of the settings that are not grayed out.

Once an option is highlighted, you can rotate the control wheel to change its settings quickly or press OK (either the center button or multi-selector) to produce a screen with all the options. Use directional buttons and the OK button to select the option you want. The Quick Navi screen is, in effect, a more fully featured Function menu. When the Quick Navi display is visible on the LCD monitor, you must compose images using the electronic viewfinder.

Going Topside

The top surface of the a7R III has several frequently accessed controls of its own. They are labeled in Figure 2.10:

- **Focal plane indicator.** Precision macro and scientific photography sometimes requires knowing exactly where the focal plane of the sensor is. The symbol etched on the top of the camera marks that plane.

- **Multi-interface shoe.** This "standard" accessory shoe is used for electronic flash units and contains extra electrical contacts for use with Sony-brand microphones, such as the Sony ECM-XYSTM1 microphone and other accessories. However, it is also compatible with the ISO-518 hot shoe used by virtually all other camera manufacturers.

The multi-interface shoe replaces the non-standard Minolta-style proprietary "iISO" shoe used by Sony for many of its cameras until about 2012. The older shoe required adapters to use non-Sony accessories. The new multi-interface connector can still be used with older Sony flash units and accessories, but it requires an adapter of its own for backward compatibility. If you own no older Sony electronic flash or accessories, you can simply move forward and purchase gear for the new, more standard hot shoe.

Figure 2.10

- **Stereo microphones.** A pair of microphones on the top panel of the camera can capture stereophonic audio while making movies.

- **Speaker.** Sounds emanating from your camera emerge here.

- **Mode dial/Mode Dial Lock Release button.** Press the center Lock Release button and rotate this dial to select Shooting modes including Manual exposure, Shutter Priority, Aperture Priority, Program Auto, Intelligent Auto, Slow Motion/Quick Motion (S&Q), Movie mode, and the Memory Recall positions, numbered 1, 2, and 3 (which each allow you to choose from up to four predefined groups of settings).

- **Exposure Compensation dial.** Rotate this dial to add or subtract up to three stops' worth of exposure.

- **On/Off switch.** Rotate to the right to turn the camera on; to the left to switch it off.

- **Shutter release button.** Partially depress this button to lock in exposure and focus. Press it all the way to take the picture. Hold this button down to take a continuous stream of images when the drive mode is set for Continuous shooting. Tapping the shutter release when the camera's power save feature has turned off the autoexposure and autofocus mechanisms reactivates both. When a review image or menu screen is displayed on the LCD, tapping this button removes that display, returning the camera to the standard view and reactivating the autoexposure and autofocus mechanisms.

- **Custom 1 button.** By default, this summons the white balance menu. The Custom 1 button can also be re-defined to perform any of several different functions, such as metering mode, creative style, drive mode, focus mode, flash mode, flash compensation, focus area, exposure compensation, and more than 50 (count 'em!) other behaviors. You can also select Not Set to deactivate it entirely. In Chapter 4, I'll show you how to redefine this button in the Custom Key Settings entry of the Camera Settings II-8 menu.

- **Custom 2 button.** By default, this button activates focus area (described in more detail in Chapter 8) but can be redefined to other functions.

Underneath Your Sony a7R III

The bottom panel of your a7R III has only a few components, illustrated in Figure 2.11.

- **Tripod socket**. Attach the camera to a vertical grip, flash bracket, tripod, monopod, or other support using this standard receptacle. The socket is positioned roughly behind the optical center of the lens, a decent location when using a tripod with a pan (side rotating) movement, compared to an off-center orientation. For most accurate panning, the socket would ideally be placed a little forward (in *front* of the camera body) so the pivot point is located *under* the optical center of the lens, but you can't have everything. There are special attachments you can use to accomplish this if you like.

Figure 2.11

- **Battery compartment door.** Slide the door open to access the battery. This door can be removed when you attach an optional battery grip.
- **Connection plate cover.** When using the Sony AC-PW20 AC adapter, the connection plate replaces the battery in the camera body, and the cord passes through the opening protected by this cover.

What's the Fuss about BSI?

So far, I've given you an introduction to the most important physical components of your a7R III—except for the camera's truly impressive sensor. Traditionally, packing more pixels into a given sensor size yields higher resolution, but results in smaller pixels with less surface area to gather light. So, the a7R III's prodigious 42MP resolution surely must have required squeezing even tinier photosites into your camera's (roughly 36mm × 24mm) sensor, right?

Fortunately for us, not so! The Sony a7R III has an innovative back-side illuminated (BSI) sensor. (Some call this sensor configuration *back-illuminated*, but the term *back-side illuminated* is the more common industry term.) This sensor gives the a7R III remarkable low-light performance with reduced noise, compared to most other high-resolution sensors. The secret to all this good stuff is flipping the electronics around so the light-sensitive photosites are larger and closer to the incoming photons, thanks to the BSI configuration.

As I mentioned earlier, packing more light-gathering "pixels" (photodiodes) onto a sensor to produce high resolution requires using the tiniest "pixels" possible. Smaller pixels are less efficient at collecting light (photons) and processing the captured image to increase sensitivity results in more random artifacts. We call that "high ISO" noise. (A second type of visual noise is produced from long exposures.)

The a7R III reduces high ISO noise by *increasing* the relative size of the photosites. That's possible because with a traditional front-illuminated sensor (shown at left in Figure 2.12), the chip's image-processing circuitry occupies much of the surface, leaving only a small photosensitive area at the bottom of a deep "well." Sony's BSI sensor reverses the position of the circuitry and photodiode components, so that a larger area can be occupied by the photosites, with the electronics positioned *underneath*, closer to the back of the camera, rather than closer to the rear of the lens. (See Figure 2.12, right.)

The figure shows a super-simplified rendition of what happens. (Actual sensors look nothing like this; the diagram includes only one set of three red, green, and blue photosites, is not to scale, and I show only three "beams" of light arriving at the sensor, when photons actually come from multiple directions.) With the conventional front-illuminated sensor at left, incoming light passes through microlenses that focus it on the photosites, which are located at the bottom of a well that resides between the on-chip aluminum circuitry. Even accounting for the microlens's focusing properties, the relative angles that result in light falling on the photosensitive area collected from the edges of the incoming image can be rather steep. Other photons (not shown) strike the sides of the wells or the area of the chip occupied by electronic circuitry and bounce back or around.

This limitation on the angle of incidence accounts for why vendors have been forced to develop "digital" lenses, which, unlike lenses designed for film cameras, focus light on the sensor from less steep angles. That explains, in general, why the a7R III functions better in this regard than most other digital cameras when using older "non-digital" lenses.

Figure 2.12 A conventional front-illuminated sensor (left), and a back-illuminated sensor (right).

At right in the figure is a representation of a back-illuminated sensor. Like the conventional sensor, it includes microlenses that focus the illumination before it passes through a red, green, or blue filter to the photosite. But because those photosites are larger, the minuscule focusing optics are larger, too, providing *gapless microlenses* that gather virtually all the illumination falling on the sensor. And, unlike the front-illuminated sensor, there is no deep well, and, without the need for intervening circuitry, the photosensitive area (shown in magenta for both types of sensors) is much larger. The electronics—faster copper (not aluminum) circuitry with lower resistance—have been moved to the back side of the sensor.

A typical conventional full-frame sensor captures only 30 to 80 percent of the light striking it, whereas a BSI sensor can grab nearly 100 percent of the photons. The angle of incidence is not nearly as crucial, making BSI sensors more similar in that respect to old-time film grain technology. The combination of larger photosensitive surface area and improved acceptable angles for incoming photons are the main factors in the Sony a7R III's superior low-light performance. The speedy copper wiring and enhanced processing algorithms in the digital image processor chip also help—and give the camera its speedy continuous shooting speeds, as well. This camera is as close as you can get to a "do-everything" model, featuring high resolution, reduced noise, and continuous shooting suitable for the fastest action.

I don't normally venture so deeply into techie territory in my camera guides, but BSI sensors (which previously have been used in other devices with especially tiny sensors, such as cell phone cameras) will henceforth play a major part in enthusiast photography technology.

3

Camera Settings I Menu

The a7R III has a remarkable number of features and options you can use to customize the way your camera operates. Not only can you change settings used at the time the picture is taken, but you can adjust the way your camera behaves. This chapter and the next three will help you sort out the settings for all the menus. These include the Camera Settings I, Camera Settings II, Network, Playback, and Setup menus, plus the My Menu custom menu screen. This chapter details options with the Camera Settings I menu; the Camera Settings II menu will be covered in Chapter 4; the Network and Playback menus in Chapter 5; and the Setup and My Menu options will be addressed in Chapter 6.

Why four entire chapters just on the menus, when other sources may have just a single chapter with a line or two about each menu entry explaining what they do? As you're discovering, the a7R III is an incredibly versatile camera with a mind-numbing number of different menu entries, many of which have submenus and multiple options. Even if you're a Sony veteran or an advanced photo enthusiast, you want more than just a brief explanation of what all the menu options do. You also need to know what they *don't* do, *when* to use each one, and, most importantly, when *not* to use them.

And, I'll bet, you purchased this book because you also wanted to know *my* personal preferences for settings and how I use these features. When I share what I know in person at workshops and other sessions with groups of photographers, I always tell them my informal motto: *I make terrible mistakes, so you don't have to!* I like to push cameras to their limits and, in the process, discover exactly what they can do, and what they can't.

So, like most of the rest of this book, Chapters 3 to 6 will cover both aspects in some detail. I'm not going to waste a lot of space on some of the more obvious menu choices in these chapters, especially those with only On/Off or Enable/Disable options. Instead, I'll concentrate on the more complex aspects of setup, such as autofocus. I'll start with an overview of using the camera's menus themselves.

Anatomy of the Menus

The menu system is quite easy to navigate. Pressing the MENU button takes you to a screen like the one shown in Figure 3.1. Rotate the rear dial to move from one main menu or tab to the next. Each tab is assigned a color: Camera Settings I (red), Camera Settings II (purple), Network (green), Playback (blue), and Setup (yellow). When a tab is active its highlight color will be bright, and the hues of the other tabs more subdued, as you can see in the figure. To navigate among menu entries:

- **Change tabs.** When only the tab is highlighted (that is, none of its entries are highlighted in orange), you can quickly move from one main menu tab to the next by using the left/right controls—either the control wheel's directional buttons or by pressing the multi-selector left/right. You can also rotate the rear dial to travel from tab to tab.

- **Select a menu entry.** To choose a menu entry within a main menu tab, use the up/down controls of the control wheel's directional buttons or the multi-selector joystick. You can also rotate the front dial or control wheel to highlight a specific menu entry.

- **Change menu pages.** Each main menu tab has multiple pages. When any entry in a menu tab is highlighted you can move from one page within that tab to the next using the left/right controls or rear dial. When you reach the last page of a tab's menus, additional movement wraps over to the first page of the next tab. The current page within a tab is shown by a numeric value (such as 1/14) and by a series of boxes at the bottom of the screen (you'll find both in Figure 3.1).

  For example, if you are using the Camera Settings I menu, the right key will take you from Camera Settings I-1 to Camera Settings I-2, and thence onward to the Camera Settings I-3 to I-14 tabs. Pressing the right key an additional time takes you onward to the Camera Settings II-1 page.

- **Make adjustments.** When a menu entry is highlighted, press the control wheel's center button or the multi-selector to view options. After making adjustments, press the button again to confirm and exit, or MENU to cancel.

> **Note**
>
> Note that each of the main tabs may have several sub-tabs: the Camera Settings I menu has tabs 1 to 14; Camera Settings II menu has tabs 1 to 9; Network has two tabs; Playback menu has 3; and the Setup menu boasts tabs 1 to 7. The advantage to having so many menu tabs is that all the entries for a given page can be shown on a single screen, with no downward scrolling required.

Camera Settings I menu   Camera Settings II menu   Network menu   Playback menu   Setup menu   My menu

Use left/right controls or rotate the rear dial to move from one main menu or tab to the next

Figure 3.1
Navigating the a7R III's menu system. This is the Camera Settings I-1 (Quality/Image Size 1) menu.

Main menu or tab

Page number within tab

Current value

Use up/down controls or rotate front dial or control wheel to highlight a specific menu entry

Press center button or multi-selector to view options for highlighted menu entry

Menu entry

Quality/Image Size1   1/14 ▸

File Format   JPEG
RAW File Type   Compressed
JPEG Quality   Fine
JPEG Image Size   L:42M
Aspect Ratio   3:2
APS-C/Super 35mm

Selected menu entry   *Page number within tab*   *Press MENU button to cancel and exit*

Press the down button or rotate the front dial or the control wheel to move the highlighting down into the selected tab to the entry you want to work with. You can choose any item in the displayed tab and press the center button to produce a screen where you can adjust the highlighted entry. While navigating any menu tab, use the left/right keys or control wheel to move to the next tab in that menu group, and then to wrap around to the first tab in the next group.

Of course, not everything has to be set using these menus. The a7R III has some convenient direct setting controls, such as the buttons of the control wheel that provide quick access to the drive modes, display information, and the ISO options. These and other buttons can be assigned other direct-access functions—more than 50 different functions in all. These control features allow you to bypass the multi-tabbed menus for many of the most commonly used camera functions.

There is also a Function menu that appears when you press the Fn button, with a set of shooting setting options, as I described in Chapter 2. Although the Fn menu has a default set of 12 functions, you can redefine those entries as well. Your a7R III offers a remarkable degree of customization. If a menu entry is unavailable, it will be "grayed out." Often this happens when you really *want* to use the feature, too. Scroll down to the grayed-out entry and press the center button. A help screen will generally pop up explaining what the problem is. Within this book, I'll also try to tell you the conditions that disable a particular feature.

ABOUT THOSE ICONS

Menu entries are preceded by an icon, such as the "mountain" icon shown next to the first five entries in Figure 3.1. A mountain icon indicates that the particular menu entry applies *only* to still photography; an icon resembling a film frame shows that the menu entry applies *only* to movie making. Presumably, entries without any icon can be used with both. A few menu entries, such as Memory Recall, Proxy Recording, Slow and Fast Motion, Enlarge, and Language are preceded by their own graphic or text icons, and are apparently used just for decorative purposes.

Camera Settings I Menu Entries

Figure 3.1, earlier, shows the first screen of the Camera Settings I menu. As you can see, at most only a half-dozen items are displayed at one time. The items found in this menu are shown in Table 3.1.

Table 3.1 Camera Settings I Menus

Quality/Image Size

File Format (Stills)	Aspect Ratio (Stills)	High ISO Noise Reduction (Stills)
RAW File Type (Stills)	APS-C/Super 35mm	Color Space (Stills)
JPEG Quality (Stills)	Long Exposure Noise Reduction (Stills)	Lens Compensation
JPEG Image Size (Stills)		

Shoot Mode/Drive

Drive Mode	Memory Recall	Register Custom Shooting Set
Bracket Settings	Memory	
Pixel Shift Multi Shooting	MR Select Media	

Autofocus

Focus Mode	Center Lock-on AF	AF Area Registration (Stills)
Priority Setting in AF-S	Set Face Priority in AF	Delete Registered AF Area (Stills)
Priority Setting in AF-C	AF Tracking Sensitivity (Stills)	AF Area Auto Clear
Focus Area	AF System (Stills)	Display Continuous AF Area
Focus Settings	AF with Shutter (Stills)	Phase Detect, Area
Switch Vertical/Horizontal AF Area (Stills)	Pre-AF (Stills)	AF Micro Adjustment
AF Illuminator (Stills)	Eye-Start AF (Stills)	

Table 3.1 Camera Settings I Menus (continued)

Exposure

Exposure Compensation	Metering Mode	AEL with Shutter
Reset Exposure Compensation	Face Priority Multi Metering	Exposure Standard Adjustment
ISO	Spot Metering Point	
ISO Auto Minimum Shutter Speed	Exposure Step	

Flash

Flash Mode	Exposure Compensation Setting	Wireless Flash
Flash Compensation		Red Eye Reduction

Color/White Balance/Image Processing

White Balance	DRO/Auto HDR	Picture Effect
Priority Setting in Auto White Balance	Creative Style	Picture Profile

Focus Assist

Focus Magnifier	Initial Focus Magnification (Stills)	Manual Focus Assist (Stills)
Focus Magnification Time	AF in Focus Magnification (Stills)	Peaking Setting

Shooting Assist

Anti-Flicker Shooting	Face Registration	Registered Face Priority

File Format (Stills)

Options: RAW, RAW & JPEG, JPEG

Default: JPEG Fine

My preference: RAW & JPEG

This menu item lets you choose the file format setting that will be used by the a7R III to store its still photo files. You have three options: RAW, RAW & JPEG, and JPEG. The two entries that follow this one allows you to specify the RAW file type (compressed or uncompressed), and JPEG quality (Extra Fine, Fine, and Standard). Sony has separated these options; previous a7-series cameras combined format and quality in a single Image Quality entry.

Should you select RAW, JPEG, or both? You can elect to store only JPEG versions of the images you shoot, or you can save your photos as "unprocessed" RAW files, which consume several times as much space on your memory card. Or, you can store both file types at once as you shoot.

Many photographers elect, as I do, to shoot *both* a JPEG and a RAW file (RAW & JPEG), so they'll have a JPEG version that might be usable as-is, as well as the original "digital negative" RAW file in case they will later want to make some serious editing of the photo with imaging software for reasons discussed shortly. If you use the RAW & JPEG option, the camera will save two different versions of the same file to the memory card: one with a .JPG extension, and one with the .ARW extension that signifies Sony's proprietary ARW 2.3 RAW format that consists of raw data. (In Chapter 6, I'll show you how to save JPEG files to one slot, and RAW files to the other, using the Recording Mode entry in the Setup 5 menu.)

JPEG vs. RAW

You'll sometimes be told that RAW files are the "unprocessed" image information your camera produces, before it's been modified. That's nonsense. RAW files are no more unprocessed than old-school camera film is after it's been through the chemicals to produce a negative or transparency. A lot can happen in the developer that can affect the quality of a film image—positively and negatively—and, similarly, your digital image undergoes a significant amount of processing before it is saved as a RAW file. Sony even applies a name (BIONZ) to the digital image processor used to perform this magic in Sony cameras.

A RAW file is closer in concept to a film camera's processed negative. It contains all the information, with no compression, no sharpening, no application of any special filters or other settings you might have specified when you took the picture. Those settings are stored with the RAW file, so they can be applied when the image is converted to JPEG or another format compatible with your favorite image editor. However, using RAW converter software such as Adobe Camera Raw (in Photoshop, Elements, or Lightroom) or Sony's Image Data Converter (available for download from various Sony websites worldwide), you can override a RAW photo's settings (such as White Balance and Saturation) by applying other settings in the software. You can make essentially the same changes there that you might have specified in your camera before taking a photo.

Making changes to settings such as White Balance is a non-destructive process in a RAW converter since the changes are made before the photo is fully processed by the software program. Making a change in settings does not affect image quality, except for changes to exposure, highlight or shadow detail, and saturation; the loss of quality is minimal however, unless the changes you make for these aspects are significant. The RAW format exists because sometimes we want to have access to all the information captured by the camera, before the camera's internal logic has processed it and converted the image to a standard file format.

A RAW photo does take up more space than a JPEG and, in uncompressed mode, preserves all the information captured by your camera after it's been converted from analog to digital form. Since we can make changes to settings after the fact while retaining optimal image quality, errors in the settings we made in-camera are much less of a concern than in JPEG capture. When you shoot JPEGs, any modification you make in software is a destructive process; there is always some loss of image quality, although that can be minimal if you make only small changes or are skilled with the use of adjustment layers.

JPEG provides smaller files by compressing the information in a way that loses some image data. The lost data is reconstructed when you open a JPEG in a computer, but this is not a perfect process. If you shoot JPEGs at the highest quality (Extra Fine) level (JPEG Quality choices are explained below), the compression (and loss of data) is minimal; you might not be able to tell the difference between a photo made with RAW capture and a Large/Fine JPEG. If you use the lower quality level, you'll usually notice a quality loss when making big enlargements or after cropping your image extensively.

So, why don't we always use RAW? Although some photographers do save only in RAW format, it's more common to use either RAW plus the JPEG option or to just shoot JPEG and eschew RAW altogether. While RAW is overwhelmingly helpful when an image needs to be modified, working with a RAW file can slow you down significantly. The RAW images take longer to store on the memory card, so you cannot shoot as many in a single burst. Also, after you shoot a series, the camera must pause to write them to the memory card, so you may not be able to take any shots for a while (or only one or two at a time) until the RAW files have been written to the memory card. When you come home from a trip with numerous RAW files, you'll find they require more post-processing time and effort in the RAW converter, whether you elect to go with the default settings in force when the picture was taken or make minor adjustments.

Those who often shoot long series of photos in one session, or want to spend less time at a computer, may prefer JPEG over RAW. Wedding photographers, for example, might expose several thousand photos during a bridal affair and offer hundreds to clients as electronic proofs on a DVD. Wedding shooters take the time to make sure that their in-camera settings are correct, minimizing the need to post-process photos after the event. Given that their JPEGs are so good, there is little need for them to get bogged down working with RAW files in a computer. Sports photographers also avoid RAW files because of the extra time required for the camera to record a series of shots to a memory card and because they don't want to spend hours in extra post-processing. As a bonus, JPEG files consume a lot loss memory in a hard drive.

My recommendation: When shooting sports, I'll switch to shooting Large/Extra Fine JPEGs (with no RAW file) to minimize the time it takes for the camera to write a series of photos to the card; it's great to be able to take another burst of photos at any time, with little or no delay. I also appreciate the fact that I won't need to wade through long series of photos taken in RAW format.

In most situations however, I shoot virtually everything as RAW & JPEG. Most of the time, I'm not concerned about filling up my memory cards, as I usually carry at least three 64GB or 128GB memory cards with me. If I know I may fill up all those cards (say, on a long trip), I'll also carry my notebook computer and an external 2 terabyte hard drive to back up my files.

RAW File Type (Stills)

Options: Compressed, Uncompressed

Default: Compressed

My preference: Uncompressed

This option allows selecting either 12-bit compressed RAW format, or 14-bit uncompressed RAW, as described above. I tend to favor the 14-bit uncompressed mode to avoid the artifacts that can appear in 12-bit compressed images. In practice, however, it's unlikely you'll notice the difference, and you may want to use the compressed format to save some storage space, as uncompressed RAW files, at about 84MB, are roughly twice the size of the compressed version (42MB).

JPEG Quality (Stills)

Options: Extra Fine, Fine, Standard

Default: Fine

My preference: Extra fine

To reduce the size of your image files and allow more photos to be stored on a given memory card, the camera's processor uses JPEG compression to squeeze the images down to a smaller size. This compacting reduces the image quality a little, so you're offered your choice of Extra Fine, Fine, and Standard compression. Standard compression is quite aggressive; the camera discards a lot of data. While Fine is, well, just fine, you'll find that Extra Fine provides even better results, so it should really be your *standard* when shooting JPEG photos.

For most work, extra compression (or lower resolution, described next) is false economy. You never know when you might need that extra bit of picture detail. Your best bet is to have enough memory cards to handle all the shooting you want to do until you have the chance to transfer your photos to your computer or a personal storage device.

JPEG Image Size (Stills)

Options: L, M, S

Default: L

My preference: L

Here you can choose between the a7R III's Large, Medium, and Small settings for JPEG still pictures. The larger the size that's selected, the higher the resolution: the images are composed of more megapixels. (If you select RAW or RAW & JPEG for File Format, you'll find that the Image Size option is grayed out, because the camera will always shoot large photos.)

As you scroll among the options, you'll note that the size for Large, Medium, and Small is shown in megapixels, as shown for the a7R III in Table 3.2. The number of pixels will vary, depending on the *aspect ratio* you've chosen. For example, with the a7R III, you'll get 42MP in Large mode using the 3:2 aspect ratio, and 36MP in Large mode using the 16:9 aspect ratio. If you are using the cropped APS-C/Super 35mm mode (explained in Chapter 12), with the a7R III, the image is cropped, giving you an 18MP Large image at 3:2 aspect ratio, or a 15MP image with the 16:9 aspect ratio. The a7R III's resolutions at various sizes and with/without the APS-C/Super 35mm crop are shown in Table 3.2.

As I noted earlier, there are some limited advantages to using the Medium and Small resolution settings, and similar space-saving benefits accrue to the Standard JPEG compression setting. All these options help stretch the capacity of your memory card, so you can shoehorn quite a few more pictures onto a single card. That can be useful when you're away from home and are running out of storage, or when you're shooting non-critical work that doesn't require full resolution (such as photos taken for real estate listings, web page display, photo ID cards, or similar applications).

Scroll to this Image Size menu item, press the center button, and scroll to the desired option: L, M, or S. Then press the center button to confirm your choice. As I noted, the actual size of the images depends on the aspect ratio you have chosen in the subsequent menu item (discussed below), either the standard 3:2 or the wide-screen 16:9 format.

There are few reasons to use a size other than Large with this camera, even if reduced resolution is sufficient for your application, such as photo ID cards or web display. Starting with a full-size image gives you greater freedom for cropping and fixing problems with your image editor. An 800 × 600–pixel web image created from a full-resolution (large) original often ends up better than one that started out as a small JPEG.

Of course, the Medium and Small settings make it possible to squeeze more pictures onto your memory card. Indeed, the a7R III images at medium resolution still amount to 18MP and 15MP, respectively, and that's nothing to sneeze at; both approach the *maximum* of some very fine dSLR cameras that were available a few years ago. The smaller image sizes might come in handy in situations where your memory cards are almost full, and/or you don't have the opportunity to offload the pictures you've taken to your computer. For example, if you're on vacation and plan to make

Table 3.2 Image Sizes Available

Image Size	Megapixels 3:2 Aspect Ratio	Resolution 3:2 Aspect Ratio	Megapixels 16:9 Aspect Ratio	Resolution 16:9 Aspect Ratio
Full Frame				
Large (L)	42MP	7952 × 5304 pixels	36MP	7952 × 4472 pixels
Medium (M)	18MP	5168 × 3448 pixels	15MP	5168 × 2912 pixels
Small (S)	11MP	3984 × 2656 pixels	8.9MP	3984 × 2240 pixels
APS-C				
Large (L)	18MP	5168 × 3448 pixels	15MP	5168 × 2912 pixels
Medium (M)	11MP	3984 × 2656 pixels	9MP	3984 × 2240 pixels
Small (S)	4.5MP	2592 × 1728 pixels	3.8MP	2592 × 1456 pixels

only 4 × 6–inch snapshot prints of the photos you shoot, setting a lower resolution will stretch your memory card's capacity. Even then, it makes more sense to simply buy and carry memory cards with higher capacity and use your a7R III camera at its maximum resolution.

Aspect Ratio (Stills)

Options: 3:2, 16:9 aspect ratios

Default: 3:2

My preference: 3.2; you can always crop to 16:9 in your image editor

The aspect ratio is simply the proportions of your image as stored in your image file. The standard aspect ratio for digital photography is approximately 3:2; the image is two-thirds as tall as it is wide, as shown by the outer green rectangle in Figure 3.2. These proportions conform to those of the most common snapshot size in the USA, 4 × 6 inches. Of course, if you want to make a standard 8 × 10 inch enlargement, you'll need to trim some of the length of the image area since this format is closer to square; you (or a lab) would need 8 × 12 inch paper to print the full image area. The 3:2 aspect ratio was also the norm in photography with 35mm film.

If you're looking for images that will "fit" a wide-screen computer display, or a high-definition television screen, you can use this menu item to switch to a 16:9 aspect ratio, which is much wider than it is tall. The camera performs this magic by cutting off the top and bottom of the frame (as illustrated by the yellow boundaries in Figure 3.2) and storing a reduced resolution image (as shown in Table 3.1). Your 42MP image becomes a 36MP shot if you set the camera to shoot in 16:9 aspect ratio instead of using the default 3:2 option. If you need the wide-screen look, this menu option will save you some time in image editing, but you can achieve the same proportions (or any other aspect ratio) by trimming a full-resolution image with your software. The 16:9 option is most useful if you plan to take a *lot* of photos that will work best in that format. Only the JPEG version of a shot is cropped; the RAW file retains its full image area, which will be trimmed by your RAW converter when you import the image into your image editor.

Figure 3.2

The 3:2 aspect ratio is shown by the outer green box. The yellow bars indicate the 16:9 aspect ratio (achieved either in-camera or later by cropping in software).

APS-C/Super 35mm

Options: On, Off, Auto

Default: Auto

My preference: N/A

This entry tells the a7R III whether to automatically switch to the APS-C/Super 35mm "crop" mode when a lens not designed for full-frame coverage is mounted on the camera. (APS-C is a still-image format; Super 35mm is a movie format.) In Chapter 12, I'll fully explain crop mode, which effectively captures pictures using only the center portion of the image, corresponding to the APS-C area used by Sony cameras that are *not* full-frame models and for Super 35mm film mode. There are three options within this menu entry:

- **On.** The camera *always* captures only the APS-C size area. If you're using a non-FE E-mount lens, then the image will correspond to what you'd see with an ASP-C camera, such as the Sony a6500. The cropped image will have the same field of view as a lens with 1.5X the actual focal length. That is, if you're using the Sony 16-50mm f/3.5-5.6 power zoom "kit" lens often supplied with the a6500 and other models, the effective focal length will be 24-75mm, and the cropped image will have a resolution of 18MP on the a7R III. Because the On setting always activates the cropping effect, even if you're using a full-frame FE lens (such as the Sony FE 70-200mm f/4 lens), the effective focal length will be 105-200mm. This APS-C crop "boost" works well with the a7R III, because its 18MP image in crop mode in the 3:2 aspect ratio is still quite respectable.

- **Off.** With this setting, the camera *never* crops the image. If you are using a non-FE, non-full-frame lens, you'll probably end up with severe vignetting in the corners. (I'll show you this effect in Chapter 12.) I sometimes use this setting when working with lenses intended for APS-C cameras, because some lenses do cover the full frame (even if just barely) at some focal lengths.

- **Auto.** When you use this setting, the a7R III will (often) detect whether you've mounted an FE or APS-C E-mount lens, and either crop or not crop as appropriate. It may not detect *all* E-mount lenses, particularly those from third-party vendors, so it's often safest to use the On option when you know you will be using an APS-C type lens and want to avoid vignetting.

Long Exposure NR/High ISO NR (Stills)

Long Exposure NR: Options: On/Off; **Default:** On

High ISO NR: Options: Normal, Low, Off; **Default:** Normal

My preference: Off for both

I've grouped these two menu options together, the first in the second page of the Camera Settings I menu (see Figure 3.3), because they work together, each under slightly different circumstances. Moreover, the causes and cures for noise involve some overlapping processes. Digital noise is that awful graininess that shows up as multicolored specks in images, and these menu items help you

Figure 3.3

The Camera Settings I-2 (Quality/Image Size 2) menu page.

manage it. In some ways, noise is like the excessive grain found in some high-speed photographic films. However, while photographic grain is sometimes used as a special effect, it's rarely desirable in a digital photograph.

The visual noise-producing process is something like listening to music in your car, and then rolling down all the windows. You're adding sonic noise to the audio signal, and while increasing the volume may help a bit, you're still contending with an unfavorable signal-to-noise ratio that probably mutes tones (especially higher treble notes) that you really want to hear.

The same thing happens when the analog signal is amplified: You're increasing the image information in the signal but boosting the background fuzziness at the same time. Tune in a very faint or distant AM radio station on your car stereo. Then turn up the volume. After a certain point, turning up the volume further no longer helps you hear better. There's a similar point of diminishing returns for digital sensor ISO increases and signal amplification as well.

Your a7R III can reduce the amount of grainy visual noise in your photo with noise reduction processing. That's useful for a smoother look, but NR processing does blur some of the very fine detail in an image along with blurring the digital noise pattern. These two menu items let you choose whether to apply noise reduction to exposures of longer than one second and how much noise reduction to apply (Normal or Low) when shooting at a high ISO level (at roughly ISO 1600 and above).

High ISO NR is grayed out when the camera is set to shoot only RAW format photos. The camera does not use this feature on RAW format photos since noise reduction—at the optimum level for any photo—can be applied in the software you'll use to modify and convert the RAW file to JPEG or TIFF. (If you shoot in RAW & JPEG, the JPEG images, but not the RAW files, will be affected by this camera feature.) As well, high ISO Noise Reduction is never applied when the camera is set to continuous shooting or continuous bracketing, or when the ISO is set to Multi Frame Noise Reduction.

Digital noise is also created during very long exposures. Extended exposure times allow more photons to reach the sensor but increase the likelihood that some photosites will react randomly even though not struck by a particle of light. Moreover, as the sensor remains switched on for the longer exposure, it heats up, and this heat can be mistakenly recorded as if it were a barrage of photons. To minimize the digital noise that can occur during long exposures, the a7R III uses a process called "dark frame subtraction." After you take the photo, the camera fires another shot, at the same shutter speed, with the shutter closed to make the so-called dark frame. The processor compares the original photo and the dark frame photo and identifies the colorful noise speckles and "hot" pixels. It then removes (subtracts) them so the final image saved to the memory card will be quite "clean."

Context-Sensitive

The a7R III has a novel "context-sensitive" noise-reduction algorithm that examines the image to identify smooth tones, subject edges, and textures, and apply different NR to each. This processing works best with areas with continuous tones and subtle gradations and does a good job of reducing noise while preserving detail. Because the BIONZ X digital processing chip is doing so much work, you may see a message on the screen while NR is underway. You cannot take another photo until the processing is done and the message disappears. If you want to give greater priority to shooting, set Long Exposure NR and High ISO NR to Off.

Long Exposure NR works well, but it causes a delay; roughly the same amount of time as the exposure itself. That would be a long 10 seconds after a 10-second exposure. During this delay the camera locks up, so you cannot take another shot. You may want to turn this feature off, as I do, to eliminate that delay when you need to be able to take a shot at any time. This feature is Off by default in continuous shooting and bracketing modes.

You might want to turn off noise reduction for long exposures and set it to a weak level for high ISO photos to preserve image detail. (NR processing blurs the digital noise pattern, but it can also blur fine details in your images.) Or, you simply may not need NR in some situations. For example, you might be shooting waves crashing into the shore at ISO 200 with the camera mounted on a tripod, using a neutral-density filter and long exposure to cause the pounding water to blur slightly. To maximize detail in the non-moving portions of your photos, you can switch off long exposure noise reduction.

Color Space (Stills)

Options: sRGB, Adobe RGB
Default: sRGB
My preference: sRGB

The Sony a7R III's Color Space option gives you two different color spaces (also called *color gamuts*), named Adobe RGB (because it was developed by Adobe Systems in 1998), and sRGB (supposedly because it is the *standard* RGB color space). These two color gamuts define a specific set of colors that can be applied to the images your a7R III captures.

You're probably surprised that the Sony a7R III doesn't automatically capture *all* the colors we see. Unfortunately, that's impossible because of the limitations of the sensor and the filters used to capture the fundamental red, green, and blue colors, as well as that of the phosphors used to display those colors on the LEDs in your camera and computer monitors. Nor is it possible to *print* every color our eyes detect, because the inks or pigments used don't absorb and reflect colors perfectly.

On the other hand, the a7R III does capture quite a few more colors than we need. A 14-bit RAW image contains a possible 281 *trillion* different hues (16,384 colors per red, green, or blue channel), which are condensed down to a mere 16.8 million possible colors when converted to a 24-bit (eight bits per channel) image.

The set of colors, or gamut, that can be reproduced or captured by a given device (scanner, digital camera, monitor, printer, or some other piece of equipment) is represented as a color space that exists within the larger full range of colors. That full range is represented by the odd-shaped splotch of color shown in Figure 3.4, as defined by scientists at an international organization back in 1931. The colors possible with Adobe RGB are represented by the black triangle in the figure, while the sRGB gamut is represented by the smaller white triangle. The location of the corners of each triangle represent the position of the primary red, green, and blue colors in the gamut.

A third color space, ProPhoto RGB, represented by the yellow triangle in the figure, has become more popular among professional photographers as more and more color printing labs support it. While you cannot *save* images using the ProPhoto gamut with your a7R III, you can convert your

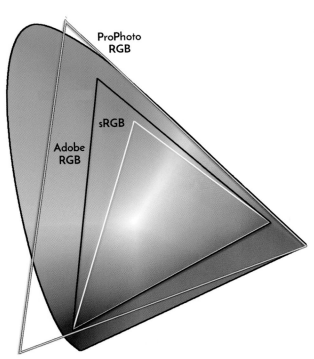

Figure 3.4

The outer curved figure shows all the colors we can see; the outlines show the boundaries of Adobe RGB (black triangle), sRGB (white triangle), and ProPhoto RGB (yellow triangle).

photos to 16-bit ProPhoto format using Adobe Camera RAW when you import RAW photos into an image editor. ProPhoto encompasses virtually all the colors we can see (and some we can't), giving advanced photographers better tools to work with in processing their photos. It has richer reds, greens, and blues, although, as you can see from the figure, its green and blue primaries are imaginary (they extend outside the visible color gamut). Those with exacting standards need not use a commercial printing service if they want to explore ProPhoto RGB: many inkjet printers can handle cyans, magentas, and yellows that extend outside the Adobe RGB gamut.

Regardless of which triangle—or color space—is used by the a7R III, you end up with some combination of 16.8 million different colors that can be used in your photograph. (No one image will contain all 16.8 million! To require that many, only about two pixels of any one color could be the same in a 42-megapixel image!) But, as you can see from the figure, the colors available will be *different.*

Adobe RGB, like ProPhoto RGB, is an expanded color space useful for commercial and professional printing, and it can reproduce a wider range of colors. It can also come in useful if an image is going to be extensively retouched, especially within an advanced image editor, like Adobe Photoshop, which has sophisticated color management capabilities that can be tailored to specific color spaces. As an advanced user, you don't need to automatically "upgrade" your a7R III to Adobe RGB, because images tend to look less saturated on your monitor and, it is likely, significantly different from what you will get if you output the photo to your personal inkjet. (You can *profile* your monitor for the Adobe RGB color space to improve your on-screen rendition using widely available color calibrating hardware and software.)

While both Adobe RGB and sRGB can reproduce the exact same 16.8 million absolute colors, Adobe RGB spreads those colors over a larger portion of the visible spectrum, as you can see in the figure. Think of a box of crayons (the jumbo 16.8 million crayon variety). Some of the basic crayons from the original sRGB set have been removed and replaced with new hues not contained in the original box. Your "new" box contains colors that can't be reproduced by your computer monitor, but which work just fine with a commercial printing press. For example, Adobe RGB has more "crayons" available in the cyan-green portion of the box, compared to sRGB, which is unlikely to be an advantage unless your image's final destination are the cyan, magenta, yellow, and black inks of a printing press.

The other color space, sRGB, is recommended for images that will be output locally on the user's own printer, as this color space matches that of the typical inkjet printer fairly closely. You might prefer sRGB, which is the default for the Sony a7R III and most other cameras, as it is well suited for the range of colors that can be displayed on a computer screen and viewed over the Internet. If you plan to take your image file to a retailer's kiosk for printing, sRGB is your best choice, because those automated output devices are calibrated for the sRGB color space that consumers use.

BEST OF BOTH WORLDS

If you plan to use RAW+JPEG for most of your photos, go ahead and set sRGB as your color space. You'll end up with JPEGs suitable for output on your own printer, but you can still extract an Adobe RGB version from the RAW file at any time. It's like shooting two different color spaces at once— sRGB and Adobe RGB—and getting the best of both worlds.

Of course, choosing the right color space doesn't solve the problems that result from having each device in the image chain manipulating or producing a slightly different set of colors. To that end, you'll need to investigate the wonderful world of *color management*, which uses hardware and software tools to match or *calibrate* all your devices, as closely as possible, so that what you see more closely resembles what you capture, what you see on your computer display, and what ends up on a printed hardcopy. Entire books have been devoted to color management, and most of what you need to know doesn't directly involve your Sony a7R III, so I won't detail the nuts and bolts here.

To manage your color, you'll need, at the bare minimum, some sort of calibration system for your computer display, so that your monitor can be adjusted to show a standardized set of colors that is repeatable over time. (What you see on the screen can vary as the monitor ages, or even when the room light changes.) I use the Spyder5 Pro monitor color correction system from Datacolor (www.datacolor.com) for my computer's three 26-inch wide-screen LCD displays. The unit checks room light levels every five minutes and reminds me to recalibrate every week or two using a small sensor device, which attaches temporarily to the front of the screen and interprets test patches that the software displays during calibration. The rest of the time, the sensor sits in its stand, measuring the room illumination, and adjusting my monitors for higher or lower ambient light levels.

If you're willing to make a serious investment in equipment to help you produce the most accurate color and make prints, you'll want a more advanced system (up to $500) like the various other Spyder products from Datacolor or Colormunki from X-Rite (www.colormunki.com).

Lens Compensation

Options: Auto, Off
Default: Shading/Chromatic Aberration: Auto; **Distortion:** Off
My preference: Auto for all three

This trio of submenus optimizes lens performance by compensating for optical defects; they're useful because very few lenses in the world are even close to perfect in all aspects. All three items work only with E-mount lenses and not when using A-mount lenses with an adapter accessory.

Shading

One key defect is caused by a phenomenon called *vignetting*, which is a darkening of the four corners of the frame because of a slight amount of fall-off in illumination at those nether regions. This menu option allows you to activate built-in "shading" compensation, which partially (or fully) compensates for this effect. Depending on the f/stop you use, the lens mounted on the camera, and the focal length setting, vignetting can be non-existent, slight, or may be so strong that it appears you've used a too-small hood on your camera. (Indeed, the wrong lens hood can produce a vignette effect of its own.)

Vignetting, even if pronounced, may not be much of a problem for you. I actually *add* vignetting, sometimes, in my image editor when shooting portraits and some other subjects. Slightly dark corners tend to focus attention on a subject in the middle of the frame. On the other hand, vignetting with subjects that are supposed to be evenly illuminated, such as landscapes, is seldom a benefit. Figure 3.5, left shows an image without shading correction at top, and a corrected image at the bottom. I've exaggerated the vignetting a little to make it more evident on the printed page. Note that this effect is applied to both RAW and JPEG images.

Figure 3.5 Vignetting (top left) is undesirable in a landscape photo, but the camera's shading correction feature can fix dark corners (bottom left). Lateral chromatic aberration, which shows as color fringes (top right), can also be corrected (bottom right).

Chromatic Aberration

The second defect involves fringes of color around backlit objects, produced by *chromatic aberration*, which comes in two forms: *longitudinal/axial*, in which all the colors of light don't focus in the same plane, and *lateral/transverse*, in which the colors are shifted in one direction. (See Figure 3.5, top right.) When this feature is enabled, the camera will automatically correct images taken with one of the supported lenses to reduce or eliminate the amount of color fringing seen in the final photograph. (See Figure 3.5, bottom right.)

Distortion

Distortion is the tendency of some lenses to bow outward (most often wide-angle lenses) or curve inward (found in some telephoto lenses). Figure 3.6, left, shows an exaggerated version of the outward-curving variety, called *barrel distortion*, exhibited by many wide-angle lenses—especially in fisheye optics, where the distortion is magically transformed into a feature. This feature works with most E-mount lenses, but not with all.

In Figure 3.6, right, you can see inward bowing, or *pincushion distortion*, as found in many telephoto lenses. Both types can be partially fixed using Photoshop's Lens Correction or Photoshop Elements' Correct Camera Distortion filters. Or, you can apply this in-camera feature to fix mild distortion. You should realize that correcting lens distortion involves warping pixels, mostly at the edges of the frame, providing a little less sharpness in those areas. The image area of your final picture will be slightly smaller than the frame you composed, and, during playback the active focus point is not shown in the review image.

Figure 3.6 Left: Barrel distortion in wide-angle lenses becomes a useful feature with fisheye lenses. Right: Pincushion distortion causes straight lines at the edges of the frame to curve inward.

In addition, applying distortion correction involves extra processing, which can reduce the number of consecutive shots possible. Because the correction is applied *after* you take the picture, the effect is not displayed on the screen when shooting in live view.

Drive Mode

Options: Single Shooting; Cont. Shooting (Hi+, H, Mid, Lo); Self-timer (2/5/10 seconds); Self-timer Continuous (2/5/20 seconds with 3 or 5 shots); Continuous Bracket/Single Bracket (3, 5, or 9 images at 0.3/0.5/0.7/1.0 EV increments; 3 or 5 images at 2.0/3.0 EV increments); White Balance Bracket (Lo/Hi), DRO Bracket (Lo/Hi)

Default: Single Shooting

My preference: N/A

This is the first entry on the Camera Settings I-3 (Shoot Mode/Drive 1) page (see Figure 3.7). Just as with the Drive (left directional) button on the back of the camera, there are several choices available through this single menu item. Your choices include:

- **Single shooting.** Takes one shot each time you press the shutter release button. You must use this mode or one of the self-timer modes (described shortly) if you want to use the a7R III's built-in Auto HDR (high dynamic range) feature or take a Bulb (long exposure) setting when working with Manual exposure.

- **Continuous Shooting.** Captures images at a rate of either 5 or 2.5 frames per second. When this option is highlighted, press the left/right directional buttons to switch among Hi+ (up to 10 fps), Mid, Hi (up to 8 fps), or Lo (up to 3 fps). The continuous speed will slow down if shooting uncompressed RAW, or when e-Front Curtain Shutter is set to Off when using Hi, Mid, or Lo speeds. The Hi+ speed is maintained, but the viewfinder/LCD monitor don't display the image in real time. You'll be viewing a slightly delayed image as the camera churns away capturing high-speed images. (Remember, you're shooting 10 frames per second at 42MP!)

Figure 3.7
The third page of the Camera Settings I menu.

When an f/stop smaller than f/8 is in use, exposure is set for the first shot, and retained for subsequent images as long as you hold down the shutter button, because of the extra time needed to open and close the small aperture. Focus can adjust during the burst if you set Focus Mode to Continuous AF and AEL w/Shutter to Off or Auto. If you want to keep track of your remaining shots, the Continuous Shooting Length indicator can be activated using the Camera Settings II-7 (Display/Auto Review 2) menu entry, which I'll describe in Chapter 4.

Continuous shooting is disabled when Picture Effect is set to Rich-Tone Mono or when using Auto HDR. You'll find more on continuous shooting in Chapter 9.

- **Self Timer (2 sec./5 sec./10 sec.).** Takes a single picture after two, five, or ten seconds have elapsed. When this choice is highlighted, press the left/right buttons to switch among the three durations.

- **Self-Timer Continuous.** The self-timer counts down, and then takes either 3 or 5 images, after delays of 2, 5, or 10 seconds. The left/right buttons cycle among the choices. You can cancel the timer by pressing the Drive button and selecting Single Shooting, or by tapping the shutter button a second time. Note that if you're using any of the single or continuous self-timer options, manual Bulb exposures produce an exposure time of 1/10th second.

- **Continuous Bracket.** Captures 3, 5, or 9 images in one burst when the shutter release is held down, bracketing them 0.3, 0.5, 0.7, or 1.0 stops apart. Increments of 2.0 or 3.0 stops apart are also available, but only 3 or 5 images can be taken. Use the left/right buttons to select the increment and number of shots.

  In Manual exposure (when ISO Auto is disabled), or in Aperture Priority, the shutter speed will change. If ISO Auto is set in Manual exposure, the bracketed set will be created by changing the ISO setting. In Shutter Priority, the aperture will change. Use continuous mode when you want all the images in the set to be framed as similarly as possible, say, when you will be using them for manually assembled high dynamic range (HDR) photos. You can use an external flash when continuous bracketing is active, but, because of the time required for the flash to recycle, you'll need to press the shutter button each time to take subsequent images (effectively switching the camera into Single Bracket mode, described next).

  Only the last shot in the set is displayed when using Auto Review. With all types of bracketing, the exposure/bracket scale at the bottom of the EVF or LCD monitor (in Display All Info mode) will display indicators showing the number of images shot and the relative amount of under/overexposure. Don't forget that you can dial in exposure compensation, and *that* will affect the amount of over/underexposure applied while bracketing. Continuous bracketing (and Single Bracketing) is disabled when using Intelligent Auto.

- **Single Bracket.** Captures one bracketed image in a set of 3, 5, or 9 shots each time you press the shutter release, bracketing them 0.3, 0.5, 0.7, 1.0 stops apart. Only 3 and 5 shots are available with the 2.0 or 3.0 EV increments. The left/right buttons are used to select the increment and number of shots. In this mode, you can separate each image by an interval of your choice. You might want to use this variation when you want the individual images to be captured at slightly different times, say, to produce a set of images that will be combined in some artistic way.

SELF-TIMER IN BRACKET MODES

You can set continuous and single bracket modes, and still make use of the self-timer. Access Bracket Settings (discussed next) and activate Self-Timer During Bracket.

- **White Balance Bracket.** Shoots three image adjustments to the color temperature. While you can't specify which direction the color bias is tilted, you can select Lo (the default) for small changes, or Hi, for larger changes using the left/right buttons. Only the last shot taken is displayed during Auto Review.
- **DRO Bracket.** Shoots three image adjustments to the dynamic range optimization. While you can't specify the amount of optimization, you can select Lo (the default) for small changes, or Hi, for larger changes, using the left/right buttons. Again, only the last shot taken is displayed during Auto Review.

Bracket Settings

Options: Self-timer during Bracketing: Off, 2 sec., 5 sec., 10 sec.; Bracket Order: 0-+, -0+
Default: Off, 0-+
My preference: N/A

This item has two entries that let you customize how bracketing is applied.

- **Self-timer during bracketing.** You can choose delays of 2, 5, or 10 seconds before bracketing begins, or disable the self-timer during bracketing. This clever option solves a problem: how to use the self-timer (say, to avoid shaking a camera mounted on a tripod) when bracketing (which resides in the same Drive menu). With continuous bracketing, all exposures will be taken after the self-timer delay; if you're using single bracketing, the delay takes place before each shot in the bracket set is exposed.
- **Bracket order.** The default is metered exposure > under exposure > over exposure. However, if you're shooting photos that will later be manually assembled into an HDR photo, you might find it more convenient to expose in order of progressively more exposure: under exposure > metered exposure > over exposure. The order you choose will also be applied to white balance bracketing.

Pixel Shift Multi Shooting

Options: Off; On, Shooting Intervals (1, 2, 3, 4, 5, 10, 15, 30 seconds)
Default: Off
My preference: N/A

If 42MP resolution isn't enough for you, your a7R III can capture images with greater effective resolution by grabbing four RAW images and then manipulating the pixels within them to produce a

100MP shot using Sony's free Imaging Edge (Remote) or (Viewer) software. You'll need to mount the camera on a tripod, so the four images can be aligned. This entry simply allows you to turn the Pixel Shift feature on or off and specify a shooting interval between shots of 1 to 5 seconds, plus 10, 15, or 30 seconds. Pixel Shift Multi Shooting is explained in more detail in Chapter 9.

MR Recall

Options: Select register to store settings

Default: None

My preference: N/A

Sony throws a curve ball by making its three Memory register entries as confusing as possible. They are listed in the Camera Settings I-3 (Shoot Mode/Drive 1) menu in the wrong order and described in the Sony Help Guide in entirely different places (pages 158 and 278!). The menu icons are wrong, too, as shown earlier in Figure 3.7. The icons show Camera 1/Camera 2 and omit/Camera 3. Before I describe how to use all three entries, I'm going to give you a quick overview of what each does.

The Memory feature allows you to save almost all the settings that you use for a particular shooting situation, including shutter speed and aperture (but *not* Program Shift adjustments), and then recall them quickly. There are three "slots" (labeled 1, 2, and 3) on the mode dial, and each slot can be loaded with default settings stored in the camera, *or* in four additional sets of settings you can store on a memory card, giving you seven groups of settings in all. The Memory feature lets you save custom-crafted sets that you can activate at any time. Simply activate the set that fits your current needs. For example, you might set up Register 1 with the settings you use while shooting volleyball in an indoor arena, Register 2 for use in landscape photography outdoors, and Register 3 for street photography. Whenever you encounter any of those three types of scenes, activate the memory channel with the suitable settings for that situation. You can then begin shooting immediately.

The three menu entries that you use to save and retrieve these memorized settings are as follows:

- **MR Recall.** If you want to use the settings already stored in the camera's memory for a particular slot, you don't need to use this menu entry. Just rotate the mode dial to the 1, 2, or 3 position. However, if you'd rather use one of the four *alternate* settings stored on your memory card, select the 1, 2, or 3 slots and then access MR Recall. (It's available only when the mode dial is set to one of the three numbered slots.) You can then use the multi-selector or left/right buttons to select M1, M2, M3, or M4. These settings reside on a memory card and are only available when that card is inserted in the a7R III.

- **MR Memory.** This entry allows you to store or *register* your camera's current settings to one of the three physical memory slots (1, 2, or 3) or to one of the four files (M1, M2, M3, or M4) on your memory card.

- **MR Select Media.** This entry tells the a7R III which memory card slot is active and contains the M1, M2, M3, or M4 settings files.

Note that you can *store* sets of settings when using any shooting modes (using the Memory entry that follows). But to *recall* a set of stored settings, you must rotate the mode dial to one of the three Memory positions, marked with a 1, 2, or 3 on the dial and then either use the settings already stored or, optionally, use this menu entry to load the additional settings saved in M1, M2, M3, or M4 files on your memory card. I'll explain recalling settings here and show you how to store them under the next menu entry, Memory.

To recap, there are two ways to activate saved settings:

■ **Mode dial.** Simply rotate the mode dial to the 1, 2, or 3 position. A set of settings for each of those positions is stored internally in the camera. When the mode dial is switched to 1, 2, or 3, the settings in that camera register automatically become active.

■ **MR Recall.** This menu entry allows you to recall *additional* memory settings, numbered M1, M2, M3, and M4, which are stored on the memory card currently in the camera. You can load the M1, M2, M3, or M4 settings into the 1, 2, or 3 mode dial positions. That may be confusing at first, but the bottom line is that the a7R III can use *any of three memory registers* (1, 2, and 3), but any of those three can be loaded with each of four sets of settings *on your current memory card*. Switch memory cards, and you can access four more! Remove your card (or reformat it), and those extra four settings are lost! (Smart move, Sony.)

SETTINGS LIBRARY

You can keep separate memory cards for each type of photography you like to do, and store M1, M2, M3, and M4 settings on each of them. But remember when you reformat the card, those settings are lost. The settings are stored in a folder on the card labeled /PRIVATE/SONY/SETTING with a sub-folder for each different camera you use. The filenames end in .DAT.

To recall settings previously stored on your memory card using Memory Recall, just follow these steps:

1. **Rotate the mode dial to the 1, 2, or 3 positions.** Select the position containing the settings you would like to recall.

2. **Access the Memory Recall entry.** Navigate to this menu entry. When you press the center button, a screen like the one shown in Figure 3.8, left appears.

3. **Review your stored settings.** The 1 highlighted in orange in the figure indicates that the mode dial has been set to the 1 position, and the settings displayed show the values currently stored for that slot. While the 1 is highlighted, you can scroll down the list with the up/down controls and review all the settings that have been stored.

4. **Change to settings on memory card.** If you want to use settings stored on your memory card instead, highlight any of the M1, M2, M3, and M4 entries, which represent four different sets of settings registered to your card. You can review the M1 to M4 settings by scrolling, as described in Step 3. If no settings have been stored for a particular M1 to M4 register, the message No File appears.

5. **Confirm.** If a selected set is satisfactory, press the center button or multi-selector to confirm your choice and exit. Your settings are now active in the camera.

MR Memory

Options: Store settings on your memory card

Default: None

My preference: N/A

This entry registers your camera's current settings, either to one of the three physical memory registers in your a7R III or to one of the card-based M1 to M4 files. The power of the memory feature stems from the fact that so many shooting settings can be saved for instant recall in any memory register.

Before you access the MR Memory item in the menu, make the desired settings in terms of camera operating mode, drive mode, ISO, white balance, exposure compensation, metering mode, and focus mode. Then, to save your current settings on your memory card in one of the M1, M2, M3, or M4 slots, just follow these steps:

1. **Set up your camera.** Set your camera to the shooting mode and adjust the camera to use the settings you'd like to store. The register can preserve shooting mode, aperture, shutter speed, and settings from the Camera Settings I menu.

2. **Navigate to Memory entry.** Select the Memory entry in the Camera Settings I-3 (Shoot Mode/Drive 1) menu and press the center button. A screen like the one shown in Figure 3.8, right, appears.

3. **Review settings.** Use the up/down buttons to scroll through the current settings to make sure they are satisfactory. A great deal more information is available than is shown in the figure (note the scroll bar at right). You can press the up/down buttons to view additional screens with detailed listings of your current settings. Exit and change desired settings, then start again at Step 2.

4. **Choose Register.** Press the left/right buttons to select which of the memory locations you'd like to store your current settings in.
   - If you choose 1, 2, or 3, the settings will be loaded into the camera's memory and will be available regardless of which memory card is in the camera.
   - If you choose M1, M2, M3, or M4, the settings will be stored on the memory card and will be available *only* when that memory card resides in the camera.

Figure 3.8 Recall settings stored on your memory card (left). Store settings in the 1, 2, or 3 mode dial positions, or as M1, M2, M3, or M4 on your memory card (right).

5. **Proceed or cancel.** Press the center button to confirm and store your settings, or the MENU button to cancel.

6. **Activate register.** To use your stored settings, rotate the mode dial to Register 1 or Register 2.

MR Select Media

Options: Slot 1, Slot 2
Default: Slot 1
My preference: N/A

This entry allows you to select which memory card slot contains the media with your M1 to M4 settings files. It does not have to be the memory card you are using to store your images. In fact, it is often a good idea to choose the *other* card slot, as that allows you to change your "main" card while retaining the stored settings in the other card. With that configuration you can also change the memory card with your M1 to M4 settings files as often as you like and keep shooting on your "main" card.

Register Custom Shooting Set

Options: Recall Custom Hold 1, 2, or 3
Default: Custom Hold 1
My preference: N/A

This function is an expansion of the Memory feature and available when using PASM exposure modes. It allows storing sets of settings for *temporary* recall at the press of a custom key, and lets you choose to store *some* settings and ignore others. You can register three groups of settings but can assign only one at a time to your defined key. The Custom Shooting set is active only while you are holding down the defined key; when you release it the a7R III returns to its previous settings.

You might want to use this feature to switch quickly and temporarily from one set of registered settings to another. Perhaps you're shooting landscapes and unexpectedly spy a rare raptor swooping by. If you've registered a set of parameters for "birds in flight" you can press your custom button, capture the bird, then release it and continue with your landscape shooting.

There are three available slots (Recall Custom Hold 1–3) and you can assign each of the three to a different button, giving you three settings available at the press of a defined button, three settings available from the 1, 2, and 3 physical mode dial positions, and four settings stored as M1 to M4 on your current memory card. Here's how to use this feature, which is available only when PASM modes are active:

1. **Access this setting from the Camera Settings I-4 (Shoot Mode/Drive 2) menu.** It's the only entry on that page (not shown). The screen shown in Figure 3.9, left, appears.

2. **Choose registration number in which to store your settings.** Select from Custom Hold 1 to Custom Hold 3.

3. **Check current settings.** You can view the current settings of the camera. Only the settings that can be registered are shown. Use the up/down controls to scroll.

4. **Adjust or disable settings.** There are two columns in the settings display: Enabled/Disabled (represented by a checked/unchecked box) and setting name/and current setting. (See Figure 3.9, center.) The left/right controls switch you from the Enable/Disable column to the Setting Name/Setting column.

5. **To disable registration of a setting.** Highlight the left column of a setting listing and press the center button to add/remove the checkmark.

6. **To change a setting.** Highlight the right column of a setting listing and press the center button. A screen will appear with the available options. For example, for Shoot Mode you can switch from the current mode to Program Auto, Aperture Priority, Shutter Priority, or Manual exposure.

7. **Store settings.** Scroll down to the bottom of the screen and highlight Import Current Setting. Press the center button. The screen shown in Figure 3.9, right, appears.

Figure 3.9 Select a Custom Hold register number (left). Review settings (center). Register settings (right).

8. **Register additional numbers.** Highlight Register to return to the screen seen in Figure 3.9, left, to register additional groups of settings.

9. **Assign a Custom Key.** To use this feature, you must assign a button to the Recall Custom Hold *x* (1, 2, or 3) behavior. Use the Custom Key entry in the Camera Settings II-8 (Custom Operation 1) menu, which I'll describe in Chapter 4. Note that you can define settings for all three Custom Hold registration numbers and can *define separate buttons* for each one. That means you can instantly (and temporarily) recall three additional sets of memory settings using custom keys, if you can spare that many from other duties.

10. **Use Custom Shooting Set.** Press the defined key to activate the Custom Hold settings assigned to that key, then press the shutter release down all the way to take a picture using those settings. When you release the custom key, your a7R III will return to its previous settings.

Focus Mode

Options: Single-shot AF (AF-S), Automatic AF (AF-A), Continuous AF (AF-C), DMF (Direct Manual Focus), MF (Manual Focus)

Default: Single-shot AF (AF-S)

My preference: Automatic AF (AF-A)

This menu item is the first in the Camera Settings I-5 (AF 1) menu (see Figure 3.10). This menu item can be used to set the way in which the camera focuses. I'll discuss focus options in detail in Chapter 8.

∎ **Single-shot AF (AF-S).** With this default setting, the camera will set focus and it will keep that focus locked as long as you maintain slight pressure on the shutter release button; even if the subject moves before you take the photo, the focus will stay where it was set. If you use this setting for still photos and then switch to Movie mode, the camera switches temporarily to AF-C.

Figure 3.10
The Camera
Settings I-5(AF 1)
menu.

- **Automatic AF (AF-A).** Begins to focus using AF-S but will switch to continuous autofocus (AF-C) if your subject is moving. This is a good all-purpose setting when you aren't sure whether your subject will suddenly begin moving around as you shoot.

- **Continuous AF (AF-C).** The camera will continue to adjust the focus if the camera-to-subject distance changes, as when a cyclist approaches your shooting position. The camera will constantly adjust focus to keep the subject sharply rendered. It uses predictive AF to predict the moving subject's position at the time you'll take the next shot and focusing at that distance. This option is useful when you're photographing sports, active children, animals, or other moving subjects, making it possible to get a series of sharply focused shots.

- **Direct Manual Focus (DMF).** Press the shutter button halfway down to let the camera start the focusing process; then, keeping the button pressed halfway, turn the focusing ring to fine-tune the focus manually. You might want to use DMF when you are focusing from a short distance on a small object and want to make sure the focus point is exactly where you want it. If you use this setting for still photos and then switch to Movie mode, the camera switches temporarily to AF-C.

- **Manual Focus (MF).** If you select Manual Focus, you turn the focusing ring on the lens to achieve the sharpest possible focus. With both DMF and Manual Focus, the camera will show you an enlarged image to help with the focusing process, if you have the MF Assist option turned on in the Camera Settings I-13 (Focus Assist) menu (described later).

Priority Set in AF-S/Priority Set in AF-C

Options: AF, Release, Balanced Emphasis

Default: Balanced Emphasis

My preference: Release

These are two separate entries, one for AF-S and one for AF-C autofocus, but functionally they are identical, differing only in the autofocus mode they are applied to. It makes sense to describe them together.

This feature lets you specify whether the camera *waits* to actually take the picture until it has achieved sharp focus (when using an autofocus mode, not manual focus mode); whether it takes the picture immediately, even if sharp focus is not guaranteed; or using a balanced approach somewhere between the two. For most kinds of candid photography, sports, or photojournalism, most of us would rather get the shot rather than lose a fleeting moment, and so Release is often your best choice. If you have a little more time, and the shot won't be affected by a short delay (perhaps half a second, on average), Balanced Emphasis, the default, will do the job. If you're looking for the best sharpness your camera can provide, the AF choice might be your best option.

The three choices are as follows:

- **AF.** The shutter is not activated until sharp focus is achieved. This is best for subjects that are not moving rapidly.

  - **AF-S.** When using AF-S, most prefer to set this to AF, because in this focus mode the subject is usually not moving rapidly, and it makes sense to allow a slight extra delay to get the best focus possible. However, I find that with the a7R III, when equipped with a lens having a built-in focus motor, in combination with the hybrid AF system, focus is fast enough that I can choose Release instead. If your camera/lens combination is slower to focus, you'll want to stick with the AF setting.

  - **AF-C.** When working in AF-C focus mode, if you select AF, the a7R III will continue to track your subjects' movement, but the camera won't take a picture until focus is locked in. An indicator in the viewing screen will flash green until focus can be achieved. You might miss a few shots, but you will have fewer out-of-focus images. Sports shooters probably won't choose AF priority for AF-C. Instead, they'll select release priority, discussed next.

- **Release.** When this option is selected, the shutter is activated when the release button is pushed down all the way, even if sharp focus has not yet been achieved. As I noted, I prefer this option for AF-C mode, as Continuous Focus focuses and refocuses constantly when autofocus is active, and even though an image may not quite be in sharpest focus, at least I got the shot. Use this option when taking a picture is more important than absolute best focus, such as fast action or photojournalism applications. (You don't want to miss that record-setting home run, or the protestor's pie smashing into the governor's face.) Using this setting doesn't mean that your image won't be sharply focused; it just means that you'll get a picture even if autofocusing isn't *quite* complete. If you've been poised with the shutter release pressed halfway, the camera probably has been tracking the focus of your image.

- **Balanced Emphasis.** In this mode, the shutter is released when the button is pressed, with a slight pause if autofocus has not yet been achieved. It can be selected for both AF-S and AF-C modes and is probably your best choice if you want a good compromise between speed of activation and sharpest focus. However, you would not want to use this setting if the highest possible continuous shooting rates are important to you.

Focus Area

Options: Wide, Zone, Center, Flexible Spot, Expand Flexible Spot, Lock-On AF
Default: Wide
My preference: Wide for general use; Lock-On AF Wide for sports and action

When the camera is set to Autofocus, use this menu option to specify where in the frame the camera will focus when you compose a scene in still photo mode, using the focus area selection you specify. I'll explain these options, the special requirements, and include illustrations of the focusing areas in Chapter 8.

- **Wide.** The camera uses its own electronic intelligence to determine what part of the scene should be in sharpest focus, providing automatic focus point selection. A green frame is displayed around the area that is in focus. Even if you set one of the other options, Wide is automatically selected in certain shooting modes, including both Auto and all SCN modes.

- **Zone.** Select one of nine focus areas (described in Chapter 9), and the camera chooses which section of that zone to use to calculate sharp focus. You can move the focus zone with the multi-selector joystick.

- **Center.** Choose this option if you want the camera to always focus on the subject in the center of the frame. Center the primary subject (like a friend's face in a wide-angle landscape composition); allow the camera to focus on it; maintain slight pressure on the shutter release button to keep focus locked; and re-frame the scene for a more effective, off-center, composition. Take the photo at any time and your friend (who is now off-center) will be in the sharpest focus. Use this option instead of manually selecting a focus point to quickly lock focus on the center of the frame, then press the defined AF lock button to fix the focus at that point so you can recompose the image as you prefer.

- **Flexible Spot.** This mode allows you to move the camera's focus detection point (focus area) around the scene to any one of multiple locations using the multi-selector joystick. When this option is highlighted, use the left/right directional buttons or control wheel to change the size range of the spot among Small (S), Medium (M), and Large (L).

  This mode can be useful when the camera is mounted on a tripod and you'll be taking photos of the same scene for a long time, while the light is changing, for example. Move the focus area to cover the most important subject, and it will always focus on that point when you later take a photo.

- **Expand Flexible Spot.** If the camera is unable to lock in focus using the selected focus point, it will also use the eight adjacent points to try to achieve focus. You can move the spot using the multi-selector joystick.

- **Lock-On AF.** In this mode, the camera locks focus onto the subject area that is under the selected focus spot when the shutter button is depressed halfway. Then, if the subject moves (or you change the framing in the camera), the camera will continue to refocus *on that subject*. You can select this mode only when the focus mode is set to Continuous AF (AF-C). Note that Lock-On AF is different from Center Lock-On AF, discussed in this chapter, and in more detail in Chapter 8.

  This option is especially powerful because you can activate it for any of the five focus area options described above. That is, once you've highlighted Lock-On AF on the selection screen, you can then press the left-right directional buttons and choose Wide, Zone, Center, Flexible Spot, or Expand Flexible Spot.

Focus Settings

Options: Move focus frame; select focus area

Default: None

My preference: Assign to a key of your choice using Custom Keys in the Camera Settings II-8 (Operation 1) menu.

This entry allows you to move the focus frame around when using the Zone focus area mode, or the focus spot when using Flexible Spot or Expand Flexible Spot area mode. It's not available when the a7R III is set to Wide, or Center area mode. It's most useful when you define one of the Custom keys or another button to activate it without wending through the menu thicket. When it's active, you can quickly make focus adjustments using the front and rear dials, and control wheel:

- In any Autofocus (AF-S, AF-A, AF-C) or Direct Manual focus mode:
  - **Front dial/up/down controls.** Moves the focus frame up/down.
  - **Rear dial/left/right controls.** Moves the focus frame left/right.
  - **Control wheel.** Rotating the wheel selects a specific focus area mode from any of the choices described in the Focus Area entry above.
- You can use Focus Settings in Manual focus mode, too:
  - **Front dial/up/down buttons.** Moves the magnified focus area up/down.
  - **Rear dial/left/right buttons.** Moves the magnified focus area left/right.
  - **Control wheel.** Rotating the wheel moves the magnified area up/down.

Switch Vertical/Horizontal AF Area

Options: Off, AF Point Only, AF Point+AF Area

Default: Off

My preference: Depends on subject

Here you can choose whether the Focus Area mode and the location of the focusing area within the frame adjusts when you change the camera's orientation from horizontal to vertical. It's especially useful when you want to change orientation frequently for the same type of subject matter. For example, when I am photographing family and individual portraits I might shoot one set of images with the camera held horizontally to capture several members of a group, then rotate to use a vertical frame to capture a head-and-shoulders image of an individual. Many sports, such as basketball, involve the same sort of adjustment—a horizontal photo showing two or three players fighting for the ball, followed by a vertically oriented picture of a pair of roundballers going after a rebound off the boards.

Here are some things to consider:

■ **You can/must set the Focus Area mode and/or focus point for each orientation individually.** That is, you must choose a Focus Area mode/focus point for horizontal orientation, then shift to each of the two vertical orientations and select a different location for either/both. If you don't specify a new location, the Focus Area and focus point remain where they were.

■ **Only three orientations available.** They are horizontal, rotated 90 degrees clockwise with the shutter release on the lower half of the camera, and rotated 90 degrees from horizontal with the shutter release on the upper half of the camera. The horizontal/upside down orientation is the same as the conventional horizontal orientation. When the camera is pointed straight up (toward the sky) or straight down (towards your feet), the a7R III has no idea about how it is otherwise oriented.

■ **AF Area Mode/Focus Point Switching Disabled.** Changes in orientation are ignored if you are using Intelligent Auto, Movie, or S&Q Motion shooting modes. The feature is also disabled if you press the shutter halfway down (and then change orientations), during autofocus, continuous shooting, self-timer countdown, or Focus Settings adjustments. Using the Focus Magnifier also disables the feature.

You have three options for this feature:

• **Off.** The Focus Area mode and Focus Point (Frame) remain the same regardless of camera orientation. If you've selected a particular Focus Area mode and you've placed the focus at the lower-left area of the frame when shooting horizontally (as seen in Figure 3.11, center), it will remain in the equivalent position when you rotate the a7R III 90 degrees counter-clockwise (Figure 3.11, left), or 90 degrees clockwise. (See Figure 3.11, right.)

• **AF Point Only.** The Focus Area mode remains the same while the Focus Point adjusts to the camera orientation. (See Figure 3.12.)

• **AF Point+AF Area.** Both the Focus Area mode and Focus Point adjust, so you can use a different Focus Area mode for each orientation.

Figure 3.11
When the feature is turned off, the focus points remain in the same relative position as the camera is rotated.

Figure 3.12
When switching is enabled, you can position the focus points in different locations within the frame for each of the three orientations. You can also optionally specify a different Focus Area mode for each presentation.

AF Illuminator (Stills)

Options: Auto, Off

Default: Auto

My preference: Auto

This entry is the first in the Camera Settings I-6 (AF 2) menu (see Figure 3.13). The AF illuminator is a light activated when there is insufficient light for the camera's autofocus mechanism to zero in on the subject. This light emanates from the same lamp on the front of the camera that provides the indicator for the self-timer. The extra blast from the AF illuminator provides a bright target for the AF system to help the camera set focus for subjects roughly no farther away than 10 feet. When you're shooting in environments so dark that conventional focusing is difficult, the a7R III will ignore the focus area you've specified and instead focus on whatever the AF assist lamp is able to illuminate. This menu item is a still-photos-only option, as the illuminator does not operate while shooting conventional or Slow & Quick motion movies.

Figure 3.13
The Camera Settings I-6 (AF 2) menu.

The default setting, Auto, allows the AF illuminator to work any time the camera judges that it is necessary. Turn it off when you would prefer not to use this feature, such as when you don't want to disturb the people around you or call attention to your photographic endeavors. The AF illuminator doesn't work when the camera is set for manual focus or when using AF-C or AF-A while the subject is moving. It is also disabled when using the Focus Magnifier, or one of the EA-LA adapters (which allow using A-mount lenses on the a7R III).

Note: Some Sony flash units (currently only the HVL-F45RM and HVL-F60RM) include a white LED video light that the a7R III will use as an AF illuminator lamp if the flash is mounted on the camera and powered up.

Center Lock-On AF

Options: On, Off

Default: Off

My preference: Off

This setting tells the camera to detect a subject positioned in the center of the frame and then adjust focus as the camera tracks its movement. A pair of white boxes appear in the EVF and LCD monitor. Move the camera to center the box on the subject you want to track and press the center button. The camera will then track that object as you reframe, or the subject moves, until you take a picture. Center Lock-On AF is not available at all when focus is set to manual.

Like the Focus Magnifier function, this feature isn't "live" all the time once you've set it. It requires a trip to the Camera Settings I-6 (AF 2) menu each time you want to use it, unless you define a custom key to summon it. There are two ways to use a custom key for that purpose (I'll show you how to redefine controls in Chapter 4):

- **Assign a custom key to Focus Standard.** If you use Center Lock-On a lot, you might want to assign a custom key to the Focus Standard behavior. Several buttons are available, including C1–C4 and the multi-selector button (that is, pressing down on the multi-selector). That option activates Center Lock-On immediately but prevents you from redefining the selected control for another behavior. The chief drawback is that this option works only when Focus Area is set to Wide or Center.

- **Assign Center Lock-On to a key.** I don't use the feature frequently, but I still like to have it available, so I use the down button, which has no default behavior of its own and is therefore not used by the a7R III in Shoot mode. When I press the down button, the Center Lock-On menu pops up, and I can select On by pressing the center button. Although it involves an additional step to activate, it works in all Focus Area modes except for Lock-on.

Keep in mind that this feature is different from the Lock-On AF option, described in Chapter 4. The key differences:

■ **Menu/Key Access.** Center Lock-On AF must be selected from this menu or summoned with an assigned custom key. Lock-On AF, when active, can be triggered simply by pressing the shutter release halfway.

■ **Fixed Zone.** Center Lock-On AF always uses the center of the frame to lock onto a subject. Lock-On AF can be set for any of the available focus area options, including Wide, Zone, Center, Flexible Spot, and Expand Flexible Spot.

■ **Available in Movie Mode.** Center Lock-On AF, unlike Lock-On AF, can be used in Movie mode. However, it is not available when shooting conventional movies or S&Q movies with a frame rate of 120/100 fps, or when using digital zoom.

Set Face Priority in AF

Options: Face Priority in AF (On, Off); Face Detect Frame Display (On, Off)

Default: Face Priority in AF: On; Face Detect Frame Display: Off

My preference: On for both only when photographing people

When you're photographing people, the a7R III can optionally look for faces and base its autofocus decisions on the faces it locates. Even better, you can give certain countenances a higher priority than others by registering them with the camera, so, say, if your significant other is ensconced in the frame, the camera will favor that person as its AF focus (so to speak) over other humans in the frame. Using the Set Face Priority in AF sub-entry, you can choose On (the a7R III gives a higher priority to detected faces) or Off (AF will proceed without looking for faces). Up to eight faces, if present, may be detected.

A second sub-entry is Face Detect Frame Display, also with On/Off options. When you select On, a gray selection box appears around detected faces. The box around the face used for autofocus turns white. If there are several faces in the frame and you've registered and prioritized some or all of them, the boxes around the other faces turn reddish-purple. If you find the boxes distracting, you can turn them off, and face detection, if enabled as described earlier, will still be active. However, a green focusing frame will still be displayed over a face that is detected and in focus.

When using Intelligent Auto, Face Priority in AF is automatically enabled and cannot be turned off. The feature is not available when shooting conventional movies or S&Q video with a frame rate of 120/100 fps. It's also disabled when using any of the digital zoom options, the focus magnifier, or the Posterization Picture Effect. I'll show you how to register faces and select their priority order later in this chapter.

AF Tracking Sensitivity (Stills)

Options: 5 (Responsive) to 1 (Locked On)

Default: 3 (Standard)

My preference: 4

This feature determines how quickly the camera unlocks focus from the subject it is currently tracking and focuses instead on another subject that intervenes. For example, if you're shooting a football game as a running back is breaking through the line and a referee bolts along the sideline in front of you. With this feature set to Responsive, the camera will very quickly switch to the ref, and then should return its attention to the running back—but often, not quickly enough. A better choice would be to use Locked On, so that the camera briefly ignores the referee, who is likely to have moved on in a second or two. Focus tracking will remain on your running back. Your options include:

- **Responsive.** At the 4 and 5 settings, the camera quickly responds to new subjects that cross the frame. This is the best setting to use for fast-moving subjects, such as sports or frenetic children, *as long as you don't expect intervening subjects.* The camera will smoothly follow your subjects. It works well when subjects within the frame are at significantly different distances.
- **Standard.** At the 3 setting, response to movement is a bit slower, so that the camera doesn't constantly refocus as subjects move about the frame. This is the default and should be used when there is only moderate movement, and especially if the movement is across the width or height of the frame (rather than coming toward you or away from you), and when you're using a small f/stop, because the increased depth-of-field will eliminate the need for most re-focusing.
- **Locked On.** At the 1 and 2 settings, the a7R III will lock onto the initial subject and follow it until it leaves the frame. Use this setting when you know you'll have intervening subjects often and are certain that you want to ignore them. Many sports events fall into this category.

AF System (Stills)

Options: Phase Detection AF, Contrast Detection AF

Default: Phase Detection AF

My preference: N/A

This stills-only item lets you choose whether you want to use phase detection or contrast detection autofocus *when you're using a compatible A-mount lens* with the Sony LA-EA1 or LA-EA3 A-mount to E-mount adapter. The available adapters and the lenses they can be used with is complicated, so I'm devoting some of Chapter 12 to explaining what works, and when. I'll explain the difference between phase detection and contrast detection in Chapter 9. As I write this, both adapters are getting long in the tooth, but still work very well with the a7R III. If Sony introduces a replacement during the life of this book (and follows its current numbering scheme) it is likely to be named the *LA-EA5*. It should function exactly like the earlier adapters in all respects.

■ **LA-EA1/LA-EA3 adapters only.** This menu entry is available *only* if you are using the LA-EA1 or LA-EA3 A-mount adapters. The EA1 version allows you to use APS-C A-mount lenses, while the EA3 model has a larger opening that makes it possible to use full-frame lenses on the a7-series cameras like the a7R III. In both cases, full autoexposure features are available.

Neither adapter has autofocus capabilities built in (unlike the current EA2 and EA4 versions) and *must* use either the phase detection or hybrid phase/contrast detection system built into the a7R III. This entry allows you to select which mode will be used.

■ **Compatible lenses only.** Autofocus operates *only* if the A-mount lens has a built-in autofocus motor (designated SSM or SAM) so the EA1 or EA3 adapter can adjust focus electronically.

If your A-mount lens uses a screw drive connection between the camera body (look for a "slot" on the lens's mount, roughly opposite the electronic contacts), then you *must* use the EA2 or EA4 adapters (or any replacement, likely to be given the EA6 name), which have their own internal phase detect AF system and AF motor needed to focus the lenses. I'll explain these details in Chapter 12.

This menu item is not available if you are using an E-mount lens, or your adapter/A-mount lens doesn't meet the above requirements. By default, the entry activates the hybrid Phase Detection system, which uses the 399 phase detect AF points on the a7R III sensor *plus* the 425 on-sensor contrast detection points (a significant step up from the 25 contrast detect zones in the predecessor, a7R II) to produce the speediest autofocus available with your camera/lens combination. If you are experiencing slow autofocus, switch to Contrast Detection AF instead, and you may find that the "slower" method works faster than the hybrid system. As always, your results may vary.

Note that when Phase Detection AF is active, only Wide, Center, and Flexible Spot focus area modes are available. You cannot choose Zone, Expand Flexible Spot, Lock-On AF, or Center Lock-On AF. In addition, only AF or Release priorities can be selected in Priority Set in AF-S (described earlier in this chapter). If you have previously chosen Balanced Emphasis, the camera will switch to AF.

But wait, there's more! If you choose Contrast AF with this entry, then the only autofocus mode available is AF-S (Single Autofocus). AF-C (Continuous AF) and DMF (Direct Manual Focus) are disabled. Further, if you want to use manual focus you must select it using the lens's AF/MF switch. Your a7R III camera has impressive autofocus capabilities, but the permutations can be mind-boggling. I'll be looking at other parameters in Chapter 8.

AF with Shutter (Stills)

Options: On/Off

Default: On

My preference: N/A

As you know, a gentle touch on the shutter release button causes the camera to begin focusing when using an autofocus mode. There may be some situations in which you prefer that the camera not re-focus every time you touch the shutter release button, such as when you want to work with *back button focus*, which I'll explain in detail in Chapter 8.

Let's say you are taking multiple pictures in a laboratory or studio with the subject at the same distance; you have no need to refocus constantly, and there is no need to put an extra burden on the autofocus mechanism and on the battery. But, you don't want to switch to manual focus. Instead, you can set AF w/Shutter to Off. From then on, the camera will never begin to autofocus, or to change the focus when the shutter release is pressed. You can still initiate autofocus by pressing the AF-On button or another key that you've assigned the AF-On function (as I'll describe later under Custom Keys). The AF-On button will start autofocus at any point, independent of the shutter release. Pressing the shutter release still locks *exposure,* unless you've disabled that function, too, using the AEL w/Shutter entry in the Camera Settings I-10 (Exposure 2) entry discussed later in this chapter.

Pre-AF (Stills)

Options: Off, On

Default: Off

My preference: N/A

This is the first entry in the Camera Setting I-7 (AF 3) menu. (See Figure 3.14.) It tells the camera to attempt to adjust the focus even before you press the shutter button halfway, giving you a head

Figure 3.14
Camera Settings I-7 (AF 3) menu.

This menu item allows choosing a value from –20 (to focus closer to the camera) to +20 (to change the focus point to farther away). You can enable/disable the feature, and clear the value set for each lens. The camera stores the value you dial in for the lens currently mounted on the camera and can log up to 30 different lenses (but each lens must be different; you can't register two copies of the same lens). Once you've "used up" the available slots, you'll need to mount a lesser-used lens and clear the value for that lens to free up a memory slot. This adjustment works reliably only with Sony, Minolta, and Konica-Minolta A-mount lenses. I'll show you how to use this feature in Chapter 12.

A-MOUNT ADAPTERS ONLY

You'll note that no such adjustment is supplied for E-mount lenses. That's because the a7R III calculates focus using *actual data collected at the sensor*—whether operating in contrast detect or phase detect mode. Front- or back-focus issues don't exist. The LA-EA2 and LA-EA4 adapters, on the other hand, use their separate SLT-style AF sensors, and slight alignment issues *can* make a difference. Sony recognizes this and has kindly provided this feature.

Exposure Compensation

Options: From +5 to –5
Default: 0.0
My preference: N/A

This is the first entry on the Camera Settings I-9 (Exposure 1) page (see Figure 3.15). It is one of three ways to specify exposure compensation:

- **This menu entry.** Here you can adjust EV values from +5 to –5 using the directional buttons, the multi-selector joystick, or by rotating the control wheel, rear dial, or front dial. It is available *only* when the Exposure Compensation dial on the top-right surface of the camera is set to 0.

- **Function menu.** Press the Fn button and navigate to the Exposure Compensation icon (located by default in the top row, fourth from the left). If the Exposure Compensation dial is set to 0, you can use the same controls described above to make adjustments.

- **Exposure Compensation dial.** If you elect to use the physical dial you can choose only values from +3 to –3. If those are a broad enough range for you (and most of the time that's all you'll really need), the dial is the fastest option. Any setting you make with the dial overrides an adjustment made with the menus.

Scroll until you reach the value for the amount of compensation you want to set to make your shots lighter (with positive values) or darker (with negative values). When shooting movies, only +2 to –2 values are valid. I'll discuss exposure compensation in more detail in Chapter 9.

Figure 3.15
The Camera
Settings I-9
(Exposure 1) menu.

Remember that any compensation you set with the physical dial will stay in place until you change it, even if the camera has been powered off in the meantime. It's worth developing a habit of checking your display to see if any positive or negative exposure compensation is still in effect; return to 0.0 before you start shooting. If you like, EV settings set using the two menu options can be "sticky" and survive a power off/on cycle, using Reset EV Compensation (discussed next).

Exposure compensation cannot be used when the camera is set to Intelligent Auto. In Manual exposure mode, the EV settings only apply if ISO has been set to ISO Auto. The EV changes you make with the menus will be in either 1/3 or 1/2 EV increments, depending on the step size you specify in the Exposure Step entry, which I'll explain shortly. When using the physical dial, increments are locked at 1/3 EV steps.

Reset EV Compensation

Options: Reset, Maintain

Default: Reset

My preference: Reset

While EV compensation set using the physical dial is locked in until you rotate the dial to a different position, any adjustments you make using the menus can be automatically zeroed out when the camera is powered off. That ability, plus the broader +5 to –5 adjustment range is a good reason to use the (faster, but less flexible) dial. I like to use the default Reset option, as it eliminates a lot of unintended exposure errors caused when you're unknowingly using compensation set for an earlier subject. If you're shooting under the same conditions for a period of time and think you'll be turning the camera on and off frequently, use Maintain instead.

ISO

Options: ISO Auto (with upper/lower limits), Settings from 50 to 102400

Default: ISO Auto

My preference: ISO Auto, set to ISO 100 Minimum/ISO 1600 Maximum

This menu item can also be accessed by pressing the right (ISO) button on the control wheel. It allows you to use the ISO setting (sensor sensitivity) in one of two ways:

- **ISO Auto.** The Auto ISO setting is at the top of the scrolling list. When it's highlighted, press the right button and choose a minimum ISO to be used as well as the maximum ISO applied (which prevents the camera from taking a clutch of pictures at, say, ISO 25600, unbeknownst to you). For general shooting, I use ISO 100 and ISO 1600 for my limits and raise the upper end to ISO 3200 or 6400 for indoor subjects (especially sports, which can benefit from faster shutter speeds and/or smaller f/stops). (See Figure 3.16.)

- **Fixed ISO settings.** You can select ISO settings from 50 to 102,400, and the camera will take all its shots at that sensitivity. Strictly speaking, ISO 100 is the lowest real sensitivity the camera can produce; that's the "native" sensitivity of the sensor. The 50/64/80 settings are "interpolated" and produce slightly higher contrast and lower quality. The a7R III places horizontal bars above and below the number for those values as a "warning." Similarly, the same bars sandwich ISO settings above 32000 to let you know that quality is reduced at the loftier settings.

I recommend using the interpolated lower values only when you really need a lower sensitivity, say, to use a wider f/stop in very bright conditions, or when you want to use a slower shutter speed to intentionally produce blur of, perhaps, a waterfall. A neutral-density filter attached to your lens can also reduce the amount of light reaching the sensor. The upper extended settings are best reserved for situations where you really need high ISO sensitivity and are willing to accept the visual noise that results. I'll explain noise reduction in a little more detail in Chapter 7.

Figure 3.16
ISO Auto allows specifying minimum and maximum ISO sensitivity.

When making fixed ISO adjustments you can scroll up and down the list in 1/3-stop increments with the up/down directional controls (the up/down buttons and multi-selector), and by rotating the control wheel or front dial. Rotate the rear dial to make adjustments in full 1 EV steps.

Your choices are restricted when you're using movies or S&Q video (only ISO 100 to 32000, plus ISO Auto are available) or Intelligent Auto (ISO Auto is set automatically). (If you've selected a higher sensitivity when you switch to movie-making mode, the camera will automatically change to 12800.)

Surprise! You can use ISO Auto in Manual exposure mode, giving you an "automatic" exposure mode. You still select the shutter speed and aperture and the a7R III will increase or decrease ISO sensitivity to produce an appropriate metered exposure within the Minimum ISO and Maximum ISO settings you specify. The ISO Auto label will appear at lower right of the viewfinder or LCD monitor screen, indicating that sensitivity is being set automatically.

ISO Auto Minimum Shutter Speed

Options: Faster, Fast, STD, Slow, Slower, 1/8000th–30 seconds
Default: STD (Standard)
My preference: STD (Standard)

Use this entry with the a7R III to specify the shutter speed that activates the ISO Auto feature described above. You'll want to use ISO Auto most frequently to avoid having the camera select a blur-inducing slow shutter speed when using P (Program Auto) or A (Aperture Priority) modes. (*You always select the shutter speed yourself in S and M modes.*) Depending on how well you can hand-hold the camera, or your level of trust for the lens and/or in-body image stabilization, you can choose which shutter speed you deem "too slow," and your a7R III will boost the ISO sensitivity as required when ISO Auto is active. You can choose from values that the camera calculates, or supply a specific shutter speed, below which Auto ISO will start to do its stuff.

The camera-calculated minimum speeds are very cool because they are based on the focal length of your lens, giving you faster minimum speeds with telephoto lenses, and longer minimum speeds with wide angles. The Fast and Fastest settings increase the minimum shutter speed by 1 and 2 stops (respectively) from the standard setting for a particular focal length. The Slow and Slower settings lower the minimum shutter speed for that focal length by 1 and 2 stops (respectively).

- **Faster/Fast.** When you highlight this entry, you can press the left/right directional buttons to choose between Faster and Fast, STD (Standard), Slow, or Slower. The a7R III will activate ISO Auto at shutter speeds that are faster than the "standard" setting (which is calculated individually based on the focal length or zoom setting of your lens). This is a more conservative setting.

- **STD (Standard).** The camera detects the current focal length/zoom setting and selects a minimum shutter speed that takes into account the effect the focal length has in magnifying the degree of blur. That is, a 200mm lens calls for higher shutter speeds than, say, a 50mm lens.

- **Slow/Slower.** This is a more liberal setting that allows slightly slower shutter speeds than specified by STD before ISO Auto kicks in. Use if you have an extraordinarily steady hand.

- **1/8000th–30 seconds.** You can bypass the camera's internal algorithm mumbo-jumbo and directly select a shutter speed that you want to use to activate ISO Auto. If you choose 1/8000th second, ISO Auto will effectively be active all the time (except when 1/8000th second is used as the shutter speed). Select 30 seconds, and ISO Auto will not activate at all.

Metering Mode

Options: Multi, Center, Spot (Standard, Large), Entire Screen Averaging, Highlight
Default: Multi

My preference: Multi

The metering mode determines how the camera will calculate the exposure for any scene. The camera is set by default to Multi, which is a multi-zone or multi-segment metering approach. No other options are available in Intelligent Auto mode or when you're using digital zoom. You'll find more information on these modes in Chapter 7, where exposure considerations are discussed in detail.

- **Multi.** Evaluates 1,200 individual segments of the scene using advanced algorithms; often, it will be able to ignore a very bright area or a very dark area that would affect the overall exposure. It's also likely to produce a decent (if not ideal) exposure with a light-toned scene such as a snowy landscape, especially on a sunny day. While it's not foolproof, Multi is the most suitable when you must shoot quickly and don't have time for serious exposure considerations. **Note:** When Face Priority in Multi Metering (discussed next) is On, this metering mode will base exposure on faces detected, if any.

- **Center.** Center-weighted metering primarily considers the brightness in a large central area of the scene, while still taking into account the average value of the rest of the frame. This approach ensures that a bright sky that's high in the frame, for example, will not severely affect the exposure. However, if the central area is very light or very dark in tone, your photo is likely to be too dark or too bright (unless you use exposure compensation).

- **Spot.** When using Spot metering, the camera measures only the brightness in a very small central area of the scene; again, if that area is very light or very dark in tone, your exposure will not be satisfactory; it's important to spot meter an area of a medium tone. Use this mode to zero in on a specific area of your image, such as a performer on a darkened stage.
  - **Size of spot.** When Spot is highlighted, press the left/right controls to change from a standard-sized spot to a larger spot.
  - **Position of spot.** By default, the metering spot is placed in the center of the frame. You can optionally link the spot to the current focus point using the Spot Metering Point entry in the Camera Settings I-10 (Exposure 2) menu, discussed shortly.
- **Entire Screen Averaging.** The a7R III calculates exposure based on the average brightness of the entire frame. This setting is useful if the overall scene has similar brightness values throughout; you can recompose slightly, or your subject can move within the frame and the exposure will not change.
- **Highlight.** In this mode, the camera adjusts the exposure to avoid blowing out the highlights, if at all possible. Use this setting if the highlights of a scene are the most important and you don't care if some shadow detail is lost. You can give Highlight metering some extra muscle by activating D-Range Optimizer or Auto HDR. The a7R III will segment the image into small areas and analyze the difference between the light and dark areas, preserving the highlights but also keeping as much shadow detail as possible.

Face Priority in Multi Metering

Options: On, Off

Default: On

My preference: Off

When you choose On, this setting tells the a7R III to adjust its Multi metering to prioritize exposure for any faces in the scene. Select Off, and the standard 1,200-zone evaluative metering system is used. For most shooting I disable this feature, as Multi metering does a good job of exposing so that faces and other parts of the image are well exposed. I turn it on when I am photographing individuals or groups and their surroundings are extra bright or dark and I want to make sure the faces receive optimal exposure.

Spot Metering Point

Options: Center, Focus Point Link

Default: Center

My preference: Focus Point Link

This is the first entry in the Camera Settings I-10 (Exposure 2) menu. (See Figure 3.17.) If Focus Area is set to Flexible Spot or Expand Flexible Spot, and Spot metering is selected as the Metering Mode, then the Spot metering area can be linked to the focus point, rather than locked in the center. Just choose Focus Point Link here. If Center is selected instead, the focus point is locked in the center of the frame.

Note: Focus Point Link also works when Focus Area is set to Lock-On Flexible Spot or Expand Lock-On Flexible Spot, but the spot metering area is moved to the starting area and does not move once tracking begins. All these AF nuances are explained in Chapter 8.

Exposure Step

Options: 1/3 EV, 1/2 EV

Default: 1/3 EV

My preference: 1/3 EV

This setting specifies the size of the exposure change for both exposure compensation and flash exposure compensation. The 1/3-stop default allows fine-tuning exposure more precisely, while selecting 1/2 EV lets you make larger adjustments more quickly, which is useful when you are trying to capture more dramatic exposure changes. The actual difference between 1/3-stop and 1/2-stop changes is relatively small, so this setting is primarily a convenience feature that's most useful when

Figure 3.17
The Camera Settings I-10 (Exposure 2) menu.

you plan to, say, use exposure compensation and want to move from 0.0 to plus or minus several whole stops in bigger jumps. I'm never in that much of a hurry, so I opt for the greater precision of the 1/3 EV steps.

Autoexposure Lock with Shutter (Stills)

Options: Auto, On, Off

Default: Auto

My preference: On

This item allows the a7R III to lock the exposure (as well as the focus in AF-S mode) when you apply light pressure to the shutter release button. Point the camera at your primary subject and maintain contact with the button while re-framing for a better composition. This technique will ensure that both focus and exposure are optimized for the primary subject.

There are three modes to choose from:

- **Auto.** Adjusts focus and then locks in exposure in AF-S mode when you press the shutter release down halfway. In AF-A mode, the camera will do the same thing if the subject is stationary. If the subject is moving (that is, the camera switches to AF-C mode) or you are shooting continuously in burst mode, exposure is *not* locked. However, even if Auto is activated, pressing the AEL lock button overrides this behavior.

- **On.** Exposure is locked when you press the shutter release halfway.

- **Off.** Pressing the shutter release halfway locks only focus. Exposure is not locked when you press the shutter release halfway, and exposure will be adjusted automatically during continuous shooting. Exposure isn't locked until you press the shutter release down all the way to take the photo, or your press the AEL lock button. Use this setting when you prefer to lock exposure manually using the AEL button or when taking the actual picture.

You might want to choose the Off option to lock focus on one subject in the scene while locking the exposure for an entirely different part of the scene. To use this technique, focus on the most important subject and keep the focus locked by keeping your finger on the shutter release button while you recompose. You can then point the lens at an entirely different area of the scene to read the exposure, and lock in the exposure with pressure on the AEL button. Finally, reframe for the most pleasing composition and take the photo.

In your image, the primary subject will be in sharpest focus while the exposure will be optimized for the area that you metered. This technique makes the most sense when your primary subject is very light in tone like a snowman or very dark in tone like a black Lab dog. Subjects of that type can lead to exposure errors, so you might want to expose for an area that's a middle tone, such as grass. I'll discuss exposure in detail in Chapter 5; then, the value of this menu option will be more apparent.

Exposure Standard Adjustment

Options: Adjust Multi, Center, Spot, Entire Screen Averaging, or Highlight metering

Default: None

My preference: None

This setting is a powerful adjustment that allows you to dial in a specific amount of exposure compensation that will be applied to every photo you take using each of the five metering modes. No more can you complain, "My a7R III always underexposes by 1/3 stop!" If that is the case, and the phenomenon is consistent, you can use this menu adjustment to compensate.

Exposure compensation is usually a better idea (does your camera *really* underexpose that consistently?), but this setting does allow you to "recalibrate" your camera yourself. You can fine-tune exposure separately for each of the metering modes. However, you have no indication that fine-tuning has been made, so you'll need to remember what you've done. After all, you someday might discover that your camera is consistently *over*exposing images by 1/3 stop, not realizing that your Exposure Standard Adjustment setting is the culprit.

In practice, it's rare that the a7R III will *consistently* provide the wrong exposure in any of the five metering modes, especially Multi metering, which can alter exposure dramatically based on the camera's internal database of typical scenes. This feature may be most useful for Spot metering, if you always take a reading off the same type of subject, such as a human face or 18 percent gray card. Should you find that the gray card readings, for example, always differ from what you would prefer, go ahead and fine-tune optimal exposure for Spot metering, and use that to read your gray cards. To use this feature:

1. **Select Exposure Standard Adjustment.** Select this menu entry from the Camera Settings I-10 (Exposure 2) page.

2. **Consider yourself warned.** In the screen that appears, choose OK after carefully reading the warning that Sony insists on showing you every time this option is activated.

3. **Select metering mode to correct.** Choose Multi metering, Center, Spot, Entire Screen Averaging, or Highlight-weighted metering in the screen that follows by highlighting your choice and pressing the center button. You can set the standard adjustment separately for each exposure mode.

4. **Specify amount of correction.** Press the up/down buttons to dial in the exposure compensation you want to apply. You can specify compensation up to + 1 or −1 stops in increments of 1/6 stop, half as large a change as conventional exposure compensation. This is truly *fine-tuning.*

5. **Confirm your change.** Press the center button when finished to return to the previous menu. You can repeat the action to fine-tune the other exposure modes if necessary. When finished, press MENU to exit. **Note:** the values you set will survive using the Reset option of the Setting Reset entry in the Setup 7 menu but will be canceled if you choose Initialize instead.

Flash Mode

Options: Flash Off, Auto Flash, Fill Flash, Slow Sync., Rear Sync., Wireless

Default: Depends on shooting mode

My preference: N/A

The first entry in the Camera Settings I-11 (Flash) menu (see Figure 3.18), this item offers options for the several flash modes that are available. Not all the modes can be selected at all times, as shown in Table 3.3. I'll describe what these modes do, and the use of flash in detail in Chapter 13.

Figure 3.18
Flash Mode is the first entry in the Camera Settings I-11 (Flash) menu.

Table 3.3 Flash Modes

Exposure Mode	Flash Off	Auto Flash	Fill Flash	Slow Sync.	Rear Sync.	Wireless	Flash Exposure Compensation	Red-Eye Reduction
Intelligent Auto	Yes	Yes	Yes	No	No	No	No	Yes
Program Auto	No	No	Yes	Yes	Yes	Yes	Yes	Yes
Aperture Priority	No	No	Yes	Yes	Yes	Yes	Yes	Yes
Shutter Priority	No	No	Yes	Yes	Yes	Yes	Yes	Yes
Manual Exposure	No	No	Yes	Yes	Yes	Yes	Yes	Yes

Flash Compensation

Options: −3 to +3 in 1/3 or 1/2 EV steps
Default: 0.0
My preference: N/A

This feature controls the flash output. It allows you to dial in plus compensation for a brighter flash effect or minus compensation for a subtler flash effect. If you take a flash photo and it's too dark or too light, access this menu item. Scroll up/down to set a value that will increase flash intensity (plus setting) or reduce the flash output (minus setting) by up to three EV (exposure value) steps. You can select between 1/3 and 1/2 EV increments in the Exposure Step entry described later in this chapter. Flash compensation is "sticky" so be sure to set it back to zero after you finish shooting. This feature is not available when you're using Intelligent Auto mode. I'll discuss this and many other flash-related topics in detail in Chapter 13.

Exp. Comp. Set

Options: Ambient & Flash, Ambient Only
Default: Ambient & Flash
My preference: Ambient & Flash

When this item is at the default setting, any exposure compensation value that you set will apply to both the ambient light exposure and to the flash exposure when using flash. You'd want to stick to this option in flash photography when you find that both the available-light exposure and the flash exposure produce an image that's too dark or too light. Setting plus or minus exposure compensation will affect both. However, in another situation when using flash, you might want to control only the brightness of the light exposure and not the flash exposure.

The Ambient Only option allows you to control only the brightness of the background such as a city skyline behind a friend when you're taking flash photos at night in a scene of this type. Setting exposure compensation will now allow you to get a brighter or a darker background (at a + and − setting, respectively) without affecting the brightness of your primary subject who will be exposed by the light from the flash. (Any exposure compensation you set will have no effect on the flash intensity.)

Wireless Flash

Options: Off, On

Default: Off

My preference: N/A

Sony is still playing catch-up in the electronic flash arena, having supported only optically trig-gered wireless flash until recently, but now offers radio-controlled wireless flash using the Sony AF-WRC1M/FA-WRR1 wireless radio commander/receiver combination or radio-compatible external flash units like the Sony HVL-45RM. This entry allows you to enable/disable both optical and radio wireless modes. I'll explain these and other flash options in Chapter 13.

Red Eye Reduction

Options: On, Off

Default: Off

My preference: Off

When flash is used in a dark location, red-eye is common in pictures of people, and especially of animals. Unfortunately, your camera is unable, on its own, to totally *eliminate* the red-eye effects that occur when an electronic flash bounces off the retinas of your subject's eyes and into the cam-era lens. The effect is worst under low-light conditions (exactly when you might be using a flash) as the pupils expand to allow more light to reach the retinas. The best you can hope for with this option is to *reduce* or minimize the red-eye effect. After all, the feature is called red-eye *reduction,* not red-eye *elimination.*

It's fairly easy to remove red-eye effects in an image editor (some image importing programs will do it for you automatically as the pictures are transferred from your camera or memory card to your computer). But, it's better not to have glowing red eyes in your photos in the first place.

To use this feature, you first have to attach an external flash to the multi-interface shoe. When Red Eye Reduction is turned on through this menu item, the flash issues a few brief bursts prior to tak-ing the photo, theoretically causing your subjects' pupils to contract, reducing the red-eye syn-drome. It works best if your subject is looking toward the flash. Like any such system, its success ratio is not great.

White Balance

Options: Auto WB, Daylight, Shade, Cloudy, Incandescent, Fluorescent (4 options), Flash, Underwater Auto, C.Temp/Filter, Custom 1–3, Custom Setup
Default: Auto (AWB)
My preference: AWB

This is the first entry in the Camera Settings I-12 (Color/WB/Image Processing) menu. (See Figure 3.19.) The various light sources that can illuminate a scene have light that's of different colors. A household lamp using an old-type (not daylight balanced) bulb, for example, produces light that's quite amber in color. Sunlight around noon is close to white but it's quite red at sunrise and sunset; on cloudy days, the light has a bluish bias. The light from fluorescents can vary widely, depending on the type of tube or bulb you're using. Some lamps, including sodium vapor and mercury vapor, produce light of unusual colors.

The Auto White Balance feature works well, particularly outdoors and under artificial lighting that's daylight balanced. Even under lamps that produce light with a slight color cast such as green or blue, you should often get a pleasing overall color balance. One advantage of using AWB is that you don't have to worry about changing it for your next shooting session; there's no risk of having the camera set for, say, incandescent light, when you're shooting outdoors on a sunny day.

The a7R III also lets you choose a specific white balance option—often called a preset—that's appropriate for various typical lighting conditions, because the AWB feature does not always succeed in providing an accurate or the most pleasing overall color balance. Your choices include:

- **Daylight.** Sets white balance for average daylight.
- **Shade.** Compensates for the slightly bluer tones encountered in open shade conditions.
- **Cloudy.** Adjusts for the colder tones of a cloudy day.

Figure 3.19
The Camera Settings I-12 (Color/WB/Image Processing) menu.

- **Incandescent.** Indoor illumination is typically much warmer than daylight, so this setting compensates for the excessive red bias.
- **Fluorescent (four types).** You can choose from Warm White, Cool White, Day White, and Daylight fluorescent lighting.
- **Flash.** Suitable for shooting with the a7R III's external electronic flash unit.
- **Underwater Auto.** Although you may find a vendor offering an underwater housing for your a7R III, it's more likely that your "underwater" shooting will involve photographing fish and other sea life through the glass of an aquarium of the commercial variety. This setting partially tames the blue-green tones you can encounter in such environments (see Figure 3.20, left), producing a warmer tone that some (but not all) may prefer (see Figure 3.20, right).
- **C.Temp/Filter/Custom/Custom Setup.** These advanced features provide even better results once you've learned how to fine-tune color balance settings, which I'll explain in Chapter 9.

When any of the presets are selected, you can press the right button to produce a screen that allows you to adjust the color along the amber (yellow)/blue axis, the green/magenta axis, or both, to fine-tune color rendition even more precisely. The screen shown in Figure 3.21 will appear, and you can use the up/down and left/right controls to move the origin point in the chart shown at lower right to any bias you want. The amount of your amber/blue and/or green/magenta bias are shown numerically to the left of the chart. You'll find more information about White Balance in Chapter 9.

My recommendation: If you shoot in RAW capture, though, you don't have to be quite as concerned about white balance, because you can easily adjust it in your software after the fact. Here again, as with ISO and exposure compensation, the white balance item is not available in Intelligent Auto mode; the camera defaults to Auto White Balance.

Figure 3.20 The Underwater Auto setting can reduce the blue cast of typical subsurface photos.

Picture Profile

Options: Picture Profiles PP1–PP10, Off

Default: Off

My preference: Off

Picture Profiles are a great tool for advanced movie shooters. You can customize the picture quality, including color and gradation of your movies by defining the parameters included in each of ten different Picture Profiles. To make these adjustments, connect the camera to a TV or monitor using the HDMI port, and use the picture on the screen as a guide while making your changes. After connecting the camera to your HDTV/monitor, navigate to this menu entry and select which Picture Profile you want to modify. Press the right button to access the index screen, then press the up/down buttons to select the parameter to be changed. Then make your adjustments and press the center button to confirm.

Even a short course in how each of the parameters affects video images, and a discussion of how to select the best settings would require a chapter or two of technical discussion and is thus beyond the scope of this book. I'm going to provide a quick listing of each type of setting for a reminder; your Sony manual provides more information about each of these. The ten Picture Profile presets already have default values:

- **PP1:** Example setting using [Movie] gamma
- **PP2:** Example setting using [Still] gamma
- **PP3:** Example setting of natural color tone using the [ITU709] gamma
- **PP4:** Example setting of a color tone faithful to the [ITU709] standard
- **PP5:** Example setting using [Cine1] gamma
- **PP6:** Example setting using [Cine2] gamma
- **PP7:** Example setting using [S-Log2] gamma
- **PP8:** Example setting using [S-Log3] gamma with the Picture Profile's Color Mode set to [S-Gamut3.Cine]
- **PP9:** Example setting using [S-Log3] gamma with the Picture Profile's Color Mode set to [S-Gamut3]
- **PP10:** Example setting for HDR Movies using [HLG2] gamma

The list that follows is not for the faint-of-heart. As I noted, you can find entire books and motion picture school classes on color grading and adjusting these parameters:

- **Black Level.** Sets the black level (–15 to +15). Black level is the level of brightness at which no light is emitted from a screen, resulting in a pure black screen. Adjustment of this parameter ensures that blacks are seen as black, and not a dark shade of gray.

- **Gamma.** Selects a gamma curve, a formula that corrects for the nonlinear relationship between the brightness (*luminance*) captured by a sensor and the brightness of the image as it's displayed on a monitor. In other words, correction is needed to make what you see on a screen more closely resemble what the camera captured in real life. You can choose from 14 different gamma curves.

- **Black Gamma.** Corrects gamma in low-intensity areas, using Range and Level controls.

- **Knee.** Sets "knee point" and slope for video signal compression to prevent overexposure by limiting signals in high-intensity areas of the subject to the dynamic range of your camera. In short, a higher knee level produces more detail in the highlights; a lower knee level produces fewer details in the highlights. Your adjustments include:
  - **Mode.** In Auto mode, the knee point and slope are set automatically; in Manual mode, they are set manually.
  - **Auto Set.** Even when the Mode is set to Auto, you can still choose maximum point for the knee point, from 90 to 100 percent, and Sensitivity, from High, Medium, or Low.
  - **Manual Set.** When Mode is set to manual, you specify a knee point (75 to 105 percent), and Slope from gentle (–5) to steep (+5).

- **Color Mode.** Sets type and level of colors, from among Movie, Still, Cinema, Pro, ITU-709 Matrix, Black & White, and S-Gamut, S-Gamut3.Cine, S-Gamut3, PT-2020, and 709.

- **Saturation.** Sets the color saturation, from –32 to +32 values.

- **Color Phase.** Sets the color phase (–7 to +7).

- **Color Depth.** Sets the color depth for each color phase.

- **Detail.** Sets parameters including Level, and Detail adjustments including Mode, Vertical/ Horizontal Balance, B/W Balance, Limit, Crispning (sic), and Hi-Light Detail.

- **Copy.** Copies the settings of the picture profile to another picture profile number.

- **Reset.** Resets the picture profile to the default setting. You cannot reset all picture profile settings at once.

Focus Magnifier

Options: Activate

Default: Off

My preference: N/A

This is the first entry in the Camera Settings I-13 (Focus Assist) menu. (See Figure 3.23.) If you like to focus manually, this is a very useful aid, one of several that Sony generously offers to enhance the chore of achieving sharp focus without using autofocus features. While you will probably find the focus magnifier most useful when using Manual focus, it is also available when using autofocus. I'm going to explain its use in MF mode first.

To use the Focus Magnifier for Manual focus, just follow these steps:

1. **Switch to manual focus.** You can use the AF/MF switch on your lens, if present, or by pressing the Fn button and using the Function menu to choose MF from among the focus mode choices. Manual focus can also be chosen by accessing the Focus Mode entry in the Camera Settings I-5 (AF 1) menu, described earlier in this chapter.

2. **Access Focus Magnifier.** You can activate the Focus Magnifier from this menu entry, but it's usually more convenient to assign the magnification behavior to a custom key, as I'll explain in Chapter 4. When activated, the image will be enlarged within a screen like the one shown in Figure 3.24, left.

3. **Press the center of the multi-selector to zoom in.** The image first is enlarged to 6.2X and then to 12.4X. (A third press exits magnified view.) A navigation window appears at lower left showing an orange rectangle that represents the current location of the blown-up section (as seen in Figure 3.24, right). You can also use the control wheel's center button to zoom in.

Figure 3.23
The Camera Settings I-13 (Focus Assist) menu.

Figure 3.24 The Focus Magnifier can be zoomed from 1X (left) to 6.2X (right) and 12.4X.

4. **Adjust the magnified area.** A quartet of triangles surrounds the image, indicating that you can move the enlarged window around with the frame. Press and release the multi-selector button or the center button, and then use the left/right/up/down directional controls to move the enlarged area.

5. **Center the magnifier.** You can press the Trash button to center the magnified section back in the center of the frame.

6. **Manually focus.** Rotate the lens's focus ring to achieve sharp focus. A scale along the bottom of the screen shows the approximate focus distance.

7. **Take the picture.** When you press the shutter release down all the way to take the picture, Focus Magnification is canceled when you're using manual focus.

8. **(Optional) Return to autofocus.** Remember to return to autofocus when you no longer want to focus on your subject manually.

TOUCH FOCUS

Your a7R III's touch screen may be a faster way to invoke the Focus Magnifier. You'll need to enable Touch Operation, which is found in the Setup 2 menu. I'll explain all the settings for the touch screen in Chapter 6. When enabled, simply double-tap the LCD monitor to select the area to focus on. You can then use a finger on the monitor screen to drag the focused area around. Double tap the monitor again to exit (if you're using manual focus) or by pressing the shutter release down halfway (if you're using the Focus Magnifier with autofocus). You'll need to enable the Focus Magnifier for autofocus using the AF in Focus Magnification entry of this menu, which I'll explain a few menu entries after this one.

Focus Magnifier Time

Options: 2 sec., 5 sec., No Limit

Default: 2 sec.

My preference: 5 sec.

This entry can be used to specify the length of time that the Focus Magnifier will magnify the image during manual focusing. If you find that it takes you longer than two seconds to manually focus using MF Assist, you can change the time to five seconds, or to No Limit; the latter will cause the image to remain magnified until you tap the shutter release button (you don't need to actually take a picture), press the center button/multi-selector button again to return to full frame, or double tap the LCD monitor if you have enabled Touch Operation.

Initial Focus Magnification (Stills)

Options: 1.0X, 6.2X (or 4X in APS-C/Super 35mm mode)

Default: 1.0X

My preference: 6.2X

You can specify the initial magnification presented when the Focus Magnifier is invoked. The default is 1.0X (no magnification), which is fine if your first step is frequently to move the magnification window around in the frame before zooming in. At 1.0X, you see the entire frame and can position the window anywhere you like. I prefer to skip that step and jump right in at 6.2X, which usually positions the window close enough that I can go ahead and move it within the frame if I want. The 6.2X magnification is automatically used if you have enabled Touch Operation and double tap the LCD monitor to zoom in. If you're using APS-C/Super 35mm crop mode, the initial focus magnification is 4.0X instead of 6.2X.

AF in Focus Magnification (Stills)

Options: On, Off

Default: Off

My preference: Off when not shooting macro/close-up images.

As I mentioned earlier, the Focus Magnifier works just fine in autofocus mode. You can use it to view an enlarged image to confirm that correct focus has been achieved automatically, or to fine tune focus when working with Direct Manual Focus (DMF) mode.

Once you've enabled the AF focus magnification option, activate the Focus Magnifier as described earlier and adjust the enlarged area using the directional controls and the navigation box. Avoid positioning the enlarged area at the edges of the frame, as the camera may be unable to focus at those positions. When you're ready, press the shutter release halfway. In any AF mode or DMF, the a7R III will focus on the center of the enlarged area. If you're using DMF, you can fine-tune focus with the lens's focus ring. Then press the shutter release down all the way to take the photo.

Autofocus using focus magnification cannot be used when shooting movies; when the Focus mode is set to AF-C; when using AF-A and continuous shooting; or a shooting mode other than P, A, S, or M. The feature is also disabled when using one of the EA-LA mount adapters. Certain autofocus features are disabled when using the focus magnifier, including Eye-AF, Center Lock-on AF, Eye-Start AF, Pre-AF, and Face Priority in AF.

Manual Focus Assist (Stills)

Options: On, Off

Default: On

My preference: On

Forget about the need to activate the Focus Magnifier manually. Set this entry to On and any time you are using manual focus or manual focus in the DMF mode, the a7R III will automatically enlarge the screen so you can better judge by eye whether the important part of your subject is in sharp focus. As you begin to focus manually by rotating the focus ring on the lens, the image on the LCD will appear at 6.2X its normal size (press the multi-selector or center button to zoom in to 12.4X). This version of the Focus Magnifier is available only for still photography. You can then scroll around the image using the directional controls. As with the manually activated Focus Magnifier, this feature makes it easier to check whether the most important subject area is in the sharpest focus. When you stop turning the focus ring, the image on the LCD display will revert back to normal (non-magnified) so you can see the entire area that the camera will record. You can turn this feature Off however, if you find that you don't need it, and adjust the magnifier time-out using Focus Magnification Time, the entry described previously.

Peaking Setting

Options: Peaking Display (On, Off); Peaking Level (High, Mid, Low); Peaking Color (Red, Yellow, White)

Default: Off, Mid, White

My preference: On, High, Red

This is a useful manual focusing aid (available only when focusing in Manual and Direct Manual modes) that's difficult to describe and to illustrate. You're going to have to try this feature for yourself to see exactly what it does. *Focus peaking* is a technique that outlines the area in sharpest focus with a color; as discussed below, that can be red, white, or yellow. The colored area shows you at a glance what will be very sharp if you take the photo at that moment. If you're not satisfied, simply change the focused distance (with manual focus). As the focus gets closer to ideal for a specific part of the image, the color outline develops around hard edges that are in focus. You can choose how much peaking is applied (High, Medium, and Low), select a specific accent color (Red, Yellow, or White) or turn the feature off.

Figure 3.25
You can choose any of three colors for peaking color (for manual focus), but only if you have activated the Peaking Level item. For these blossoms, red was a better choice than white or yellow.

Peaking Color allows you to specify which color is used to indicate peaking when you use manual focus. White is the default value, but if that color doesn't provide enough contrast with a similarly hued subject, you can switch to a more contrasting color, such as red or yellow. (See Figure 3.25.)

Anti-Flicker Shooting (Stills)

Options: Off, On

Default: Off

My preference: Off, unless shooting under flickering light source

This is the first of only three entries in the Camera Settings I-14 (Shooting Assist) menu, which is not illustrated with a separate figure. Novice sports photographers often ask me why shots they take in certain gymnasiums or arenas have inconsistent exposure, wildly varying color, or banding. The answer is that certain types of artificial lighting actually have a blinking cycle that is imperceptible to the eye, but which the camera can capture. This setting, when enabled, detects the frequency (it's optimized for 100 to 120 Hz illumination) of the light source that is blinking, and takes the picture at the moment when the flicker has the least effect on the final image. It cannot be used in live view or movie shooting.

You may experience a slight shutter release time lag as the camera "waits" for the proper instant, and your continuous shooting speed may be reduced, which makes this setting a necessary evil for sports and other activities involving action. Your results may vary when using P or A modes, because the shutter speed can change between shots as proper exposure requires. You're better off using S or M mode, so the shutter speed remains constant.

A handy Flicker warning will appear, alerting you that the feature is enabled, except in Intelligent Auto mode. This feature may not work as well with dark backgrounds, a bright light within the image area, when using wireless flash, and under other shooting conditions. I recommend taking test shots to see how effective the feature is under the light source you are working with. The feature is not available at all when using Bulb exposures or shooting movies. If you have Priority Set in AF-S or AF-C is set to Release or Balanced Emphasis, the camera will focus and shoot immediately when you press the shutter release down all the way. You'll need to use a half-press first to give Anti-Flicker a chance to do its thing.

Face Registration

Options: New Registration, Order Exchanging, Delete, Delete All

Default: None

My preference: N/A

This menu entry is used to log into your camera's Face Detection memory the visages of those you photograph often. New Registration allows you to log up to eight different faces. Line up your victim (subject) against a brightly lit background to allow easier detection of the face. A white box appears that you can use to frame the face. Press the shutter button. A confirmation message appears (or a Shoot Again warning suggests you try another time). When Register Face? appears, choose Enter or Cancel, and press the MENU button to confirm.

The Order Exchanging option allows you to review and change the priority in which the faces appear, from 1 to 8. The a7R III will use your priority setting to determine which face to focus on if several registered faces are detected in a scene. You can also select a specific face and delete it from the registry (say, you broke up with your significant other!) or delete *all* faces from the registry (your SO got custody of the camera). Face data remains in the camera when you delete individual faces but is totally erased when you select Delete All.

Registered Face Priority

Options: On, Off

Default: On

My preference: Off

This entry simply tells the a7R III whether it should give a higher priority to registered faces during the autofocus process when Face Priority in AF (discussed earlier) has been set to On.

4

Camera Settings II Menu

Additional shooting options are available from the Sony a7R III's Camera Settings II menu. These settings are adjustments that you generally don't make during a particular shooting session but need to tweak more often than those in the Setup menu, which is described in Chapter 6. This menu has some very cool features, including the ability to assign as many different behaviors to a variety of buttons and controls on your camera or lens. Sony has moved many menu items for the a7R III when compared to its predecessor a7 II–series cameras, grouping some (but not all) related settings together more logically.

Camera Settings II Menu Entries

Figure 4.1 shows the first screen of the Camera Settings II menu. As you can see, at most, only a half-dozen items are displayed at one time. The items found in this menu are shown in Table 4.1.

Exposure Mode (Movies)

Options: Program Auto, Aperture Priority, Shutter Priority, Manual Exposure

Default: Program Auto

My preference: Program Auto works well for me when shooting movies

This setting is the first on the Camera Settings II-01 (Movie 1) menu. It is available only when the mode dial is in the Movie position and allows you to specify which exposure mode is used (from among P, S, A, and M options) when shooting movies; the mode you select can be different from the one set for still photography or S&Q modes.

Table 4.1 Camera Settings II Menus

Movie

Exposure Mode (Movies)	Exposure Mode (S&Q)	File Format (Movies)
Record Setting (Movies)	S&Q Settings (S&Q)	Proxy Recording
AF Drive Speed (Movies)	AF Track Sensitivity (Movies)	Auto Slow Shutter (Movies)
Audio Recording	Audio Recording Level	Audio Level Display
Audio Out Timing	Wind Noise Reduction	Marker Display (Movies)
Market Settings (Movies)	Video Light Mode	Movie with Shutter

Shutter/SteadyShot

Silent Shooting (Stills)	e-Front-Curtain Shutter	Release without Lens
Release without Card	SteadyShot	SteadyShot Settings

Zoom

Zoom	Zoom Setting	Zoom Ring Rotate

Display/Auto Review

DISP Button	Finder/Monitor	Finder Frame Rate (Stills)
Zebra Setting	Grid Line	Exposure Setting Guide
Live View Display	Continuous Shooting Length	Auto Review

Custom Operation

Custom Key (Stills)	Custom Key (Movies)	Custom Key (Playback)
Function Menu Settings	Dial Setup	Av/Tv Rotate
Dial EV Compensation	MOVIE Button	Lock Operation Parts
Audio Signals		

Figure 4.1

The Camera Settings II-1 (Movie 1) menu.

Exposure Mode (S&Q Motion)

Options: Program Auto, Aperture Priority, Shutter Priority, Manual Exposure
Default: Program Auto
My preference: Program Auto

This setting is identical to the previous entry, except that it applies only to S&Q (Slow-motion and Quick-motion) capture and is grayed out if the mode dial is not set to the S&Q position. As before, the mode you select here can be different from the one set for still photography or movie shooting modes.

File Format (Movies)

Options: XAVC S 4K, XAVC S HD, AVCHD
Default: XAVC S HD
My preference: AVCHD

The a7R III offers full HD (high-definition) video recording in the AVCHD format. Advanced video shooters can also choose from the XAVC S 4K or XAVC S HD formats, which support faster recording speeds for improved quality, as I'll explain in Chapter 10.

By default, movies are recorded in XAVC S HD, but this menu item allows you to switch to XAVC S 4K AVCHD. In any case, you'll need a fast memory card of at least 64GB capacity to support the higher frame rates possible with these pro formats. The XAVC S 4K format is especially demanding because of its ultra-high 3840 × 2160–pixel resolution (roughly four times that of full HD).

AVCHD clips are limited to roughly 2GB in size; when your movie file reaches that limit, the a7R III will continue recording using a new file that it creates automatically. Note that when shooting 4K video, if APS-C/Super 35 is set to Auto, the 1.5X crop factor will apply. If you're using an external recorder, video monitor, or other device using the a7R III's HDMI connection, the real-time image is *not* displayed on the camera's LCD monitor as you shoot.

Record Setting (Movies)

Options: Varies
Default: XAVC S: 60p 50M
My preference: XAVC S: 60p 50M

This item allows you to choose from various options if you are using XAVC S 4K, XAVC S, or AVCHD. Your choices are shown in the left-hand column of each of the tables that follow. Note that the frame rates apply to countries using the NTSC system, such as the US, Japan, and some other countries. For countries that use the PAL system, 25, 50, and 100 frame rates replace 30, 60, and 120 fps respectively. I'll explain frame rates, scanning, and bit rates in Chapters 10 and 11. All the terminology and concepts will make more sense when you read Chapters 10 and 11, which provide more of an education on many aspects of movie making. (See Table 4.2.)

Table 4.2 Camera Settings II Menus

Record Setting	Bit Rate	Resolution
XAVC S 4K		
30p 100M/25p 100M	100 Mb/sec	3840 × 2160
30p 60M/25p 60M	60 Mb/sec	3840 × 2160
24p 100M	100 Mb/sec	3840 × 2160
24p 60M	60 Mb/sec	3840 × 2160
XAVC S		
60p 50M/50p 50M	50 Mb/sec	1920 × 1080
60p 25M/50p 25M	25 Mb/sec	1920 × 1080
30p 50M/25p 50M	50 Mb/sec	1920 × 1080
30p 16M/25p 16M	16 Mb/sec	1920 × 1080
24p 50M/50p 50M	50 Mb/sec	1920 × 1080
120p 100M/100p 50M	100 Mb/sec	1920 × 1080
120p 60M/100p 60M	60 Mb/sec	1920 × 1080
AVCHD		
60i 24M/50i 24M (FX)	24 Mb/sec	1920 × 1080 interlaced
60i 17M/50i 17M (FH)	17 Mb/sec	1920 × 1080 interlaced

S&Q Settings (S&Q Motion)

Options: Record Setting: 60p, 30p, 24p (NTSC); Frame Rate: 120, 60, 30, 15, 8, 4, 2, 1 frames per second.

Default: 30p, 120 fps

My preference: N/A

This is a great feature if you want to shoot some slow-motion movies as a special effect, analyze the dynamics of a particular motion, or speed up a sequence to provide a humorous herky-jerky appearance. Sony's implementation of high/slow frame rate photography, which it now calls slow-motion/quick-motion, allows you to capture a *silent* (no sound) slow-motion video at up to 120 frames-per-second rate (100 fps for PAL). It will play back 4X or 5X slower, depending on whether you select 30p/25p or 24p as your Record Setting option within this menu entry. You can also record at slower speeds (down to 1 frames per second). Here are your options, and how it works:

- **Record setting.** This parameter is labeled a bit misleadingly. It determines the *playback* speed of your video clip and, therefore, how much of a slow-motion/fast-motion effect you will see when viewing the movie. Your choices are 60p, 30p or 24p when using the NTSC television system. Think of this setting as a *factor,* which, when dividing the Frame Rate, determines the motion effect you get. All will become clear in a moment.

■ **Frame rate.** Here you select the number of frames per second captured in S&Q mode. You can select 120, 60, 30, 15, 8, 4, 2, and 1 frames per second. (Scroll down to find the last two options.) When the frames per second is divided by the record setting, you will arrive at the slow-motion effect or speed factor. I'll show you some typical results next.

Slow-Motion

When you capture video at any frame rate and then play it back at a *slower* frame rate, the result is slow-motion. For example, if you choose 120 fps for the Frame Rate, a 10-second video will include 1,200 individual frames (120 fps × 10). If you've chosen 30 fps for your Record Setting, those frames will require 40 seconds to play back (1,200 frames divided by 30). The playback time is increased 4X. Other playback times involve different amounts of slow-motion: 24 fps gives you 5X playback. (When shooting at 120 fps, the 60 fps Record Setting is not available.) Table 4.3 shows the amount of slow motion you get with each combination of frame rates from 30 to 120, and playback settings of 60, 30, and 24 frames per second.

Quick Motion

Frame rates *slower* than 30 fps gives you speeded-up quick-motion instead of slow-motion. For example, with a Frame Rate of 4 frames per second you'll capture just 40 frames in 10 seconds. When viewed at a Record Setting of, say, 24 fps that 10-second clip will be compressed into only 1.7 seconds of viewing time. Obviously, because of the speed-up factor, you'll get the maximum effect when you shoot longer sequences that can be displayed very, very quickly. Look over Table 4.3, and the explanation that follows to calculate your own slow/quick-motion effects.

To calculate the *slow-motion* effects you can look forward to, multiply any of the figures labeled "slow-motion" by the number of seconds captured in your original clip. For example, if you shot a two-minute, 120 fps sequence and played it back at 30p (4X slow-motion) you'd need 8 minutes to

Table 4.3 Slow-Motion/Quick-Motion Effects

Capture Frame Rates	60p Playback	30p Playback	24p Playback
120 fps	Not possible.	4X slow-motion	5X slow-motion
60 fps	1X standard speed	2X slow-motion	2.5X slow-motion
30 fps	2X quick-motion	1X standard speed	1.25X quick-motion
15 fps	4X quick-motion	2X quick-motion	1.6X quick-motion
8 fps	7.5X quick-motion	3.75X quick-motion	3X quick-motion
4 fps	15X quick-motion	7.5X quick-motion	6X quick-motion
2 fps	30X quick-motion	15X quick-motion	12X quick-motion
1 fps	60X quick-motion	30X quick-motion	24X quick-motion

watch the whole thing. Going the other way, a two-minute clip captured at 4 fps and played back at 30p, would zip by in four seconds of frantic action.

Obviously, in real life you probably won't be shooting slow-motion video for two whole minutes (a golf swing or sports action sequence can be captured in a few seconds), and will be shooting quick-motion, time-lapse-like clips (such as a blooming flower or the march of the stars across the night sky) for longer periods so you'll have time to enjoy what you see. As you work with this cool feature, you may have to experiment to see which combination of frame rate capture speeds and the three possible playback speeds work best for you in a given situation. Also, keep in mind that many video-editing programs can handle clips captured at various frame rates and output them at a different rate for playback.

All movies are recorded in XAVC S HD format, and, as noted earlier, are silent. When shooting slow-motion video, TC Run and TC Output (under TC/UB Settings, described later), and 4K Output Selection are disabled. And, obviously, fast frame rates require shorter shutter speeds, so be ready to boost your ISO settings if necessary to cope.

Proxy Recording

Options: On, Off

Default: Off

My preference: Off

If you like, you can record a compact, low-bit-rate version of your XAVC S movies simultaneously while capturing your main movie. Although lower in quality, these "proxy" recordings are suitable for emailing, display on a smartphone or tablet, or uploading online.

While capturing your full HD (1920 × 1080) video, the a7R III also saves a standard HD (1280 × 720) version at a paltry 9 Mb/second, using the same frame rate (that is, 60/50p, 30/25p, or 24p) selected for the main video. You must use the XAVC S HD record setting with a frame rate other than 120/100p. A "Px" label appears over a main movie's icon during image review to indicate that a proxy movie was recorded at the same time (the proxy itself cannot be displayed or edited in-camera). Any time you delete the main movie from your memory card the proxy is erased, too.

AF Drive Speed (Movies)

Options: Fast, Normal, Slow

Default: Normal

My preference: Normal for most scenes, Fast for sports and action

This entry is the first in the Camera Settings II-2 (Movie 2) menu. It is a movies-only setting for the a7R III that is used to adjust how quickly the camera focuses while capturing video. It's used in conjunction with AF Track Sensitivity (Movies), described next. Unlike stills, when focus changes while shooting movies it is apparent in the clip and can be undesirable.

Figure 4.2
The Camera
Settings II-2
(Movie 2) menu.

Your three options are as follows:

- **Fast.** The camera focuses as quickly as possible, but with slightly less precision. This setting is good for sports, action, photojournalism, and street photography, and any situation where it's important to keep the main subjects in focus as they move around. In such situations, the automatic focus adjustments add to the feeling of following the action; any delay in refocusing would be disconcerting.

- **Normal.** The AF responds smoothly to subject movement by refocusing gradually. With scenes that are not filled with constant action, this mode may be the least noticeable to the viewer.

- **Slow.** Focusing is much less speedy and is a good choice if your subjects are moving at a constant rate of speed and direction. This setting will allow the a7R III to smoothly follow focus. Choose Slow to be on the safe side, in such situations, particularly when using older lenses that are themselves somewhat pokey in achieving focus.

AF Track Sensitivity (Movies)

Options: Responsive or Standard

Default: Standard

My preference: Standard

This entry works hand-in-hand with the AF Drive Speed entry above. It is another movies-only setting and determines how quickly the camera unlocks focus from the subject it is currently tracking and focuses instead on another subject that intervenes. For example, if you're shooting a football game as a running back is breaking through the line and a referee bolts along the sideline in front of you. With this feature set to High, the camera will very quickly switch to the ref, and then should return its attention to the running back—but often, not quickly enough. A better choice would be to use Normal, so that the camera briefly ignores the referee, who is likely to have moved on in a second or two. Focus tracking will remain on your running back.

Your options include:

- **Responsive.** The camera quickly responds to new subjects that cross the frame. This is the best setting to use for fast-moving subjects, such as sports or frenetic children, *as long as you don't expect intervening subjects.* The camera will smoothly follow your subjects, especially if AF Drive Speed has been set to Fast, too.

- **Standard.** Response to movement is a bit slower, so that the camera doesn't constantly refocus as subjects move about the frame. This is the default and should be used when there is only moderate movement, and especially if the movement is across the width or height of the frame (rather than coming toward you or away from you), and when you're using a small f/stop, because the increased depth-of-field will eliminate the need for most re-focusing.

Auto Slow Shutter (Movies)

Options: On, Off

Default: On

My preference: Off

When shooting movies in very dark locations, the best way to ensure that the video clips are bright is to use a slow shutter speed. When this menu item is On, the camera can automatically switch to a slower shutter speed than its default. This is a useful feature, since it works in any camera operating mode; there's no need to use S mode and set a slow shutter speed yourself in dark locations. I like to leave it off, because when I am capturing video with a slow shutter speed, I want to make sure I have the camera mounted on a tripod, and the need to activate this feature manually is a reminder to me that I need to do so.

Audio Recording

Options: On, Off

Default: On

My preference: On

Use this item to turn off sound recording when you're shooting videos, if desired. In most cases you'll want to leave the setting On, to capture as much information as possible; the audio track can be deleted later, if desired, with software. However, there could be occasions when it's useful to disable sound recording for movies, for example, if you know ahead of time that you will be dubbing in other sound, or if you have no need for sound, such as when panning over a vista of the Grand Canyon. At any rate, this option is there if you want to use it.

Audio Rec Level

Options: On, Off

Default: On

My preference: On

You can adjust the recording level of the camera's built-in or external microphones using this entry, which also enables/disables the audio level overlay on the screen while movies are captured. To use this feature, just follow these steps:

1. Rotate the mode dial to the Movie position.
2. Navigate to the Camera Settings II-2 menu, highlight Audio Rec Level, and press the center button.
3. The screen shown in Figure 4.3 appears. Rotate the front or rear dials or control wheel or use the left/right controls to adjust the volume level up or down.
4. Press the center button to confirm and exit the screen.
5. Alternatively, you can use the up/down buttons to highlight Reset to return the recording level to the default value. Then press MENU to exit.
6. If Audio Recording and Audio Level Display are set to On, an overlay appears at the lower left of the EVF or LCD monitor showing the current audio levels for the left/right channels (Ch1/Ch2).

Figure 4.3 Set Audio level.

Audio Level Display

Options: On, Off

Default: On

My preference: N/A

This entry, available only when in Movie mode, enables/disables display of audio level indicator bars, so you can monitor sound recording levels visually. The volume bars do not appear when Audio Recording is set to Off, or the DISP setting is set to No Disp. Info., or you are recording slow-motion or quick-motion video. When in movie standby mode, the bars will display so you adjust the sound level before starting to capture.

Audio Out Timing

Options: Live, Lip Sync

Default: Live

My preference: Live

This is the first entry in the Camera Settings II-3 (Movie 3) menu (see Figure 4.4). With the a7R III, *audio out* refers to the sound signal you hear when monitoring the recording through the camera's headphone jack. In this mode, the sound you hear may be slightly out of sync with the video, because the video must be processed by the camera's digital processing chip before you see it on the LCD or EVF. Sony offers two different audio modes that can ignore or compensate for this lag.

- **Live mode.** Allows you to hear the sound being recorded in real time, with no delay. Use this mode if you are watching the action in the scene directly, rather than through the viewfinder or EVF.

- **Lip Sync mode.** In this mode, the audio and video shown while the movie is being captured are delayed by the same amount and will be in sync with each other if you monitor using headphones in conjunction with the EVF or LCD.

Wind Noise Reduction

Options: On, Off

Default: Off

My preference: Off

Designed to muffle the howling sound produced by a loud wind passing over the built-in microphones, this item (when On) is for use when recording video. It's off by default because Wind Noise Reduction (provided by the camera's processor) does degrade sound quality, especially bass tones, and the recording volume is reduced. I recommend setting it to On only when shooting in a location with loud wind noises.

Figure 4.4

The Camera Settings II-3 (Movie 3) menu.

Marker Display (Movies)

Options: On, Off

Default: Off

My preference: N/A

When shooting video that will end up being displayed in other than HDTV's 16:9 ratio, it's useful to know exactly where the boundaries of other types of frames are, so the image can be composed to keep important subject matter contained within those boundaries. This setting lets you turn the display of any of four different types of markers on or off, as described in the Market Settings entry that follows.

Marker Settings (Movies)

Options: Center, Aspect Ratio, Safety Zone, Guide Frame

Default: Center

My preference: N/A

This entry allows you to choose which markers are displayed during video capture. You can select any or all of the following, if you like, although using more than one or two markers is likely to be confusing. Your choices (shown in Figure 4.5) are as follows:

- **Center—On/Off.** Whether or not the center marker is shown in the middle of the shooting screen. The default value is Off.

- **Aspect Ratio—Off/4:3 /13:9/14:9/15:9/1.66:1/1.85:1/2.35:1.** This activates a marker showing your preferred aspect ratio. The default is Off.

- **Safety Zone—Off/80%/90%.** Sets the safety zone display that represents the standard range that can be received by a household standard-definition television.

- **Guide Frame—On/Off.** Enables/disables a guide frame that can be used to verify whether a subject is parallel or perpendicular.

Figure 4.5
Video guide
markers.

Center   4:3 Aspect Marker   13:9 Aspect Marker

Safety Zone   Guide Frame

Video Light Mode

Options: Power Link, REC Link, REC Link & Standby, Auto

Default: Power Link

My preference: Auto

Sony offers video lighting units for its camcorders and digital cameras, such as the HVL-LVPC (about $200), which is a battery-operated LED video light. This menu entry allows you to control when the light illuminates. Your choice is a matter of personal preference, depending on how you operate. Your choices are as follows:

- **Power Link.** Turns on when the camera is powered up, and off when the camera is powered down. Use this if you'll be shooting more or less continually and don't need to save battery power between sequences.
- **REC Link.** Video light turns on when movie recording starts, and off when you stop capture. This setting will preserve your battery. I like to use it when I definitely want to use the video light at all times during movie capture, such as when I am shooting exclusively indoors, or am outdoors and want some fill light to illuminate shadows for close-ups.
- **REC Link & STBY.** Illuminates when movie capture is underway and dims at other times. Operates like the previous choice but stretches the life of your battery.
- **Auto.** The video light turns on under dim lighting conditions. You might want to use this if you intend to shoot movies under both dim and bright lighting conditions (say, indoors and out) and want the light to come on only under reduced illumination.

Movie with Shutter

Options: On, Off

Default: Off

My preference: Off

Your a7R III gives you the option of using the shutter release to start and stop shooting movies as an alternate to the Movie button located to the right of the viewfinder. Select On, and either button can be used; choose Off, and only the movie button will activate/stop movie capture. It's usually easier to find the shutter release, which is larger and located on top of the camera, when your eye is up to the viewfinder. It's easy to press the AF-ON or even AEL button by mistake. If your current session will be confined to video capture, you'll probably decide that using the shutter button will be more convenient.

I like this option when I am capturing movies hand-held. If the a7R III is mounted on a tripod and I am generally framing, composing, or focusing using the LCD monitor, I'll usually use either the Movie button or a remote release like the Sony RMT-DSLR2 to stop/start video capture. (The latter helps avoid camera motion from "stabbing" the Movie button with a finger.)

Silent Shooting (Stills)

Options: On, Off

Default: Off

My preference: Off

This is the first entry in the Camera Settings II-4 (Shutter/Steady Shot) menu. (See Figure 4.6.) Because the a7R III model has an electronic front-curtain shutter (described next), you can take still photographs without the audible clunk that the physical shutter makes. Silent Shooting is available only in P, S, A, or M shooting modes.

However, the most important limitation of silent shooting is that you can't use electronic flash when in this mode. There's a whole list of other functions that are not available in quiet mode. You can't use it when making Bulb exposures, using Auto HDR, Picture Effect, or Picture Profile settings, nor when using Long Exposure noise reduction. It's also disabled if you have the electronic front-curtain shutter enabled. Bracket shooting is not available when shooting RAW or RAW & JPEG formats when you've specified Uncompressed for your JPEG format.

You can turn the silent shutter feature on or off using this menu entry. Note that even with silent shutter activated, the camera will not be totally silent. The opening and closing of the aperture as the f/stop changes may make a faint noise, and the focusing motor and zoom motor (in power zoom lenses) may also be heard. However, I've spooked a few colleagues when they saw me take a picture and could not hear the familiar shutter click.

The "rolling shutter" in silent shooting mode (the camera records the 5,304 lines in a full-resolution image, one line after another) may produce distortion with moving subjects, because as a subject crosses the frame, the portion at the top of the frame will be in a different position from the part of the subject at the bottom of the frame. This "jello" effect may be most noticeable when shooting uncompressed RAW images. To reduce the distortion, change the RAW file type to Compressed, and use continuous shooting. You'll get the best results, however, capturing in JPEG mode.

Figure 4.6
The Camera Settings II-4 (Shutter/SteadyShot) menu.

e-Front-Curtain Shutter

Options: On, Off

Default: On

My preference: N/A

This feature reduces the lag time between when you press the shutter, and when the picture is actually taken. It can also reduce a certain type of blurring due to slight camera motion when the physical shutter "clunks" open. When set to On, the electronic front shutter curtain is used by the camera at the start of the exposure, rather than the mechanical shutter. (The physical rear shutter curtain is still used to conclude the exposure.)

Although e-front-curtain shutter usually works very well, when you are using an unusually wide aperture, such as the Sony/Zeiss T* FE 55mm f/1.8 ZA lens, for example, and a very fast shutter speed, areas of the photo may exhibit a secondary (ghost) image and bokeh (the out-of-focus portion of the image) may be affected. When that happens, set this menu item to Off and the camera will use only its mechanical shutter mechanism, and the problem will not occur. Sony also recommends turning the e-curtain Off when you are using a lens made by another manufacturer, as exposure may be uneven or incorrect.

The problems pop up because the e-curtain is, in effect, *too* fast. It reduces the shutter lag to the point that the iris may not have sufficient time to close completely before the exposure begins. So, the f/stop used at the beginning of the exposure can be different from the one used for the rest of the exposure (after the iris closes down to the correct aperture completely). The overall exposure will thus be incorrect, regardless of shutter speed. In addition, at higher shutter speeds, *exposure grading,* can occur. At those higher speeds, the "slit" (the gap between the front and rear curtains) is increasingly small as the shutter speed becomes faster, and parts of the image exposed initially will receive more exposure than those exposed later.

Exposure grading is worse with lenses that need a longer time to close their irises, and so is more likely with non-Sony lenses, older Sony lenses, and Sony/Minolta/third-party A-mount lenses used with one of the LA-EA adapters. The irises of those lenses aren't designed to respond at the speeds demanded by an electronic front-curtain shutter. In addition, even theoretically compatible lenses may have slower iris response due to dust/grit infiltration. You'll want to use newer, good condition E-mount lenses, or adapted lenses that are manually stopped down to the "taking" aperture prior to exposure.

Release w/o Lens

Options: Disable, Enable

Default: Enable

My preference: Enable

By default, the a7R III will refuse to try to take a photo when a lens is not mounted on the camera; this is a logical setting, especially for distracted folks who fail to notice that they have a lensless camera body hanging around their necks. If you chose Enable, however, the camera will open its shutter when you depress the shutter release button when no lens is mounted. This option will be useful if you attach the camera to some accessory such as a telescope or a third-party optic that's not recognized as a lens. I prefer to select Enable, because I frequently use oddball third-party and "foreign" lenses on my camera, such as my favorite Lensbaby distortion lens or a fisheye lens designed with a different camera mount.

Release w/o Card

Options: Disable, Enable
Default: Enable
My preference: Disable

The ability to trip the shutter without having a memory card installed is not especially useful, unless you want to hand your camera to someone for demonstration purposes and do not want to give them the capability of actually taking a picture. This happens frequently at trade shows, where vendors want you to try out their equipment, but would prefer you not leave the premises with any evidence/image samples, especially if the memory card in question belongs to the vendor rather than you.

On the contrary, it's more likely that you'd prefer to have your own camera inoperable if you've forgotten to insert a memory card. It's easy to miss the orange No Card warning that flashes when the non-picture is taken. Disabling release when a card is absent can help you avoid losing a card (you removed it to load some pictures onto someone else's computer) or having to sheepishly ask the bride and groom if they would be willing to re-stage their wedding.

SteadyShot

Options: On, Off
Default: On
My preference: On

Sony introduced in-body image stabilization (IBIS) with its a7 II–series cameras. So, the a7R III has both in-body image stabilization (the awesome 5-axis SteadyShot that so many of us are crazy about), and the ability to use optical image stabilization (Optical SteadyShot or OSS) built into certain lenses. Both systems work well with each other and can be used simultaneously. If for some reason you want to disable SteadyShot, you can use this menu entry. Some lenses, like the new Sony FE 24-105 f/4 G OSS have an Optical SteadyShot On/Off Switch. If so, this menu setting is not available.

SteadyShot is on by default to help counteract image blur that is caused by camera shake, but you should turn it off when the camera is mounted on a tripod, as the additional anti-shake feature is not needed, and slight movements of the tripod can sometimes "confuse" the system. In other situations, however, I recommend leaving SteadyShot turned on at all times.

SteadyShot Settings

Options: Auto, Manual

Default: Auto

My preference: Auto

This setting allows the camera to adjust the behavior of SteadyShot, based on the amount of image stabilization typically required at particular focal lengths. That is, telephoto lenses "magnify" camera shake and thus can benefit from more aggressive image stabilization. Indeed, this aspect is one reason why in-lens IS is often touted as superior to in-body stabilization. Your a7R III gives you the opportunity to benefit from both! This setting is not available if you have disabled SteadyShot using the entry above or turned off Optical SteadyShot with a switch available on some lenses.

- **Auto.** When this default setting is chosen, the camera receives focal length information electronically from the lens and can activate the appropriate amount of SteadyShot anti-shake.

- **Manual.** You can enter the focal length of the lens or the zoom position from the range 8mm to 1000mm. This is especially useful if you're working with a teleconverter, which produces magnification beyond that which the camera can detect from the supplied lens data alone. It's also a good option if you are using a lens (possibly a "foreign" lens with an adapter) that cannot communicate focal length to the a7R III.

Zoom

Options: Smart or ClearImage Zooming in shooting mode

Default: None

My preference: None

This is the first entry in the Camera Settings II-5 (Zoom) menu. (See Figure 4.7.) The feature adds an ersatz "power zoom" control to the a7R III, which otherwise lacks one. It's useful once you understand what it does and how it works, but Sony has done its best to make the feature as confusing as possible.

Figure 4.7
The Camera Settings II-5 (Zoom) menu.

Some other cameras in the Sony mirrorless lineup, such as the a5100, have a physical zoom lever located concentrically with the shutter release. None of the a7R III–series models has this feature. But, in effect, you still have *five* different ways to zoom while you're taking still photographs or movies. This list will sort out the options for you:

- **Optical zoom with zoom ring.** Zoom lenses always have a ring around their barrel that can be rotated back and forth to zoom in or out on your subject. The sole exception is lenses that have a power zoom lever that takes the place of the zoom ring.

- **Optical Power Zoom.** Certain E-mount lenses include a PZ (power zoom) designation in their name. These include the Sony E PZ 16-50mm f/3.5-5.6 OSS lens, Sony E PZ 18-200mm f/3.5-6.3 OSS lens, and Sony E PZ 18-105mm f/4 G OSS lens. They all have a zooming motor built in that can be activated by sliding a switch on the lens barrel itself. Alternatively, you can zoom these lenses using a camera's zoom switch (if you own a model that has one).

- **Smart Zoom.** This is one of three zoom options that take you beyond the true optical zoom range of your lens into the realm of digitized zooming, which produces a zoom *effect* by taking the pixels in the center of the original image and filling the frame with them.

  Smart Zoom is available only when you have set the camera to M (medium) or S (small) image size. It provides a limited amount of zooming, but, technically, requires no quality-reducing interpolation. The camera simply produces each "zoomed" image by cropping the photo to the zoomed size. The resolution of your final image corresponds to the resolution of the Medium or Small image size, as explained in Chapter 2. When using Smart Zoom, an S label appears in the viewfinder or LCD monitor zoom scale to indicate that the feature is in effect.

- **ClearImage Zoom.** When using this option, some quality is lost, as this kind of zooming doesn't produce any actual additional information; it just *interpolates* the pixels captured optically to simulate a zoomed-in perspective. Pixels are created to fill the frame at the resolution of the given Image Size setting (Large, Medium, or Small). ClearImage Zoom has many options, and I'll explain them later in this chapter. When a zoom scale is shown in the viewfinder or on the LCD monitor, a C label appears whenever you leave optical zooming behind and enter the ClearImage realm. When ClearImage Zoom is used alone, you'll typical achieve 1X to 2X magnifications *over and above* whatever optical zoom setting you've used.

- **Digital Zoom.** This option gives you even higher magnifications than ClearImage Zoom, with an additional decrease in image quality. When a zoom scale is shown in the viewfinder or on the LCD monitor, and a D label appears when you are using digital zoom. I'll explain the options later in the chapter. When Digital Zoom is active, it takes up where ClearImage Zoom leaves off, giving you up to 4X magnification *beyond* the optical zoom focal length you've selected when using Large image size. At Medium image size, you can zoom up to 6.2X; with Small image size, up to 8X.

Using Zoom

My basic recommendation is to use optical zoom only most of the time, and this feature might not be available. If you've set the camera for Optical Zoom Only in the Zoom Settings entry which follows this one, then this Zoom feature is not available at all if Image Size is set to Large. If ClearImage Zoom is set to On, you can use ClearImage zooming; if Digital Zoom is set to On, you can use both. When Image Size is set to Medium or Small, then Smart Zoom is also available for all three Zoom Settings options. After you've sorted out which of the zoom methods you want to use, using the Zoom feature while shooting is fairly easy. Just follow these steps:

1. **Navigate to the Camera Settings II-5 (Zoom) menu.** Select Zoom and press the center button.

2. **Preview image.** A live view of your sensor image appears in the EVF and LCD monitor, with a zoom scale at lower right, as shown in Figure 4.8.

3. **Zoom in or out.** You can rotate the control wheel or use the left/right directional controls to zoom in or out.

4. **Change zoom steps.** Press the up/down controls to change the size of the zoom increment, from 1X to 1.4X and thence all the way up to 8X.

5. **Confirm or cancel.** When you're satisfied with the zoom level, press the center button to confirm, or the MENU button to cancel. You can then continue to shoot at the new zoomed magnification.

Figure 4.8 The zoom scale shows the amount of magnification and type of zoom in use.

Zoom Setting

Options: Optical Zoom Only, ClearImage Zoom, Digital Zoom

Default: Optical Zoom Only

My preference: Optical Zoom Only

The a7R III series has three different types of zoom settings: Optical Zoom, ClearImage Zoom, and Digital Zoom, and you can choose any *one* of them here. My preference is to stick with optical zoom only. I own lots of great lenses, and don't hesitate to switch to one of them when I need some extra reach. Neither ClearImage nor Digital Zoom give me the image quality I am looking for. However, if you don't own a lens with enough telephoto magnification and/or don't need the best quality for some applications, the two electronic zoom modes are available.

They are most practical with a camera like the a7R III, as its 42.2-megapixel sensor has resolution to waste. Of course, you can always shoot without the electronic zoom features and crop to the effective magnification you want in your image editor. ClearImage Zoom and Digital Zoom are not available when Image Quality is set to RAW or RAW & JPEG. When working with those ersatz zooms, the metering mode is locked at Multi, and Focus Area setting is disabled (the focus area frame in the zoomed image is shown by a dotted line).

Zoom Ring Rotate

Options: Left/Right (Wide-Tele), Right/Left (Wide-Tele)
Default: Left (W), Right (T)
My preference: N/A

This setting controls whether power zooming (with PZ-designated lenses that have a power zoom feature) proceeds from wide-angle to telephoto settings when the zoom control is pressed from left to right, or in the reverse direction, from right to left. The setting is compatible only with power zoom lenses that support this feature.

DISP. Button

Options (Monitor): Graphic Display, Display All Info., No Disp. Info., Histogram, Level, For Viewfinder, Monitor Off
Options (Viewfinder): Graphic Display, Display All Info., No Disp. Info., Histogram, Level
My preference: Activate all but Graphic Display

This is the first entry in the Camera Settings II-6 (Display/Auto Review 1) menu. (See Figure 4.9.) Use this item to specify which of the available display options will—and will not—be available in Shooting mode when you use the LCD or viewfinder and press the DISP button to cycle through the various displays. Choose from Monitor or Viewfinder and mark or unmark the screens you want to enable or disable. The Monitor selection includes a For Viewfinder option that displays a text/graphic display of your current settings on the back-panel LCD.

Figure 4.9
The Camera Settings II-9 (Display/Auto Review 1) menu.

You can use this menu item to deselect one or more of the display options, so it/they will never appear on the LCD when you press the DISP button. To make that change, scroll to an option and press the center button to remove the check mark beside it. Naturally, at least one display option must remain selected. If you de-select all of them, the camera will warn you about this and it will not return to Shooting mode until you add a check mark to one of the options. If you turn the camera off while none are selected, the camera will interpret this as a Cancel command and return to your most recent display settings.

The same screens shown at left in Figure 4.10 are also available for the electronic viewfinder, except For Viewfinder and Monitor Off. (See Figure 4.10, right.) The viewfinder versions have some slight differences; for example, at the bottom of the viewfinder version is an analog exposure indicator. You can select a different set of displays for the viewfinder and monitor. That is, you can choose to view the Graphic Display in the EVF and Display All Info on the LCD monitor. Here's a recap of the available display options for the monitor.

- **Graphic Display.** When selected, this display shows basic shooting information, plus a graphic display of shutter speed and aperture (except when Sweep Panorama is the mode in use). If you learn how to interpret it, you'll note that it indicates that a fast shutter speed will freeze motion, that a small aperture (large f/number) will provide a great range of acceptably sharp focus, and other information of this type. (See Figure 4.11, left.)

- **Display All Info.** The default screen when you first turn the camera on, this option displays data about current settings for a complete overview of recording information. (See Figure 4.11, right.) Not all the information in the figure may be displayed at one time, and there are additional icons not shown because they occupy the same space on the screen as another indicator.

- **No Disp. Info.** Despite its name, this display option provides the basic shooting information as to settings, in a conventional size. (See Figure 4.12, left.)

- **Histogram.** Activate this option if you want to be able to view a live luminance histogram to assist you in evaluating the exposure before taking a photo, a feature to be discussed in Chapter 9. The basic shooting data will appear in addition to the histogram. (See Figure 4.12, right.)

- **Level.** This display shows how much the camera is rotated around the lens axis (horizontal tilt) as well as how far it is tilted forward and backward. When the camera is not perfectly level, orange indicators show the amount of forward/backward and horizontal tilt. (See Figure 4.13.) When the camera is level in both directions, the indicators turn green. (See Figure 4.14.)

- **For Viewfinder.** This display can be shown only on the LCD monitor. When visible, you can press the Fn button to produce the Quick Navi screen, which I explained in Chapter 2. (See Figure 4.15.)

- **Monitor Off.** When this option is selected, pressing the DISP. button eventually takes you to a blank monitor screen, which you might need to use when a brightly lit LCD is distracting or intrusive.

Figure 4.10 Select which display screens are shown on the LCD monitor (left) or viewfinder (right).

Figure 4.11 Graphic Display (left); Display All Information (right).

Figure 4.12 No Display Information (left); Histogram Display (right).

Forward/back tilt

Figure 4.13
Orange indicators show the amount of tilt.

Horizontal tilt

Figure 4.14
When the camera is level, the indicators turn green.

Figure 4.15
For Viewfinder Display.

FINDER/MONITOR

Options: Auto, Viewfinder, Monitor
Default: Auto
My preference: N/A

This also uses the eye sensor located above the viewfinder window, but it controls only whether the camera turns off the LCD and switches the view to the viewfinder when your eye comes near the EVF. With the default setting of Auto, the screen goes blank and the viewfinder activates when your eye (or any other object) approaches the Eye-Start sensor. Helpfully, the eye sensor is *disabled* when you tilt the LCD monitor away from the camera body, presumably because in that mode you'll be working exclusively with the LCD and do not want the a7R III to switch to viewfinder mode if your hand (or any other object) passes in front of the sensor.

Switch to the Viewfinder or Monitor options and the eye sensor no longer initiates a switch from one display to the other. The display is then *always* sent to the viewing device you selected, and the other one is turned off. You might want to use the Monitor option if you are doing work involving critical focusing using the LCD, and as you examine the screen closely, your face will frequently be close to the back of the camera where the Eye-Start sensor might detect it. Or, perhaps, you are shooting at a concert or other venue where the bright LCD can be distracting to others. Choose Viewfinder, and the shooting preview, menus, photos displayed for review during playback, and so forth will be shown only in the EVF.

Of course, if you disable automatic switching between the two, you'll still want to have the option of activating the viewfinder or monitor displays manually. To do that, you'll need to assign the FINDER/MONITOR switching function to a key. I'll show you how to do that later in this chapter, when I describe the Custom Key option in the Camera Settings II-08 (Custom Operation) menu.

Finder Frame Rate (Stills)

Options: Standard, High
Default: Standard
My preference: Standard

The a7R III sports an advanced Quad-VGA OLED EVF with a maximum resolution of approximately 3,686k dots (1280 × 960) and includes a Zeiss T* coating to reduce reflections. To reduce a slight jerkiness in the EVF when shooting action, you can switch from the default Standard (60 fps) frame rate to a blistering High (120 fps) rate that displays fast-moving subjects more smoothly. The tradeoff is a reduced resolution view at the highest frame rate. Standard is automatically invoked when reviewing images or video in playback mode, when viewing using an HDMI connection, or when the temperature inside the camera body is high. I tend to stick with the higher-resolution Standard frame rate, except when tracking sports or action subjects.

Zebra

Options: On, Off, IRE 70, 75, 80, 85, 90, 95, 100, 100+

Default: Off, **Zebra Level:** 70

My preference: 80

This feature warns you when highlight levels in your image are brighter than a setting you specify in this menu option. It's somewhat comparable to the flashing "blinkies" that digital cameras have long used during image review to tell us, after the fact, which highlight areas of the image we just took are blown out.

Zebra patterns are a much more useful tool, because you are given an alert *before* you take the picture and can specify exactly how bright *too bright* is. The Zebra feature has been a staple of professional video shooting for a long time, as you might guess from the moniker assigned to the unit used to specify brightness: IRE, a measure of video signal level, which stands for *Institute of Radio Engineers.*

When you want to use Zebra pattern warnings, access this menu entry and specify an IRE value from 70 to 100, or 100+. Once you've been notified, you can adjust your exposure settings to reduce the brightness of the highlights, as I'll describe in Chapter 7.

So, exactly how bright *is* too bright? A value of 100 IRE indicates pure white, so any Zebra pattern visible when using this setting (or 100+) indicates that your image is extremely overexposed. Any details in the highlights are gone and cannot be retrieved. Settings from 70 to 90 can be used to make sure facial tones are not overexposed. Generally, Caucasian skin generally falls in the 80 IRE range, with darker skin tones registering as low as 70, and very fair skin or lighter areas of your subject edging closer to 90 IRE. Once you've decided the approximate range of tones that you want to make sure do *not* blow out, you can set the camera's Zebra pattern sensitivity appropriately and receive the flashing striped warning on the LCD of your camera. (See Figure 4.16.) The pattern does not appear in output to a device through the HDMI port, nor in your final image, of course—it's just an aid to keep you from blowing it, so to speak.

Grid Line

Options: Rule of 3rds Grid, Square Grid, Diag.+Square Grid, Off

Default: Off

My preference: Off

This feature allows you to activate one of three optional grids, so it's superimposed on the LCD or EVF display. The grid pattern can help you with composition while you are shooting architecture or similar subjects. I sometimes use the Rule of Thirds grid to help with composition, but you might want to activate another option when composing images of scenes that include diagonal, horizontal, and perpendicular lines. (See Figure 4.17.)

Figure 4.16 The flashing stripes show an area is overexposed.

Figure 4.17 Grid lines can help you align your images on the LCD or EVF.

Exposure Setting Guide

Options: On, Off

Default: Off

My preference: N/A

This feature is of most use to those with poor eyesight, but a convenience for all. All it does is show a scrolling scale on the LCD or viewfinder with an enlarged rendition of the current shutter speed or aperture highlighted in orange. It more or less duplicates the display of both that already appears on the bottom line of the screen, but in a larger font and with the next/previous setting flanking the current value. In Aperture Priority, the scale shows f/stops. In Shutter Priority, you see shutter speeds. In Program mode, both are visible. When using Manual exposure, a single scrolling line appears showing shutter speed *or* aperture, depending on whether you rotate the rear or front dials. I like to leave it switched on, as the display is a reminder of which parameter I'm fooling with at the moment.

Live View Display

Options: Setting Effect ON, Setting Effect OFF

Default: Setting Effect ON

My preference: Setting Effect ON, unless using flash in manual mode

This is the first entry in the Camera Settings II-7 (Display/Auto Review 2) menu (see Figure 4.18). As a mirrorless camera, the a7-series cameras are always in a "live view" mode, showing you what the sensor sees. This entry lets you specify whether the camera should apply any exposure settings or effects that you've selected to the image before presenting it to you as a preview.

There are times when you don't want to see the effects of the settings you've made on the screen/EVF. For example, when you are using flash in manual mode, the camera has no way of knowing exactly how much light will be illuminating your scene. That f/16 aperture may be ideal for a shot exposed by your studio strobes, but the a7R III will, when Setting Effect is set to ON, show you a preview based on the ambient light, rather than the flash. The result? Your viewfinder or LCD monitor image is very, very dim. You'll want to select Setting Effect OFF so the camera will boost the electronic image to viewable levels.

When Setting Effects are active, the live view display in the EVF or the LCD reflects the *exact* effects of any camera features that you're using to modify the view, including as exposure compensation and white balance. In that mode, this allows for an accurate evaluation of what the photo will look like and enables you to determine whether the current settings will provide the effects you want.

Figure 4.18

The Camera Settings II-7 menu.

The ON option can be especially helpful when you're using any of the Picture Effects, because you can preview the exact rendition that the selected effect and its overrides will provide. It's also very useful when you're setting some exposure compensation, as you can visually determine how much lighter or darker each adjustment makes the image. And when you're trying to achieve correct color balance, it's useful to be able to preview the effect of your white balance setting.

If you'd like to preview the image without the effect of settings visible, you can set this feature to OFF. Naturally, the display will no longer accurately depict what your photo will look like when it's taken. So, for most users, ON is the most suitable option. Unfortunately, this setting has caused more than a few minutes of head-scratching among new users who switch to Manual exposure mode and find themselves with a completely black (or utterly white) screen. The black screen, especially, may fool you into thinking your camera has malfunctioned.

Continuous Shooting Length

Options: Always Display, Shooting-Only Display, Not Displayed

Default: Not Displayed

My preference: Shooting-Only Display when shooting action

Your a7R III has a much larger buffer than its predecessor, the a7R II, and can store an impressive 76 full-resolution 42MP JPEG or RAW photos (or 28 uncompressed 14-bit RAW files) before it fills, slowing down the camera while images are dumped to your memory card. (A message, "SLOW," appears on the screen.) At 10 frames per second, you might encounter a full buffer with a burst of less than 8 seconds. This entry can enable a useful "thermometer"-type indicator at the left side of the screen that graphically shows the status of the a7R III's buffer. You can choose Always Display, which pops up the indicator any time the camera is set to Continuous Shooting. In that mode, it also serves as a reminder that you're shooting bursts. I prefer to use Shooting-Only Display, but only when I am photographing sports or other action. If I'm just using continuous shooting to allow me to take short bursts of shots—say, when photographing urban street scenes—it's screen clutter that I don't need. You can dispense with the indicator entirely by selecting Not Displayed.

Auto Review

Options: Off, 2 sec., 5 sec., 10 sec.

Default: Off

My preference: N/A

When this item is set to 2, 5, or 10 seconds, the camera can display an image on the LCD or viewfinder for your review immediately after the photo is taken. (When you shoot a continuous or bracketed series of images, only the last picture that's been recorded will be shown.) During this display, you can press the Zoom In button to get a closer look at your image, delete a disappointing shot by pressing the Delete button, or cancel picture review by tapping the shutter release button or performing another function. (You'll never be prevented from taking another picture because you were reviewing images.) This option can be used to specify whether the review image appears for 2, 5, or 10 seconds, or not at all.

Depending on how you're working, you might want a brief display, or you might prefer to have time for a more leisurely examination (when you're carefully checking compositions). Other times, you might not want to have the review image displayed at all, such as when you're taking photos in a darkened theater or concert venue, and the constant flashing of images might be distracting to others. Turning off picture review or keeping the duration short also saves battery power. You can always review the last picture you took at any time by pressing the Playback button.

Custom Key (Stills)

Options: More than 80 different definitions for Control Wheel, Custom Buttons 1, 2, 3, 4, Multi-selector Center Button, Center Button, Left/Right/Down Buttons, AEL Button, Focus Hold Button (on lens)

Default: Various

My preference: N/A

This is the first entry on the Camera Settings II-8 (Display/Auto Review 2) menu. (See Figure 4.19.) It allows customization of as many as 11 buttons of the camera, the control wheel, and one additional button, Focus Hold, found on some lenses. Indeed, the following is a list of the only buttons on the camera that you *cannot* redefine to perform some other function:

- **Shutter release.** It is always used to take a picture and will initiate autofocus (although you can assign AF-ON and other AF functions to a different key).

- **Up directional button.** It is used to change your information display in shooting and Playback modes, and as a directional button in menus.

Figure 4.19
The eighth page of the Camera Settings II menu.

- **Playback button.** Activates picture review.
- **Fn (Function) button.** (Almost) always summons the Function menu, and in Playback mode sends the current image to a smart device. However, you *can* redefine the Fn button to FTP Transfer when in Playback mode (only).
- **Movie button.** Starts/stops movies. However, you can specify whether you want the button to commence video capture always, or only when the mode dial is set to the Movie position.

Your custom key definitions override any default definitions for those buttons when in Shooting mode; they retain their original functions in Playback mode (unless you redefine them, as I'll describe shortly). Because button definition is such a personal choice, I steer away from recommending particular definitions for each of the buttons, even though certain functions can be accessed *only* by assigning them to a custom key setting. Our fingers and agility vary, so, while buttons like the AF-ON button are traditionally used for something like back button focus, you may prefer to assign that function to a different key.

When assigning definitions to keys, keep in mind that certain behaviors can be used *only* if you have made them available using a custom key definition. For example, if you want to use the Bright Monitoring feature, which temporarily turns the Live View Setting Effect to Off to increase the brightness level of the screen in dark locations, you must assign it to a key.

Each of the customizable buttons (except the down button) have a default behavior assigned for shooting mode, listed below. In Movie mode, these buttons have the exact same behavior, unless you choose a different option. In Playback mode, only the Fn button and C1–C3 buttons can be redefined, with Custom 3 having the only default behavior (Protect).

- Custom 1: White Balance
- Custom 2: Focus Area
- Custom 3: Focus Mode (Protect in Playback mode)
- Custom 4: Touch Operation Select
- Multi-selector Center button: Focus Standard
- Control Wheel Center button: Eye AF
- Left button: Drive Mode
- Right button: ISO
- Down button: Not Set
- Up button: DISP. (Not customizable)
- Focus Hold (on lens): Focus Hold

Basic Functions

These functions are all available for Custom buttons 1, 2, 3, 4, and the AF-ON and Focus Hold buttons. The whole list, *except* for In-Camera Guide, can be assigned to the Multi-selector center button, Control wheel center button, and AEL buttons. In all cases, choosing Not Set deactivates that button.

- File Format
- JPEG Quality
- JPEG Image Size
- Aspect Ratio
- APS-C/Super 35/Full Frame
- Drive Mode
- Self-timer During Bracket
- Pixel Shift
- Memory Recall
- Recall Custom Hold 1
- Recall Custom Hold 2
- Recall Custom Hold 3
- Focus Mode
- AF/MF Control Hold
- AF/MF Ctrl Toggle
- Focus Standard
- Focus Area
- Focus Settings
- Register AF Area Hold
- Register AF area toggle
- Register AF Area+AF-ON
- Center Lock-on AF
- Face Priority in AF
- Eye AF
- AF On
- Focus Hold
- Exposure Comp
- ISO

- ISO Auto Min SS
- Metering Mode
- Face Priority in Multi Metering
- AEL Hold
- AEL Toggle
- AEL Spot Hold
- AEL Spot Toggle
- Flash Mode
- Flash Compensation
- Wireless Flash
- FEL Lock hold
- FEL Lock toggle
- FEL Lock/AEL Hold
- FEL Lock/AEL toggle
- White Balance
- Priority Set in AWB
- DRO/Auto HDR
- Creative Style
- Picture Effect
- Picture Profile
- Focus Magnifier
- Peaking Display Selection
- Peaking Level
- Peaking Color
- Anti-Flicker Shooting
- In-Camera Guide
- Movie
- S&Q Frame Rate

- Audio Rec Level
- Audio Level Display
- Marker Display Settings
- Silent Shooting
- SteadyShot
- SteadyShot Adjustments
- SteadyShot Focal Length
- Zoom
- Aperture Preview
- Shot Result Preview
- Finder/Monitor Selection
- Finder Frame Rate
- Zebra Display Select
- Zebra Level
- Grid Line
- Live View Display Selection
- Bright Monitoring
- Audio Signals
- Sent to Smartphone
- FTP Transfer
- Playback
- Monitor Brightness
- Gamma Display Assist
- Touch Operation Select
- TC/UB Display Switch
- Prioritize Record Media
- Not Set

Other Buttons

The other buttons have limitations on the functions that can be assigned to them. In all cases, selecting Not Set deactivates that button.

- **Left, Right, Down buttons.** All the basic functions listed above are available, except for the 17 following behaviors, which require holding the button down to access the feature. They are: Recall Custom Hold 1, Recall Custom Hold 2, Recall Custom Hold 3, AF/MF Control Hold, Focus Standard, Register AF Area Hold, Register AF Area+AF-ON, Eye AF, AF On, Focus Hold, AEL Hold, AEL Spot Hold, FEL Lock hold, FEL Lock/AEL Hold, In-Camera Guide, Aperture Preview, Shot Result, Preview.

- **Control wheel.** The *only* functions that can be assigned to the rotation of the control wheel for Shooting mode are Move AF Point Left/Right, Move AF Point Up/Down, Aperture, Shutter Speed, ISO, White Balance, Creative Style, Picture Effect, and Not Set.

- **Center button.** All the basic functions can be assigned, plus Standard, which leaves the control wheel at its standard behavior as an OK/Enter button.

VARIATIONS ON A THEME

You have several options for assigning the very useful autoexposure lock (AEL) functions to one of the definable keys.

- **AEL hold.** Exposure is locked while the button is held down.

- **AEL toggle.** The AEL button can be pressed and released, and the exposure remains locked until the button is pressed again.

- **Center Point AEL hold.** Exposure is locked on the center point of the frame while the button is held down.

- **Center Point AEL toggle.** Toggles exposure lock on/off using the center point of the frame.

Other Useful Key Definitions

Here are some other possible custom key definitions you might find useful:

- **FINDER/MONITOR switch.** If you turn off automatic switching between finder and monitor, you'll want to have a button that will quickly toggle between the two. The down button has no default behavior, and FINDER/MONITOR is a good choice.

- **Fast ISO change.** Assign ISO to the control wheel, and as you shoot you can spin the wheel to adjust your ISO setting on the fly. While the a7R III's Auto ISO feature works well (especially when you're shooting fast and quickly), at times the photographer can do a better job of adjusting sensitivity to suit the task at hand.

- **More pairs.** The control wheel and its center button can also be assigned pairs of related functions. For example, if you've set the control wheel to change ISO sensitivity, the center button can be used to specify ISO Auto Minimum Shutter Speed when you select ISO Auto with the wheel. Image Size/Quality is another good pair for the wheel/center button combination.

- **Freed-up keys.** Once you assign ISO to the control wheel, that leaves the right button, formerly used to set ISO, free for a new definition. You could assign it to Metering Mode or another function.

Custom Key (Movies)

Options: More than 80 different definitions for Control Wheel; Custom Buttons 1, 2, 3, 4; Multi-selector Center Button; Center Button; Left/Right/Down Buttons; AEL Button; Focus Hold Button (on lens)

Default: Follow Custom (Stills)

My preference: N/A

You can assign *different* functions to each of the customizable controls when shooting movies, assuming you have such a need and an excellent memory. The default definition for those controls is Follow Custom (Stills), which uses whichever behaviors you have assigned using the Custom Key (Stills) entry.

Custom Key (Playback)

Options: Definitions for Custom Buttons 1, 2, and 3, plus Fn/Send to Smartphone button

Default: Varies

My preference: N/A

Only a limited number of controls and functions are available using this entry. The Custom 1, 2, and 3 buttons can be assigned behaviors during Playback, most of them options from the Playback menu itself. C1 and C2 follow the setting made for Stills/Movie mode (unless you choose another behavior), while C3 has a default setting of Protect during image review. The Fn button, which by default sends the displayed image to your smartphone, can also be defined to switch to FTP settings.

Function Menu Settings

Options: 36 different Function menu settings

Default: Top row: Drive Mode, Focus Mode, Focus Area, Exposure Compensation, ISO, Metering mode; Bottom row: Flash Mode, Flash Compensation, White Balance, Creative Style, Prioritize Record Media, Shoot Mode

My preference: N/A

When you press the Fn button when in Shooting or Movie modes, a screen like the one shown in Figure 4.20, left, pops up, with six settings each in two rows arrayed along the bottom. The default options are illustrated. This entry allows you to change the function of any of the 12 positions in the Function menu, so you can display only those you use most, and arrange them in the order that best suits you. There are 506 different functions available, including Not Set. Browse through the list below and decide which 12 you want to display on the Function menu.

When you highlight Function Menu Set. and press OK, the first of two screens appears, as shown in Figure 4.20, right. The screen has an entry for each of the positions in the top row, along with the current function (the second screen shows the positions in the bottom row). Highlight the position you want to modify and press OK. You can then select from among these options, all explained in detail elsewhere in this book:

- File Format
- JPEG Quality
- JPEG Image Size
- Aspect Ratio
- APS-C/Super 35 Shooting
- APS-C/Super 35 Shooting: Manual
- Drive Mode
- Self-timer During Bracket
- Pixel Shift
- Focus Mode
- Focus Area
- Center Lock-On AF
- Face Priority in AF
- Exposure Compensation
- ISO
- ISO Auto Minimum Shutter Speed

- Metering Mode
- Face Priority in Multi Metering
- Flash Mode
- Flash Compensation
- Wireless Flash
- White Balance
- Priority Set in AWB
- DRO/Auto HDR
- Creative Style
- Picture Effect
- Picture Profile
- Peaking Display
- Peaking Level
- Peaking Color
- Anti-Flicker
- S&Q Frame Rate
- Audio Recording Level

- Audio Level Display
- Marker Display
- Silent Shooting
- SteadyShot
- SteadyShot Adjust
- SteadyShot Focal Length
- Finder Frame Rate
- Zebra Display
- Zebra Level
- Grid Line
- Live View Display
- Audio Signals
- Gamma Display Assist
- Touch Operation
- Prioritize Record Media
- Shoot Mode
- Not Set

Figure 4.20 Function menu default settings (left). Function menu settings (right).

Note that you can select Not Set to leave a position blank if you want to unclutter your screen, or even duplicate an entry in multiple positions, accidentally or on purpose. Don't underestimate the power of this function. You can, in effect, create your own pop-up Function menu using any of more than four *dozen* different functions.

Dial Setup

Options: Reverse functions

Default: Front Dial: Aperture; Rear Dial: Shutter Speed

My preference: N/A

By default, in Manual exposure mode the front dial controls the f/stop, and the rear dial adjusts the shutter speed. This entry allows you to reverse those functions for Manual exposure only if you prefer. Either the front or rear dials can be used to adjust shutter speed (in Shutter Priority mode) and aperture (in Aperture Priority mode). You may have a special reason for wanting to reverse the dial directions, but you're better off leaving it alone.

Av/Tv Rotate

Options: Normal, Reverse functions

Default: Normal

My preference: N/A

This entry lets you specify the direction of rotation of the front and rear dials, plus the control wheel when using them to adjust the aperture or shutter speed. When the default Normal is in effect, rotating the appropriate dial clockwise produces a smaller f/stop or faster shutter speed; rotating counterclockwise sets a larger f/stop or slower shutter speed. Choose Reverse, and clockwise rotation sets a larger f/stop or slower shutter speed, while counterclockwise produces a smaller f/stop or faster shutter speed. This is a personal preference setting.

Dial EV Compensation

Options: Off, Front Dial, Rear Dial
Default: Off
My preference: N/A

This is the first entry of the Camera Settings II-9 (Custom Operation 2) menu. (See Figure 4.21.) If you like, you can use the front *or* rear dial to control exposure compensation whenever the exposure compensation dial is set to zero. Or, select Off and neither will have the Ev comp function. Assigning the exposure compensation behavior to a dial overrides any other function you might have defined for that dial. Moreover, dialing in exposure comp with a dial takes priority over any exposure compensation you might have set using a menu. In Manual exposure mode, the defined dial is disabled if ISO sensitivity is set to ISO Auto.

MOVIE Button

Options: Always, Movie Mode Only
Default: Always
My preference: Always

Movie recording can be started in any operating mode by pressing the Movie record button. This feature is on by default, but if you find that you occasionally press the button inadvertently, you might want to choose the Off option. After you do so, pressing the button will have no effect; when you want to record a movie, you'll need to rotate the mode dial to the Movie position. I prefer Always, because I find that impromptu video-capture situations are more frequent than accidental movie start-ups.

Figure 4.21
Camera Settings
II-9 (Custom
Operation 2) menu.

Lock Operation Parts

Options: Off, Multi-Selector Only, Dial+Wheel, All

Default: Off

My preference: Off

If you want to avoid accidentally changing settings by inadvertently using the front/rear dials, multi-selector, or control wheel, you can implement this locking option. Choose Lock and the specified dial or dials are frozen whenever the Fn button is pressed and held down. A "Locked" indicator appears on the screen. If the default Off option is selected, pressing the Fn button has no effect on the controls. You can choose to freeze the multi-selector (only), the front/rear control dials *plus* control wheel, or all four controls.

Audio Signals

Options: On, Off

Default: On

My preference: Off

Enables and disables the beeping/chirping sounds the camera makes when various operations happen, such as achieving autofocus or the self-timer countdown. Most of the time I don't require the feedback and, on the contrary, want to blend in without calling attention to myself, so I disable the noises. The self-timer countdown is especially noticeable, even in environments with a moderate amount of noise. Couple this setting with Silent Shooting and you can often take pictures virtually unnoticed.

5

Network and Playback Menus

Your a7R III is equipped with a built-in wireless communication system that includes a whole collection of impressive abbreviations, acronyms, and buzzwords—and functions to match! Wi-Fi, NFC, Bluetooth, and FTP have arrived, so you can easily and quickly transfer files from your camera to a smartphone or computer, upload to Facebook, control your camera remotely, and perform other tasks. This chapter provides an introduction to connecting your camera to other devices using the Network menu. Then, we'll move on to the Playback menu to discuss some of the options available when reviewing images.

Using the Network Menu

The section explains the basic functions on the Network menu, in order, although you probably won't be using them in this order. For example, you should make Wi-Fi Settings or assign a name to a device in the Network 2 menu *before* you use the functions in the Network 1 menu. (See Figure 5.1.) I'll summarize all the entries first, and then later cover the major options in logical/functional order rather than the order they appear in the menus. Detailed networking/information technology topics and software operation discussions (including configuring and using PlayMemories Home on your computer) are beyond the scope of this book, which is primarily a *photography* tome, so some sections may provide just an overview. The Network menu entries are shown in Table 5.1.

Figure 5.1 The Network 1 and 2 menus.

Table 5.1 Network Menu		
Send to Smartphone Function	Control with Smartphone	Location Info Link Settings
Send to Computer	Airplane Mode	Edit Device Name
FTP Transfer Function	Wi-Fi Settings	Import Root Certificate
View on TV	Bluetooth Settings	Reset Network Settings

Send to Smartphone Function

Options: Send to Smartphone (Select on This Device, Select on Smartphone); Sending Target (Proxy Only, Original Only, Proxy & Original)

Using the PlayMemories Mobile app on your smart device, you can transfer still photographs, XAVC X video, and slow- or quick-motion movies from your camera's memory card. This entry lets you specify whether the files to be transferred are selected on the camera or on the smart device, and whether you transfer the original file only, or, in the case of videos, a proxy (lower-quality, faster transfer) movie only, or both the original and proxy. (See Chapter 4 for a description of proxy recordings in the Camera Settings I-9 menu.)

The PlayMemories Mobile app allows you to choose the Image Copy Size for stills, either original, 2MB, or VGA, so you can speed up transfer, if necessary, by selecting a smaller file size. RAW files are converted to JPEG before transmission. 4K video, XAVC S movies recorded at 120/100p, and AVCHD movies cannot be transferred at all.

Send to Computer

Options: Slot 1, Slot 2

You can transfer images stored on your memory card to a computer through a wireless access point or broadband router connection using the PlayMemories Home application *on your computer.* PlayMemories Home is the Windows/Mac counterpart to the PlayMemories Mobile app on your smart device. Don't confuse the two! You can choose the memory card slot that contains the files to be transferred. Proxy movies cannot be transferred using this facility.

FTP Transfer Function

Options: FTP Transfer, Display FTP Result, Select FTP Server, Define FTP Server 1–3

IT techies can transfer images from the camera to a networked FTP (File Transfer Protocol) server, view the results, select which server to send to, and define up to three different FTP servers. Only JPEG and RAW files can be transferred using FTP.

View on TV

Options: Connect to TV

You don't need to hardwire your network-enabled smart TV to the a7R III to transfer still images. This entry allows you to set up displays and slide shows wirelessly, selecting images, the display interval, playback size, and any special effects. Movies cannot be transferred using this facility. Operations controlled from the TV vary by model, so you'll need to consult your DLNA-compatible smart TV's manual to make the best use of this feature.

Control with Smartphone

Options: Control with Smartphone (On, Off); Display QR Code; Always Connected (On, Off)

You can control your camera using your smart device and a Wi-Fi connection. This entry turns the feature on or off, displays a QR code to quickly link the camera and device, and specifies whether, once activated, the camera remains connected to the smartphone at all times (draining your battery significantly), or maintains the link only when you connect manually.

Airplane Mode

Options: On, Off

Enables/disables wireless functions. Use this to save power, or when required (as when boarding an airplane).

Wi-Fi Settings

Options: WPS Push, Accent Point Settings, Display MAC Address, SSID/PW Reset

This entry includes features for connecting the a7R III to a Wi-Fi access point, either semi-automatically using WPS Push, or by manually registering by entering the SSID name of the access point and entering security information. You can also view the device's MAC Address. Each device on a network has a unique Media Access Control number. You generally have no need to know this, unless you want to block a device from your network and use the MAC address to identify the unwanted device.

SSID/PW Reset deletes the current SSID and password. You might want to do this for security reasons (say, you load/give/sell your a7R III to someone else) or need to start over in registering your camera with a network. Reset Network Settings removes all network settings from the camera. I'll describe the key components of the Wi-Fi Settings screen later in the chapter.

Bluetooth Settings

Options: Bluetooth Function (On, Off); Pairing; Display Device Address

Your a7R III can access the GPS information available from your smartphone and embed that data in your image files using low-energy Bluetooth connectivity. Use this, and you no longer have to wonder where you took a photo; the GPS data can be displayed by many applications, including Lightroom's Map tab. This entry allows you to turn off Bluetooth sharing, pairing your phone with your camera, and displaying the device's address. Keep in mind that when you initialize your camera, as described in Chapter 6, pairing settings are canceled as well.

Location Information Link Setting

Options: Location Info Link, Auto Time Correction, Auto Area Adjustment

This entry allows the a7R III to access the location information from your smartphone, after you've enabled Bluetooth connectivity in the previous entry. One of the cool features is to use the Auto Time Correction option to allow your smartphone's (very) accurate time information to be used to set the time and date used by your camera. It's the "let's synchronize our watches" version for the 21st century. You can also activate Auto Area Adjustment, so the camera "knows" where it is and uses the correct time zone. Turn this on if you want to embed in your image files the local time when you took a picture; turn if off if you'd prefer the time reflect your "back home" norm.

Edit Device Name

Options: Change Device Name

By default, the label applied to your camera is ILCE-RM3. You can change it to something else, if, say, you own three or four a7R III's and want to differentiate between them—or simply want to personalize your camera's "name."

Import Root Certificate

Options: Import certificate

Encrypted communications with an FTP server may require verification using a root certificate. This entry allows you to import that certificate.

Reset Network Settings

Options: Reset and Reboot

Changes all network settings to their factory defaults and reboots your a7R III.

Making a Connection

For this section, I'm basing my descriptions in this chapter on the assumption that you are *not* an IT specialist, and don't need (or want) to compare the advantages of WEP versus WPA security, would rather not set IP addresses yourself, and don't care much about root certificates. Alternatively, I will assume that if you *are* an IT specialist and find these topics compelling, you already know most of what you need and would rather not hear it from me, again. As Thoreau once said, "Simplify, simplify!" (but without explaining the redundant "Simplify.")

If you want to connect using your smartphone or tablet, the first thing you should do is venture over to your smart device's app store and download the PlayMemories Mobile app. Then follow the instructions that follow for connecting through NFC or Wi-Fi. The a7R III has an additional option for linking your smartphone to the camera through Bluetooth so GPS information can be embedded in your photographs.

Camera/Device: NFC Connection

If you have an Android device, connecting with NFC is your simplest option. NFC stands for *Near Field Communication*, a wireless access method found in Android-based smartphones and tablets. It's not available with iOS devices, although Apple Pay uses it to send your money hither and yon. Once you've installed the PlayMemories Mobile app on your device, linking the a7R III and the device is as simple as tapping the area on your phone containing its transceiver with the camera's transceiver (located under the "N" mark on the right side).

Camera/Device: Wi-Fi Connection

Wi-Fi connections are slightly more complicated and can be used both for Android and iOS smartphones. Just follow these steps:

1. Make sure Ctrl w/Smartphone is set to On in the Network 1 menu.
2. Choose Connection in the same menu. The a7R III will display a QR code on the LCD monitor.

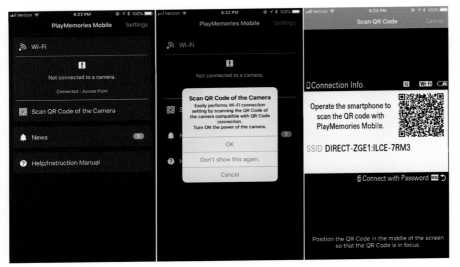

Figure 5.2

Connecting using PlayMemories Mobile.

3. Launch PlayMemories Mobile. You'll see a screen like the one at left in Figure 5.2. Tap Scan QR Code of the camera.

4. An instructional screen appears (see Figure 5.2, center). Tap OK or Don't Show This Again to proceed.

5. A capture window will appear on the smartphone. Center it over the QR code on the LCD monitor of the a7R III to allow the smartphone to capture the code. (See Figure 5.2, right.)

6. A message "Scanning Complete" appears on the smartphone. Tap OK to confirm.

7. Follow the remaining instructions to install a profile on your smartphone for the camera connection. You may have to enter your device's passcode and confirm installation.

8. When installation is complete, you will be instructed to select the a7R III's "hot spot" as your Wi-Fi connection, and then restart PlayMemories Mobile.

Using WPS Push

Wi-Fi Protected Setup works only when you're in range of a network provided by a wireless router that is equipped with a WPS button. Not all are. Examine your router and look for a button labeled WPS, or with a 🔄 symbol. Or, find the owner's manual for your router or use a Google search (try "*routername* manual PDF") to locate the WPS button, if one is available. Some routers that support WPS provide it with software instead of a physical button; in that case, you'll need to access the router's control panel using a computer and click the button on the WPS page. The WPS Push tactic is great, but it would not work at a Wi-Fi hotspot in a supermarket, for instance, since the network owner is unlikely to use the WPS feature for hundreds of customers.

WHAT'S WPS?

The abbreviation WPS indicates Wi-Fi Protected Setup. This is a security standard that makes it easier and quicker to connect a device, including your a7R III, to a wireless home network. It eliminates the need to key in the password. Because it's possible for an aggressive hacker to recover the WPS PIN number, some experts suggest turning the router's WPS feature off when you're not actually using it; this may not be possible with all router models but check the owner's manual for the one you own.

Just follow these steps:

1. **Access Network 1 menu and choose Wi-Fi Settings.** If your router provides WPS, scroll to the WPS Push item in the camera's Wi-Fi settings menu and press the center button.

2. **Press router's WPS button.** A screen will appear advising you to press the router's WPS button within 2 minutes. When you press the button (or use the software) to do so, the camera should be able to establish connectivity.

3. **Confirm registration.** Once the connection is established, a screen reporting "Registered. SSID *network name*" appears. Press the center button to confirm.

Registering Manually

You can also select an access point manually when within range of a wireless network; you'll need to know the network password, if one is in place, to do so. Just follow these steps:

1. **Access the Network 2's Wi-Fi entry and scroll to Access Point Set.** Press the center button. A Wi-Fi Standby screen will appear confirming that the camera is searching for available access points.

2. **Wait for the camera to find your network.** The a7R III will find the nearby access points (networks) in less than a minute. (See Figure 5.3.) If there is more than one network or available access point, all of those found will be shown. If your smartphone has a hotspot feature and it's turned on, that "network" may appear as well.

   When several networks are displayed, some may belong to nearby businesses or your neighbors, and you can ignore them (their signal strength is probably weaker than your own network in any case, even if your neighbor's network is not protected by a password). In my case, my wireless router resides in my office; in other, more distant rooms is a wired access point, and, on the second floor, a wireless repeater. Scroll to the one you intend to use and press the center button to confirm.

3. **Input the password (if necessary).** The next screen that appears may have a field for entering your network password, if your router/access point is set up to require one. If not, proceed to Step 4. Otherwise, press the center button and a virtual keyboard will appear. Using this keyboard, enter the password for your network. The keyboard works a bit like the physical multi-tap keyboard found on some (older) cell phones. Use the directional buttons to highlight a letter

Figure 5.3
Access Point Settings can be used to select an access point/hotspot. The camera displays the available networks that are within range.

group, such as abc, def, ghi, and press the center button once to enter the first character in the group, twice for the second character, three times for the third character, and four times for the fourth. Some of the virtual keys allow you to backspace, delete characters, and toggle between uppercase and lowercase. When finished, highlight OK and press the center button.

4. **IP Address Setting.** The next screen will appear, showing the IP Address Setting as Auto and Priority Connection as Off. These defaults should work perfectly. Select OK and press the center button. A screen will appear showing the camera trying to connect to the network.

   If the Auto IP Address Setting option does not work, and you have some networking expertise, change from Auto to Manual, and a screen appears that allows you to enter the IP address, Subnet Mark, and Default Gateway. You can safely leave the Priority Connection parameter set to Off. Fortunately, you probably won't have to resort to these additional steps.

5. **Confirm connectivity.** After the Wi-Fi connectivity has been made, a screen will appear confirming that your network has been registered. The screen will look like the one in Figure 5.3, but an orange dot will appear next to the connected network. If you get a screen with a note stating *cannot authenticate*, or that the *input value is invalid*, you'll need to start again at step 1; make sure you have the correct password for the network and be extra careful when keying it in. Remember that when a capital letter is required, you must use the shift feature (an arrow pointing upward) on the virtual keyboard.

6. **Try it again later.** After you have established Wi-Fi connectivity, you can revert to using the a7R III as usual; a touch of the shutter release button returns it to shooting mode. The camera will retain the connection to the network until you turn it off or it goes into power-saving sleep mode; Wi-Fi is then temporarily disconnected. When you're ready to use Wi-Fi again, activate the a7R III while in range of the same network, scroll to Access Point Settings in the Wireless menu, and press the center button. The camera will quickly find your network to re-establish Wi-Fi connectivity.

If you're connecting to a public Wi-Fi hotspot, the steps should be the same, but you'll most likely find a screen that requires you to agree to the hotspot's terms and conditions. Some hotspots may not require you to enter a password.

Selecting an Access Point Manually

If the desired access point (network) is not displayed on the screen as described in Step 2 above, you may need to enter it yourself. Just follow these steps:

1. **Choose Manual Setting.** Scroll down to Manual Setting and press the center button. The screen shown in Figure 5.4 appears.

2. **Select Manual Registration.** Press the center button to begin the manual registration process. The screen shown in Figure 5.5 appears.

3. **Enter SSID.** On the Manual Registration screen, there's a field for entering the SSID name of the access point (network) you plan to use. Press the center button when this field is visible, and the virtual keyboard appears. Enter the data. When you're finished press the center button.

4. **Change Security (if necessary).** Again, if you have some networking expertise, you'll know if the security setting on your router is WPA (Wi-Fi Protected Access, the default), WEP (Wired Equivalent Privacy, an older, easily "hacked" protection scheme), or None (effectively, no security). If you want to change the Security setting, highlight that field and press the center button. Select your choice and press the MENU button to return.

5. **Enter password.** The next screen will ask for your password, which you can enter using the virtual keyboard.

6. **Enter WPS PIN (if necessary).** If your WPS connection requires a PIN, you can enter it.

Take care not to lose the network connection by inadvertently using the Initialize or the Reset Network Settings item of the Wireless menu. If you do so, the camera will eliminate all your network settings and you'll need to repeat the steps in this section.

Figure 5.4 Manual registration requires you to complete extra steps.

Figure 5.5 Enter the SSID (network/access point name).

Sending Photos to a Smart Device

To transfer photos from your camera to a smartphone or tablet, the device must be running the free PlayMemories Mobile app for Android or iOS; you can get it from your usual app store. After you have downloaded the PlayMemories Mobile app (for iOS or Android) and are running it in your smart device, you can send one or more images to the smart device. (The app, and hence the camera's Wi-Fi features like this one, are not available in a few countries where many aspects of Internet use are restricted.) This feature does not work for video clips. Here are the steps you'll follow:

1. **Turn on the camera and the smart devices.** Ensure that both the a7R III and the smart device have found your network. With the a7R III, you'll do so using the Access Point Settings as discussed earlier.

2. **Use the View on Smartphone item.** Access this Wireless 1 menu item in the camera. (The term smartphone actually means smart *device* since it works with a tablet computer, too, in the same manner.) The a7R III will display a screen with three options: This Image, All Images on This Date, and All Images in the Device. Scroll to the one that specifies the types of files you want to transfer to the smart device and press the center button.

3. **Enter the SSID and password in the smart device.** At this point, the a7R III will be displaying both its unique ID (SSID) and a Password. Using the smart device's virtual keyboard, enter the SSID and password that your a7R III is displaying. Remember, it's all case sensitive so use capital letters when necessary. If you get an *incorrect password* message from the smart device, start again using greater care to be accurate. Click on Join or whatever command your device requires to proceed.

4. **Run the PlayMemories Mobile app in the smart device.** After starting the app in your smartphone or tablet, wait for it to find the a7R III. Your device's screen will indicate that it's searching for the camera. When that's finished, the image transfer from the camera to the smart device will begin.

5. **View the Images.** After the smart device has completed importing files from the a7R III, you can view the thumbnails on its screen. Naturally, you can enlarge any photo so it fills the device's screen.

6. **Use the smart device to send photos, etc.** You can now use any of the smart device's capabilities: modify any of the images, send it to friends via e-mail, upload it to any website, and so on.

Wi-Fi Transfer to a Computer

You can transfer photos from the a7R III to a computer that's also connected to the same wireless network. Do note that you must first install Sony's PlayMemories Home for Windows, or Sony's Wireless Auto Import for Mac to your computer.

Use this Wireless menu item when you're ready to transfer images from the a7R III via Wi-Fi to a computer that is connected to the network. (Review the items under the Networks heading for advice on establishing Wi-Fi connectivity between your camera and a network.)

Before you can transfer photos to a computer with Wi-Fi, be sure to install the PlayMemories Home software on a Windows or Mac computer. Then, you'll need to register the a7R III in the software; this will also instruct the camera as to where photos should be sent in future, using Wi-Fi. The process is automatic after you connect the camera to the computer with the USB cable; the software will recognize it after a few seconds and proceed to register it. Afterward, image transfer will be possible without cable connection.

Use the following steps. These are based on the ones I used with PlayMemories Home in a Windows PC; they may be slightly different if you own a Mac computer and are using the Wireless Auto Import software.

1. **Begin to authenticate your a7R III.** Before using Wi-Fi, you must sync the two devices. Launch the Sony software, connect the camera to the computer with the USB cable, and turn the camera on to start the process. (If any auto run wizard opens, offering to transfer images, close it.) The Sony Software in the computer will recognize the a7R III and confirm it; you'll also see a screen on your computer monitor indicating that a compatible device has been found. If the computer software displays a screen indicating that the USB mode must be changed (to Mass Storage), click on Yes. (Surprisingly, this was necessary for me although the USB mode in the camera was at Auto, which should have worked without any problem.)

2. **Proceed with the software-recommended step.** When you see the screen on your computer monitor asking how you want to set up Wi-Fi import, the Recommended item will be checked. Click on Next. A Settings Completed screen will appear. Click on Finish.

3. **Disconnect the camera.** Since you'll be sending photos from the a7R III to the computer using Wi-Fi, there's no need for any cable connection from this point on.

4. **Access the Send to Computer menu item.** Turn the a7R III on, access the Wireless menu and scroll to this item; then, press the center button. The camera will find the network and connect to it; it will then find your computer and make that connection, using Wi-Fi. This can take a minute or two. The camera's LCD will display a confirmation that files are being shared with the computer via Wi-Fi. PlayMemories Home in your computer will display a bar on your monitor confirming the wireless connection to the a7R III and that it's importing (bringing in) the files on the memory card.

5. **Wait for the file transfer to finish.** There is no method for importing only certain files to a computer. The transfer process can be very time consuming if the memory card contains numerous images, especially RAW photos and long movie clips. The camera should shut down automatically after saving the files to your computer; if not, turn it off yourself.

6. **Confirm that the files have arrived.** Use any software to access the drive/folder that was the destination for the photos and video clips. You should find them in the expected location, in individual folders. Delete any files that you do not want to keep.

BYPASS SECURITY SOFTWARE

If, during Step 4, you get a note on the a7R III's display screen indicating that the camera could not connect to your computer, the problem is being caused by a computer firewall and you'll need to make a change to allow incoming data to be received. For example, my Norton 360's firewall was set by default to Block incoming data. I changed that to Allow and then all went exactly as discussed in the steps. After the data transfer has been completed, it's essential that you re-activate the blocking features of the firewall, so it will again provide full security.

FTP Transfer

Transfer to a remote FTP server is an extremely useful feature, especially for photojournalists who want to upload still images to their organizations for immediate editing and distribution. Considerable knowledge of the technology is required, and beyond the scope of this book, but Sony offers an additional FTP Help Guide at http://helpguide.sony.net/di/ftp/v1/h_zz/index.html.

Viewing Images on a TV

As with any current digital camera, it's possible to view JPEG photos and video clips on an HDTV when you connect the a7R III to the TV using an HDMI cable. This is an extra-cost accessory. Buy the Type D cable with a micro HDMI connector at one end (for plugging into the camera) and a conventional HDMI plug (to connect to the TV's HDMI port). An inexpensive cable is fine; there's no need to pay more for one of the premium brands unless you need a cable that's longer than about 6 feet. Make the cable connection and you can now display photos and movies on the oversized screen.

After the Wi-Fi connection has been made with a Digital Living Network Alliance/DLNA-compatible (network-enabled or Wi-Fi Direct-enabled) HDTV, you can use this menu item, on the second screen of Wireless options. Use it to display photos on the HDTV without cable connection after Wi-Fi connectivity has been confirmed. The benefit of Wi-Fi Direct is that you do not need to register your access point on the camera before doing so; in other words, the TV need not be connected to the network if you are using Wi-Fi Direct. Movie clips cannot be transferred to a TV for display over Wi-Fi; to show those, connect the camera to the HDTV using an optional Type D HDMI cable.

Use the menu options to instruct the camera as to which device (TV) it should send to, which photos to display (all or only those in a specific folder), and whether the display time should be long or short if using the slide show feature. Press the center button if you do want to use the slide show feature. At any time, you can move to another image for the display by scrolling to the left or right.

It's also possible to transfer JPEG photos, but not videos, to an HDTV without cable connection. If you have a networked TV (or a network-friendly game machine such as PlayStation or xBox), you can view the images in your camera on that display without using the HDMI cable.

Of course, the HDTV must be DLNA (Digital Living Network Alliance) compliant and it must first be connected to your home network via Wi-Fi as per the instructions that came with the device. The a7R III must also be communicating with your network via Wi-Fi, of course. (Use the steps provided earlier.)

> **Note**
>
> There is an exception to the DLNA rule. Some HDTVs are Wi-Fi Direct enabled; if yours is, then it need not be connected to your network. Mine is not, so I have not been able to try this feature.

There are simply too many types of Wi-Fi-enabled HDTV's to provide full specifics on exactly how you'll transfer JPEGs to the device. Sony's published documents specifically recommend their Bravia HDTV, as you might expect, but you can use any DLNA (or Wi-Fi Direct) enabled TV. A Bravia HDTV does provide a few extra display features that are possible only when using a Sony camera.

In any event, start by accessing the View on TV item in the camera's Network menu and press the center button. The camera will confirm the Wi-Fi connection to your network and it will search for a compatible TV. Be sure to consult your TV's instructions for setting the media display component to receive information from the camera. When connectivity with the TV has been confirmed, you can begin the sharing process using connection controls like those described earlier in this chapter.

Remote Control

Shooting photos remotely with your a7R III is the next best thing to shooting tethered using Lightroom. All you need is your camera and your smartphone. You can also shoot remotely using the new, free Imaging Edge software, which you can download from your country's Sony website. For casual remote-control shooting, whether you want to exercise some creative options (to get unusual viewpoints), you are stalking wildlife, or are a double-naught spy, your smartphone and camera will do the job.

Once you've connected your camera to the smartphone, the screen shown at left in Figure 5.6 appears. There are a limited number of settings you can make from the smartphone, but you can always use the controls *on the camera itself* to make additional adjustments. You're stuck with the exposure mode already set on the a7R III, but can change White Balance, switch from single to continuous shooting, select an f/stop or shutter speed if using Aperture Priority, Shutter Priority (respectively), or Manual exposure. Adjust ISO, make exposure compensation settings, activate the self-timer, and use a menu like the one shown at right in the figure. Note the GPS indicator at center left (it looks like a satellite) indicating that location information from your linked smartphone is

Figure 5.6
Shooting by remote control.

being recorded. Tap the "shutter button" icon at bottom center and take a picture. If you have specified Always Connected under the Control with Smartphone entry in the Network 1 menu, you'll always be ready to go when the camera and smartphone are in proximity.

Playback Menu

This menu controls functions for deleting, protecting, displaying, and printing images. **Tip:** While you can access the Playback menu at any time using the Menu system, you can bring it up on your screen more quickly just by pressing the Playback button first, then the MENU button, which causes the *most recent* Playback menu page you've accessed to appear. The entries available in the three Playback menus are shown in Table 5.2.

Table 5.2 Playback Menu		
Protect	Photo Capture	Image Index
Rotate	Enlarge Image	Display Continuous Shooting
Delete	Enlarge Initial Magnification	Group
Rating	Enlarge Initial Position	Display Rotation
Rating Set (Custom Key)	Slide Show	Image Jump Setting
Specify Printing	Select Playback Media	
Copy	View Mode	

Protect

Options: Multiple Images, All with Current View Mode, Cancel All Images

This is the first entry in the Playback menu. (See Figure 5.7.) You might want to protect certain images or movie clips on your memory card from accidental erasure, either by you or by others who may use your camera from time to time. This menu item enables you to tag one or more images or movies for protection, so a delete command will not delete it. (Formatting a memory card deletes everything, including protected content.) This menu item also enables you to cancel the protection from all tagged photos or movies. If all you want to do is protect/unprotect the image currently on the screen, just press C3 during playback.

To use this feature, make sure to specify whether you want to do so for stills or movies; use the View Mode item in the Playback 3 menu (described later) to designate the desired view mode. There, you can select from Date View, Folder View (Still), AVCHD View, XAVC S HD View, or XAVC S 4K View to see only items matching that parameter.

Then, access the Protect menu item, choose Multiple Images, and press the center button. An image (or thumbnail of a movie) will appear; scroll among the photos or videos using the control wheel to reach the photo you want to tag for protection; press the center button to tag it with an orange check mark at the bottom-left corner of the image. (If it's already tagged, pressing the button will remove the tag, eliminating the protection you had previously provided.)

After you have marked all the items you want to protect, press the MENU button to confirm your choice. A screen will appear asking you to confirm that you want to protect the marked images; press the center button to do so. Later, if you want, you can go back and select the Cancel All Images option to unprotect all the tagged photos or movies.

Figure 5.7
Playback 1 menu.

Rotate

Options: None

When you select this menu item, you are immediately presented with a new screen showing the current or most recently reviewed image along with an indication that the center button can be used to rotate the image. (This feature does not work with movies.) Scroll left/right to reach the image you want to rotate. Successive presses of the center button will now rotate the image 90 degrees at a time. The camera will remember whatever rotation setting you apply here. You can use this function to rotate an image that was taken with the camera held vertically, when you have set Display Rotation to Manual. Press the MENU button to exit.

Delete

Options: Multiple Img., All with Current View Mode

Sometimes we take pictures or video clips that we know should never see the light of day. Maybe you were looking into the lens and accidentally tripped the shutter. Perhaps you really goofed up your settings. You want to erase that photo *now,* before it does permanent damage to your reputation as a good photographer. Unless you have turned Auto Review off in the Camera Settings II-9 (Display/Auto Review 2) menu, you can delete a photo immediately after you take it by pressing the Trash key (Delete button). Also, you can use that method to delete any individual image that's being displayed on the screen in Playback mode.

However, sometimes you need to wait for an idle moment to erase all pictures that are obviously not "keepers." I sometimes do this during halftime when shooting sports, to eliminate a series of continuous shots I know were a waste of storage space. This menu item makes it easy to remove selected photos or video clips (Multiple Images), or to erase all the photos or video clips taken, sorted by your currently active view mode (such as folder or date). (Change the type of view using the View Mode option, described later.) Note that there is no delete method that will remove images tagged as Protected.

To remove one or more images (or movie files), select the Delete menu item, and use the up/down directional buttons, front dial, rear dial, or the control wheel to choose the Multiple Images option. Press the center button, and the most recent image *using your currently active view* (Date View, Folder View (Still), Folder View (MP4), or AVCHD View) will be displayed on the LCD.

Scroll left/right through your images and press the center button when you reach the image you want to tag for deletion; a check mark then appears beside it and an orange check mark appears in the bottom-right corner of the screen. You can press the DISP button to see more information about a particular image. You can also press the AEL/Thumbnail button to view thumbnails of multiple images and select them in that mode.

The number of images marked for deletion is incremented in the indicator at the lower-right corner of the LCD, next to a trash can icon. When you're satisfied (or have expressed your dissatisfaction with the really bad images), press the MENU button, and you will be asked if you're sure you want to proceed. To confirm your decision, press the center button. The images (or video clips) you had tagged will now be deleted. If you want to delete *everything* on the memory card, it's quicker to do so by using the Format item in the Setup menu, as discussed in Chapter 6.

Rating

Options: One to five stars, Off

This setting lets you apply a quality rating to still images (but not movies) you've shot. You can also use the rating system to represent some other criteria. Simply select this menu item (or define a custom key as a dedicated Rating button, as described next). You can use this entry to give images one, two, three, four, or five stars, or turn the rating off. The Image Jump function (described later in this chapter) can display only images that have been given a specific rating, or any rating at all. Suppose you were photographing a track meet with multiple events. You could apply a one-star rating to jumping events, two stars to relays, three stars to throwing events, four stars to hurdles, and five stars to dashes. Then, using the Image Jump feature, you could review only images of one type. I personally find this type of use more helpful than simply critiquing my own work.

With a little imagination, you can apply the rating system to all sorts of categories. At a wedding, you could classify pictures of the bride, the groom, guests, attendants, and parents of the couple. If you were shooting school portraits, one rating could apply to first grade, another to second grade, and so on. Given a little thought, this feature has many more applications than you might think. Ratings can be used to specify images for a slide show, too, or to select images in Digital Photo Professional.

To use the Ratings menu entry, follow these steps:

1. Choose the Rating menu item.
2. The most recently viewed image appears.
3. Press the center button, and an icon appears, flanked by left/right triangles. (See Figure 5.2, left.)
4. Use the left/right controls to scroll among Off, and the individual star settings available. (You can specify which ratings can be applied, as I'll describe shortly.)
5. Press MENU to confirm and exit.
6. The star rating (if any) that you've applied will henceforth be overlaid on the image each time you review it.

Rating Set (Custom Key)

Options: Activate any (or all) star ratings

This is a clever option that allows you to specify *which* star ratings can be applied when rating images using a defined Custom Key for the Rating function. For example, if you're rating by quality and don't deign to mark your really bad images, you can disable the * or ** star values. Thereafter, you'll only need to consider ***, ****, or **** ratings.

For this to work, you must apply the Rating behavior to a custom key of your choice, as I described in Chapter 4. After that, you can visit this menu entry, shown in Figure 5.8, right, and highlight individual star values. Press the center button to mark/unmark them, then highlight Enter and press the center button again to confirm and exit. When rating an image using the Custom Key, just press the key multiple times. The ratings change to the next available value each time you press the key. (This should be your default way of applying ratings!)

Figure 5.8 You can apply one to five stars or turn ratings off (left). If you rarely use a particular star value, you can deactivate it when using a Custom Key.

Specify Printing

Options: Multiple Images, Cancel All, Print Setting

Most digital cameras are compatible with the DPOF (Digital Print Order Format) protocol, which enables you to tag JPEG images on the memory card (but not RAW files or movies) for printing with a DPOF-compliant printer; you can also specify whether you want the date imprinted as well. Afterward, you can transport your memory card to a retailer's digital photo lab or do-it-yourself kiosk or use your own DPOF-compatible printer to print out the tagged images in the quantities you've specified.

Choose multiple images using the View Mode filters described earlier to select to view either by Date or by Folder. Press the center button to mark an image for printing with an orange check mark, and the MENU button to confirm when you're finished. The Print Setting entry lets you choose to superimpose the date onto the print. The date will be added during printing by the output device, which controls its location on the final print.

Copy

Options: Copy all images in current view mode to other card

This menu entry is the first in the Playback 2 menu (see Figure 5.9). The ability to work with two memory cards is a great feature. One of the best uses for your two slots is to make back-up images while traveling, or at any other time that your computer isn't easily accessible. Here are some examples of what I do:

- **Make a copy.** Use this Copy facility to make a copy of images you shot on one card to your second card.

- **Make copies to distribute.** I bought a bunch of 8GB memory cards for $4 each and find it's quick and easy to make multiple copies of photos, not for backup, but for distribution either on the spot, say, to provide models I've hired with some raw (not RAW) images or to send by snail mail to colleagues, friends, or family. No computer required!

- **Leave your laptop or external storage at home.** When I use a camera with dual memory card slots, I leave my hard disk/personal storage device with its built-in reader or my laptop at home more often. If I am going to be gone for only a day or two, it's easier to just make copies in the camera, and not bother with another external device.

Figure 5.9
Playback 2 menu.

The process is simple: just select Copy and the a7R III will take all the images visible *in your current View Mode* and copy them from the memory card slot that you specified using Select Playback Media (described later in this chapter) to the other memory card slot. Note that the process takes awhile, especially if you have many images, so you should be prepared to wait, and have a fully-charged battery installed. Use the View Mode entry to choose the type of files to copy, using Date View, Folder View (Still), Folder View (MP4), AVCHD View, XAVC S HD View, or XAVC S 4K View. You can interrupt transfer at any time (say, a UFO lands nearby) by pressing the center button to cancel.

If you have any XAVC S movies on the source card, you will not be able to copy them to a card that is not fast enough to support XAVCS S video. When that conflict happens, you'll see a message: "Cannot copy in the current memory card combination. Insert an SDXC Class 10 or USH-I/UHS II compatible memory card in the slot of the device where the copies are to be saved." Substitute another card, or switch to a View Mode that excludes XAVC S clips. If you have "stacked" images in a continuous shooting group using Display Continuous Shooting Group (described shortly), they will not be grouped when copied to the other memory card.

Photo Capture

Options: Capture video frame

This menu entry can be accessed only when you're playing back a video clip. You can use it to extract a still frame from a movie you've captured. Just follow these steps:

1. **Select the movie.** In Playback mode, navigate to the movie you want to clip from.
2. **Press MENU.** Choose Photo Capture from the Playback 2 menu. The first frame of the video will appear, along with a display offering playback controls.
3. **Play video.** Press the center button to start playback of the video at normal speed.
4. **Pause.** Press the center button again to pause playback when you reach the approximate location containing the desired frame.
5. **Select frame.** Use one of the following controls to navigate to the exact frame you want to extract:
   - **Up button.** Plays back slowly so you can monitor the action easily.
   - **Forward/Reverse.** Press the left/right buttons to move to the next frame/previous frame.
   - **Down button.** Saves the currently displayed frame to your memory card.

Enlarge Image

Options: Zoom On, Zoom Out

Whenever you are playing back still images (not movies), you can use this menu entry to magnify the image. (You can also double-tap the touch screen to zoom in.) The a7R III will try to zoom in on the point used to focus the image, if possible, and will zoom into the center of the frame if not.

Press the Index/Reduce/AEL button to zoom out, and the Magnify/AF-MF button to zoom in. The MENU button exits. Use the control wheel to zoom in and out, and you can scroll around inside the enlarged image using the control wheel's direction controls. Rotate the front or rear dials to view the next or previous image (respectively) at the same magnification. Press MENU or the center button to exit. The initial magnification of the image is set using the entry that follows.

Enlarge Initial Magnification

Options: Standard Magnification, Previous Magnification

Here you can choose the initial magnification used by the Enlarge Image entry. Use Standard Magnification to always see any image you magnify at the same zoom level. This is a good choice if you magnify from time to time to closely examine an image and may want to zoom in or out to view more or less of your subject matter. When you select Previous Magnification, the enlargement resumes at the most recent level used. For example, if you are checking focus of your images as you shoot and zooming in tightly, it's convenient to return to the same zoom level for each successive image.

Enlarge Initial Position

Options: Focused Position, Center

By default, whenever you magnify an image during playback, the a7R III centers the enlargement around the area in the frame where focus was achieved. That's often the best choice, because when evaluating an image during playback, focus is the parameter most often checked. However, I prefer the enlargement positioned in the center of the frame, so I can move the magnifying window around anywhere I like. That setting potentially minimizes the amount of "travel" if the previous area I examined is located some distance in the frame from my new area of interest.

Slide Show

Menu Options: Repeat (On/Off), Interval: 1 second, 3 seconds, 5 seconds, 10 seconds, 30 seconds

Use this menu option when you want to display all the still images on your memory card in a continuous show. You can display still images in a continuous series, with each one displayed for the amount of time that you set. Choose the Repeat option to make the show repeat in a continuous loop. After making your settings, press the center button and the slide show will begin. You can scroll left or right to go back to a previous image or go forward to the next image immediately, but that will stop the slide show. The show cannot be paused, but you can exit by pressing the MENU button.

Select Playback Media

Options: Slot 1, Slot 2

This is the first entry in the Playback 3 menu. (See Figure 5.10.) Your a7R III has two memory card slots, with useful labels on the reverse side of the memory card door to help you sort them out. You can specify which slot has precedence when reviewing images. Select either Slot 1 or Slot 2 here to register your preference.

- **See images on preferred card.** Once you've selected a slot, when you press the Playback button, images in that card matching your current view mode will be displayed. If no images are available in that view, a sidebar appears at the left of the LCD/viewfinder. You can press the up/down buttons to change to a different view mode.

- **Card not inserted.** If you press Playback and no card is inserted in your preferred slot, you'll see a message "No memory card inserted. Slot #".

- **Switching slots.** To change active *playback* slot, you'll need to use this menu entry. Note that if you want to change the active *recording* slot to use during shooting, you can define a button for the Select Recording Media behavior with the Custom Key (Shooting) entry in the Camera Settings II-8 menu, as described in Chapter 4.

View Mode

Options: Date View, Folder View (Still), AVCHD View, XAVC S HD View, XAVC S 4K View

Adjusts the way the camera displays image/movie files, which is useful for reviewing only certain types of files, or for deleting only particular types, as described above. You can elect to display files by Date View, Folder View (still photos only), AVCHD View (just AVCHD movies), or XAVCS clips in both HD (high-definition) and 4K modes.

Figure 5.10
Playback 3 menu.

Image Index

Options: 9, 25

You can view an index screen of your images on the camera's LCD by pressing the down directional button (Index button) while in Playback mode. By default, that screen shows up to 9 thumbnails of photos or movies; you can change that value to 25 using this menu item. Remember to use the View Mode menu item first, to identify the folder that the index display should access; by default, it will show thumbnails of still photos, but you might want to view thumbnails of your movie clips instead. When viewing an index, highlight the bar at the left side of the screen and use the control wheel's directional controls to move quickly among available thumbnails. Press the center button to switch View Mode quickly.

Display Continuous Shooting Group

Options: On, Off

If you shoot sports, you'll love this feature. The a7R III is smart enough to know that when you shoot a burst of images in continuous shooting mode it would be helpful to group them all together. That makes it easy to evaluate the first shot in a particular set of images captured sequentially, without having to wade through all of them. When set to On, the camera groups images in a burst together, and overlays a "stack" icon on the group, so you'll know you are viewing/evaluating only the first image in that burst. The View Mode must be set to Date View to use this feature. Set this option to Off and you'll be shown every picture you captured, one by one, during image review.

Display Rotation

Options: Auto, Manual, Off

You can use this function to determine whether a vertical image is rotated automatically during picture review. If you want to rotate the image more, use the Rotate entry, described earlier.

- **Auto.** The image will be shown in the orientation indicated by information in the image, no matter how the camera itself is rotated during picture review. For example, a vertical image will be shown in the correct orientation, as shown at top left in Figure 5.11 when the camera is held horizontally. It will be shown smaller in size to fit the long dimension of the image into the short dimension of the screen. Rotate the camera 90 degrees, and the a7R III will automatically rotate the photo so it's *still* shown in the correct orientation, but it will now fill the LCD screen, as you can see in Figure 5.11, top right.

Figure 5.11
Display Rotation configurations.

Display Rotation: Auto

Display Rotation: Manual

Display Rotation: Off

- **Manual.** With this setting, the image is always displayed on the LCD in the same orientation it was taken. That is, a vertically oriented photo will be displayed in a smaller size, just as it is when using Auto, as shown at center left in Figure 5.11. However, when you rotate the camera during picture review, the a7R III does *not* automatically rotate the image at the same time, so it will be shown with an incorrect orientation (see Figure 5.11, center right).

- **Off.** With this setting, both vertical and horizontal images are displayed to fill the screen as much as possible with the image. Vertical shots are larger, as shown at bottom left in Figure 5.11, but the camera must be rotated to view them in the correct orientation. (see Figure 5.11, bottom right).

Image Jump Setting

Options: Select Dial (Front, Rear); Image Jump Method (One by One, Protect Only, Rating Only (All), Rating Only (1–5 stars, or Without Rating Only)

You can select which dial to use when scrolling among images during playback. The default method, One by One, is usually most convenient, but it would have been nice if Sony had provided options other vendors use that allow jumping ahead by 10 or 100 images. This feature is much better than nothing, as you can elect to jump only between Protected images, images that have been rated, or images with particular star ratings. That allows you to "mark" images that you want to evaluate later, using either the protection attribute or a star rating.

6

Setup and My Menus

Even more options are available from the Sony a7R III's Setup menu, providing control over settings that you typically won't change during a particular shooting session. For example, you can adjust the brightness of the LCD monitor or viewfinder, change your HDMI parameters to direct your camera's output to an external screen or recorder, and enter copyright information to be embedded in each image file. I'll wind up this chapter with a description of how you can build your own list of commands using the My Menu feature.

Setup Menu

Other than the Format and Cleaning mode commands listed below, you probably won't make frequent changes to any of these settings. Language, date/time, power-saving options, and many others are likely to be "set and forget" adjustments over the long term. The complete list of entries is as follows:

Monitor Brightness

Options: Manual, Sunny Weather

Default: Manual

My preference: Manual

This is the first entry on the Setup 2 menu. (See Figure 6.1.) When you access this menu item, two controls appear. The first is a Brightness bar (shown just above the grayscale/color patches in Figure 6.2). It's set to Manual adjustment by default but press the center button and you can change it to Sunny Weather for a brighter display. You might resort to this setting if you're shooting outdoors in bright sun and find it hard to view the LCD even when shading it with your hand.

Table 6.1 Setup Menu

Monitor Brightness	Touch Pad Settings	Copyright Info
Viewfinder Brightness	Demo Mode	Format
Finder Color Temperature	TC/UB Settings	File Number
Gamma Display Assistance	Remote Control	Set File Name
Volume Settings	HDMI settings	Record Media Settings
Delete Confirm	4K Output Selection (Movies)	Select Recording Folder
Display Quality	USB Connection	New Folder
Power Save Start Time	USB LUN Setting	Folder Name
Auto Power Off Temperature	USB Power Supply	Recover Image Database
NTSC/PAL Selector	PC Remote Settings	Display Media Information
Cleaning Mode	Language	Version
Touch Operation	Date/Time Setup	Setting Reset
Touch Panel/Pad	Area Setting	

Figure 6.1
The first page of the Setup menu.

Figure 6.2
Adjust monitor brightness.

If you set Sunny Weather, the LCD brightness will automatically increase, making the display easier to view in very bright light. This makes the display unusually bright and less suitable for judging exposure and color, so use it only when it's really necessary. In such bright conditions, you're usually better off using the electronic viewfinder. Remember too that it will consume a lot more battery power, so have a spare battery available.

The grayscale steps and color patches can be used as you manually adjust the screen brightness using the left/right directional buttons. Scroll to the right to make the LCD display brighter or scroll to the left to make the LCD display darker, in a range of plus and minus 2 (arbitrary) increments. As you change the brightness, keep an eye on the grayscale and color chart to visualize the effect your setting will have on various tones and hues. The zero setting is the default and it provides the most accurate display in terms of exposure and color, but you might want to dim it when the bright display is distracting while shooting in a dark theater, perhaps. A minus setting also reduces battery consumption but makes your photos appear to be underexposed (too dark).

I prefer to choose Manual but then leave the display at the zero setting. This ensures the most accurate view of scene brightness on the LCD for the best evaluation of exposure while previewing the scene before taking a photo. Note that this setting (and the next) are ignored when shooting 120/100 fps slow-motion in S&Q mode or when capturing 4K video. If you've boosted the output brightness, your display dims in those modes.

Viewfinder Brightness

Options: Auto, Manual

Default: Auto

My preference: Manual+1

This entry is similar to Monitor Brightness control but adds an Auto setting that adjusts the viewfinder's output based on the a7R III's reading of the ambient light falling on the full-frame sensor. No Sunny Weather option is available, but I still like a slightly brighter viewfinder, so I prefer Manual with a +1 boost. A notice will appear on the LCD monitor advising you to look through the viewfinder and make your settings.

Finder Color Temperature

Options: +2 to –2

Default: 0

My preference: N/A

While looking through the viewfinder, press the left/right buttons to adjust the color balance of the finder to make it appear warmer (using the left button) or colder/bluer (using the right button), according to your preference.

Gamma Display Assist

Options: Off, Auto, S-Log2->709 (800%), S-Log3->709 (800%), HLG (BT.2020), HLG (709)

Default: Off

My preference: N/A

As you'll learn in Chapter 10, the a7R III is capable of recording movies using Picture Profiles (which were introduced in Chapter 3). These profiles can use gamma correction to extend the dynamic range (range of tones from black to white) recorded during video capture. Movies captured using gamma profiles appear to be very low in contrast until processed using software on your computer. As a result, reviewing these clips in the camera can be difficult. This menu entry allows selecting options that will adjust the display of extended dynamic range clips so they appear *in the camera* with a more normal look, which is useful if you use live view to evaluate your captures. The display is not changed if you're viewing through a device such as an external monitor plugged into the HDMI port, and you'll still need to process the video in your video-editing software.

You can turn Gamma Display Assist off, allow the camera to select an appropriate adjustment automatically, or manually set the assist feature to use the gamma you are using. Your choices include S-Log2 and S-Log3, and two HLG (Hybrid Log Gamma) settings, which are used for delivery of video to high dynamic range TVs that are currently the rage. These are a bit esoteric for the average a7R III user who isn't heavily into professional-quality video capture.

Volume Settings

Options: 0–15

Default: 7

My preference: N/A

This menu item affects only the audio volume of movies that are being played back in the camera (and not the beeps or other noises the a7R III emits). When you select Volume Settings, the camera displays a scale of loudness from 0 to 15; scroll up/down to the value you want to set, and it will remain in effect until changed.

You might want to use this menu item to pre-set a volume level that you generally prefer. However, you can also adjust the volume whenever you're displaying a movie clip, to set it to just the right level. To do so, press the down directional button and use the up/down directional buttons to raise or lower the volume.

Delete Confirm

Options: Delete First, Cancel First

Default: Cancel First

My preference: Delete First

Determines which choice is highlighted when you press the trash button to delete an image. The default Cancel First is the safer option, as you must deliberately select Delete and then press the center or trash buttons to actually remove an image. Delete First is faster; press the trash button, then the center button, and the unwanted image is gone. You'd have to scroll down to Cancel if you happened to have changed your mind or pressed the trash button by mistake.

Display Quality

Options: Standard (60 fps), High (120 fps)

Default: Standard

My preference: Standard, except when shooting sports

This is the first entry on the second page of the Setup menu. (See Figure 6.3.) You can specify the image quality of the EVF display, switching from the default Standard of 60 fps to High, which at 120 fps, uses more battery power and reduces the resolution of the display. While you might discern a small difference when viewing on an external monitor, most of the time the camera display isn't reliable for judging images anyway, so sticking to Standard quality is usually your best bet. However, if you shoot sports in continuous mode, you might want to use High Quality to reduce the tiny lag in displaying the image in the viewfinder.

Figure 6.3
The Setup 2 menu.

Power Save Start Time

Options: 30 minutes, 5 minutes, 2 minutes, 1 minute, 10 seconds

Default: 1 minute

My preference: 5 minutes

Although the NP-FZ100 battery is more powerful than the one used in the a7R III's predecessor, you'll still want to avoid wasting juice when the camera is idle. This item lets you specify the exact amount of time that should pass before the camera goes to "sleep" when the eye sensor next to the viewfinder window indicates you're not actively taking photos. The default of 1 minute is a short time, useful to minimize battery consumption. You can select a much longer time before the camera will power down, or a much shorter time. I use 5 minutes most of the time to avoid having to "waken" the camera frequently. If I'm wandering around with long periods of time between shots or the camera is mounted on a tripod, I may set it to 2 or 5 minutes. In street photography or sports mode, I use 30 minutes to make sure my camera will always be ready for action. But, of course, I tend to carry at least two spare batteries with me at all times, and in a pinch will use my RavPower 16,750 mAh power pack linked to the camera with a USB-C cable for long-term non-stop shooting.

You'll need to keep in mind that this setting will be ignored if the camera is linked to an external monitor or video recorder through the HDMI port, and shutoff will be postponed while you are uploading images over a Wi-Fi connection.

Auto Power Off Temperature

Options: Standard, High

Default: Standard

My preference: Standard

Your camera may overheat if operated continuously (as when shooting movies) for periods of time and continued use after that point can result in damage. The a7R III can turn itself off when its internal temperature gets too high, which is particularly useful if the camera is mounted on a tripod so that your hands don't feel the increasing warmth. Shooting 4K video, for example, can generate a lot of heat and deplete your battery rather quickly. This option allows you to stretch the safe operating time by switching from the default Standard mode to High (which allows operation when the camera is hotter than normal). Sony recommends not holding the camera in your hands when you've activated the High setting.

NTSC/PAL Selector

Options: NTSC, PAL
Default: Depends on the country where the camera is sold
My preference: N/A

Allows you to switch the camera between the two major television video systems, NTSC (used in North and South America, Korea, Japan, and some other Pacific countries), and PAL, which is used in Europe, the Middle East, and elsewhere. To switch from one video system to another, Sony says you must be using a memory card that was formatted while the camera was using that video system. You'll be prompted to reformat the card or use a different card. However, the a7R III *does not* reformat the card for you (whew!). However, if you try to shoot a video using the "new" system, you will be forced to reformat.

Your camera will be set up at the factory to default to the video system used in your country. If you switch to the alternate system, the start-up screen will display a message "Running on NTSC" or "Running on PAL" to make sure you're aware of the change. Note that a few countries in South America (Brazil, Argentina, Paraguay, and Uruguay) use a modified PAL system, while others, including Bulgaria, France, Greece, Guiana, Iran, Iraq, Monaco, Russia, and Ukraine use a third system, called SECAM.

Cleaning Mode

Options: Enter, Cancel
Default: Cancel
My preference: N/A

Access this entry when you want to use the camera's auto image sensor cleaning feature. You'll hear a buzzing sound as the camera gives the sensor a good shake. Your tip-off that the sensor needs cleaning will be blurry spots and artifacts that show up in less detailed areas of the image (such as the sky) in photos taken at small f/stops (the extra depth-of-focus makes them more obvious). If the a7R III's own sensor cleaning isn't sufficient, you can use a "rocket"-style blower, special sensor cleaning brushers, or wet-wipe swabs available online and from photo retailers.

Touch Operation

Options: On, Off
Default: Off
My preference: On, once you've mastered touch controls

This entry allows you to disable touch operations completely. You should leave touch operation Off until you've practiced using the feature; otherwise, the touch pad/panel's functions can be confusing.

Touch Panel/Pad

Options: Touch Panel+Pad, Touch Panel Only, Touch Pad Only, Off

Default: Touch Panel Only

My preference: Touch Panel+Pad

This is the first entry on the third page of the Setup menu. (See Figure 6.4.) As I described in Chapter 2, the a7R III has a touch-sensitive LCD. With this setting, you can define whether the LCD-oriented Touch Panel or EVF-oriented Touch Pad, or *both* are active. You can also choose Off to deactivate touch controls. The dual screen/pad modes are used because the touch feature can be used in two different ways: as a touch *screen* or *panel* when you are using the LCD monitor to compose your photos, and as a touch *pad* that you can tap when the camera is raised to your eye and you're using the electronic viewfinder.

Unfortunately, the touch features are limited to the ability to specify a focus *point* when shooting stills and videos. You still have to press the shutter release halfway or the AF-ON (or other defined key) to initiate focus. You can't select menu entries, type in text, scroll through playback views, or pinch/expand with your fingertips to zoom in and out during image review. However, the touch focus feature is quite useful, especially when shooting movies, as it allows selecting a focus area with a gentle tap. There are two modes:

■ **Touch screen.** When active and you're using the LCD monitor to compose, you can select a focus point or zone anywhere that the a7R III is able to achieve autofocus (that is, most of the frame other than the edges). You can tap the screen or hold down your finger and slide the focus area around. Cancel your focus selection by pressing the center button. A quick tap may not register; this function requires a firm press. I'll explain the various AF area modes in Chapter 8.

Figure 6.4
The Setup 3 menu.

■ **Touch pad.** When touch pad mode is active and you're using the electronic viewfinder to compose, you can touch the LCD monitor screen to specify the focus area. You don't have to tap the exact area (actually, that's impossible, because you're not actually looking at the LCD). Instead, when you touch the pad, a focus point appears in the viewfinder *relative to the location on the LCD*. That is, if you tap the center of the sensitive area, the focus point appears in the center; tap to the right or left, and the focus area appears to the right or left side. As I'll explain shortly, that mode is needed because you can change the size of the sensitive area of the LCD screen. Once the focus area is displayed, keep your finger on the screen and slide it around to the position you want, using your view through the EVF as your reference.

Select whether you want the touch screen *and* touch pad, or only one to be used, depending on your preference.

Touch Pad Settings

Options: Operation in vertical orientation (On, Off); Touch position mode (Absolute Position, Relative Position); Operation Area (Whole Screen, Right or Left 1/2 or 1/4, upper/lower Right or Left)

Default: Operation in vertical orientation (Off); Touch position (Absolute Position); Operation Area (Whole Screen)

My preference: Vertical orientation (Off); Touch Position mode (Absolute Position); Operation Area (Whole Screen)

This entry has three options:

■ **Operation in Vertical Orientation.** Here you can specify whether touch controls are available when the camera is oriented in the vertical position, or only when the camera is held in horizontal orientation. The touch feature can be a little awkward to use when rotated vertically, so some prefer to disable touch control for that mode.

■ **Touch Position Mode.** This controls whether your touch places the focus point in the Absolute Position on the screen, from whence you can optionally move it to a different location or Relative Position. In the latter mode, you tap anywhere on the screen and then drag the focus point that appears to the location you want. This is the best mode to use when working with the touch pad and your eye at the viewfinder. You can tap anywhere on the panel's sensitive operation area (set up as described next), and then move the focus point while viewing through the EVF.

■ **Operation Area.** By default, the entire touch pad is sensitive when using the EVF, and that works well for most people. However, if your left eye is dominant (i.e., you're "left-eyed"), your nose will touch the screen, and the a7R III registers that as a finger press. To fix that, you can limit sensitivity of the touch *pad* to the right or left 1/2 or 1/4 of the screen, or the upper/lower left and right corners. The "relative" orientation remains the same but is limited to that reduced area.

Demo Mode

Options: On, Off

Default: Off

My preference: N/A

This is a semi-cool feature that allows your camera to be used as a demonstration tool, say, when giving lectures or showing off at a trade show. When activated, if the camera is idle for about one minute it will begin showing a protected AVCHD movie, which is not impressive on the camera's built-in LCD, but can have a lot more impact if the camera is connected to a large-screen HDTV through the HDMI port.

You may not have seen this feature discussed much in other guides; they tend to dismiss it as a retailer-only feature. But it can be quite useful. Previously, it could only be activated when using the optional AC-PW20 AC Adapter, but I've found that it works perfectly if you connect your a7R III to an external power source through a USB port. My RavPower pack is perfect, and doubles as a power source for time-lapse images. If you're properly equipped, just follow these steps:

1. Use the File Format entry in the Camera Settings II-1 (Movie 1) menu and select AVCHD as the movie format, as explained in Chapter 3. Demo Mode works only with AVCHD files.

2. Shoot the clip that you want to use as your demonstration, in AVCHD format.

3. In the Playback 3 menu, access the View Mode and select AVCHD View so that only AVCHD videos will appear.

4. In the Playback 1 menu, choose Protect and select the demo clip, which must reside on Slot 1, and must be the video with the oldest recorded date and time. (If you have some older clips on your card, you should move or delete them.)

5. Connect the camera to the optional AC-PW20 AC adapter or to a power source using the USB-C port. Because Demo Mode uses a lot of juice, it operates only when one of these external power sources is connected.

6. Demo Mode will no longer be grayed out in the Setup 2 menu. Select it and choose On.

7. After about one minute of idling, the demo clip will begin playing. Note that, because the external source is connected, your automatic power-saving setting is ignored, and Demo Mode will not operate if no movie file is stored on your memory card.

TC/UB Settings

Options: TC/UB Display Settings, TC Preset, UB Preset, TC Format, TC Run, TC/UB Time Rec., TC Make

Default: TC/UB Display Settings: Counter

My preference: N/A

The Time Code (TC) and User Bit (UB) settings are information that can be embedded and used to sync clips and sound when editing movies, especially those captured by multiple cameras. I'll describe this advanced feature in a little more detail in Chapter 11, including what each of these options do, but pro movie-making techniques are largely beyond the scope of this book.

Remote Control

Options: On, Off

Default: Off

My preference: N/A

The a7R III can be operated at distances of about 20 feet (indoors) or 6 feet (outdoors in full sunlight) using infrared signals using the Sony RMT-DSLR1 and RMT-DSLR2 Wireless Remote Commander controls. It can also be triggered with an array of third-party remotes, and smartphones with an infrared transmitter and accompanying remote control app. Constantly "looking" for the IR signal using the sensor on the front of the camera can sap battery power (because the a7R III does not go into power save mode), so it's wise to turn the remote control feature on only when it's actually needed. Choose On, and you can take pictures using the Shutter, 2 Sec., Start/Stop buttons on the RMT-DSLR1/2 controls, plus the Movie button found on the RMT-DSLR2 control. For best performance, make sure a lens hood or other object doesn't interfere with the IR signal reaching the a7R III's sensor. If the camera is set for an autofocus mode, the a7R III will attempt to focus when your press the Shutter or 2 Sec. buttons. If it cannot focus, the picture won't be taken.

HDMI Settings

Options: HDMI Resolution, 24/60p Output, HDMI Info. Display, TC Output, REC Control, CTRL for HDMI

Default: HDMI Resolution: Auto; 24/60p Output: 60p; HDMI Info. Display: On; TC Output: Off; CTRL for HDMI: On

My preference: N/A

Several HDMI settings that previously had their own menu entries with earlier a7-series cameras, plus several new ones, have been combined under this heading. You can view the display output of your camera on a high-definition television (HDTV) when you connect it to the a7R III if you make the investment in an HDMI cable (which Sony does not supply); get the Type C with a mini-HDMI connector on the camera end. (Still photos can also be displayed using Wi-Fi, without cable connection.) When connecting HDMI-to-HDMI, the camera automatically makes the correct settings. If you're lucky enough to own a TV that supports the Sony Bravia synchronization proto-col, you can operate the camera using that TV's remote control when this item is On. Just press the Link Menu button on the remote, and then use the device's controls to delete images, display an image index of photos in the camera, display a slide show, protect/unprotect images in the camera, specify printing options, and play back single images on the TV screen.

- **HDMI Resolution (Auto, 2160/1080p, 1080p, 1080i).** The camera can adjust its output for display on a high-definition television when at the Auto setting. This usually works well with any HDTV. If you have trouble getting the image to display correctly, you can set the resolution manually here to 2160/1080p (for 4K and Full HD), 1080p, or 1080i. I had to make a manual selection so my BlackMagic Intensity Shuttle (a screen capture device) could accept my a7R III's output.

- **24p/60p Output.** You can select either 60p or 24p output to the HDMI port when connected to a 1080 60i–compatible device and Record Setting (described in Chapter 4) has been set to 24p 24M (FX), 24p 17M (FH), or 24p 50M. The frames of the 24p video are duplicated to play back at a 60 fps rate. If a different setting was used, this setting is ignored, and the output conforms to the HDMI Resolution setting above instead.

- **HDMI Info. Display.** Choose On or Off. Choose On if you want the shooting information to display when the camera is connected to an HDTV television/monitor or other device using an HDMI cable. For example, I left this setting On when capturing screen shots of live view images, so all the overlaid icons appear. Select Off if you don't want to show the shooting information on the display.

- **TC Output.** Choose on or off to enable/disable including time code in the HDMI output signal. Use On if you are outputting to professional video equipment and want to include the time code information. Note that the time code is *data* and will not actually appear on the screen. If this setting is on and you are sending the signal to a television or some other device, the image may not appear properly. Change this setting to off when outputting to devices not equipped to handle TC information.

- **REC Control.** This setting is available only when TC Output is set to on. Choose on or off. The setting allows you to start and stop REC Control–compatible external video recorders connected to the camera. A REC or STBY icon will be displayed on the camera's screen as appropriate.

- **CTRL for HDMI.** This option can be useful when you have connected the camera to a non-Sony HDTV and find that the TV's remote control produces unintended results with the camera. If that happens, try turning this option Off, and see if the problem is resolved. If you later connect the camera to a Sony Bravia sync-compliant HDTV (vendors other than Sony also use it), set this menu item back to On. Be aware that not all so-called Bravia-friendly devices conform completely, so you should be prepared to turn the function off if necessary.

keypads in the pre-smartphone era: highlight a button and press the center button multiple times to enter a particular character. For example, if you highlight the "abc" button, pressing once inserts an a, twice a b, and three times a c. When finished, highlight OK and press the center button to return to the initial screen, where you can highlight OK again and press the center button a last time to confirm.

■ **Set Copyright.** Define your copyright terms, such as *Cpr. 2018 David D. Busch.* Strictly speaking, "Cpr." should be used rather than a lowercase c between two parentheses. Text is entered as described above.

■ **Disp. Copyright Info.** Displays whatever copyright information you've specified.

Format

Options: OK, Cancel

Default: None

My preference: N/A

As you'd guess, you'll use Format to re-format your memory card while it's in your a7R III. To proceed with this process, choose the Format menu item and select "OK" and press the center button to confirm, or Cancel to chicken out.

Use the Format command to erase everything on your memory card and to set up a fresh file system ready for use. This procedure removes all data that was on the memory card and reinitializes the card's file system by defining anew the areas of the card available for image storage, locking out defective areas, and creating a new folder in which to deposit your images. It's usually a good idea to reformat your memory card in the camera (not in your camera's card reader using your computer's operating system) before each use. Formatting is generally much quicker than deleting images one by one. Before formatting the card however, make sure that you have saved all your images and videos to another device; formatting will delete everything, including images that were protected.

File Number

Options: Series, Reset

Default: Series

My preference: N/A

The default for the File Number item is Series, indicating that the a7R III will automatically apply a file number to each picture and video clip that you make, using consecutive numbering; this will continue over a long period of time, spanning many different memory cards, and even if you reformat a card. Numbers are applied from 0001 to 9999; when you reach the limit, the camera starts back at 0001. The camera keeps track of the last number used in its internal memory. So, you could take pictures numbered as high as 100-0240 on one card, remove the card and insert another, and the next picture will be numbered 100-0241 on the new card. Reformat either card, take a picture, and the next image will be numbered 100-0242. Use the Series option when you want all the photos you take to have consecutive numbers (at least, until your camera exceeds 9999 shots taken).

If you want to restart numbering back at 0001 frequently, use the Reset option. In that case, the file number will be reset to 0001 *each* time you format a memory card or delete all the images in a folder, insert a different memory card, or change the folder name format (as described in the next menu entry). I do not recommend this since you will soon have several images with exactly the same file number.

Set File Name

Options: Choose three-letter prefix

Default: DSC

My preference: 7R3

This entry allows you to specify the first three characters in the file name applied to your images. The a7R III, like other cameras in the Sony product line, automatically applies a name like _DSC0001.jpg or DSC_0001.nef to your image files as they are created. You can use this menu option to change the names applied to your photos, but only within certain strict limitations. In practice, you can change only three of the eight characters, the *DSC* portion of the file name. The other five are mandated either by the Design Rule for Camera File System (DCF) specification that all digital camera makers adhere to or to industry conventions.

DCF limits file names created by conforming digital cameras to a maximum of eight characters, plus a three-character extension (such as .jpg, .nef, or .wav in the case of audio files) that represents the format of the file. The eight-plus-three (usually called 8.3) length limitation dates back to an evil and frustrating computer operating system that we older photographers would like to forget (its initials are D.O.S.), but which, unhappily, lives on as the wraith of a file naming convention.

Of the eight available characters, four are used to represent, in a general sense, the type of camera used to create the image. By convention, one of those characters is an underline, placed in the first position (as in _DSCxxxx.xxx) when the image uses the Adobe RGB color space, and in the fourth position (as in DSC_xxxx.xxx) for sRGB and RAW files. That leaves just three characters for the manufacturer (and you) to use. The remaining four characters are used for numbers from 0000 to 9999, which is why your a7R III "rolls over" to DSC_0000 again when the 9999-number limitation is reached.

Because the default DSC characters don't tell you much, don't hesitate to change them to something else. I use 7R3 for my a7R III. You can change the three characters to anything else that suits your purposes, including your initials (DDB_ or JFK_, for example), or even customize for particular shooting sessions (EUR_, GER_, FRA_, and JAP_ when taking vacation trips). You can also use the file name flexibility to partially overcome the 9999 numbering limitation. You could, for example, use the template 7R1_ to represent the first 10,000 pictures you take with your a7R III, and then 7R2_ for the next 10,000, and 7R3_ for the 10,000 after that. Note that you can't use the underscore as the *first* character in your file name; it's reserved for AdobeRGB files.

That's assuming that you don't rename your image files in your computer. In a way, file naming verges on a moot consideration, because, they apply *only* to the images as they exist in your camera. After (or during) transfer to your computer, you can change the names to anything you want, completely disregarding the 8.3 limitations (although it's a good idea to retain the default extensions). If you shot an image file named DSC_4832.jpg in your camera, you could change it to Paris_EiffelTower_32.jpg later.

Recording Media Settings

Options: Prioritize Recording Media (Slot 1, Slot 2); Recording Mode (Standard, Simultaneously modes for Stills, Movies, Stills/Movies; Sorted for RAW/JPEG, JPEG/RAW, Stills Movies)

Default: Prioritize: Slot 1; Recording Mode: Standard; Auto Switch Mode: Stills/Movies

My preference: N/A

This entry is the first in the Setup 6 menu. (See Figure 6.7.) It has three options that specify how the memory cards in your camera should be used. They include specifying which slots to use, what types of files should be saved on specific card slots, and what to do when switching from one card slot to another.

Figure 6.7
The Setup 6 menu.

Your choices, shown in Figure 6.8, are as follows:

■ **Prioritize Recording Media.** Use this to specify the memory card that your image and movie files are stored on by default. You'll generally want to use Slot 1, because that slot has the fastest transfer rate, useful when you're working with UHS-II media. However, if you need to use Sony Memory Stick PRO Duo media, specify Slot 2, as you cannot use Memory Sticks in Slot 1.

■ **Recording Mode.** This slightly confusing entry (because of its multiple options) is actually simple to understand. Here you choose whether you save files to two cards (for in-camera backup) or split various types of files between the two cards. Your choices include:

  • **Standard.** All files are stored on the slot you specify using Prioritize Recording Media (above).

  • **Simultaneous (Stills).** Still photos are stored on *both* memory cards (excellent for backup), while movies are stored on your default (prioritized) slot.

  • **Simultaneous (Movies).** Movies are stored on *both* memory cards, while stills are stored on your default slot. Use this if you are shooting video primarily and want to back up your work.

  • **Simultaneous (Stills/Movies).** Both still photographs and movies are stored on both slots. As with any of the other two "simultaneous" (backup) modes, storing files on both cards at the same time will slow down your continuous shooting speed.

  • **Sort (RAW/JPEG).** RAW photos are stored on your default slot, and JPEG files on the other card. This option and the next allows you to keep both file types separate. Because JPEG files are smaller than RAW files, you may be able to get away with using a memory card with less capacity in your alternate slot.

Figure 6.8
Your Recording Media Settings options.

My Menu

Options: Add Item, Sort Item, Delete Item, Delete Page, Delete All
Default: None
My preference: N/A

The My Menu feature lets you create your own customized menu containing the entries you use most often, which can save you a lot of time wading through the a7R III's many pages of menu tabs and entries. Of course, since you can create up to five My Menu screens, each with as many as five menu items, you can find you've created your own maze of entries—but, at least, it is *your* maze. Virtually any menu entry from the other main menu tabs (except for the Playback menu) and View on TV can be added to your personalized menu. The My Menu system can be handy and quick to access (if one of your My Menu pages was the one you used last, it will pop up first when you press the MENU button). But you might have used a different menu, so it would have been helpful to be able to assign My Menu to a custom key. Pay attention, Sony!

The first time you access My Menu, no custom pages will exist, so you'll see a screen similar to the one in the screen shown at left in Figure 6.9, except all the entries except Add Item will be grayed out. Press the center button, and you'll be shown a screen with a list of menu entries. Use the left/right controls to scroll among available menu pages, and up/down controls to highlight a particular entry you want to add. Press the center button and you'll be given the opportunity to choose which page to add it to, numbered from 1 through 5. (See Figure 6.10, left.)

You don't need to fill up one page before starting another one. Conceivably, you could have five My Menu pages, each with a single entry. After you've created a new My Menu page, the command function page (Add, Sort, etc.) moves to the end of the line, eventually becoming Page 6 when the other five My Menu pages have been created. Each newborn My Menu page will look something like Figure 6.10 (right), but with your personal entries included.

Figure 6.9 My Menu screens.

Figure 6.10 Adding My Menu options.

The additional options available include:

- **Sort.** Highlight a My Menu item and press the center button. You can then use the up/down controls to move it within its current menu, or the left/right controls to transport it to a different My Menu page.

- **Delete Item/Delete Page/Delete All.** Highlight an entry or page and press the center button to remove that item or page from My Menu. Delete All will remove all your My Menu items so you can start from scratch.

7

Nailing the Optimum Exposure

In the most basic sense, exposure is all about light. Exposure can make or break your photo. Correct exposure brings out the detail in the areas you want to picture, providing the range of tones and colors you need to create the desired image. Poor exposure can cloak important details in shadow or wash them out in glare-filled featureless expanses of white.

However, getting the perfect exposure requires some intelligence—either that built into the camera or the smarts in your head—because digital sensors can't capture all the tones we are able to see. If the range of tones in an image is extensive, embracing both inky black shadows and bright high-lights, we often must settle for an exposure that renders most of those tones—but not all—in a way that best suits the photo we want to produce. This chapter discusses using the full range of the camera's various shooting modes and exposure controls, so you'll be better equipped to override the default settings when you want to, or need to, and achieve spot-on exposures that produce the exact image you are looking for, every time.

Getting a Handle on Exposure

You're probably well aware of the traditional "exposure triangle" of aperture (quantity of light, light passed by the lens), shutter speed (the amount of time the shutter is open), and the ISO sensitivity of the sensor—all working *proportionately* and *reciprocally* to produce an exposure. The trio is itself affected by the amount of illumination that is available to work with. So, if you double the amount of light, increase the aperture by one stop, make the shutter speed twice as long, or boost the ISO setting 2X, with any one of those changes you'll get exactly twice as much exposure. Similarly, you can *increase* any of these factors while *decreasing* one of the others by a similar amount to keep the same exposure.

Working with any of the three controls involves trade-offs. Larger f/stops provide less depth-of-field, while smaller f/stops increase depth-of-field (and potentially at the same time can *decrease* sharpness through a phenomenon called *diffraction*). Shorter shutter speeds do a better job of reducing the effects of any camera/subject motion, while longer shutter speeds make that motion blur more likely. Higher ISO settings increase the amount of visual noise and artifacts in your image, while lower ISO settings reduce the effects of noise. (See Figure 7.1.)

Exposure determines the look, feel, and tone of an image, in more ways than one. Incorrect exposure can impair even the best-composed image by cloaking important tones in darkness, or by washing them out so they become featureless to the eye. On the other hand, correct exposure brings out the detail in the areas you want to picture and provides the range of tones and colors you need to create the desired image. Digital sensors can't capture all the tones we are able to see. Sometimes, we must settle for an exposure that renders most of those tones—but not all—in a way that best suits the photo we want to produce. You'll often need to make choices about which details are important, and which are not, so that you can grab the tones that truly matter in your image.

For example, look at the two bracketed exposures presented in Figure 7.2. For the image at top left, the highlights are well exposed, but everything else in the shot is seriously underexposed. The version at the top right, taken an instant later with the tripod-mounted camera, shows detail in the

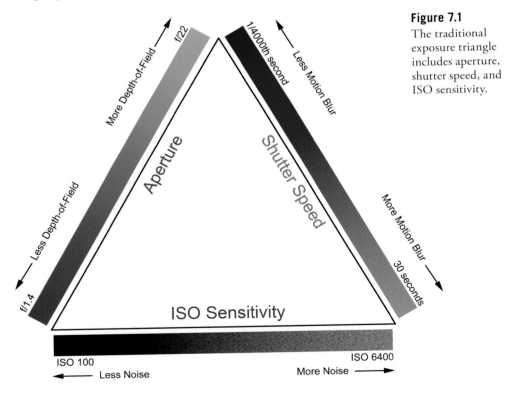

Figure 7.1
The traditional exposure triangle includes aperture, shutter speed, and ISO sensitivity.

How the a7R III Calculates Exposure

Your camera calculates exposure by measuring the light that passes through the lens and reaches the sensor, based on the assumption that each area being measured reflects about the same amount of light as a neutral gray card that reflects a "middle" gray of about 12- to 18-percent reflectance. (The photographic "gray cards" you buy at a camera store have an 18-percent gray tone; your camera is calibrated to interpret a somewhat lighter 12-percent gray. I'll explain more about this later.) That "average" 12- to 18-percent gray assumption is necessary, because different subjects reflect different amounts of light. In a photo containing, say, a white cat and a dark gray cat, the white cat might reflect five times as much light as the gray cat. An exposure based on the white cat will cause the gray cat to appear to be black, while an exposure based only on the gray cat will make the white cat washed out.

This is more easily understood if you look at some photos of subjects that are dark (they reflect little light), those that have predominantly middle tones, and subjects that are highly reflective. I'm not going to use actual cats but, rather, will include a more human figure in the frame (which is more common, unless you're a cat photographer), accompanied by a card with a trio of gray reference patches. The next figure shows what you would end up with if you exposed a set of photographs using a different gray patch for each.

Correctly Exposed

The image shown in Figure 7.4, left, represents how a photograph might appear if you inserted the patches shown at bottom left into the scene, and then calculated exposure by measuring the light reflecting from the middle gray patch, which, for the sake of illustration, we'll assume reflects approximately 12 to 18 percent of the light that strikes it. The exposure meter in the camera sees

Figure 7.4 Exposure based on the middle-gray tone in the center of the card is accurate (left). Metering the black square, the black patch looks gray, the gray patch appears to be a light gray, and the white square is seriously overexposed (center). With exposure calculated from the white patch, the photo is underexposed (right).

an object that it thinks is a middle gray (the middle patch), calculates an exposure based on that, and the patch in the center of the strip is rendered at its proper tonal value. Best of all, because the resulting exposure is correct, the black patch at left and white patch at right are rendered properly as well.

When you're shooting pictures with your a7R III camera, and the meter happens to base its exposure on a subject that averages that "ideal" middle gray, then you'll end up with similar (accurate) results. The camera's exposure algorithms are concocted to ensure this kind of result as often as possible, barring any unusual subjects (that is, those that are backlit, or have uneven illumination). The camera has five different metering modes (described in an upcoming section), each of which is equipped to handle certain types of unusual subjects, as I'll outline.

Overexposed

Figure 7.4, center, shows what would happen if the exposure were calculated based on metering the leftmost, black patch, which is roughly the same tonal value of the darkest areas of the subject's hair. The light meter sees less light reflecting from the black square than it would see from a gray middle-tone subject, and so figures, "Aha! I need to add exposure to brighten this subject up to a middle gray!" That lightens the "black" patch, so it now appears to be gray.

But now the patch in the middle that was *originally* middle gray is overexposed and becomes light gray. And the white square at right is now seriously overexposed and loses detail in the highlights, which have become a featureless white. Our human subject is similarly overexposed. You should always be *aware* when overexposure occurs but note that it's not *always* a bad thing. Some slight overexposures add a dreamy look to an image; once you know how the rules are derived, you'll know how and when to break them.

Underexposed

The third possibility in this simplified scenario is that the light meter might measure the illumination bouncing off the white patch and try to render *that* tone as a middle gray. A lot of light is reflected by the white square, so the exposure is *reduced*, bringing that patch closer to a middle gray tone. The patches that were originally gray and black are now rendered too dark. Clearly, measuring the gray card—or a substitute that reflects about the same amount of light—is the only way to ensure that the exposure is precisely correct. (See Figure 7.4, right.)

As you can see, the ideal way to measure exposure is to meter from a subject that reflects 12 to 18 percent of the light that reaches it. If you want the most precise exposure calculations, the solution is to use a stand-in, such as the evenly illuminated gray card I mentioned earlier. But, because the standard Kodak gray card reflects 18 percent of the light that reaches it and, as I said, your camera is calibrated for a somewhat lighter 12 percent tone, you would need to add about one-half stop *more* exposure than the value metered from the card. Of course, in most situations, it's not necessary to do this. Your camera's light meter will do a good job of calculating the right exposure, especially if you use the exposure tips in the next section. But, I felt that explaining exactly what is going on during exposure calculation would help you understand how your camera's metering system works.

In some very bright scenes (like a snowy landscape or a lava field), you won't have a mid-tone to meter. Another substitute for a gray card is the palm of a human hand (the backside of the hand is too variable). But a human palm, regardless of ethnic group, is even brighter than a standard gray card, so instead of one-half stop more exposure, you need to add one additional stop. That is, if your meter reading is 1/500th of a second at f/11, use 1/500th second at f/8 or 1/200th second at f/11 instead. (Both exposures are equivalent.)

Or, you might want to resort to using an evenly illuminated gray card mentioned earlier. Small versions are available that can be tucked in a camera bag. Place it in your frame near your main subject, facing the camera, and with the exact same even illumination falling on it that is falling on your subject. Then, use the Spot metering function (described in the next section) to calculate exposure.

In serious photography, you'll want to choose the *metering mode* (the pattern that determines how brightness is evaluated) and the *exposure mode* (determines how the appropriate shutter speed and aperture is set). I'll describe both aspects in later sections.

ORIGIN OF THE 18 PERCENT "MYTH"

Why are so many photographers under the impression that camera light meters are calibrated to the 18 percent "standard," rather than the true value, which may be 12 to 14 percent, depending on the vendor? You'll find this misinformation in an alarming number of places. I've seen the 18 percent "myth" taught in camera classes; I've found it in books, and even been given this wrong information from the technical staff of camera vendors. (They should know better—the same vendors' engineers who design and calibrate the cameras have the right figure.)

The most common explanation is that during a revision of Kodak's instructions for its gray cards in 1977, the advice to open up an extra half stop was omitted, and a whole generation of shooters grew up thinking that a measurement off a gray card could be used as-is. Kodak restored the proviso in 1997 during the next update of the instructions but by then it was too late

EXTERNAL METERS CAN BE CALIBRATED

The light meters built into your camera are calibrated at the factory. But if you use a hand-held incident or reflective light meter, you *can* calibrate it, using the instructions supplied with your meter. Because a hand-held meter *can* be calibrated to the 18 percent gray standard (or any other value you choose), my rant about the myth of the 18 percent gray card doesn't apply.

The Importance of ISO

Another essential concept when discussing exposure, ISO control allows you to change the sensitivity of the camera's imaging sensor. Sometimes photographers forget about this option, because the common practice is to set the ISO once for a particular shooting session (say, at ISO 100 or 200 for bright sunlight outdoors, or ISO 800 or 1600 when shooting indoors) and then forget about ISO. Or some shooters simply leave the camera set to ISO Auto. That enables the camera to change the ISO it deems necessary, setting a low ISO in bright conditions or a higher ISO in a darker location. That's fine, but sometimes you'll want to set a specific ISO yourself. That will be essential sometimes, since ISO Auto cannot set the highest ISO levels that are available when you use manual ISO selection. Indeed, when shooting movies, only ISO settings from ISO 200 to ISO 32000 can be set.

> **TIP**
>
> When shooting in the Program (P), Aperture Priority (A), and Shutter Priority (S) modes, all discussed soon, changing the ISO does not change the exposure. If you switch from using ISO 100 to ISO 1600 in A mode, for example, the camera will simply set a different shutter speed. If you change the ISO in S mode, the camera will set a different aperture, and in P mode, it will set a different aperture and/or shutter speed. In all of these examples, the camera will maintain the same exposure. If you want to make a brighter or a darker photo in P, A, or S mode, you would need to set + or – exposure compensation, as discussed later.
>
> However, when you use the Manual (M) mode, changing the ISO also changes the exposure, as discussed shortly.

The camera provides the best possible image quality in the ISO 50 to 400 range. We use higher ISO levels such as ISO 1600 in low light and ISO 6400 in a very dark location because it allows us to shoot at a faster shutter speed. That's often useful for minimizing the risk of blurring caused by camera shake, which can occur even with 5-axis image stabilization in the camera body and optical image stabilization (OSS) built into many lenses. And, of course, you must also contend with movement of the subject, which no amount of image stabilization will fix.

Although you can set a desired ISO level yourself, the a7R III also offers an ISO Auto option. When enabled, the camera will select an ISO that should be suitable for the conditions: a low ISO on a sunny day and a high ISO in a dark location. In Intelligent Auto, ISO Auto is the only available option. Over the past few years, there has been something of a competition among the manufacturers of digital cameras to achieve the highest ISO ratings. The highest announced ISO numbers have been rising annually, from 1600 to 3200 and 6400; a few cameras even allow you to choose a sensitivity setting that tops 1.6 *million*. Sony is a bit more conservative, but the a7R III offers all of the ISO options you're ever likely to need, up to 104200. Obviously, the loftiest numbers come at the cost of increased contrast and grain.

Choosing a Metering Method

The Sony a7R III has five different schemes for evaluating the light received by its exposure sensors. The quickest way to choose among them is to assign Metering Mode to a key using the Custom Key settings in the Camera Settings II-8 menu, as described in Chapter 4. Then, you can press the defined key to produce the Metering Mode screen; then scroll up/down among the options. Without a custom key, the default method for choosing a metering mode is to use the Camera Settings I-9 (Exposure 1) menu (see Figure 7.5), the Function menu, or the Quick Navi menu.

■ **Multi.** In this "intelligent" (multi-segment) metering mode, the a7R III measures the illumination falling on all the pixels in the sensor, but slices up the frame into 1,200 different zones, as shown at left in Figure 7.6. The camera evaluates the measurements to make an educated guess about what kind of picture you're taking, based on examination of exposure data derived from thousands of different real-world photos. For example, if the top section of a picture is much lighter than the bottom portions, the algorithm can assume that the scene is a landscape photo with lots of sky. This mode is the best all-purpose metering method for most pictures. A typical scene suitable for Multi metering is shown at right in Figure 7.6.

The Multi system can recognize individual elements in a very bright scene and it can automatically increase the exposure to reduce the risk of a dark photo. This will be useful when your subject is a snow-covered landscape or a close-up of a bride in white. Granted, you may occasionally need to use a bit of exposure compensation, but often, the exposure will be close to accurate even without it. (In my experience, the Multi system is most successful with light-toned scenes on bright days. When shooting in dark, overcast conditions, it's more likely to underexpose a scene of that type.)

Multi-segment metering is especially suitable for people. If you activate Face Priority in Multi Metering in the Camera Settings I-9 (Exposure 1) menu, the a7R III will use any detected faces to calculate exposure.

Figure 7.5

The a7R III cameras provide five options for metering mode: Multi (the default), Center, Spot, Entire Screen Averaging, and Highlight (left, top to bottom).

Figure 7.6
Multi metering uses 1,200 zones and is suitable for complex scenes like this one.

Figure 7.7
Center metering calculates exposure based on the full frame but emphasizes the center area.

- **Center.** This (center-weighted) metering was the only available option with cameras some decades ago. In this mode you get conventional metering without any "intelligent" scene evaluation. The light meter considers brightness in the entire frame but places the greatest emphasis on a large area in the center of the frame, as shown at left in Figure 7.7, on the theory that, for most pictures, the main subject will not be located far off-center.

Of course, Center metering is most effective when the subject in the central area is a mid-tone. Even then, if your main subject is surrounded by large, extremely bright or very dark areas, the exposure might not be exactly right. (You might need to use exposure compensation, a feature discussed shortly.) However, this scheme works well in many situations if you don't want to use one of the other modes for scenes like the one shown in at right in Figure 7.7.

- **Spot.** This mode confines the reading to a very small area in the center of the image, as shown at left in Figure 7.8. When Spot is highlighted, you can press the left/right controls to choose from a standard size spot, or a larger one.

By default, the spot is located in the center of the frame, unless you use the Spot Metering Point entry of the Camera Settings I-10 (Exposure 2) menu to link it to the current focus area. However, when you use the Flexible Spot or Expand Flexible Spot focus area options, the spot metering will *always* be at the area where the camera sets focus. So, you have the option of linking the exposure spot to the focus area *all* of the time, or only when using the two Flexible Spot settings.

The Spot meter does not apply any "intelligent" scene evaluation. Because the camera considers only a small target area, and completely ignores its surroundings, Spot metering is most useful when the subject is a small mid-tone area. For example, the "target" might be a tanned face, a medium red blossom, or a gray rock in a wide-angle photo; each of these is a mid-tone.

The Spot metering technique is simple if you want to Spot meter a small area that's dead center in the frame. If the "target" is off-center, you would need to point the lens at it and use the AE Lock technique discussed later in this chapter. (Lock exposure on your target before re-framing for a better composition so the exposure does not change.) For Figure 7.8, right, Spot metering was used to base the exposure on the train man's face.

If you Spot meter a light-toned area or a dark-toned area, you will get underexposure or overexposure respectively; you would need to use an override for more accurate results. On the other hand, you can Spot meter a small mid-tone subject surrounded by a sky with big white clouds or by an indigo blue wall and get a good exposure. (The light meter ignores the subject's surroundings so they do not affect the exposure.) That would not be possible with Center-weighted metering, which considers brightness in a much larger area.

■ **Entire Screen Averaging.** This option tells the a7R III to simply measure all the illumination in the frame and calculate exposure based on the average value. (See Figure 7.9, left.) That may not lead to the optimal exposure for an image (if some large very bright or very dark areas are present), but it does have one advantage: because only the average reflectance is used, the exposure will not change as your subjects move around in the frame. The woman's hands shown at right in Figure 7.9 darted back and forth as she worked, but the exposure remained constant for several successive images.

Figure 7.8
Spot metering calculates exposure based on a spot that's only a small percentage of the image area, such as this trainman's face.

Figure 7.9
When using Entire Screen Averaging, the exposure will not change if a subject, such as this artisan's fast-moving hands, move within the frame.

■ **Highlight.** This choice pays special attention to the highlights of an image. Figure 7.10, left, doesn't really show the active metering area, but is a graphical representation of what areas are most important in the photo at right in the figure. If your subject is surrounded by very dark areas, this metering method will help avoid overexposure.

Figure 7.10
Highlight-weighted metering will help avoid overexposure of subjects surrounded by dark areas.

INSTANT SWITCHING

If you frequently use one metering method, but occasionally like to switch to another method on the fly, you can redefine one of the a7R III's custom keys to change to your alternate mode at the press of a button, using the Custom Keys feature I explained in Chapter 4.

The really cool thing is that you can define one button for, say, Center-weighted metering, another one for Spot metering, and then set the main metering mode switch to Matrix, and thus be able to switch among those three on a whim. I've done this as a way to compare the exposure settings of the three metering methods while composing a single image in the viewfinder. I've also found the capability useful when I'm, say, working with Multi metering and want to zero in on a particular area of the frame temporarily using Spot metering.

Choosing an Exposure Mode

After you set a desired metering mode, you have several methods for choosing the appropriate shutter speed and aperture, semi-automatically or manually. Just press the mode dial's center lock button and spin the mode dial to the exposure mode that you want to use. Your choice of which is best for a given shooting situation will depend on aspects like your need for extensive or shallow depth-of-field (the range of acceptably sharp focus in a photo) or the desire to freeze action or to allow motion blur. The semi-automatic Aperture Priority and Shutter Priority modes discussed in the next section emphasize one aspect of image capture or another, but the following sections introduce you to all four of the modes that photographers often call "creative."

Aperture Priority (A) Mode

When using the A mode, you specify the lens opening (aperture or f/stop) with the front or rear dial. After you do so, the camera (guided by its light meter) will set a suitable shutter speed considering the aperture and the ISO in use. If you change the aperture, from f/5.6 to f/11 for example, the camera will automatically set a longer shutter speed to maintain the same exposure, using guidance from the built-in light meter. (I discussed the concept of equivalent exposure earlier and provided the equivalent exposure chart.)

Aperture Priority is especially useful when you want to use a particular lens opening to achieve a desired effect. Perhaps you'd like to use the smallest aperture (such as f/22) to maximize depth-of-field (DOF), to keep the entire subject sharp in a close-up picture. Or, you might want to use a large aperture (small f/number like f/4) to throw everything except your main subject out of focus, as in Figure 7.11. Maybe you'd just like to "lock in" a particular f/stop, such as f/8, because it allows your

Figure 7.11
Use Aperture Priority mode to "lock in" a wide aperture (denoted by a large f/number) when you want to blur the background.

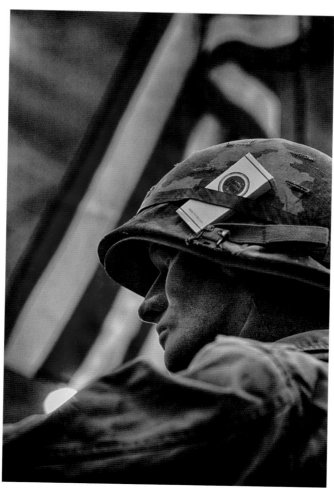

lens to provide the best optical quality. Or, you might prefer to use f/2.8 with a lens that has a maximum aperture of f/1.4, because you want the best compromise between shutter speed and optical quality.

Aperture Priority can even be used to specify a *range* of shutter speeds you want to use under varying lighting conditions, which seems almost contradictory. But think about it. You're shooting a soccer game outdoors with a telephoto and want a relatively fast shutter speed, but you don't care if the speed changes a little should the sun duck behind a cloud. Set your camera's shooting mode to A, and adjust the aperture using the front or rear dial until a shutter speed of, say, 1/1,000th second is selected at the ISO level that you're using. (In bright sunlight at ISO 400, that aperture is likely to be around f/11.) Then, go ahead and shoot, knowing that your a7R III will maintain that f/11 aperture (for sufficient DOF as the soccer players move about the field) but will drop down to 1/800th or 1/500th second if necessary should a light cloud cover part of the sun.

When the camera cannot provide a good exposure at the aperture you have set, the shutter speed numeral will turn orange. That indicator warns that the camera is unable to find an appropriate shutter speed at the aperture you have set, considering the ISO level in use and over- or underexposure will occur. That's the major pitfall of using Aperture Priority: you might select an f/stop that is too small or too large to allow an optimal exposure with the available shutter speeds.

Here are a couple of examples where you might encounter a problem. Let's say you set an aperture of f/2.8 while using ISO 400 on an extremely bright day (perhaps at the beach or in snow); in this situation, even your camera's fastest shutter speed might not be able to cut down the amount of light reaching the sensor to provide the right exposure. (The solution here is to set a lower ISO or a smaller aperture, or both, until the blinking stops.) Or, let's say you have set f/16 in a dark arena while using ISO 100; the camera cannot find a shutter speed long enough to provide a correct exposure so your photo will be underexposed. (In low light, the solution is to manually set a higher ISO or a wider aperture, or both, until the orange shutter speed indicator turns white again.) Aperture Priority is best used by those with a bit of experience in choosing settings. Many seasoned photographers leave their camera set on Aperture Priority all the time.

When to use Aperture Priority:

- **General landscape photography.** The a7R III is a great camera for landscape photography, of course, because its high resolution allows making huge, gorgeous prints, as well as smaller prints that are filled with eye-popping detail. Aperture Priority is a good tool for ensuring that your landscape is sharp from foreground to infinity, if you select an f/stop that provides maximum depth-of-field.

   If you use A mode and select an aperture like f/11 or f/16, it's your responsibility to make sure the shutter speed selected is fast enough to avoid losing detail to camera shake, or that the a7R III is mounted on a tripod. One thing that new landscape photographers fail to account for is the movement of distant leaves and tree branches. When seeking the ultimate in sharpness, go ahead and use Aperture Priority, but boost ISO sensitivity a bit, if necessary, to provide a sufficiently fast shutter speed, whether shooting hand-held or with a tripod.

- **Specific landscape situations.** Aperture Priority is also useful when you have no objection to using a long shutter speed, or, particularly, *want* the a7R III to select one. Waterfalls are a perfect example. You can use A mode, set your camera to ISO 100, use a small f/stop, and let the camera select a longer shutter speed that will allow the water to blur as it flows. Indeed, you might need to use a neutral-density filter to get a sufficiently long shutter speed. But Aperture-priority mode is a good start.

- **Portrait photography.** Portraits are the most common applications of selective focus. A medium-large aperture (say, f/5.6 or f/8) with a longer lens/zoom setting (in the 85mm–135mm range) will allow the background behind your portrait subject to blur.

- **When you want to ensure optimal sharpness.** All lenses have an aperture or two at which they perform best, providing the level of sharpness you expect from a camera with the resolution of the a7R III. That's usually about two stops down from wide open, and thus will vary depending on the maximum aperture of the aperture of the lens.

- **Close-up/Macro photography.** Depth-of-field is typically very shallow when shooting macro photos, and you'll want to choose your f/stop carefully.

Shutter Priority (S) Mode

Shutter Priority is the inverse of Aperture Priority. You set the shutter speed you'd like, using the front or rear dial, and the camera sets an appropriate f/stop considering the ISO that's in use. When you change the shutter speed, the camera will change the aperture to maintain the same (equivalent) exposure using guidance from the built-in light meter. Shutter Priority mode gives you some control over how much action-freezing capability your digital camera brings to bear in a particular situation. In other cases, you might want to use a slow shutter speed to add some blur to a sports photo that would be mundane if the action were completely frozen (see Figure 7.12).

Figure 7.12
Set a slow shutter speed when you want to introduce blur into an action shot, as with this panned image of a base runner.

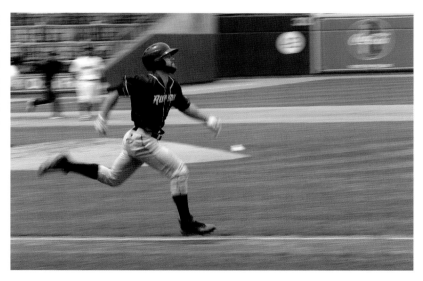

Take care when using a slow shutter speed such as 1/8th second, because you'll potentially get blurring from camera shake unless you're using a tripod or other firm support. Of course, this applies to any mode, but in most modes the camera displays a blinking camera shake warning icon when the shutter speed is long. That indicator does not blink in S mode however, perhaps because Sony assumes that users of Shutter Priority are aware of the potential problem caused by camera shake. The in-body 5-axis image stabilization and SteadyShot stabilizer in OSS-designated lenses are useful but they cannot work miracles.

As in Aperture Priority, you can encounter a problem in Shutter Priority mode; this happens when you select a shutter speed that's too long or too short for correct exposure under certain conditions. I've shot outdoor soccer games on sunny fall evenings and used Shutter Priority mode to lock in a 1/1,000th second shutter speed, only to find that my camera refused to produce the correct exposure when the sun dipped behind some trees and there was no longer enough light to shoot at that speed, even with the lens wide open.

In cases where you have set an inappropriate shutter speed, the aperture numeral will blink. When might this happen? Let's say you set 1/15th second shutter speed while using ISO 400 on that extremely bright day; in this situation, even the smallest aperture available with your lens might not be able to cut down the amount of light reaching the sensor to provide a correct exposure. (The solution here is to set a lower ISO or a faster shutter speed, or both, until the blinking stops.) Or, let's say you have set 1/250th second in the arena while using ISO 100; your lens does not offer an aperture that's wide enough to enable the camera to provide a good exposure so you'll get the blinking and your photo will be underexposed. (In low light, the solution is to set a higher ISO or a longer shutter speed, or both, until the blinking stops.)

When to use Shutter Priority:

- **To reduce blur from subject motion.** Set the shutter speed of the a7R III to a higher value to reduce the amount of blur from subjects that are moving. The exact speed will vary depending on how fast your subject is moving and how much blur is acceptable. You might want to freeze a basketball player in mid-dunk with a 1/1,000th second shutter speed or use 1/200th second to allow the spinning wheels of a motocross racer to blur a tiny bit to add the feeling of motion.

- **To add blur from subject motion.** There are times when you want a subject to blur, say, when shooting waterfalls with the camera set for a one- or two-second exposure in Shutter Priority mode.

- **To add blur from camera motion when *you* are moving.** Say you're panning to follow a base runner. You might want to use Shutter Priority mode and set the a7R III for 1/60th second, so that the background will blur as you pan. The shutter speed will be fast enough to provide a sharp image of the athlete, as shown in Figure 7.12.

- **To reduce blur from camera motion when *you* are moving.** In other situations, the camera may be in motion, say, because you're shooting from a moving train or auto, and you want to minimize the amount of blur caused by the motion of the camera. Shutter-priority is a good choice here, too.

- **Landscape photography hand-held.** If you can't use a tripod for your landscape shots, you'll still probably want the sharpest image possible. Shutter-priority can allow you to specify a shutter speed that's fast enough to reduce or eliminate the effects of camera shake. Just make sure that your ISO setting is high enough that the a7R III will select an aperture with sufficient depth-of-field, too.

- **Concerts, stage performances.** I shoot a lot of concerts with my 70-200mm f/4 lens, and have discovered that, when vibration reduction is taken into account, a shutter speed of 1/180th second is fast enough to eliminate camera shake that can result from hand-holding the camera with this lens, and also to avoid blur from the movement of all but the most energetic performers. I use Shutter-priority and set the ISO so the camera will select an aperture in the f/4-5.6 range.

Program Auto (P) Mode

The Program mode uses the camera's built-in smarts to set an aperture/shutter speed combination, based on information provided by the light meter. If you're using Multi metering, the combination will often provide a good exposure. Rotate the front or rear dial and you can switch to other aperture/shutter speed combinations, all providing the same (equivalent) exposure. The P on the screen changes to P*. You can't use Program Shift when working with flash. To reverse Program Shift, change to another exposure mode (you can immediately switch back to P mode) or turn the camera off.

In the unlikely event that the correct exposure cannot be achieved with the wide range of shutter speeds and apertures available, the shutter speed and aperture will both turn orange. (The solution is to set a lower ISO in bright light and a higher ISO in dark locations until the blinking stops.) The P mode is the one to use when you want to rely on the camera to make reasonable basic settings of shutter speed and aperture, but you want to retain the ability to adjust many of the camera's settings yourself. All overrides and important functions are available, including ISO, white balance, metering mode, exposure compensation, and others.

When to use Program mode:

- **When you're in a hurry to get a grab shot.** The a7R III will do a pretty good job of calculating an appropriate exposure for you, without any input from you.

- **When you hand your camera to a novice.** Set the a7R III to P, hand the camera to your friend, relative, or *trustworthy* stranger you meet in front of the Eiffel Tower, point to the shutter release button and viewfinder, and say, "Look through here, and press this button."

- **When no special shutter speed or aperture settings are needed.** If your subject doesn't require special anti- or pro-blur techniques, and depth-of-field or selective focus aren't important, use P as a general-purpose setting. You can still make adjustments to increase/decrease depth-of-field or add/reduce motion blur with a minimum of fuss.

Making Exposure Value Changes

Sometimes you'll want a brighter or darker photo (more or less exposure) than you got when relying on the camera's metering system. Perhaps you want to underexpose to create a silhouette effect or overexpose to produce a high-key (very light) effect. It's easy to do so by using the a7R III's exposure compensation features, available only in P, S, A, M, Panorama, and Movie modes. There are several ways to set exposure compensation:

- **Exposure compensation dial.** This dial, located at the right end of the top surface of the camera, is the fastest method for adding/subtracting exposure. It can be rotated to provide plus or minus three stops of exposure in one-third stop increments. Only plus/minus 2 stops are available when using Movie mode.

  In Manual exposure mode, exposure compensation can be dialed in only when ISO Auto is activated, as the camera will leave your shutter speed and aperture settings undisturbed and add or subtract exposure by changing ISO sensitivity instead. Unlike the mode dial, the exposure compensation dial is not "locked," so you can easily spin it with your thumb while shooting. It has click detents and is not likely to rotate accidentally.

- **Exposure Compensation menu.** If you want additional exposure compensation, venture to the Camera Settings I-9 (Exposure 1) menu, where the Exposure Comp. entry will let you set plus or minus five stops of exposure using the front or rear dials or control wheel. This option is not available if you've made a setting with the exposure compensation dial; its menu entry will be grayed out.

- **Function menu.** Unless you've redefined your Function menu to remove it, exposure compensation can also be applied by pressing the Fn button. The exposure compensation entry's default position is at the far right of the top row of functions. The Function menu entry also lets you choose up to five stops of compensation.

- **Define a key.** If you like, you can define a key as your exposure compensation button, using the Custom Keys feature described in Chapter 4. When I feel I am going to be making many exposure compensation settings, I define the down directional button as the exposure compensation button. Then, I can press the down button and rotate the control wheel to make quick adjustments.

In my experience, adding exposure compensation is the option that's most often necessary. I'll often set +2/3 when using Multi metering if the camera underexposed my first photo of a light-toned scene. With Center-weighted or Spot metering, +1.3 or an even higher level of plus compensation is almost always necessary with a light-toned subject. Since the camera provides a live preview of the scene (when Setting Effect is turned on), it's easy to predict when the photo you'll take is likely to be obviously over- or underexposed. When the histogram display is on, you can make a more accurate prediction about the exposure; I'll discuss this feature shortly. Of course, you can also use plus compensation when you want to intentionally overexpose a scene for a creative effect.

You won't often need to use minus compensation. This feature is most likely to be useful when metering a dark-toned subject, such as close-ups of black animals or dark blue buildings, for example. Since these dark-toned subjects lead the camera to overexpose, set –2/3 or –1 compensation (when using Multi metering) for a more accurate exposure. (The amount of minus compensation that you need to set may be quite different when using the other two metering modes.) Minus compensation can also be useful for intentionally underexposing a scene for a creative effect, such as a silhouette of a sailboat or a group of friends on a beach.

Any exposure compensation you set will remain active for all photos you take afterward, unless you've activated Reset EV Compensation in the Camera Settings I-9 (Exposure 1) menu, as described in Chapter 3. The camera provides a reminder as to what value is currently set in some display modes. Turning the a7R III off and then back on does not set compensation back to zero; when you no longer need to use it, be sure to do so yourself, or enable the Reset option. If you inadvertently leave it set for +1 or –1, for example, your photos taken under other circumstances will be over- or underexposed.

Manual Exposure (M) Mode

Part of being an experienced photographer comes from knowing when to rely on your a7R III's automation (including Intelligent Auto and P modes), when to go semi-automatic (with Shutter Priority or Aperture Priority), and when to set exposure manually (using M). Some photographers actually prefer to set their exposure manually. This is quite convenient, as the camera is happy to provide an indication of when your settings will produce over- or underexposure, based on its metering system's judgment. It can even indicate how far off the "correct" (recommended) exposure your photo will be at the settings you have made.

I often hear comments from novices first learning serious photography claiming that they must use Manual mode in order to take over control from the camera. While a back-to-basics approach does force you to learn photographic principles, it's not always necessary. For example, you can control all important aspects when using semi-automatic A or S mode as discussed in the previous sections. This allows you to control depth-of-field (the range of acceptable sharpness) or the rendition of motion (as blurred or as frozen). You can set a desired ISO level; that will not change the exposure. You would use exposure compensation when you want a brighter or a darker photo.

Manual mode provides an alternative that allows you to control the aperture and the shutter speed and the exposure simultaneously. For example, when I shot the windmill in Figure 7.13, I was not getting exactly the desired effect with A or S mode while experimenting with various levels of exposure compensation. So, I switched to M mode, set ISO 100, and then set an aperture/shutter speed that might provide the intended exposure. After taking a test shot, I changed the aperture slightly and the next photo provided the exposure for the interpretation of the scene that I wanted.

Manual mode is also useful when working in a studio environment using multiple flash units. The additional flash units are triggered by slave devices (gadgets that set off the flash when they sense the light from another flash, or, perhaps from a radio or infrared remote control). In some cases, M mode is the only suitable choice. Your camera's exposure meter doesn't compensate for the extra illumination, and can't interpret the flash exposure at all, so you need to set the aperture and shutter speed manually.

Figure 7.13
Manual mode allowed setting the exact exposure for this silhouette shot, by metering the subject and then underexposing.

HDR ISN'T HARD

The 1.0 to 3.0 EV options are the ones you might try first when bracketing if you plan to perform High Dynamic Range magic later on in Photoshop (with Merge to HDR), Elements (with Photomerge), or with another image editor that provides an HDR feature. That will allow you to combine images with different exposures into one photo with an amazing amount of detail in both highlights and shadows. To get the best results, mount your camera on a tripod, shoot in RAW format, and use BRK C3.0EV to get three shots with 3 EV of difference in exposure. Of course, with this camera, you also have the option of using the Auto HDR feature as well; this can provide very good results in the camera without the need to use any special HDR software.

change. You can use flash when continuous bracketing is active, but, because of the time required for the flash to recycle, you'll need to press the shutter button each time to take subsequent images (effectively switching the camera into Single Bracket mode, described next). Continuous Bracketing (and Single Bracketing) is disabled when using Intelligent Auto.

Only the last shot in the set is displayed when using Auto Review. With all types of bracketing, the exposure/bracket scale at the bottom of the EVF or LCD monitor (in Display All Info mode) will display indicators showing the number of images shot and the relative amount of under- or overexposure.

Don't forget that you can dial in exposure compensation, and *that* will affect the amount of over/underexposure applied while bracketing, too. You can bracket your exposures based on something other than the base (metered) exposure value. Set any desired exposure compensation, either a plus or a minus value. Then set the Bracketing level you want to use. The camera will bracket exposures as over, under, and equal to the *compensated* value.

Single Bracketing

This mode captures one bracketed image in a set of 3, 5, or 9 shots each time you press the shutter release, bracketing them 0.3, 0.7, 1.0 stops apart. Only 3 and 5 shots are available with the 2.0, or 3.0 EV increments. The left/right buttons are used to select the increment and number of shots. In this mode, you can separate each image by an interval of your choice. You might want to use this variation when you want the individual images to be captured at slightly different times, say, to produce a set of images that will be combined in some artistic way.

White Balance Bracketing

In this mode, the camera shoots three images, each with a different adjustment to the color temperature. While you can't specify which direction the color bias is tilted, you can select Lo (the default) for small changes, or Hi, for larger changes using the left/right buttons. Only the last shot taken is displayed during Auto Review.

DRO Bracketing

This mode takes three images, with Lo (the default) or High adjustments to the dynamic range optimization. Use the left/right buttons to specify the degree of adjustment. Again, only the last shot taken is displayed during Auto Review.

Dealing with Digital Noise

Visual noise is that random grainy look with colorful speckles that some like to use as a visual effect, but most consider to be objectionable. That's because it robs your image of detail even as it adds that "interesting" texture. Noise is caused by two different phenomena: high ISO levels and long exposures. The a7R III offers a menu item to minimize both types. In Chapter 3, I discussed the Camera Settings I-2 (Quality/Image Size 2) menu items that you can use to modify the noise reduction processing; you might want to review the sections about High ISO NR and Long Exposure NR as a refresher.

High ISO Noise

Digital noise commonly appears when you set an ISO above ISO 1600 with the a7R III. High ISO noise appears as a result of the amplification needed to increase the effective sensitivity of the sensor. While higher ISOs do pull details out of dark areas, they also amplify non-signal information randomly, creating noise.

High ISO Noise Reduction is very useful, although at default, it also tends to make images slightly softer as blurring the noise pattern also blurs some intricate details. The higher the ISO, the more aggressive the processing will be, depending on whether you've specified Normal or Low. The Low level for NR provides images that are more grainy but with better resolution of fine detail. Even if you've chosen Off, the camera still applies some noise reduction.

High ISO NR is grayed out when the camera is set to shoot only RAW-format photos. The camera does not use this feature on RAW-format photos since noise reduction—at the optimum level for any photo—can be applied in the software you'll use to modify and convert the RAW file to JPEG or TIFF. (If you shoot in RAW & JPEG, the JPEG images, but not the RAW files, will be affected by this camera feature.) I'll discuss Noise Reduction with software in more detail in the next section.

Figure 7.15 shows two pictures that I shot at ISO 6400. For the first, I used the default (Normal) High ISO NR, and for the second shot, I set the NR to Off. (I've exaggerated the differences between the two slightly so the grainy/less grainy images are more evident on the printed page. The halftone screen applied to printed photos tends to mask these differences.)

Figure 7.15
The Normal level for High ISO NR (left) produces a smoother (less grainy) image than one made with High ISO NR turned off (right).

Long Exposure Noise

A similar digital noise phenomenon occurs during long time exposures, which allow more photons to reach the sensor, increasing your ability to capture a picture under low-light conditions. However, the longer exposures also increase the likelihood that some pixels will register as random, "phantom," photons, often because the longer an imager collects photos during an exposure, the hotter it becomes, and that heat can be mistaken by the sensor as actual photons. The camera tries to minimize this type of noise automatically; there is no separate control you can adjust to add more or less noise reduction for long exposures.

CMOS imagers like the one in the a7R III, contain millions of individual amplifiers and A/D (analog to digital) converters, all working in unison though the BIONZ X digital image processor chip. Because these circuits don't necessarily all process in precisely the same way all the time, they can introduce something called fixed-pattern noise into the image data.

Long exposure noise reduction is used with JPEG exposures longer than one full second. (This feature is not used on RAW photos and in continuous shooting or bracketing modes.) When it's active, long exposure noise reduction processing removes random pixels from your photo, but some of the image-making pixels are unavoidably vanquished at the same time.

It's possible that you prefer the version made without NR, and you can achieve that simply by shooting RAW. Indeed, noise reduction can be applied with most image-editing programs. You might get even better results with an industrial-strength product like Nik Dfine, part of the Nik collection (now owned by DxO), or Topaz DNoise or Enhance (www.topazlabs.com). You can apply noise reduction to RAW photos with Sony's Image Data Converter or any other versatile converter software. Some products are optimized for NR with unusually sophisticated processing, such as Photo Ninja (www.picturecode.com) and DXO Optics Pro's version 9 or higher (www.dxo.com).

Using Dynamic Range Optimizer

Dynamic Range Optimizer (DRO), see Figure 7.16, and Auto HDR (discussed next) are features you can select from the Camera Settings I-12 menu or the Function menu, as explained in Chapter 3. When enabled, the camera will examine your images as they are exposed, and, if the shadows appear to have detail even though they are too dark, will attempt to process the image so the shadows are lighter, with additional detail, without overexposing detailed highlights. The processed image is always saved as a JPEG, so if you are shooting RAW you won't notice a difference.

Here is how the DRO and Auto HDR features work:

- **DRO Off.** No optimization. You're on your own; the camera will not apply extra processing even to your JPEG photos. Of course, if you are shooting RAW (or RAW & JPEG) photos, you can apply DRO effects to your photo when converting it with the downloadable Image Data Converter SR software. (Other programs have different tools for lightening shadow areas and/ or darkening highlight areas.) Use Off when shooting subjects of normal contrast, or when you want to capture an image just as you see it, without modification by the camera.

- **DRO.** Press the left/right buttons after scrolling to DRO Auto and you can then set a specific intensity level for the Dynamic Range Optimizer, from Level 1 through Level 5.

  If you do not want to set a specific level, simply scroll to DRO Auto and allow the camera to decide on the amount of increased dynamic range. With the Auto setting, the camera dives into your image, looking at various small areas to examine the contrast of highlights and shadows, making modifications to each section to produce the best combination of brightness and tones with detail. In my experience, Auto provides a mid level of DRO that's worth leaving on at all times.

- **HDR Auto.** In this mode, the a7R III creates a high dynamic range photo. It starts by taking three JPEG photos, each at a different exposure; the three are then composited into one by the processor using the best-exposed areas from each photo. The final image will have a high dynamic range effect, with great detail in shadow areas and increased detail in bright areas. You can specify how dramatic the effect should be.

  After scrolling to HDR Auto, press the left/right buttons and set an HDR Level, from 1.0 EV to 6.0 EV. (One EV equals one stop of exposure.) The higher the level you set, the greater the exposure difference will be among the three photos the camera will shoot to produce one with high dynamic range. There's no "best" setting; it depends on your personal preference. At a very high EV level, the effect will be dramatic, but the photo may not appear to be "natural" looking. See the section that follows for more on HDR photography.

Figure 7.16 DRO Off (upper left); Level 1 (upper right); Level 3 (lower left); and Level 5 (lower right).

Tip

The primary method for DRO processing is lightening the dark tones and mid tones of an image. The higher the level of DRO you set, the more significantly the processor will lighten those areas; that causes digital noise to be more and more noticeable, especially in photos made at ISO 800 and at higher ISO levels. This is one reason why you would not always want to set Level 4 or 5 for DRO, particularly when using a high ISO setting. The other reason is that very high DRO produces a somewhat unnatural-looking effect with all shadow areas lighter than "normal." Auto and Levels 1 to 3 retain the most natural-looking effect.

When you activate DRO, you have your choice of specifying the aggressiveness of the processing (from Level 1 through Level 5), in which case it will *always* be applied at the level you specify. Or, you can set the feature to Auto and let the camera decide the ideal amount of optimization (or even when to apply it at all). Auto is usually your best choice, because the camera is pretty smart about choosing which images to process, and which to leave alone. Indeed, the camera's programming usually does a better job than a similar feature available in the Image Data Converter SR software you may have installed on your computer.

Figure 7.16 shows an image with DRO turned off, and using Level 1, Level 3, and Level 5 optimization. (The differences between, say, Level 1 and 2, or 2 and 3 are subtle and wouldn't show up well on the printed page, so I skipped the even-numbered levels.) The printed page also doesn't show that DRO tends to increase the amount of noise in an image as it works more aggressively; it's usually a good idea to avoid using the feature at high ISO levels where noise tends to be a real problem under any conditions.

Working with HDR

High dynamic range (HDR) photography is quite the rage these days, and entire books have been written on the subject. It's not really a new technique—film photographers have been combining multiple exposures for ages to produce a single image of, say, an interior room while maintaining detail in the scene visible through the windows.

It's the same deal in the digital age. Suppose you wanted to photograph a dimly lit room that had a bright window showing an outdoors scene. Proper exposure for the room might be on the order of 1/60th second at f/2.8 at ISO 200, while the outdoors scene probably would require f/11 at 1/400th second. That's almost a 7 EV step difference (approximately 7 f/stops) and well beyond the dynamic range of any digital camera, including the Sony a7R III cameras. (An additional problem, of course, is the mixed illumination: daylight outdoors and probably tungsten or fluorescent lamps indoors. Pro photographers sometimes gel the windows with corrective film so that inside/outside illumination matches.)

Until camera sensors gain much higher dynamic ranges (which may not be as far into the distant future as we think), special tricks like DRO and HDR photography will remain basic tools. With the Sony cameras, you can create in-camera HDR exposures, or shoot HDR the old-fashioned way—with separate bracketed exposures that are later combined in a tool like Photomatix or Adobe's Merge to HDR image-editing feature. I'm going to show you how to use both.

Auto HDR

The camera's in-camera Auto HDR feature is simple and surprisingly effective in creating high dynamic range images. It's also remarkably easy to use. It can be dialed in using the DRO/Auto HDR entries found in the menu, Function menu, and any key you might define with that function.

Figure 7.17 illustrates how the three shots that the camera's Auto HDR feature merges might look. There is a one-stop differential between each of the images, from the overexposed image at top left, to the intermediate exposure at center left, and to the underexposed image at the bottom left. The in-camera HDR processing is able to combine the three to derive an image similar to the one shown at right in the figure, which has a much fuller range of tones.

To use the camera's HDR feature, select it in the Camera Settings I-12 menu's DRO/Auto HDR entry, or from the Fn menu. You can manually specify an increment from 1 EV to 6 EV or choose Auto and allow the camera to select the appropriate differential. When you press the shutter release, the camera will take all three shots consecutively, align the images (because, if the camera is hand-held, there is likely to be a small amount of movement between shots), and then save one JPEG image to your memory card. The feature does not work if you have selected RAW or RAW+JPEG formats or have activated a Picture Effect or Picture Profile.

Figure 7.17
Three bracketed images (left) can be combined to produce the merged HDR image (right).

Bracketing and Merge to HDR Pro

If your credo is "If you want something done right, do it yourself," you can also shoot HDR manually, without resorting to the camera's HDR mode. Instead, you can shoot individual images either by manually bracketing or using the camera's auto bracketing modes.

Although my goal in this book is to show you how to take great photos *in the camera* rather than how to fix your errors in Photoshop, the Merge to HDR Pro feature in Adobe's flagship image editor (and a variation also found in Photoshop Elements) is too cool to ignore. The ability to have a bracketed set of exposures that are identical except for exposure is key to getting good results with this Photoshop feature, which allows you to produce images with a full, rich dynamic range that includes a level of detail in the highlights and shadows that is almost impossible to achieve with digital cameras.

When you're using Merge to HDR Pro, you'd take several pictures, some exposed for the shadows, some for the middle tones, and some for the highlights. The exact number of images to combine is up to you. Four to seven is a good number. Then, you'd use the Merge to HDR Pro command to combine all of the images into one HDR image that integrates the well-exposed sections of each version. Here's how.

The images should be as identical as possible, except for exposure. So, it's a good idea to mount the camera on a tripod, use a remote release, and take all the exposures in one burst. Just follow these steps:

1. **Set up the camera.** Mount the camera on a tripod.

2. **Set the camera to shoot a bracketed burst with an increment of at least 2 EV.**

   You can use auto bracketing or manually change the exposure between shots. In Manual mode, make sure Auto ISO is off, and you adjust exposures *only* by changing the shutter speed. You should be very careful when you make the adjustment to avoid jostling the camera.

3. **Choose an f/stop.** Set the camera for Aperture Priority and select an aperture that will provide a correct exposure at your initial settings for the series of manually bracketed shots. *And then leave this adjustment alone!* You don't want the aperture to change for your series, as that would change the depth-of-field and, potentially, the image size of some elements. You want the camera to adjust exposure *only* using the shutter speed.

4. **Choose manual focus.** You don't want the focus to change between shots, so set the camera to manual focus, and carefully focus your shot.

5. **Choose RAW exposures.** Set the camera to take RAW files, which will give you the widest range of tones in your images. (This is an advantage of manually creating HDR files; the camera's Auto HDR feature can't be used when RAW or RAW+JPEG is active.)

6. **Take your bracketed set.** Press the button on the remote (or carefully press the shutter release or use the self-timer) and take the set of bracketed exposures.

7. **Continue with the Merge to HDR Pro steps listed next.** You can also use a different program, such as Photomatix or Nik software, if you know how to use it.

DETERMINING THE BEST EXPOSURE DIFFERENTIAL

How do you choose the number of EV/stops to separate your exposures? You can use histograms, described at the end of this chapter, to determine the correct bracketing range. Take a test shot and examine the histogram. Reduce the exposure until dark tones are clipped off at the left of the resulting histogram. Then, increase the exposure until the lighter tones are clipped off at the right of the histogram. The number of stops between the two is the range that should be covered using your bracketed exposures.

The next steps show you how to combine the separate exposures into one merged high dynamic range image.

1. **Copy your images to your computer.** If you use an application to transfer the files to your computer, make sure it does not make any adjustments to brightness, contrast, or exposure. You want the real raw information for Merge to HDR Pro to work with.

2. **Activate Merge to HDR Pro.** Choose File > Automate > Merge to HDR Pro.

3. **Select the photos to be merged.** Use the Browse feature to locate and select your photos to be merged. You'll note a check box that can be used to automatically align the images if they were not taken with the camera mounted on a rock-steady support. This will adjust for any slight movement of the camera that might have occurred when you changed exposure settings.

4. **Choose parameters (optional).** The first time you use Merge to HDR Pro, you can let the program work with its default parameters. Once you've played with the feature a few times, you can read the Adobe Help files and learn more about the options than I can present in this non-software-oriented camera guide.

5. **Click OK.** The merger begins.

6. **Save.** Once HDR merge has done its thing, save the file to your computer.

If you do everything correctly, you'll end up with a full-range high dynamic range photo. What if you don't have the opportunity, inclination, or skills to create several images at different exposures, as described? If you shoot in RAW format, you can still use Merge to HDR, working with a *single* original image file. What you do is import the image into Photoshop several times, using Adobe Camera Raw to create multiple copies of the file at different exposure levels.

For example, you'd create one copy that's too dark, so the shadows lose detail, but the highlights are preserved. Create another copy with the shadows intact and allow the highlights to wash out. Then, you can use Merge to HDR to combine the two and end up with a finished image that has the extended dynamic range you're looking for. (This concludes the image-editing portion of the chapter. We now return you to our alternate sponsor: photography.)

Exposure Evaluation with Histograms

While you may be able to improve poorly exposed photos in your image-editing software or with DRO or HDR techniques, it's definitely preferable to get the exposure close to correct in the camera. This will minimize the modifications you'll need to make in post-processing, which can be very time-consuming and will degrade image quality, especially with JPEGs. A RAW photo can tolerate more significant changes with less adverse effects, but for optimum quality, it's still important to have an exposure that's close to correct.

Instead, you can use a histogram, which is a chart displayed on the camera's screen that shows the number of tones that have been captured at each brightness level. Two types of histograms are available, a "live" histogram that appears at the lower-right corner of the screen in Shooting mode, and a larger, more detailed version that appears in Histogram mode during playback. The live version can help you make exposure decisions as you shoot, whereas the playback version is useful in determining corrections to be made before you take your next shot. I'll explain both versions, but first it's useful to understand exactly what you're seeing when you view a histogram.

The Live Histogram

The camera's live histogram offers the most reliable method for judging the exposure as you shoot (although the Zebra feature described in Chapter 4 can be used to isolate specific problems involving blown highlights). A pair of live histograms are also available for display for both the viewfinder and monitor; activate both with the DISP Button (Monitor/Finder) item in the Camera Settings II-6 menu, as discussed in Chapter 4. After activating, press the DISP button a few times to reach the display that includes the histogram, which will be shown at lower right in the viewfinder and LCD monitor screens.

In Shooting mode, you'll get a luminance (brightness) histogram that shows the distribution of tones and brightness levels across the image given the current Camera Settings I, including exposure compensation, Dynamic Range Optimizer (DRO) level in use, or the aperture, shutter speed, and ISO that you have set if using Manual mode. This live histogram (displayed before taking a photo) is useful for judging whether the exposure is likely to be satisfactory or whether you should use a camera feature to modify the exposure. When the histogram looks better, take the photo. I'll show you how to evaluate histograms later in this chapter.

The Playback Histograms

You can view histograms in Playback mode, too; press the DISP button until the display shown in Figure 7.18 appears. The top graph, called the luminance or brightness histogram, is conventional, showing the distribution of tones across the image. Each of the other three histograms is in a specific color: red, green, and blue. That indicates the color channel you're viewing in that histogram: red, green, or blue. These additional graphs allow you to see the distribution of tones in the three individual channels. It takes a lot of expertise to interpret those extra histograms and, frankly, the conventional luminance histogram is the only one that many photographers use.

Figure 7.18
The Playback histograms show you the tonal distribution of a photo you've already taken.

As a bonus in Playback mode, another feature is available when the histograms are visible: any areas of the displayed image that are excessively bright, or excessively dark, will blink. This feature, often called "blinkies," warns that you may need to change your settings to avoid loss of detail in highlight areas (such as a white wedding gown) or in shadow areas (such as a black animal's fur). The camera also includes the Zebra feature to indicate overexposure, as discussed in Chapter 4. You can use the histogram information along with the flashing blinkie and Zebra alerts to guide you in modifying the exposure, and/or setting the DRO feature (discussed earlier), before taking the photo again.

Tonal Range

Histograms help you adjust the tonal range of an image, the span of dark to light tones, from a complete absence of brightness (black) to the brightest possible tone (white), and all the middle tones in between. Because all values for tones fall into a continuous spectrum between black and white, it's easiest to think of a photo's tonality in terms of a black-and-white or grayscale image, even though you're capturing those tones in three separate color layers of red, green, and blue.

Because your images are digital, the tonal "spectrum" isn't really continuous: it's divided into discrete steps that represent the different tones that can be captured. Figure 7.19 may help you understand this concept. The gray steps shown range from 100 percent gray (black) at the left, to 0 percent gray (white) at the right, with 20 gray steps in all (plus white).

Figure 7.19
A tonal range from black (left) to white (right) and all the gray values in between.

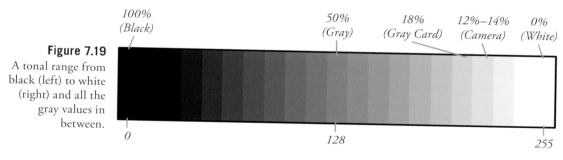

Along the bottom of the chart are the digital values from 0 to 255 recorded by your sensor for an image with 8 bits per channel. (8 bits of red, 8 bits of green, and 8 bits of blue equal a 24-bit, full-color image). Any black captured would be represented by a value of 0, the brightest white by 255, and the midtones would be clustered around the 128 marker. The actual scale may be "finer" and record say, 0 to 4,094 for an image captured when the a7R III is capturing RAW images with 14 bits per channel.

Grayscale images (which we call black-and-white photos) are easy to understand. Or, at least, that's what we think. When we look at a black-and-white image, we think we're seeing a continuous range of tones from black to white, and all the grays in between. But, that's not exactly true. The blackest black in any photo isn't a true black, because *some* light is always reflected from the surface of the print, and if viewed on a screen, the deepest black is only as dark as the least-reflective area a computer monitor can produce. The whitest white isn't a true white, either, because even the lightest areas of a print absorb some light (only a mirror reflects close to all the light that strikes it), and, when viewing on a computer monitor, the whites are limited by the brightness of the display's LCD or LED picture elements. Lacking darker blacks and brighter, whiter whites, that continuous set of tones doesn't cover the full grayscale tonal range.

The full scale of tones becomes useful when you have an image that has large expanses of shades that change gradually from one level to the next, such as areas of sky, water, or walls. Think of a picture taken of a group of campers around a campfire. Since the light from the fire is striking them directly in the face, there aren't many shadows on the campers' faces. All the tones that make up the *features* of the people around the fire are compressed into one end of the brightness spectrum—the lighter end.

Yet, there's more to this scene than faces. Behind the campers are trees, rocks, and perhaps a few animals that have emerged from the shadows to see what is going on. These are illuminated by the softer light that bounces off the surrounding surfaces. If your eyes become accustomed to the reduced illumination, you'll find that there is a wealth of detail in these shadow images.

This campfire scene would be a nightmare to reproduce faithfully under any circumstances. If you are an experienced photographer, you are probably already wincing at what is called a *high-contrast* lighting situation. Some photos may be high in contrast when there are fewer tones and they are all bunched up at limited points in the scale. In a low-contrast image, there are more tones, but they are spread out so widely that the image looks flat. Your digital camera can show you the relationship between these tones using a *histogram*.

Histogram Basics

Your a7R III's histograms are a simplified display of the numbers of pixels at each of 256 brightness levels, producing an interesting mountain range effect. Although separate charts may be provided for brightness and the red, green, and blue channels, when you first start using histograms, you'll want to concentrate on the brightness histogram.

Figure 8.2 Phase detection "lines up" portions of your image using rangefinder-like comparison to achieve focus.

Figure 8.3 Visualizing phase detection.

Figure 8.3 is another way of visualizing phase detection. (This is a greatly simplified view just for illustration purposes.) In Figure 8.3 (top left), a typical horizontally oriented focus sensor is looking at a series of parallel vertical lines in a weathered piece of wood. The lines are broken into two halves by the sensor's rangefinder prism, and you can see that they don't line up exactly; the image is slightly out of focus. The rangefinder approach of phase detection tells the camera exactly how much out of focus the image is, and in which direction (focus is too near, or too far), thanks to the amount and direction of the displacement of the split image.

HORIZONTAL PROBLEMS

You should know that each of these sensors consist of a tiny horizontal array of pixels (represented by the red and green rectangles at top in the figure) and do the best job of detecting vertical lines that intersect them at a 90-degree angle. These vertical-sensitive sensors also do a fairly good job lining up diagonally oriented features. But they are less effective when faced with horizontal features, such as the rotated example shown at bottom left in Figure 8.3. The solution would be to include some vertical, horizontal line–sensitive sensors (as in Figure 8.3, bottom right), but Sony didn't need to do this, as the a7R III's complementary contrast detection fine-tuning system handles horizontal features well. However, with very difficult subjects, if you find yourself photographing something with predominant horizontal lines, you can improve your results by rotating the camera to better align the a7R III's PDAF sensors with your subject.

The camera can snap the image into sharp focus and line up the vertical lines, as shown in Figure 8.3, top right, in much the same way that rangefinder cameras align two parts of an image to achieve sharp focus. Even better, because it knows the amount of focus travel needed, the camera is able to adjust the speed of the lens's AF motor to move the lens elements slowly or quickly, depending on how much focus adjustment is needed.

As with any rangefinder-like function, accuracy is better when the "base length" between the two images is larger, so the two split images have greater separation. (Think back to your high school trigonometry; you could calculate a distance more accurately when the separation between the two points where the angles were measured was greater.) For that reason, phase detection autofocus is more accurate with larger (wider) lens openings than with smaller lens openings, and, with the Sony a7R III, may not work at all when the f/stop is smaller than f/8 (Sony says f/9 or smaller). Obviously, the "opposite" edges of the lens opening are farther apart with a lens having an f/2.8 maximum aperture than with one that has a smaller, f/5.6 maximum f/stop, and the base line is much longer. The camera is able to perform these comparisons and then move the lens elements directly to the point of correct focus very quickly, in milliseconds.

Because of the speed advantages of phase detection, makers of mirrorless cameras have been adding on-chip phase detect points to their sensors. Sony, because it designs and makes its own sensors, has been able to do a stellar job with this. The a7R III has a whopping 399 phase detect pixels embedded in its sensor.

Comparing the Two Hybrid Components

Sony a7R III autofocus uses both phase detection autofocus (PDAF) and contrast detection autofocus (CDAF) to provide a combination of fast and accurate AF. Figure 8.4 shows the layout of the autofocus points and zones used.

- **Contrast detection zones.** The blue boxes in Figure 8.4 represent the 425 areas of the sensor used by the a7R III when deploying contrast detection in full-frame mode. Notice that a large area of the frame, roughly 60 percent, is covered by the contrast-sensitive areas of the sensor.

- **Phase detection points.** The 399 phase detect points of the a7R III, represented by the green rectangles in the figure, are spread over a wider area. The a7R III's PDAF covers roughly 40 percent of the full frame, providing extra coverage.

- **Crop mode coverage.** One often-overlooked advantage of using the a7R III APS-C/Super 35 crop mode is that both the CDAF and PDAF areas are larger, because the outside area of the sensor is cropped out. The contrast detect zones fill virtually the entire cropped frame, and the phase detect sensors' points occupy around 60 percent of the cropped image area. That can be important for sports photographers, who may have subjects in all parts of the image.

The hybrid autofocus system uses both types of AF. The process begins by rapidly focusing using PDAF, because the rangefinder approach always tells the camera whether to move focus closer or farther, and by approximately how much. No hunting is required, which is often the case with phase detection, which needs to tweak the focus point until it settles on the sharpest position.

Figure 8.4

Autofocus zones for contrast detection (blue boxes) and phase detection (green boxes).

Once the PDAF has done its stuff, contrast detection kicks in, using its finicky but more accurate focusing capabilities to fine-tune focus. So, you end up with speedy initial focus (PDAF) and slightly slower final adjustments (CDAF), providing a perfect hybrid compromise. That's why Sony didn't switch to phase detection completely. Here's a quick rundown of the advantages of a hybrid system:

- **Contrast detection works with more image types.** Contrast detection doesn't require subject matter to have lines that are at angles to the PDAF points to work optimally, as phase detection does. Any subject that has edges running in any direction can be used to achieve sharp focus.

- **Contrast detection can focus on larger areas of the scene.** Whereas phase detection focus can be achieved *only* at the points that fall on one of the special autofocus sensor pixels, with contrast detection much larger portions of the image can be used as focus zones. Focus is achieved with the actual sensor image, so focus point selection is simply a matter of choosing which part of the sensor image to use. (This point is highlighted by the fact, discussed below, that in Flexible Spot mode, you can move the Autofocus Area to many parts of the sensor, whereas with a phase detection system, you can move the Autofocus Area only to a small number of specific locations where the special autofocus sensors used for phase detection are located.)

- **Contrast detection can be more accurate with some types of scenes.** Phase detection can fall prey to the vagaries of uncooperative subject matter: if suitable lines aren't available, the system may achieve less than optimal focus. In addition, accuracy decreases as the maximum aperture baseline used for calculations becomes smaller. Although AF is always conducted with the lens wide open, a lens with a maximum aperture of f/5.6 will focus with less accuracy than one with an f/1.4 maximum aperture. Contrast detection focus is more clear-cut. In most cases, the camera is able to determine clearly when sharp focus has been achieved.

- **Phase detection "knows" which direction to focus.** The split image seen by phase detection sensors reveal instantly whether focus is too close or too far. As I mentioned earlier, there is no need to "hunt" for the focus point, as the AF system can immediately adjust in the proper direction. That boosts focus speed considerably.

TRICKY BITS

There are a couple of restrictions you need to keep in mind when using the a7R III's hybrid AF system.

- **f/8 or larger.** Sony advises that focal plane phase detection AF is disabled whenever an aperture of f/9 or smaller is used; the a7R III will rely *only* on contrast detection in that case.
- **Compatible lenses.** Not all lenses are compatible with the phase detection component. Older lenses, and lenses that need to be updated using firmware, don't support phase detection, which in turn blocks use of the Automatic AF, AF Track Duration, and AF Drive Speed features explained in Chapter 3. A-Mount lenses used with the LA-EA2 or LA-EA4 adapters do not support focal plane phase detection, although most can be used with their own phase detection.

- **Phase detection "knows" how far out of focus a subject is.** The separation between the two halves of the image let the AF system know whether the subject is grossly out of focus, or whether only a slight adjustment is needed. That means faster autofocus, too.
- **Phase detection isn't as dependent on scene brightness.** As long as the split images are illuminated well enough for the AF system to make an evaluation, greater or lesser amounts of light don't have as much of an effect on speed and accuracy. Remember, the reason phase detection systems operate less well at smaller f/stops is because the baseline diameter of the aperture is smaller.

Focus Modes and Options

Now that you understand the fundamental principles of how the a7R III achieves focus, let's discuss the practical application of these principles to your everyday picture-taking activities, by setting the various modes and options available for the autofocus system. We'll also discuss the use of manual focus, and when that method might be preferable to autofocus.

As you've come to appreciate by now, the a7R III offers many options for your photography. Focus is no exception. Of course, as with other aspects of this camera, you can set the shooting mode to either Auto option or a scene mode such as Sports Action, and the camera will do just fine in most situations, using its default settings for autofocus. But, if you want more creative control, the choices are there for you to make.

FOCUS MODES/FOCUS AREA MODES

Your camera has a lot of modes! To keep the various focus options straight, remember that *focus modes* determine *when* the camera focuses: either once or continuously using autofocus, or manually. *Focus area modes* determine *where* in the frame the a7R III collects the information used to achieve autofocus.

So, no matter what shooting mode you're using, your first choice is whether to use autofocus or manual focus. Yes, there's also a Direct Manual Focus (DMF) option, discussed in Chapter 3, but that still provides autofocus, with the option of *fine-tuning* focus manually before taking the shot. Manual focus presents you with great flexibility along with the challenge of keeping the image in focus under what may be difficult conditions, such as rapid motion of the subject, darkness of the scene, and the like. Later in this chapter, I'll cover manual focus as well as DMF. For now, I'll assume you're going to rely on the camera's conventional AF mode.

The Sony a7R III has three basic AF modes: AF-S (Single-shot autofocus) and AF-C (Continuous autofocus), as well as Automatic AF (AF-A), which switches between the two other modes as required. Once you have decided on which of these to use, you also need to tell the camera how to select the area used to measure AF. In other words, after you tell the camera *how* to autofocus, you also have to tell it *where* to direct its focusing attention. I'll explain both *AF modes* and *AF area modes* in more detail later in this chapter.

MANUAL FOCUS

When you select manual focus (MF) in the Focus Mode entry in the Camera Settings I-5 menu, using the Function menu, Quick Navi screen, or by switching using a defined button, the a7R III lets you set the focus yourself by turning the focus ring on the lens. There are some advantages and disadvantages to this approach. While your batteries will last slightly longer in manual focus mode, it will take you longer to focus the camera for each photo. And unlike older 35mm film SLRs, digital cameras' electronic viewfinders and LCDs are not designed for optimum manual focus. Pick up any advanced film camera and you'll see a big, bright viewfinder with a focusing screen that's a joy to focus on manually. So, although manual focus is still an option for you to consider in certain circumstances, it's not as easy to use as it once was. I recommend trying the various AF options first and switching to manual focus only if AF is not working for you. And then be sure to take advantage of the focus peaking feature and the automatic frame enlargement (MF Assist), which can make it easier to determine when the focus is precisely on the most important subject element. And remember, if you use the DMF mode, you can fine-tune the focus after the AF system has finished its work.

Focus Pocus

Back in the pre-AF days, manual focusing was problematic because our eyes and brains have poor memory for correct focus, which is why your eye doctor must shift back and forth between sets of lenses and ask, "Does that look sharper or was it sharper before?" in determining your correct prescription. Similarly, manual focusing involves jogging the focus ring back and forth as you go from almost in focus, to sharp focus, to almost focused again. The little clockwise and counterclockwise arcs decrease in size until you've zeroed in on the point of correct focus. What you're looking for is the image with the most contrast between the edges of elements in the image.

The Sony a7R III can assess sharpness quickly, and it's also able to remember the progression perfectly, making the entire process fast and precise. Unfortunately, even this high-tech system doesn't really know with any certainty *which* object should be in sharpest focus. Is it the closest object? The subject in the center of the frame? Something lurking *behind* the closest subject? A person standing over at the side of the picture? Many of the techniques for using autofocus effectively involve telling the camera exactly what it should be focusing on.

Adding Circles of Confusion

But there are other factors in play, as well. You know that increased depth-of-field brings more of your subject into focus. But more depth-of-field also makes autofocusing (or manual focusing) more difficult because the contrast is lower between objects at different distances. So, autofocus with a 300mm lens (or zoom setting) may be easier than at a 16mm focal length (or zoom setting) because the longer lens has less apparent depth-of-field. By the same token, a lens with a maximum aperture of f/1.8 will be easier to autofocus (or manually focus) than one of the same focal length with an f/4 maximum aperture, because the f/4 lens has more depth-of-field and a dimmer view. It's also important to note that lenses with a maximum aperture smaller than f/5.6 would give your Sony Alpha's autofocus system fits, because the smaller opening (aperture) would allow less light to enter or to reach the autofocus sensor.

To make things even more complicated, many subjects aren't polite enough to remain still. They move around in the frame, so that even if the camera's lens is sharply focused on your main subject, the subject may change position and require refocusing. An intervening subject may pop into the frame and pass between you and the subject you meant to photograph. You (or the camera) have to decide whether to focus on this new subject, or to remain focused on the original subject. Finally, there are some kinds of subjects that are difficult to bring into sharp focus because they lack enough contrast to allow the camera's AF system (or our eyes) to lock in. Blank walls, a clear blue sky, or other low-contrast subject matter may make focusing difficult even with the hybrid AF system.

If you find all these focus factors confusing, you're on the right track. Focus is, in fact, measured using something called a *circle of confusion*. An ideal image consists of zillions of tiny little points, which, like all points, theoretically have no height or width. There is perfect contrast between the point and its surroundings. You can think of each point as a pinpoint of light in a darkened room. When a given point is out of focus, its edges decrease in contrast and it changes from a perfect point to a tiny disc with blurry edges (remember, blur is the lack of contrast between boundaries in an image). (See Figure 8.5.)

Figure 8.5

When a pinpoint of light (left) goes out of focus, its blurry edges form a circle of confusion (center and right).

If this blurry disc—the circle of confusion—is small enough, our eye still perceives it as a point. It's only when the disc grows large enough that we can see it as a blur rather than as a sharp point that a given point is viewed as being out of focus. You can see, then, that enlarging an image, either by displaying it larger on your computer monitor or by making a large print, also magnifies the size of each circle of confusion. Moving closer to the image does the same thing. So, parts of an image that may look perfectly sharp in a 5 × 7–inch print viewed at arm's length, might appear blurry when blown up to 11 × 14 inches and examined at the same distance. Take a few steps back, however, and the image may look sharp again.

To a lesser extent, the viewer also affects the apparent size of these circles of confusion. Some people see details better at a given distance and may perceive smaller circles of confusion than someone standing next to them. For the most part, however, such differences are small. Truly blurry images will look blurry to just about everyone under the same conditions.

Technically, there is just one plane within your picture area, parallel to the back of the camera (actually the sensor) that is in sharp focus. That's the plane in which the points of the image are rendered as precise points. At every other plane in front of or behind the focus plane, the points show up as discs that range from slightly blurry to extremely blurry. In practice, the discs in many of these planes will still be so small that we see them as points, and that's where we get depth-of-field: the range of planes that includes discs that we perceive as points rather than blurred splotches. The size of this range increases as the aperture is reduced in size and is allocated roughly one-third in front of the plane of sharpest focus, and two-thirds behind it. (See Figure 8.6.)

Figure 8.6
The focused plane (the nose of the train) is sharp, but the area in front of (the track) and behind it (the background) are blurred because the depth-of-field (the range of acceptably sharp focus) is shallow in this image.

Your Focus Mode Options

Manual focus can come in handy, as I'll explain later in this chapter, but autofocus is likely to be your choice in the great majority of shooting situations. Choosing the right AF mode and the way in which focus points are selected is your key to success. Using the wrong mode for a particular type of photography can lead to a series of pictures that are all sharply focused—on the wrong subject.

But autofocus isn't some mindless beast out there snapping your pictures in and out of focus with no feedback from you. There are several settings you can modify to regain a fair amount of control. Your first decision should be which of the autofocus modes to select: Single-shot (AF-S), Continuous AF (AF-C), or Automatic AF (AF-A). DMF first uses autofocus, and then allows you to fine-tune focus manually. Press the MENU button, go to the Camera Settings I-5 menu, and navigate to the line for Focus Mode. Press the center button, then highlight your autofocus mode choice from the submenu, and press the center button again. You can also set autofocus mode using the Quick Navi screen or by pressing the Fn button and using the Function menu.

Single-Shot AF (AF-S) Mode

With Single-Shot AF (AF-S), the camera will lock in focus when you press the shutter release (or defined AF start button) and will not adjust focus if your subject moves or you change the distance between you and your subject, as long as you hold down the button.

In AF-S mode, focus is locked. By keeping the button depressed halfway, you'll find you can reframe the image by moving the camera to aim at another angle; the focus (and exposure) will not change. Maintain pressure on the shutter release button and focus remains locked even if you recompose, or if the subject begins running toward the camera, for example.

FOCUS INDICATOR

At the lower-left corner of your screen, you'll find a green focus confirmation indicator that's active while focusing is underway. It consists of a round green disk which may have rounded brackets at either side. If the *disk glows steadily*, the image is in focus. Only the disk appears when using AF-S; in AF-C mode, the disk is surrounded by the brackets and indicates that the focus plane may change if the subject moves. If the *brackets are flashing and no disk appears*, focusing is in progress; if the *disk is flashing*, focusing has failed. (See Figure 8.7.)

Steady:
Image
in focus
(AF-S)

Flashing:
Focus has
failed

Image in focus,
but focus may
change
(AF-C)

Focus in
progress

Figure 8.7
The focus indicator icon shows focus status.

Tip

In this chapter, I'm assuming that you're using P, A, S, or M mode where you have full control over the camera features. This is important because the camera will use *only* AF-S in either Intelligent Auto mode. And it will set Continuous AF (AF-C) only in Movie mode, regardless of what focus mode you've selected for still images.

When sharp focus is achieved in AF-S mode, the solid green focus indicator appears in the lower-left corner of the screen and you'll hear a little beep. One or more green focus confirmation frames will also appear to indicate the area(s) of the scene that will be in sharpest focus.

For non-action photography, AF-S is usually your best choice, as it minimizes out-of-focus pictures (at the expense of spontaneity). Because of the small delay while the camera zeroes in on correct focus, you might experience slightly more shutter lag. This mode uses less battery power than Continuous AF.

If you have set the a7R III for Pre-AF in the Camera Settings I-7 menu, you may notice something that seems strange: the camera's autofocus mechanism will begin seeking focus even before you touch the shutter release button. In this mode, no matter which AF method is selected, the camera will continually alter its focus as it is aimed at various subjects, *until* you press the shutter release button halfway. At that point, the camera locks focus, in Single-shot AF mode.

When using AF-S or AF-C (described next), you can specify focus priority, from AF (wait until the subject is in sharp focus), Release (take the picture *now* even if not in perfect focus), and Balanced Emphasis (compromise!). I explained these options in more detail in Chapter 3.

Continuous AF (AF-C) Mode

When Continuous AF is active, focus is constantly readjusted as your subject (or you) move. The difference between Single-shot AF and Continuous AF comes at the point the shutter release button (or defined focus start button) is pressed halfway. (See the discussion of *back-button focus* later in this chapter.)

Switch to this mode when photographing sports, young kids at play, and other fast-moving subjects. In this mode, the camera can lock focus on a subject if it is not moving toward the camera or away from your shooting position; when it does, you'll see a green circle surrounded by brackets. (There will be no beep.) But if the camera-to-subject distance begins changing, the camera instantly begins to adjust focus to keep it in sharp focus, making this the more suitable AF mode with moving subjects.

Automatic AF (AF-A) Mode

The camera begins using AF-S, and switches to AF-C if the subject begins moving. Use this mode when you're not certain that your subject will begin moving, and you'd like to take advantage of AF-S, as described earlier, until the subject does move. You might use AF-A to photograph a sleeping pet, which, if awakened by the activity, might respond with sudden movement.

Direct Manual Focus (DMF) Mode

The camera focuses using AF-S mode, then uncouples the focus motor so you can fine tune focus (if necessary) manually. For best results, use this mode with focus peaking enabled to provide you with visual feedback as you adjust.

Manual Focus

No autofocus at all. You're on your own in deciding when the image is in sharp focus but provided with extra tools, such as the focus indicator in the lower-left corner of the screen (shown earlier in Figure 8.7), focus peaking, and the a7R III's focus magnification features.

Setting the AF Area

So far, you have allowed the camera to choose which part of the scene will be in the sharpest focus using its focus detection points called *AF areas* by Sony. However, you can also specify a single focus detection point that will be active. Use the Function menu, or press the MENU button, navigate to the Focus Area item in the Camera Settings I-5 menu, press the center button, and select one of the options. Press the center button again to confirm. The Custom 2 (C2) button will summon Focus Area if you haven't redefined it to another behavior. Here is how the AF Area options work:

- **Wide.** The camera chooses the appropriate focus area(s) in order to set focus on a certain subject in the scene. There are no focus indicators visible on the screen until you press the shutter release button halfway. At that point, in AF-S mode the camera displays one or more green focus indicators to show what area(s) of the image it has used to set focus on. In AF-C mode, the indicators will continue to flicker around the frame while the camera refocuses as necessary. If Face Detection is active, the AF system will prioritize faces when making its decision as to where it should set focus. You'll see multiple focus indicators when several parts of the scene are at the same distance from the camera. When most of the elements of a scene are at roughly the same distance, the camera displays a single, large green focus bracket around the entire edge of the screen. Even if you set one of the other options, Wide is automatically selected in Intelligent Auto mode. Use this mode to give the camera complete control over where to focus. (See Figure 8.8.)

- **Zone.** Brackets representing nine different focus zones are shown on the screen—three at the top left, center, and top right of the frame, three in the equivalent positions at the bottom, and three in the middle. Each zone is populated by a 9 × 9 array of PDAF focus points. You can move the focus zone by holding down the defined Focus Settings button (the default is C2) and then using the multi-selector joystick to shift the array to one of the nine overlapping areas. Select one of those nine focus zones, and the camera chooses which sections within that zone to use to calculate sharp focus. (See Figure 8.9). Those individual focus points will be highlighted in green. Use this mode when you know your subject is going to reside in a largish area of the frame and want to allow the a7R III to select the exact focus point within your designated zone.

- **Center.** Activate this AF area and the camera will use only a single focus detection point in the center of the frame to set focus. Initially a pair of black focus brackets appears on the screen. Touch the shutter release button and the camera sets and locks focus on the subject in the center of the image area; the brackets then turn green to confirm the area that will be in the sharpest focus in your image. (See Figure 8.10.) Choose this option if you want the camera to always focus on the subject in the center of the frame. Center the primary subject (like a friend's face in a wide-angle landscape composition), allow the camera to focus on it, maintain slight pressure on the shutter release button to keep focus locked, and re-frame the scene for a more effective, off-center, composition. Take the photo at any time and your friend (who is now off-center) will be in the sharpest focus.

- **Flexible Spot.** This mode enables you to move the camera's focus detection point (focus area) around the scene to any one of multiple locations, using the directional buttons. When opting for Flexible Spot, you can use the left/right buttons to choose Small, Medium, or Large spots, which changes the size of the focus brackets in the frame. This mode can be useful when the camera is mounted on a tripod and you'll be taking photos of the same scene for a long time, while the light is changing, for example. Move the focus area to cover the most important subject, and it will always focus on that point when you later take a photo.

Figure 8.8 With Wide AF Area, the camera either displays one large green bracket indicating that most of the scene is at the same distance to the camera or it displays one or more smaller points to indicate the specific area(s) of the scene that will be in sharpest focus.

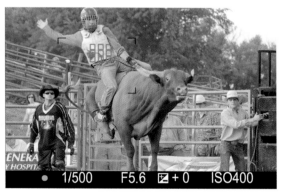

Figure 8.9 In Zone mode, brackets represent a focus zone, and you can move the zone to nine different locations on the screen. The camera selects one or more focus points within that array.

Figure 8.10 In the Center AF Area mode, the camera displays the focus brackets in the center of the screen; the brackets turn green after focus has been set.

Figure 8.11 When the Flexible Spot AF Area mode is initially selected, the active focus detection point is delineated with indicators that turn green when focus is confirmed and locked. Use the multi-selector or touch screen to specify location of the spot.

Use the multi-selector joystick to move the brackets around the screen, which allows great versatility in the placement of the active focus detection point. (See Figure 8.11.) Adjust the brackets until they cover the most important subject area and touch the shutter release button. The brackets will turn green and the camera will beep to confirm that focus has been set on the intended area.

- **Expand Flexible Spot.** If the camera is unable to lock in focus using the selected focus point, it will also use the eight adjacent points to try to achieve focus.

- **Lock-On AF.** In this mode, the camera locks focus onto the subject area that is under the selected focus spot when the shutter button is depressed halfway. Then, if the subject moves (or you change the framing in the camera), the camera will continue to refocus *on that subject*. You can select this mode only when the focus mode is set to Continuous AF (AF-C).

This option is especially powerful, because you can activate it for any of the five focus area options described above. That is, once you've highlighted Lock-On AF on the selection screen, you can then press the left-right directional button and choose Wide, Zone, Center, Flexible Spot, or Expand Flexible Spot. The camera will lock on a subject, using one of those five area modes to follow it. (See Figure 8.12.)

You cannot use this option if the mode dial is set to Movies or S&Q quick-/slow-motion video, nor if Center Lock-on AF, located in the Camera Settings I-6 menu, is activated. In that mode, you can *only* lock on a subject in the center of the frame, but you gain the ability to use lock-on AF while shooting movies. I'll describe Lock-On AF and Center Lock-On AF in more detail later in this chapter.

MOVING THE FOCUS FRAME

You can move the focus frame/point in either of two ways: use the multi-selector joystick when working with an AF mode that allows you to specify the focus area, or, if touch operations are enabled, by tapping the touch screen to indicate the focus point and/or dragging the focus point on the screen to the desired location. In manual focus mode, the same controls move the magnified focus area. If you assign Focus Standard to the multi-selector center button, pressing it will move the focusing frame back to the center of the screen.

Just as you're limited in the use of the AF mode in certain operating modes, there's a limitation with AF Area as well. For example, Flexible Spot is not available for selection in Intelligent Auto mode; the camera will always use Multi as the AF Area mode.

Face Detection and Eye AF

As hinted already, the a7R III has a couple more tricks up its sleeve for setting the AF area. In the Camera Settings I-6 menu, the Set Face Priority in AF entry allows you to turn Face Priority on or off and activate visible frames around the faces the a7R III detects. This enables the camera to attempt to identify any human faces in the scene. If it finds one or more faces, the camera will surround each one (up to eight in all) with the highest priority face outlined in white, and the others in either gray (if an unregistered face) or purple (if you have previously registered that face). In AF-S mode, an additional frame will be placed on the eyes of your subject, if detected. Press the shutter release halfway and the camera focuses on the highest priority face.

You can also specify Face Priority in Multi Metering and the a7R III will not only try to focus on faces, it will base its exposure on them as well. (In Chapter 3, I explained how to register and prioritize faces using entries in the Camera Settings I-14 menu.) When you press the shutter button halfway down to lock autofocus, the frame will turn green, confirming that they are in focus. If no faces are detected, the camera will display green indicators on the area it is using to achieve focus.

So, if the Face Detection option is grayed out on the Camera Settings I menu, check those other settings to make sure they are in effect. Personally, I often prefer to exercise my own control as to exactly where the camera should focus, but when shooting quick snaps during a party, Face Detection can be a useful feature. It's also an ideal choice if you need to hand the camera to someone to photograph you and your family or friends at an outing in the park. However, it really comes in useful when you couple it with Eye AF.

THE EYES HAVE IT

I like to use Face Detection in tandem with Eye AF. By default, the control wheel's center button activates Eye AF while you hold the button down. When active, simply point the camera at a face and press the defined key. The camera will magically identify the face and focus on the eye that's closest to the camera. If no eye is detected, the a7R III reverts to face detection. If it cannot find a face, Eye AF will fail to lock in. But if you'd like to be amazed, set your camera as follows:

- Continuous AF
- Lock-On AF: Flexible Spot
- Eye AF

The camera will almost unerringly locate faces and focus on the eye of your subject. It's great for candid portraits, weddings, or child photography.

Center Lock-On AF

The next trick the camera can perform is called Center Lock-On AF, which is a separate feature from the Lock-On AF that you can activate with a half-press of the shutter release. Center Lock-On AF must be accessed from a defined key, like Eye AF, or from its Camera Settings I-6 menu entry. It's designed to maintain focus on a specific subject as it moves around the scene that you're shooting. Don't confuse this feature with Continuous AF (AF-C), the mode you would use in action photography with a subject running toward you, for example. AF-C's *predictive focus* feature is often called "AF tracking" by other cameras and by many photographers. The a7R III offers that feature too, with AF-C mode autofocus, but it's not the same as Center Lock-On or Lock-On AF.

The Center Lock-On AF function *can* change focus as a person approaches the camera, but it's not intended for that purpose with a fast-action subject. And this feature is far more versatile than Continuous AF mode. Once the camera knows what your preferred subject is, it can maintain focus as it moves around the image area, as a person might do while mingling with a large group of friends at a party.

Turn on Center Lock-On AF in the Camera Settings I-6 menu. (You cannot do so when the camera is set for Lock-On AF in the Focus Area menu.) When it's been activated by a defined key or its menu entry, a small white square initially appears in the center of the screen. Move the position of the square with the directional controls until it covers your intended subject and press the center button. The small square now changes to a larger double square (as shown in Figure 8.12, right) that's called the *target frame*. You have instructed the camera as to your preferred subject. If the camera is set to AF-C mode, the camera tracks a focus subject when the shutter button is pressed halfway.

Figure 8.12 Left: Decide on the object the camera should track, center it, and press OK to instruct the a7R III as to your preferred target. Right: When Lock-On AF is active, the camera maintains focus on your preferred target, tracking it as it moves around the scene.

To use Center Lock-On AF, just follow these steps:

1. **Deactivate Lock-On AF.** You won't be able to activate Center Lock-On AF if its Lock-On AF cousin is enabled. Visit the Function menu and choose Wide, Zone, Center, Flexible Spot, or Expand Flexible Spot.

2. **Activate Center Lock-On AF.** Next, stop by the Camera Settings I-6 menu and enable Center Lock-On AF.

3. **Activate.** Press the center button to activate.

4. **Choose subject.** Align the camera so the subject you want to track is within the selection box. Press the center button again to select that subject.

5. **Start tracking.** Once the camera figures out which areas of the image under the selection box include your subject, it will outline the subject with a double white border. The camera will now use the live view image to track the subject and its phase detection AF system to keep that subject in focus.

   Move the camera around to change your composition or wait until your targeted subject begins moving around. Note that the target frame will remain on your subject, confirming that it will be in the sharpest focus when you take a photo. Changes in lighting, lack of contrast with the background, extra-small or extra-large subjects, and anything moving very rapidly can confuse Center Lock-On AF, but it's generally quite effective. Note that once you take a picture, you must go through the menu/custom key rigmarole again; this mode is not "sticky."

6. **Don't panic.** If your subject moves out of the frame, the a7R III will remember what it was tracking for several seconds and relock on it if it appears in the frame again within that time. If tracking is totally lost, the camera resumes its normal AF behavior until you select another subject to track.

7. **Stop tracking.** You can press the center button again to stop tracking your subject.

There are a few other benefits with Center Lock-On AF when using the camera when Face Detection is also active. Let's say you have designated the intended target as your friend Jack's face. If Jack leaves the room while being tracked and then returns to the scene, Center Lock-On AF will remember it and focus on Jack again. Whenever a face is your target, the camera can continue tracking that person even if the face is not visible; it will then make the body the target for tracking.

Center Lock-On AF allows you to choose the subject to track, rather than rely on the camera to track whatever object focus is originally locked on, as with Lock-On AF, described next. In addition, it can also be used in Movie mode, which can be very handy when you want to track a moving subject as you capture video. It cannot be used when Lock-On AF is active.

Center Lock-On may not work if the subject is moving too quickly, is too small or too large to be isolated effectively, has only reduced contrast against its background, or if the ambient light is too dark or changes dramatically while you're tracking.

Lock-On AF

Lock-On AF is the other tool for tracking a moving subject. Lock-On AF is easier than Center Lock-On AF, because you can turn it on and forget it. It does, however, only work in still photography mode; you can't use it when shooting movies. To use Lock-On AF, just follow these steps:

1. **Choose AF-C.** This feature works only when you are using continuous autofocus because, well, it refocuses continually.

2. **Deactivate Center Lock-On.** You can't use Lock-On and Center Lock-On at the same time.

3. **Activate Lock-On AF.** Use the Function menu and choose Focus Area. Scroll down past the Expand Flexible Spot entry and highlight Lock-On AF.

4. **Choose Focus Area.** Surprise! Using Lock-On AF does *not* mean you lose access to the four AF area modes. With Lock-On AF highlighted, use the left/right controls to select Wide, Zone, Center, Flexible Spot, or Expand Flexible Spot. That will give you both Lock-On AF *and* the area mode you prefer. If you switch from AF-C to AF-S, you lose the lock on capabilities, and the camera just reverts to whatever focus area mode you select here.

5. **Start tracking.** When you activate focus by pressing the shutter release halfway, the camera will use your selected focus area option to lock in focus, as always. However, now, once focus has been locked, the camera will *track* your subject as it roams around the screen. You'll see the green focus area rectangles moving as your subject moves (or you reframe the image with the camera). If a face is detected, a tracking rectangle around the face will be shown. (You'll learn more about face detection in an upcoming section.)

Using Manual Focus

As I noted earlier, manual focus is not as straightforward as with an older manual focus 35mm SLR equipped with a focusing screen optimized for this purpose and a readily visible focusing aid. But Sony's designers have done a good job of letting you exercise your initiative in the focusing realm, with features that make it easy to determine whether you have achieved precise focus. It's worth becoming familiar with the techniques for those occasions when it makes sense to take control in this area.

Here are the basic steps for quick and convenient setting of focus:

- **Select Manual Focus.** After you do so (in the Focus Mode entry in the Camera Settings I-5 menu), the letters MF will appear in the LCD display when you're viewing the default display that includes a lot of data. (You can change display modes by pressing the DISP button.)

- **Aim at your subject and turn the focusing ring on the lens.** As soon as you start turning the focusing ring, the image on the LCD is enlarged (magnified) to help you assess whether the center of interest of your composition is in focus. (That is, unless you turned off this feature, called MF Assist, through the Camera Settings II 1 menu.) Use the up/down/left/right directional controls to move around the magnified image area until you're viewing the most important subject element, such as a person's eyes. Turn the focusing ring until that appears to be in the sharpest possible focus.

  The enlargement lasts two seconds before the display returns to normal; you can increase that with the MF Assist Time menu item. In situations where you want to use manual focus without enlargement of the preview image, you can turn this feature off in the Camera Settings II menu, using the MF Assist item.

- **If you have difficulty focusing, zoom in if possible and focus at the longest available focal length.** If you're using a zoom lens, you may find it easier to see the exact effect of slight changes in focus while zoomed in. Even if you plan to take a wide-angle photo, zoom to telephoto and rotate the ring to set precise focus on the most important subject element. When you zoom back out to take the picture, the center of interest will still be in sharp focus.

- **Use Peaking of a suitable color.** On by default in Shooting mode, focus peaking provides a colored overlay around edges that are sharply focused; this makes it easier to determine when your subject is precisely focused. The overlay is white, but you can change that to another color when necessary. The alternate hue may be needed to provide a strong contrast between the peaking highlights and the color of your subject. Access the Peaking Color item of the Setup menu to adjust the color. To make the overlay even more visible, select High in the Peaking Level item; you can also turn peaking Off with this item, if desired.

- **Consider using the DMF option.** Your third option is DMF, or Direct Manual Focus. Activate it and the camera will autofocus with Single-shot AF and lock focus when you press the shutter release button halfway. As soon as focus is confirmed, you can turn the focusing ring to make fine-tuning adjustments, as long as you maintain slight pressure on the shutter release button. The MF Assist magnification will be activated immediately.

This method gives you the benefit of autofocus but gives you the chance to change the exact point of focus, to a person's eyes instead of the tip of the nose, for example. This option is useful in particularly critical focusing situations, when the precise focus is essential, as in extremely close focusing on a three-dimensional subject. Because depth-of-field is very shallow in such work, you'll definitely want to focus on the most important subject element, such as the pistil or stamen inside a large blossom. This will ensure that it will be the sharpest part of the image.

Back-Button Focus

Once you've been using your camera for a while, you'll invariably encounter the terms *back focus* and *back-button focus* and wonder if they are good things or bad things. Actually, they are *two different things,* and are often confused with each other. *Back focus* is a bad thing and occurs when a particular lens consistently autofocuses on a plane that's *behind* your desired subject. Fortunately, that's a malady only cameras with outboard AF sensors have, so you won't experience back or front focus unless you're using an EA-LA2- or EA-LA4 A-mount adapter.

Back-button focus, on the other hand, is a tool you can use to separate two functions that are commonly locked together—exposure and autofocus—so that you can lock in exposure while allowing focus to be attained at a later point, or vice versa. It's a *good* thing, although using back-button focus effectively may require you to unlearn some habits and acquire new ways of coordinating the action of your fingers.

As you have learned, the default behavior of your camera is to set both exposure and focus (when AF is active) when you press the shutter release down halfway. When using AF-S mode, that's that: both exposure and focus are locked and will not change until you release the shutter button or press it all the way down to take a picture and then release it for the next shot. In AF-C mode, exposure is locked and focus is set when you press the shutter release halfway, but the a7R III will continue to refocus if your subject moves for as long as you hold down the shutter button halfway. Focus isn't locked until you press the button down all the way to take the picture. In AF-A mode, the camera will start out in AF-S mode but switch to AF-C if your subject begins moving.

What back-button focus does is *decouple* or separate the two actions. You can retain the exposure lock feature when the shutter is pressed halfway, but assign autofocus *start* and/or autofocus *lock* to a different button. So, in practice, you can press the shutter button halfway, locking exposure, and reframe the image if you like (perhaps you're photographing a backlit subject and want to lock in exposure on the foreground, and then reframe to include a very bright background as well).

But, in this same scenario, you *don't* want autofocus locked at the same time. Indeed, you may not want to start AF until you're good and ready, say, at a sports venue as you wait for a ballplayer to streak into view in your viewfinder. With back-button focus, you can lock exposure on the spot where you expect the athlete to be and activate AF at the moment your subject appears. The a7R III gives you a great deal of flexibility, both in the choice of which button to use for AF, and the behavior of that button. You can *start* autofocus, *lock* autofocus at a button press, or *lock it while holding the button.* That's where the learning of new habits and mind-finger coordination comes in. You need to learn which back-button focus techniques work for you, and when to use them.

Back-button focus lets you avoid the need to switch from AF-S to AF-C when your subject begins moving unexpectedly. Nor do you need to use AF-A and *hope* the camera switches when appropriate. You retain complete control. It's great for sports photography when you want to activate autofocus precisely based on the action in front of you. It also works for static shots. You can press and release your designated focus button, and then take a series of shots using the same focus point. Focus will not change until you once again press your defined back button.

Want to focus on a spot that doesn't reside under one of the a7R III's focus areas? Use back-button focus to zero in focus on that location, then reframe. Focus will not change. Don't want to miss an important shot at a wedding or a photojournalism assignment? If you're set to *focus priority*, your camera may delay taking a picture until the focus is optimum; in *release priority* there may still be a slight delay. With back-button focus you can focus first and wait until the decisive moment to press the shutter release and take your picture. The a7R III will respond immediately and not bother with focusing at all.

Activating Back-Button Focus

To enable back-button focus, just follow these steps:

1. **Select an AF-ON button.** The a7R III's built-in AF-ON button performs this function by default, but if you don't care for its location next to the viewfinder, you can redefine the AEL button or another key to have the AF-ON behavior. In the Camera Settings II-8 menu, select Custom Key Settings (Stills) and define the button of your choice.

2. **Turn off shutter button AF activation.** In the Camera Settings I-6 menu, set AF/w Shutter to Off. When you want to disable back-button focus (temporarily or permanently), change it back to On.

That's all there is to it. Henceforth, pressing the shutter release will *not* activate autofocus. Auto-exposure metering will still be initiated by pressing the button halfway, as long as the AEL/w Shutter is set to Auto or On (and not Off) and pressing it all the way takes a picture.

Useful Menu Items for AF

I discussed how to set all the autofocus options, which are scattered among the Camera Settings I and Camera Settings II menus, plus how to define Custom Keys to activate certain features in Chapters 3 and 4. If you need a recap, here is a list of the a7R III autofocus features that you should keep in mind. I'll recap the most important aspects here, as a quick guide to help you locate the longer discussions. Table 8.1 provides some guidelines for particular types of subjects. Remember that some of these are also available in the Function menu.

Table 8.1 Focus Guidelines

Subject	Focus Mode	Focus Area	Priority Setup	Lock-On AF	Tracking Drive Speed	Tracking Duration	Face Detection	Eye AF
Portraits	AF-S	Flexible Spot	AF	Off	Fast	3	On	Yes
Street photography	AF-C	Wide	Balanced Emphasis	On	Fast	3	On	As needed
General sports action	AF-C	Expanded Flexible Spot	Release	On	Fast	1	Off	No
Birds in flight	AF-C	Expanded Flexible Spot	Balanced Emphasis	On	Fast	5	Off	No
Football, soccer, basketball	AF-C	Expanded Flexible Spot	Release	On	Fast	1	Off	Off
Kids, pets	AF-C	Zone	Balanced emphasis	On	Fast	2	On	Yes
Track events, auto racing	AF-C	Wide	Release	On	Fast	3	Off	No
Landscapes	AF-S	Wide	AF	Off	Slow	3	Off	No
Concerts, performances	AF-S	Flexible Spot	AF	Off	Fast	3	On	Yes

Here are your options:

- **AF Illuminator (Stills).** This Camera Settings I-6 menu item is set at Auto by default, indicating that the illuminator on the front of the camera will provide a burst of light in a dark location when using in AF-S mode. That provides a bright target for the autofocus system. Turn this feature off when you feel the red burst might be intrusive.

- **Face Registration.** Mentioned briefly earlier in this chapter, this Camera Settings I-14 menu item is quite versatile and was described in Chapter 3. You can register up to eight faces that should get priority in terms of autofocus and then specify the order of priority from the most important faces to the least important.

To register a face, point the camera at the person's face, make sure it's within the large square on the screen, and press the shutter release button. Do so for several faces. When you're taking a photo of a scene that contains more than one registered face, the camera will prioritize faces based on which were the first to be registered in the process you used.

Take advantage of the Order Exchanging option of this menu item so the faces you consider the most important are prioritized. When you access it, the camera displays the registered faces with a number on each; the lower the number the higher the priority. You can now change the priority in which the faces will be recognized, from 1 (say your youngest child) to 8 (perhaps your cousin twice removed). You can also use the Delete or the Delete All options to delete one or more faces from the registry, such as your ex and former in-laws.

- **Set Face Priority in AF (Camera Settings I-6).** Turn Face Priority on and off and specify whether frames should appear around faces detected.

- **Focus Mode (Camera Settings I-5).** Choose focus modes from AF-S, AF-C, DMF, and MF.

- **Priority Set AF-S/AF-C (Camera Settings I-5).** Select whether focus is *release priority* (take picture immediately, even if sharp focus not achieved) or *focus priority* (don't take picture until sharp focus locked in). You can also choose *balanced emphasis* as a compromise between the two. Separate entries for AF-S and AF-C.

- **Focus Area (Camera Settings I-5).** Select the number and location of autofocus points used, from Wide, Zone, Center, Flexible Spot, and Expanded Flexible Spot.

- **Focus Settings (Camera Settings I-5).** Adjust specific focus area with the front dial and multi-selector joystick and focus type of focus area with the control wheel.

- **Switch Vertical/Horizontal AF Area (Camera Settings 1-5).** Specify different AF areas for horizontal and two vertical camera orientations.

- **Center Lock-On AF (Camera Settings I-6).** When activated, automatically tracks focused subject when shooting stills and movies. Mutually exclusive with Lock-On AF.

- **AF Track Sensitivity (Stills) (Camera Settings I-6).** Select tracking response from 1 (locked on) to 5 (responsive).

- **AF System (Camera Settings I-6).** When using an A-mount lens and adapter, specify whether PDAF or CDAF is used.

- **AF with Shutter (Camera Settings I-6).** Choose On to start AF when the shutter is pressed halfway, or Off to decouple AF start from shutter release.

- **Pre-AF (Stills) (Camera Settings I-7).** Enables/disables AF initiation even before a button is pressed.

- **Eye-Start AF (Stills) (Camera Settings I-7).** When using a compatible A-mount lens and adapter, autofocus is initiated when you put your eye up to the viewfinder.

- **AF Area Registration (Stills) (Camera Settings I-7).** Allows setting a preassigned AF area location to a custom key.

- **AF Area Auto Clear (Camera Settings I-7).** Determines whether the autofocus area is displayed all the time, or only briefly before disappearing.

- **Display Continuous AF Area (Camera Settings I-7).** Enables/disables display of AF areas during continuous autofocus.

- **Phase Detect Area (Camera Settings I-8).** Displays the phase detection area when used with compatible lenses.

- **AF Micro Adjustment (Camera Settings I-8).** Fine-tune autofocus for specific A-mount lenses when used with EA-LA2 or EA-LA4 adapters.

- **AF Drive Speed (Movies) (Camera Settings II-2).** Choose between slow and accurate AF, or fast and slightly less accurate in video mode.

- **AF Track Sensitivity (Movie) (Camera Settings II-2).** Adjust how long the a7R III waits to refocus on intervening objects when shooting movies.

- **Focus Magnifier (Camera Settings I-13).** Enlarges image during manual focus.

- **MF Assist (Camera Settings I-13).** Turns manual focus magnifier on or off.

- **Focus Magnifier Time (Camera Settings I-13).** Length of time focus magnifier remains active.

- **Peaking Setting (Camera Settings I-13).** Turn peaking on or off, set the level (strength) of the effect, and the color of the outline.

9

Advanced Techniques

Now it's time to begin exploring some of the advanced techniques your a7R III has that enable you to get stunning shots that will have your family, friends, and colleagues asking you, "How did you *do* that?" These more advanced techniques include the amazing Pixel Shift feature, which deserves an entire book of their own, but there is plenty of room in this chapter to introduce you to some clever things you can do with your a7R III.

Exploring Ultra-Fast Exposures

Fast shutter speeds (such as 1/1,000th second) can stop action because they capture only a tiny slice of time: a high-jumper frozen in mid-air, perhaps. The Sony a7R III has a top shutter speed of 1/8,000th second for ambient light exposures. Electronic flash can also freeze motion by virtue of its extremely short duration—as brief as 1/50,000th second or less. When you're using flash, the short duration of the actual burst of light can freeze a moving subject; that can also give you an ultra-quick glimpse of a moving subject when the scene is illuminated only by flash.

The a7R III is fully capable of immobilizing all but the very fastest movement if you use a shutter speed of 1/8,000th second (without flash). The top speeds are generally overkill when it comes to stopping action; I can rarely find a situation where even 1/4,000th second is required to freeze high-speed motion. For example, the image shown in Figure 9.1 required a shutter speed of just 1/2,000th second to freeze the high jumper as she cleared the bar.

Virtually all sports action can be frozen at 1/2,000th second or a slower shutter speed, and for many sports a shutter speed of 1/500th of a second or even much slower is actually preferable—for example, to allow the wheels of a racing automobile or motorcycle, or the propeller on a classic aircraft, to blur realistically.

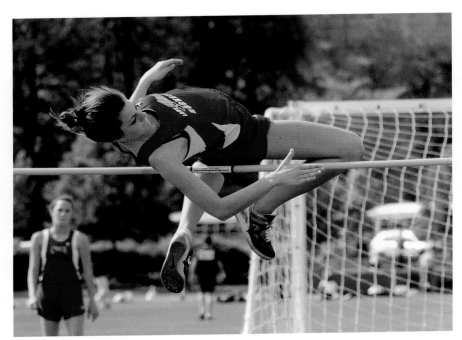

Figure 9.1
A shutter speed of 1/2,000th second will freeze most action.

There may be a few situations where a shutter speed faster than 1/4,000th second is required. If you wanted to use an aperture of f/1.8 at ISO 100 outdoors in bright sunlight, say to throw a background out of focus with the shallow depth-of-field available at f/1.8, a shutter speed of 1/4,000th second would more than do the job. You'd need a faster shutter speed only if you set a higher ISO, and you probably wouldn't do that if your goal were to use the widest aperture possible. Under *less* than full sunlight, I doubt you'd even need to use a shutter speed of 1/4,000th second in any situations you're likely to encounter.

Electronic flash works well for freezing the motion of a nearby subject when flash is the only source of illumination. Since the subject is illuminated for only a split second, you get the effect that would be provided by a very fast shutter speed and also the high level of light needed for an exposure. This feature can be useful for stopping the motion of a nearby subject.

Of course, as you'll see in Chapter 13, the tiny slices of time extracted by the millisecond duration of an electronic flash exact a penalty. To use flash, the a7R III employs a shutter speed no faster than 1/250th second, which is the fastest shutter speed—called sync speed—in conventional flash photography with your a7R III camera.

You can have a lot of fun exploring the kinds of pictures you can take using very brief exposure times, whether you decide to take advantage of the action-stopping shutter speeds (between 1/1,000th and 1/8,000th second) or the brief burst of light from flash that can freeze the motion of a nearby subject.

Here are a few ideas to get you started:

- **Take revealing images.** Fast shutter speeds can help you reveal the real subject behind the façade, by freezing constant motion to capture an enlightening moment in time. Legendary fashion/portrait photographer Philippe Halsman used leaping photos of famous people, such as the Duke and Duchess of Windsor, Richard Nixon, and Salvador Dali, to illuminate their real selves. Halsman said, "*When you ask a person to jump, his attention is mostly directed toward the act of jumping and the mask falls so that the real person appears.*" Try some high-speed portraits of people you know in motion to see how they appear when concentrating on something other than the portrait. (See Figure 9.2.)

Figure 9.2
Fast shutter speeds can freeze your subject at the top of a jump.

■ **Create unreal images.** High-speed photography can also produce photographs that show your subjects in ways that are quite unreal. A helicopter in mid-air with its rotors frozen or a moto-cross cyclist leaping over a ramp, but with all motion stopped so that the rider and machine look as if they were frozen in mid-air, makes for an unusual picture. (See the frozen rotors at top in Figure 9.3.) When we're accustomed to seeing subjects in motion, seeing them stopped in time can verge on the surreal.

■ **Capture unseen perspectives.** Some things are *never* seen in real life, except when viewed in a stop-action photograph. MIT professor Dr. Harold Edgerton's famous balloon burst photographs were only a starting point for the inventor of the electronic flash unit. Freeze a hummingbird in flight for a view of wings that never seem to stop. Or, capture the splashes as liquid falls into a bowl, as shown in Figure 9.4. No electronic flash was required for this image (and wouldn't have illuminated the water in the bowl as evenly). Instead, a clutch of high-intensity lamps bounced off a green card and an ISO setting of 1600 allowed the camera to capture this image at 1/2,000th second.

Figure 9.3
Freezing a helicopter's rotors with a fast shutter speed makes for an image that doesn't look natural (top); a little blur helps convey a feeling of motion (bottom).

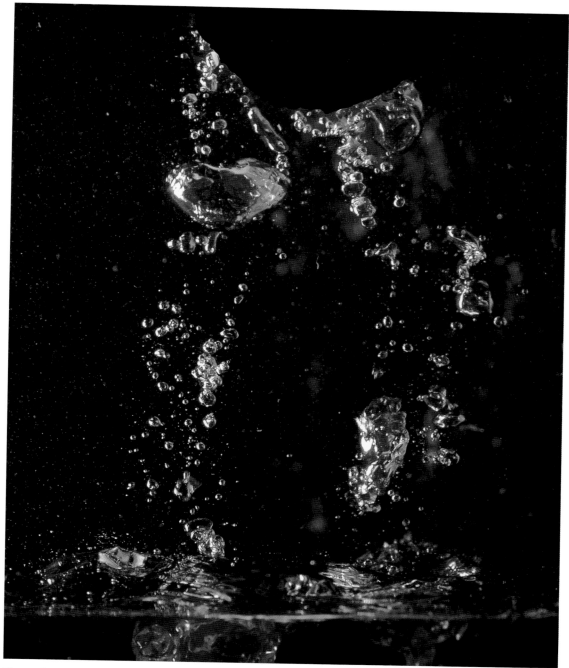

Figure 9.4 A large amount of artificial illumination and an ISO 1600 setting made it possible to capture this shot at 1/2,000th second without use of electronic flash.

Long Exposures

Longer exposures are a doorway into another world, showing us how even familiar scenes can look much different when photographed over periods measured in seconds. At night, long exposures produce streaks of light from moving, illuminated subjects like automobiles or amusement park rides, as you can see in Figure 9.5. Or, you can move the camera or zoom the lens to get interesting streaks from non-moving light sources, such as holiday lights. Extra-long exposures of seemingly pitch-dark subjects can reveal interesting views using light levels barely bright enough to see by. At any time of day, including daytime (in which case you'll often need the help of neutral-density filters to make the long exposure practical), long exposures can cause moving objects to vanish entirely, because they don't remain stationary long enough to register in a photograph.

Because the a7R III produces such good images at longer timed exposures (and at even longer bulb exposures), and there are so many creative things you can do with long-exposure techniques, you'll want to do some experimenting. Get yourself a tripod or another firm support and take some test shots with long exposure noise reduction both enabled and disabled in the Setup menu (to see whether you prefer low noise or high detail) and get started.

As I noted in Chapter 7, you can make exposures as long as 30 seconds when using P, A, or S modes. In Manual exposure mode, bulb exposures can be even longer (but not available if you're using any mode that produces multiple exposures within the same frame, such as Auto HDR). In bulb mode, hold down the shutter release for the duration of the exposure, or use a wired release with a locking button, such as the Sony RM-VPR1 ($50).

Figure 9.5

Long exposures can produce interesting streaks of light.

If you want to experiment with long exposures, here are some things to try:

- **Make people invisible.** One very cool thing about long exposures is that objects that move rapidly enough won't register at all in a photograph, whereas the subjects that remain stationary are portrayed in the normal way. That makes it easy to produce people-free landscape photos and architectural photos at night, or even in full daylight if you use one or more dark neutral-density filters to allow an exposure of at least a few seconds. At ISO 100 and f/16, for example, a pair of 8X (three-stop) neutral-density filters will allow you to make an exposure of nearly two seconds on a sunny day. Overcast days and/or even more neutral-density filtration would work even better if daylight people-vanishing is your goal. They'll have to be walking *very* briskly and across the field of view (rather than directly toward the camera) for this to work. At night, it's much easier to achieve this effect with the 20- to 30-second exposures that are possible in low light without any filter.

- **Create streaks.** If you aren't shooting for total invisibility, long exposures with the camera on a tripod can produce some interesting streaky effects. Even a single 8X ND filter will let you shoot at f/22 and 1/6th second in daylight. Indoors, you can achieve interesting streaks with slow shutter speeds, which is a technique I often use when photographing ballet dancers.

> **Tip**
>
> Neutral-density filters are gray (non-colored) filters that reduce the amount of light passing through the lens, without adding any color or effect of their own.

- **Produce light trails.** At night, car headlights, taillights, and other moving sources of illumination can generate interesting light trails. Your camera doesn't even need to be mounted on a tripod; hand-holding the camera for longer exposures adds movement and patterns to your trails. If you're shooting fireworks, a longer exposure—with the camera on a tripod—may allow you to combine several bursts into one picture.

- **Blur waterfalls, etc.** You'll find that waterfalls and other sources of moving liquid produce a special type of long-exposure blur, because the water merges into a fantasy-like veil that looks different at different exposure times, and with different waterfalls. Cascades with turbulent flow produce a rougher look at a given longer exposure than falls that flow smoothly. Although blurred waterfalls and rapids have become almost a cliché, there are still plenty of variations for a creative photographer to explore.

- **Show total darkness in new ways.** Even on the darkest, moonless nights, there is enough starlight or glow from distant illumination sources to see by, and, if you use a long exposure, there is enough light to take a picture, too. I was visiting a Great Lakes park hours after sunset but found that a several-second exposure revealed the skyline scene shown in Figure 9.6, even though in real life, there was barely enough light to make out the boats in the distance. Although the photo appears as if it were taken at twilight or sunset, in fact the shot was made at 10 p.m.

Figure 9.6 A long exposure transformed this night scene into a picture apparently taken at dusk.

Continuous Shooting

The a7R III's continuous shooting modes are indispensable for the sports photographer, and useful for anyone photographing an event in which, even if you have lightning-fast reflexes, a decisive moment may occur a fraction of a second after you've completed an exposure. The a7R III is capable of capturing images continuously at *up to* (and note that qualification) 10 frames per second, so you can shoot consecutive images non-stop until the camera's buffer fills. At an air show I covered earlier this year, I took more than 1,000 images in a couple hours. I was able to cram hundreds of Large/ Fine JPEGs on a single memory card. That's a lot of shooting. Given an average burst of about eight frames per sequence at the camera's highest frame (nobody really takes 15 to 20 shots or more of one pass, even with a slow-moving biplane as shown in Figure 9.7), I was able to capture more than 100 different sequences like the one shown before I needed to swap cards. For some types of action (such as football), even longer bursts come in handy, because running and passing plays often last 5 to 10 seconds; there's also a change in character as the action switches from the quarterback dropping back to pass or hand off the ball, then to the receiver or running back trying to gain as much yardage as possible. (See Figure 9.8.)

Figure 9.7
Air shows make a perfect subject for continuous bursts.

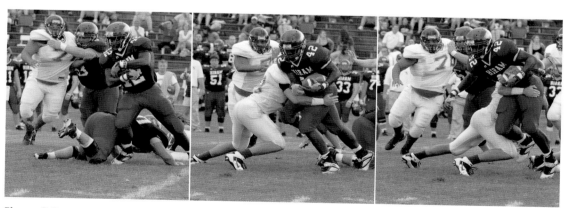

Figure 9.8 Continuous shooting allows you to capture an entire sequence of exciting moments as they unfold.

To use the a7R III's continuous advance mode, press the drive button (left directional button), access the Function menu, or go to the Drive Mode entry in the Camera Settings I-3 menu. Then navigate to the Cont. Shooting option. Press the left/right buttons to select Hi+ (10 fps), Hi (8–9 fps), Mid (7 fps), or Lo (3–4 fps). The camera takes advantage of the electronic front curtain shutter to produce the highest frame rates, and actually slows down in Hi, Mid, or Lo modes if you have turned it off.

If you set the AF mode (in the Function submenu) to AF-C (Continuous autofocus) and AEL w/Shutter in the Camera Settings I-10 menu to Off or Auto, then autofocus will be available in all continuous drive modes, but only as long as the subject is covered by the active focus detection point(s). This feature is useful when a moving subject is approaching the camera or moving away from it; the a7R III will continuously adjust to focus on the subject as the distance changes, so the entire set of photos should be sharply focused. When using Hi+, Hi, or Mid and an f/stop smaller than f/8 (f/11 and beyond), the a7R III focuses for the first image in a burst, then keeps that focus point for subsequent shots. Moreover, in Hi+ and Hi modes, the image is not displayed in real time (you see a previous shot); in Mid or Lo modes, you'll be looking at the actual image as it is captured.

Surprise! Your a7R III is fast enough to shoot continuously even when capturing RAW, although the shooting speed will be slower if you're grabbing uncompressed RAW images. In addition, at the Hi+ setting, the camera captures 12-bit RAW rather than full-range 14-bit RAW files to reduce the size of the files it must write to the memory card. However, the buffer is large enough to handle up to 76 images in a burst without pausing for both RAW, JPEG, and RAW & JPEG files. Its capacity drops to 28 images, though for uncompressed RAW/uncompressed RAW & JPEG.

The reason the cameras cannot let you shoot hundreds of photos in a single burst is that continuous images are first shuttled into the a7R III's internal memory buffer, then doled out to the memory card as quickly as the card can write the data. Technically, the a7R III takes the data received from the digital image processor and converts it to the output format you've selected—either JPEG or RAW—and deposits it in the buffer ready to store on the card.

The internal "smart" buffer can suck up photos much more quickly than the memory card and, indeed, some memory cards are significantly faster or slower than others. When the buffer begins to fill, the framing speed slows significantly; eventually the buffer fills and then you can't take any more continuous shots until the a7R III has dumped some of them to the card, making more room in the buffer.

Remember that if you need a reminder of how much space remains in your buffer, you can opt to display the Continuous shooting length indicator using the entry in the Camera Settings II-7 menu, as explained in Chapter 4. Continuous shooting is not available when DRO/Auto HDR is set to Auto HDR or Picture Effect is set to Soft Focus. Continuous shooting may also be disabled if your battery level is low.

Customizing White Balance

Back in the film days, both color transparency and color negative ("print") films were standardized, or balanced, for a particular "color" of light. Most were balanced for daylight but you could also buy "tungsten" balanced color negative and transparency film for shooting under incandescent lamps that produced light of an amber color. This type of film had a bluish color balance, intended to moderate the effect produced by light that was amber. Digital cameras like the Sony a7R III can be adjusted for specific white balance options suitable for particular types of illumination.

This is important because various light sources produce illumination of different "colors," although sometimes we are not aware of the difference. Indoor illumination tends to be somewhat amber when using lightbulbs that are not daylight balanced, while noonday light outdoors is close to white, and the light early and late in the day is somewhat red/yellow.

White balance is measured using a scale called color temperature. Color temperatures were assigned by heating a theoretical "black body radiator" (which doesn't reflect any light; all illumination comes from its radiance alone) and recording the spectrum of light it emitted at a given temperature in degrees Kelvin. So, daylight at noon has a color temperature in the 5,500- to 6,000-degree range. Indoor illumination is around 3,400 degrees. Hotter temperatures produce bluer images (think blue-white hot) while cooler temperatures produce redder images (think of a dull-red glowing ember). Because of human nature, though, bluer images are actually called "cool" (think wintry day) and redder images are called "warm" (think ruddy sunset), even though their color temperatures are reversed.

Take a photo indoors under warm illumination with a digital camera sensor balanced for cooler daylight and the image will appear much too red/yellow. An image exposed outdoors with the white balance set for incandescent (tungsten) illumination will seem much too blue. These color casts may be too strong to remove in an image editor from JPEG files. Of course, if you shoot RAW photos, you can later change the WB setting to the desired value in RAW converter software; this is a completely "non-destructive" process so full image quality will be maintained.

Mismatched white balance settings are easier to achieve accidentally than you might think, even for experienced photographers. I'd just arrived at a Charlie Musselwhite concert after shooting some photos indoors with electronic flash and had manually set WB for Flash. Then, as the concert began, I resumed shooting using the incandescent stage lighting—which looked white to the eye—and ended up with a few shots like Figure 9.9, left. Eventually, I caught the error during picture review and changed my white balance. Another time, I was shooting outdoors, but had the camera white balance still set for incandescent illumination. The excessively blue image is shown in Figure 9.9, right.

The Auto White Balance (AWB) setting, available from the White Balance entry in the Camera Settings I-5 menu, Function menu, or a key defined with that function, examines your scene and chooses an appropriate value based on its perception of the color of the illumination and even the colors in the scene. However, the process is not foolproof (with any camera). Under bright lighting

Figure 9.9 An image exposed indoors with the WB set for electronic flash will appear too reddish (left); using the incandescent setting outdoors makes an image too blue (right).

conditions, it may evaluate the colors in the image and still assume the light source is daylight and balance the picture accordingly, even though, in fact, you may be shooting under extremely bright incandescent illumination. In dimmer light, the camera's electronics may assume that the illumination is tungsten, and if there are lots of reddish colors present, set color balance for that type of lighting. With mercury vapor or sodium lamps, correct white balance may be virtually impossible to achieve with any of the so-called presets. In those cases, you should use flash instead, or Custom WB with JPEGs, or shoot in RAW format and make your corrections after importing the file into your image editor with a RAW converter.

The a7R III provides many WB presets, each intended for use in specific lighting conditions. You can choose from Daylight, Shade, Cloudy, Incandescent (often called Tungsten by photographers), four types of Fluorescent (Warm White, Cool White, Day White, and Daylight), and Flash. However, the a7R III also offers a method for setting a desired color temperature/filter as well as a custom WB feature.

The Daylight preset provides WB at 5,200K, while the Shade preset uses 7,000K to give you a warming effect that's useful in the bluish light of a deeply shaded area. The chief difference between direct sun and an area in shade, or even incandescent light sources, is nothing more than the proportions of red and blue light. The spectrum of colors used by the a7R III is continuous, but it is biased toward one end or the other, depending on the white balance setting you make.

10

Movie-Making Basics

As we've seen during our exploration of its features so far, the a7R III is superbly equipped for taking still photographs of very high quality in a wide variety of shooting environments. But this camera's superior level of performance is not limited to stills. It's highly capable in the movie-making arena as well. It can shoot Full HD (high-definition) and 4K (ultra-high-definition) clips. Sony has also provided overrides for controlling all important aspects of a video clip.

So, even though you may have bought your camera primarily for shooting stationary scenes, you acquired a device that's also great for recording high-quality video clips. Whether you're looking to record informal clips of the family on vacation, the latest viral video for YouTube, or a set of scenes that will be painstakingly crafted into a cinematic masterpiece using editing software, the a7R III will perform admirably.

This camera can shoot HD video at 1920 × 1080 resolution using Sony's AVCHD encoding, plus MP4 video, which allows both 1920 × 1080 full HD and 1280 × 7210 standard HD. It also can capture HD video in the newer XAVC S format. The a7R III adds the ability to capture superior 4K video *internally* using XAVC S 4K.

The camera also uses something called *Picture Profiles*, to tailor color, saturation, sharpness, and some video-centric attributes. You can visualize Picture Profiles as Creative Styles for video. This chapter will show you the fundamentals of shooting video; in the next chapter, you'll learn about some of your camera's more advanced features, including the XAVC S format in HD and 4K options.

This chapter and the next deal with conventional video; S&Q (slow- and quick-motion video) settings were explained in Chapter 4.

Some Fundamentals

Recording a video with the a7R III is extraordinarily easy to accomplish—just press the black button with the red dot located on the back of the camera to the immediate right of the viewfinder window. Sony has placed it there to minimize the chance that you'll start recording a movie accidentally. That's because video can be captured in *any* exposure mode; there's no need to activate a special Movie mode. After you press the button, the camera will confirm that it's recording with a red REC and numerals showing the elapsed time in the EVF and LCD monitor. Press the button again when you want to stop recording.

Before you start, though, there are some settings to prepare the camera to record the scene the way you want it to. I'll show you how to optimize your settings before you start shooting video, but here are some considerations to be aware of as you get started. Many of these points will be covered in more detail later in this chapter:

- **Use the right card.** Because movie capture, is, basically, full-time "continuous" shooting, you'll need to use a memory card with sufficient capacity and a fast enough write speed to handle the streams of video you'll be shooting. I recommend SDXC memory cards 64GB or larger. Keep in mind that Slot 1 is the faster of your two slots and supports speedy UHS-II memory cards.

  The camera can shoot a continuous movie of just under 30 minutes when shooting HD video (a limitation on cameras not classified as camcorders), or 20 minutes for MP4/MPEG4 (a limitation imposed by the maximum 4GB file size allowed by that format). If you reach either limit, you can stop recording and start shooting the next clip right away; this assumes there's enough space on the memory card and adequate battery power. Of course, you will miss about 30 seconds of the action. (Also see the later item about keeping the camera cool.)

- **Avoid extraneous noise.** Try not to make too much noise when changing camera controls or when using a conventional zoom lens's mechanical zooming ring (power zooms with a zoom lever on the lens are typically relatively quiet). And don't make comments that you will not want to hear on the audio track.

- **Minimize zooming.** While it's great to be able to use the zoom for filling the frame with a distant subject (especially the power zoom on lenses equipped with that feature), think twice before zooming. The sound made by a mechanical zoom ring rotating will be picked up and it will be audible when you play a movie. (As I noted, lenses with power zoom are virtually silent.) As well, remember that any more than the occasional minor zoom will be very distracting to friends who watch your videos. And while digital zoom will definitely degrade video quality, the effect is minimized when shooting video because your final video frame (in Full HD mode) will be just 1920 × 1080 pixels. Digital zoom *is* useful as a way of mimicking a power zoom, as, when activated in the Camera Settings II-5 Zoom Setting entry, you can "zoom" quietly and digitally by pressing the right button, and then pressing and holding again to zoom continuously. (You can't do this if you have a lens with a power zoom lever.)

■ **Use a fully charged battery.** A fresh battery will allow about one hour of filming at normal (non-winter) temperatures, but that can be shorter if there are many focus adjustments. Individual clips can be no longer than 29 minutes, however.

■ **Keep it cool.** Video quality can suffer terribly when the imaging sensor gets hot so keep the camera in a cool place. When shooting on hot days especially, the sensor can get hot more quickly than usual; when there's a risk of overheating, the camera will stop recording and it will shut down about five seconds later. A thermometer icon will appear on the screen as a warning. Give the sensor time to cool down before using the camera again. This limitation generally won't affect serious movie-makers, who tend to shoot a series of short scenes that are assembled into a finished movie with an editor. But if you plan to set up your camera and photograph your kid's school pageant non-stop for an hour, you're out of luck.

■ **Press the Movie button.** You don't have to hold it down. Press it again when you're done to stop recording. It's recessed so you will not press it inadvertently.

Preparing to Shoot Video

First, here's what I recommend you do to prepare for a *basic* recording session. More advanced detail settings will be addressed later:

■ **Choose your file format.** Go to the File Format entry in the Camera Settings II-1 menu (as discussed in Chapter 3) and select the file format for your movies. You can set it to AVCHD, XAVC S HD, or, with the a7R III, XAVC S 4K. File formats determine the transfer rate (roughly equivalent to JPEG compression), which, with resolution, determines the quality of your video. You'll learn more about these formats later.

■ **Choose record setting.** Also, in the Camera Settings II-1 menu, you'll find the Record Setting item, which allows you to choose the size, frame rate, and image quality for your movies. Tables 10.1 to 10.4 later in this chapter spell out your choices.

Which of the many options should you choose? It depends in part on your needs. If your plan is to primarily shoot videos that you'll show to friends and family on an HDTV set, choose AVCHD. For more professional productions, you'll want to select XAVC S HD or (with the a7R III) XAVC S K. I'll explain the differences later.

■ **Activate proxy recording (optional).** If you are shooting an XAVC S or AVCHD movie, you can elect to record a lower 9 Mb/sec. bit-rate (reduced quality) Standard HD (1280 × 720) movie simultaneously, giving you a video optimized for viewing on a smart device or website. Use the Proxy Recording entry in the Camera Settings II-1 menu. You'll definitely want to use a larger memory card when working with this option. When you review your images, the proxy video isn't displayed, viewable, or editable in the camera; the "main" movie will have a Px indicator overlaid on its icon to show you that the clip is paired with a proxy counterpart. Deleting or protecting the main clip deletes/protects the proxy at the same time.

- **Preview the movie's aspect ratio for stills.** There's an item in the Image Size menu for Aspect Ratio and it's at 3:2 by default, but you can change that to 16:9. *The setting in this item won't affect your video recording.* Setting the 16:9 option will merely cause the camera to display the preview of the scene when you are shooting stills, before you start movie recording, in the format that will be used for the video clip. This gives you a better feel for what will be included in the frame after you press the record button.

- **Turn on autofocus.** Make sure autofocus is turned on through the Focus Mode entry of the Camera Settings I menu. You also have the option of using manual focus, or even Direct Manual Focus, with focus peaking. I find that manual focus is fine for situations such as a stage play where the actors will usually be at roughly the same distance to your position during the entire performance, and for more professional productions where precise focus is a must, or when changing focus during a shot (*focus pulling*) is used creatively. In other cases, however, you'll probably want to rely on the camera's effective full-time continuous autofocus ability while recording a video clip.

- **Try Flexible Spot AF Area.** As in still image making, you can use the Flexible Spot AF Area (discussed in Chapter 8) while recording a video clip. This feature is most suitable for a static scene you'll record with the camera on a tripod, where an important small subject is off-center and will remain in the same location. By placing the AF Area exactly on that part of the scene, you'll be sure that the focus will remain on the most important part of the scene during the entire recording. (In truth, you could use manual focus for the same purpose.)

  If you decide to try this, compose the scene as desired before pressing the record button. Set the Focus Area to Flexible Spot in the Camera Settings I-5 menu. Brackets will appear on the screen, indicating the current location of the active focus detection point. Move the brackets with the directional buttons so they cover the primary subject and press the center button to confirm. You can now begin recording the video, confident that the focus will always be on your primary subject (assuming it does not move while you're recording).

- **Set useful functions.** Before you start recording, you can set a desired ISO, white balance, Creative Style, Picture Profiles (explained in the next chapter), a Picture Effect (for special effects), any of the three metering modes, and the level of exposure compensation. You can also set an override in the Creative Style for a specific level of sharpness, contrast, and saturation, if desired, or use a Picture Profile for more advanced parameters. The DRO and Auto HDR features will not be available, however. You'll recall that these functions are not available in fully automatic modes; if you set them while using another mode and then switch to a fully automatic mode for recording the video, the camera will revert back to the defaults.

- **Decide on a shooting mode.** You can choose an exposure mode (P, S, A, or M) for your movies, either using a menu entry or by rotating the mode dial.

  The P mode works well, allowing the camera to set the aperture/shutter speed and giving you access to the other features discussed above. Program shift (to other aperture/shutter speed combinations) can be used before you start recording, but it will not be available during actual recording.

You might prefer to use Aperture Priority (A) mode for full control over the specific aperture; in that case, you can preset a desired aperture and you can also change it anytime while recording. Be careful however, especially if you have set a specific ISO level. If you switch to a very small aperture while recording in low light, your movie clip may darken; this is particularly likely if you're using a low ISO level. And if you switch to a very wide aperture on a sunny day, especially if using a high ISO, your video will become too bright. Of course, you can see the change in brightness in the live view display before recording a movie and while you're recording.

Switch to S mode if you want control over the shutter speed; this is a more advanced technique in Movie mode. You can preset a shutter speed and you can change it while recording. Again, be careful as to your settings to avoid a very dark or overly bright video, especially if you have set a specific ISO level. The live view display before and during recording will help to guide you. I don't recommend using the Manual (M) mode initially but you might want to experiment with it later.

■ **Press the record button.** You don't have to hold it down. Press it to start recording and press it again when you're done. Shoot a short test clip and view it to make sure that the settings you made are producing the overall effect you want. If not, change some settings (White Balance or Creative Style or Exposure Compensation, for example) and try again.

Steps During Movie Making

Once you have set up the camera for your video session and pressed the Movie button, you have done most of the technical work that's required of you for basic movie clips. Now your task is to use your skills at composition, lighting, scene selection, and, perhaps, directing actors, to make a compelling video production.

■ **Zoom, autofocus, and autoexposure all work.** If you're new to the world of high-quality still cameras that also take video, you may just take it for granted that functions such as autofocus continue to work normally when you switch from stills to video. But until recently, most such cameras performed weakly in their video modes; they would lock their exposure and focus at the beginning of the scene, and you could not zoom while shooting the video. The a7R III has no such handicaps, and, in fact, it is especially capable in these areas.

Indeed, this camera allows you to choose any exposure mode, including Manual exposure, Auto ISO, shutter speed, and aperture. You can change settings while shooting, and lock exposure with the AEL button.

Autoexposure works very well, modifying the exposure as the scene brightness changes; the method used depends on the metering mode that you're using. You can zoom to your heart's content (though I recommend that you zoom sparingly). Best of all, AF-C autofocus works like a charm; the camera can track moving subjects and quickly snap them back into sharp focus with speedy continuous AF. Manual focus is also available, with focus peaking to help you zero in on a focus plane. Don't limit yourself based on the weaknesses of past cameras; the a7R III opens up new horizons of video freedom.

- **Exposure compensation works while filming.** I found this feature to be quite remarkable. Although the autoexposure system works very well (especially with Multi metering) to vary the aperture when the ambient lighting changes, you can certainly dial in exposure compensation when you need to do so or want to do so for a certain effect. You could even use this function as a limited kind of "fade to black" in the camera, though you probably won't be able to fade quite all the way to black.

  If the preview display (when Live View Display is set to Setting Effect On in the Setup menu) suggests that your movie will be dark (underexposed) and if it does not get brighter after you set plus compensation, there's another problem: the camera cannot provide a good exposure for the movie at the ISO that you have set (as discussed earlier). Switch to a higher ISO level until the brightness is as desired or switch to ISO Auto to enable the camera to set a higher ISO level to prevent the "underexposure."

- **Use AE Lock instead.** Occasionally, you may find that you start having an exposure problem during recording; this might happen when pointing the lens toward a light-tone area that causes the camera to begin underexposing. While plus compensation will allow you to increase brightness, it's preferable to use the defined AE Lock button (either the physical AEL button or one you specify using Custom Keys in the Setup menu) to maintain a pleasing exposure during the entire video clip.

  Why would you need this feature? Let's say you're filming entertainers against grass and foliage, but you're moving the camera and will soon be filming a second group against a white sky. As soon as you do so, the backlighting will cause the video to get darker. Don't let that happen. Before pointing the lens toward the backlit area, press AEL and keep it depressed. This will prevent the exposure from changing as you point the lens toward the backlit part of the scene. This is preferable to waiting until an underexposure problem starts and then setting plus exposure compensation that suddenly makes the video brighter.

- **Don't be a flash in the pan.** With HD video, there is a possibility of introducing artifacts or distortion if you pan too quickly. (This effect is called rolling shutter distortion or the "Jell-O effect.") That is, because of the way the lines of video are displayed in sequence, if the camera moves too quickly in a sideways motion, some of the lines may not show up on the screen quickly enough to catch up to the rest of the picture. As a result, objects in your video can become somewhat distorted or you may experience a jiggling effect and/or loss of detail. So, if at all possible, make your pans smooth and steady, and slow them down to a comfortable pace.

More About Frame Rates and Bit Rates

Both videos and stills are captured in much the same way, but the technology used for the sensor can cause problems that are most evident when shooting movies. To understand why, it's necessary to understand the difference between a *rolling shutter* and a *global shutter*, and how *interlacing* differs from *progressive scan*.

An image (still or video) captured by the sensor consists of rows and columns of pixels. With the a7R III, there are 5,304 different rows, each row consisting of 7,952 individual pixels. A "rolling" shutter captures each row one after the other, so that, effectively, the pixels in the top row are captured at a different moment in time than those in the bottom row. This gap is very brief, and typically isn't noticeable in still photographs. But with video this difference can manifest itself as anomalies such as wobble when the camera is moving or vibrating, skew (which is a diagonal bending of an image due to wobble), smear (produced when part of the image, such as an automobile tire, is rotating), and other defects.

A "global" shutter, on the other hand, captures the entire image in one instant, eliminating these problems. Although your a7R III *does* have a rolling shutter, the high speed of its sensor (aided by the improved on-sensor copper wiring of the 42M sensor) and BIONZ digital image processing chip minimizes the rolling shutter effects.

Frame Rates

That leads us to progressive scanning versus interlacing. With a rolling shutter, line-by-line scanning during capture and playback can be done in one of two ways. With *interlaced scanning*, odd-numbered lines (lines 1, 3, 5, 7, and so forth) are captured with one pass, and then the even-numbered lines (2, 4, 6, 8, and so forth) are grabbed. With the 1080/60i format, roughly 60 pairs of odd/even line scans, or 60 *fields* are captured each second. (The actual number is 59.94 fields per second.) Interlaced scanning was developed for and works best with analog display systems such as older television sets. It was originally created as a way to reduce the amount of bandwidth required to transmit television pictures over the air. Modern LCD, LED, and plasma-based HDTV displays must de-interlace a 1080i image to display it. (See Figure 10.1.)

Newer displays work better with a second method, called *progressive scanning* or *sequential scanning,* and progressive scan modes are the only choices when shooting XAVC S video. Instead of two interlaced fields, the entire image is scanned as consecutive lines (lines 1, 2, 3, 4, and so forth). This happens at a rate of 120, 60, 30, or 24 frames per second (not fields). (All these numbers apply to the NTSC television system used in the United States, Canada, Japan, and some other countries; other places use systems like PAL, where the nominal scanning figures are 100/50/25 rather than 120/60/30. The 24 fps rate applies to both NTSC or PAL.)

One problem with interlaced scanning appears when capturing video of moving subjects. Half of the image (one set of interlaced lines) will change to keep up with the movement of the subject while the other interlaced half retains the "old" image as it waits to be refreshed. Flicker or *interline twitter* results. That makes your progressive scan (p) options a better choice for action photography. Interlaced video frame rates are indicated with an (i) designation; for example, within the AVCHD choices, 60i 24M (FX) indicates interlaced video, while 60p 28M (PS) represents progressive scan video. (I'll explain the 24M/28M part in the next section.)

Figure 10.1
The inset shows how lines of the image alternate between odd and even in an interlaced video capture.

Computer-editing software like Final Cut Pro can handle either type, and convert between them (although AVCHD, XAVC S 4K, and XAVC S HD may not be compatible with the other software you own). The choice between 24 fps and 60 fps (NTSC), or 25 fps and 50 fps (PAL) is determined by what you plan to do with your video. The short explanation is that, for technical reasons I won't go into here, shooting at 24 fps (or 25 fps) gives your movie more of the so-called "cinematic" look that film would produce, excellent for showing fine detail. However, if your clip has moving subjects, or you pan the camera, 24 fps (or 25 fps) can produce a jerky effect called "judder." The 60 fps (or 50 fps) option produces a home-video look that some feel is less desirable, but which is smoother and less jittery when displayed on an electronic monitor. I suggest you try both and use the frame rate that best suits your tastes and video-editing software.

ABOUT 120/100p

You'll note that when shooting XAVC S HD, you can select 120p (at 100 Mbs transfer rates; NTSC only) or 120/100p (at 60 Mbs transfer rate; both NTSC and PAL). These high frame rates—amounting to 120 and 100 frames per second—produce video that can be converted to play back at conventional speeds, either 30/25 fps (four times slower than recorded) or 24 fps (five times slower than recorded; NTSC only). Specify the playback speed using the Movie/HFR entry of the Camera Settings menu, as explained in Chapter 3. The slow-motion video that results can be used for special effects, including clichés like two long-lost lovers running toward each other on a beach.

Bit Rates

Bit rates represent the speed of transfer from your camera to your memory card or external video recorder. The higher the bit rate, the more demands made on your media in storing that data quick enough to keep pace with the video capture. Higher average bit rates range from 6 Mbps (megabits per second) for 1280 × 720 (720p) MP4 movies, to as much as 28 Mbps maximum for AVCHD, 60p full-HD clips. When using XAVC formats, the demands are even higher: 50 Mbps with XAVC S HD and 60 to 100 Mbps with XAVC S 4K (with the a7R III only). Tables 10.1 to 10.4 show the frame rates, bit rates, and resolution of the various recording settings for video. Note that frame rates of 30/25, 60/50, and 120/100 represent NTSC/PAL systems, respectively.

Table 10.1 XAVC S 4K

Record Setting	Resolution	Bit Rate
30p/25p 100M	3840 × 2160	Approx. 100 Mbps
30p/25p 60M	3840 × 2160	Approx. 60 Mbps
24p 100M (NTSC only)	3840 × 2160	Approx. 100 Mbps
24p 60M (NTSC only)	3840 × 2160	Approx. 60 Mbps

Table 10.2 XAVC S HD

Record Setting	Resolution	Bit Rate
60p/50p 50M	1920 × 1080	Approx. 50 Mbps
30p/25p 50M	1920 × 1080	Approx. 50 Mbps
24p 50M (NTSC only)	1920 × 1080	Approx. 50 Mbps
24p 50M (NTSC only)	1280 × 720	Approx. 50 Mbps
120p/100p 50M	1280 × 720	Approx. 50 Mbps

Table 10.3 AVCHD

Record Setting	Resolution	Bit Rate
60i/50i 24M (FX)	1920 × 1080	Approx. 24 Mbps
60i/50i 17M (FH)	1920 × 1080	Approx. 17 Mbps
60p/50p 28M (PS)	1920 × 1080	Approx. 28 Mbps
24p/25p 24M (FX)	1920 × 1080	Approx. 24 Mbps
24p/25p 17M (FH)	1920 × 1080	Approx. 17 Mbps

Table 10.4 MP4

Record Setting	Resolution	Bit Rate
60p/50p 28M	1920 × 1080	Approx. 28 Mbps
30p/25p 16M	1920 × 1080	Approx. 16 Mbps
30p/25p 6M	1280 × 720	Approx. 6 Mbps

Choosing Metering/Exposure Modes

You can use Multi, Center, or Spot metering when shooting movies. I recommend sticking with Multi metering, unless you have a special reason for, say, Spot metering, as I explained in Chapter 7. Next, you'll want to select exposure mode, from among Program, Aperture Priority, Shutter Priority, or Manual. Rotate the mode dial to the Movie position and specify which of these modes is used for movies using the Movie/S&Q Motion entry or Exposure Mode entry in the Camera Settings II-1 menu page, as explained in Chapter 4. The mode you select will be used when the mode dial is in the Movie position. Of course, using the Movie position on the mode dial isn't mandatory, as you can use any exposure mode for movie recording. If the mode dial is in the P, A, S, or M positions, that setting will override the value you set in the Movie/HFR screen.

- **Program mode.** The P mode works well for movies, allowing the camera to set the aperture/shutter speed. Program shift (to other aperture/shutter speed combinations) can be used before you start recording, but it will not be available during actual recording.

- **Aperture Priority.** You might prefer to use Aperture Priority (A) mode for full control over the specific aperture; in that case, you can preset a desired aperture and you can also change it anytime while recording. However, remember that your shutter speed may change in Aperture Priority mode, and when shooting movies, it is often desirable to use a specific shutter speed (as I'll explain in an upcoming section).

- **Shutter Priority.** Switch to S mode if you want control over the shutter speed; this is a more advanced technique in Movie mode. You can preset a shutter speed and you can change it while recording. Again, be careful as to your settings to avoid a very dark or overly bright video, especially if you have set a specific ISO level. The live view display before and during recording will help to guide you. I recommend Shutter Priority highly, especially for beginners.

- **Manual Exposure.** Manual exposure may be best when you want to maintain tight control over shutter speed and aperture, say, to maintain exposure as lighting conditions change, or to keep the same depth-of-field in a scene under changing conditions.

As you work, you'll discover that the a7R III's Zebra feature in the Camera Setting II-6 (Display/Auto Review 1, as explained in Chapter 4) can be a marvelous aid in monitoring your exposure. If you are using Shutter Priority, as I recommended, you'll have the shutter speed fixed and, based on what you see in the viewfinder or LCD monitor and Zebra display feedback, adjust the aperture or

ISO sensitivity to get the exposure you want. As I explained in Chapter 4, you can adjust the Zebra feature's threshold setting, perhaps specifying 95% so that you're alerted only when the brightest highlights start to clip (making the stripes less distracting) or use 85% so you'll know when human skin starts to be overexposed. Zebra display may not work for you when using S-Log2/S-Log3 gamma settings (described later in this chapter), as those very low contrast renditions don't lend themselves to that kind of monitoring.

Should you need to adjust exposure from what the camera recommends, exposure compensation works quite well while filming. Although the autoexposure system does a good job (especially with Multi metering) to vary the aperture when the ambient lighting changes, you can certainly dial in exposure compensation when you need to do so or want to do so for a certain effect. You could even use this function as a limited kind of "fade to black" in the camera, though, as I mentioned earlier, you probably won't be able to fade quite all the way to black.

If the preview display (when Live View Display is set to Setting Effect On in the Camera Setting II-7 menu) suggests that your movie will be dark (underexposed) and if it does not get brighter after you set plus EV compensation, there's another problem: the camera cannot provide a good exposure for the movie at the ISO that you have set (as discussed earlier). Switch to a higher ISO level until the brightness is as desired or switch to ISO Auto to enable the camera to set a higher ISO level to prevent the "underexposure."

You can also "lock" exposure to keep the same exposure settings as lighting changes or you reframe your scene. Occasionally, you may find that you start having an exposure problem during recording; this might happen when pointing the lens toward a light-tone area that causes the camera to begin underexposing. While plus compensation will allow you to increase brightness, it's preferable to use the defined AE Lock button (either the physical AEL button or one you specify using Custom Key (Movie) options in the Camera Settings II menu) to maintain a pleasing exposure during the entire video clip.

Why would you need this feature? Let's say you're filming entertainers against grass and foliage, but you're moving the camera and will soon be filming a second group against a white sky. As soon as you do so, the backlighting will cause the video to get darker. Don't let that happen. Before pointing the lens toward the backlit area, press AEL and keep it depressed. This will prevent the exposure from changing as you point the lens toward the backlit part of the scene. This is preferable to waiting until an underexposure problem starts and then setting plus exposure compensation that suddenly makes the video brighter.

Stop That!

Both Manual Exposure and Shutter Priority modes allow you to explicitly choose a shutter speed. You might think that setting your camera to a faster shutter speed will help give you sharper video frames. But the choice of a shutter speed for movie making is a bit more complicated than that. As you might guess, in most cases it's best to leave the shutter speed at 1/30th or 1/60th second and allow the overall exposure to be adjusted by varying the aperture and/or ISO sensitivity.

Effectively, you're better off working in Shutter Priority mode, so that the aperture or ISO settings are your only way of adjusting the exposure. A "slow" 1/30th or 1/60th second shutter speed doesn't mean your movies will have the same amount of blur that a typical still photograph will have using those shutter speeds. We don't normally stare at a video frame for longer than 1/30th or 1/24th second, so while the shakiness of the *camera* can be disruptive (and often corrected by your camera's in-lens and in-body image stabilization), if there is a bit of blur in our *subjects* from movement, we tend not to notice. Each frame flashes by in the blink of an eye, so to speak, so a shutter speed of 1/30th or 1/60th second works a lot better in video than it does when shooting stills. Even shots with lots of movement, such as the frame shown in Figure 10.2, are often sufficiently sharp at 1/60th second.

Higher shutter speeds actually introduce problems of their own. If you shoot a video frame using a shutter speed of 1/250th second, the actual moment in time that's captured represents only about 12 percent of the 1/30th second of elapsed time in that frame. Yet, when played back, that frame occupies the full 1/30th of a second, with 88 percent of that time filled by stretching the original image to fill it. The result is often a choppy/jumpy image, and one that may appear to be *too* sharp.

The reason for that is more social imprinting than scientific: we've all grown up accustomed to seeing the look of Hollywood productions that, by convention, were shot using a shutter speed that's half the reciprocal of the frame rate (that is, 1/48th second for a 24 fps movie). Movie cameras use a rotary shutter (achieving that 1/48th second exposure by using a 180-degree shutter "angle"), but the effect on our visual expectations is the same. For the most "film-like" appearance, use 24 fps and 1/60th second shutter speed.

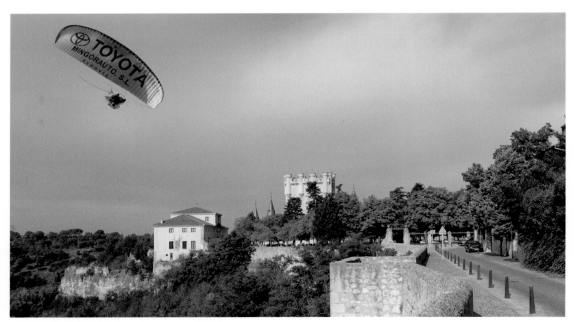

Figure 10.2 Movement adds interest to a video clip.

Faster shutter speeds do have some specialized uses for motion analysis, especially where individual frames are studied. The rest of the time, 1/30th or 1/60th of a second will suffice. If the reason you needed a higher shutter speed was to obtain the correct exposure, use a slower ISO setting, or a neutral-density filter to cut down on the amount of light passing through the lens. A good rule of thumb is to use 1/60th second or slower when shooting at 24 fps; 1/60th second or slower at 30 fps; and 1/125th second or slower at 60 fps.

In choosing between 30p and 60p, there are several considerations. The 30p frame rate allows you to use a reduced ISO setting for improved grain compared to 60p at a higher ISO value. That's an advantage under low light. However, as I mentioned earlier, at 60p you can safely use a higher shutter speed of 1/125th second, which can produce smoother video of moving subjects. Video editors can *transcode* 60p video to give you 30p video (with files suitable for uploading to websites) as well as the 60i video you might need for DVD/Blu-Ray productions.

Choosing an Autofocus Mode

As I said in Chapter 8, you'll generally want sharp focus in your image—somewhere—but exactly where and how focus is achieved can be an important part of your creative process. On the one hand, while shooting certain types of scenes—particularly action scenes—you'll want the camera to automatically retain focus on your main subjects and keep them tightly in focus. Other times, you'll want to use selective focus to emphasize a subject and de-emphasize the background, or "pull" focus to dramatically change the focus (so to speak) of the scene, say, refocusing to cause a blurry subject to suddenly come into sharp relief.

As with still photography, you have both manual focus and autofocus tools at your disposal, which allow you to specify *when* to focus and what to focus on. An important step before shooting is to ensure autofocus is turned on through the Focus Mode entry of the Camera Settings or Function menus. Only Continuous AF (AF-C) and Manual Focus (MF) can be used when shooting movies. Here are some points to consider.

- **AF-C or MF.** If the mode dial is in the Movie position, only AF-C and MF are available.

- **Presto change-o.** If the mode dial is *not* in the Movie position, and you have selected a focus mode other than AF-C or MF, when you begin shooting movies, the a7R III will automatically switch to AF-C.

- **Lock focus.** As video is captured, the a7R III's Continuous autofocus will refocus as you move the camera, or subjects in the frame change location. To lock focus, press the shutter release halfway, or use a key you've assigned that function. When you release the button, the camera will refocus. Ordinarily, it does an excellent job of not refocusing constantly, and changes focus only when the a7R III detects camera or subject movement.

■ **Manual focus.** If you prefer manual focus, you'll need to set it before commencing video capture. I find that manual focus is fine for situations such as a stage play where the actors will usually be at roughly the same distance to your position during the entire performance, and for more professional productions where precise focus is a must, or when changing focus during a shot (*focus pulling*) is used creatively. In other cases, however, you'll probably want to rely on the camera's effective full-time continuous autofocus ability while recording a video clip.

■ **Focus area modes.** You can use all focus area modes, as described in Chapter 8, except for Lock-On AF. Center Lock-On, however, can be used. Try Flexible Spot AF. As in still image making, you can use the Flexible Spot AF Area (also discussed in Chapter 8) while recording a video clip. This feature is most suitable for a static scene you'll record with the camera on a tripod, where an important small subject is off-center and will remain in the same location.

By placing the Focus Area exactly on that part of the scene, you'll be sure that the focus will remain on the most important part of the scene during the entire recording. (In truth, you could use manual focus for the same purpose.) If you decide to try this, compose the scene as desired before pressing the record button. Set the Focus Area to Flexible Spot in the Camera Settings I-5 menu. When you press the center button (or designated Focus Standard button), locator brackets will appear on the screen, indicating the current location of the active focus detection point. Move the bracket with the directional buttons so they cover the primary subject and press OK (the center button) to confirm. You can now begin recording the video, confident that the focus will always be on your primary subject (assuming it does not move while you're recording).

Tips for Movie Making

I'm going to close out this introductory movie chapter with a general discussion of movie-making concepts that you need to understand as you move toward more polished video production. In the chapter that follows, I'll explain some of the a7R III's features that allow you to produce more sophisticated movies. Here are some basic tips:

■ **Keep things stable and on the level.** Camera shake's enough of a problem with still photography, but it becomes even more of a nuisance when you're shooting video. While the a7R III's in-body five-axis stabilization and stabilizer found in lenses with the OSS designation can help minimize this, neither can work miracles. Placing your camera on a tripod will work much better than trying to hand-hold it while shooting. One bit of really good news is that compared to pro dSLRs, the a7R III can work very effectively on a lighter tripod, due to the camera's light weight. On windy days however, the extra mass of a heavy tripod is still valuable.

■ **Use a shooting script.** A shooting script is nothing more than a coordinated plan that covers both audio and video and provides order and structure for your video. A detailed script will cover what types of shots you're going after, what dialogue you're going to use, audio effects, transitions, and graphics.

■ **Plan with storyboards.** A storyboard is a series of panels providing visuals of what each scene should look like. While the ones produced by Hollywood are generally of very high quality, there's nothing that says drawing skills are important for this step. Stick figures work just fine if that's the best you can do. The storyboard just helps you visualize locations, placement of actors/actresses, props, and furniture, and also helps everyone involved get an idea of what you're trying to show. It also helps show how you want to frame or compose a shot. You can even shoot a series of still photos and transform them into a "storyboard" if you want, such as in Figure 10.3.

Today's audience is used to fast-paced, short-scene storytelling. In order to produce interesting video for such viewers, it's important to view video storytelling as a kind of shorthand code for the more leisurely efforts print media offers. Audio and video should always be advancing the story. While it's okay to let the camera linger from time to time, it should only be for a compelling reason and only briefly.

It only takes a second or two for an establishing shot to impart the necessary information. For example, many of the scenes for a video documenting a model being photographed in a rock 'n' roll music setting might be close-ups and talking heads, but an establishing shot showing the studio where the video was captured helps set the scene.

Figure 10.3 A storyboard is a series of simple sketches or photos to help visualize a segment of video.

- **Provide variety.** Provide variety too. Change camera angles and perspectives often and never leave a static scene on the screen for a long period of time. (You can record a static scene for a reasonably long period and then edit in other shots that cut away and back to the longer scene with close-ups that show each person talking.)

- **When editing, keep transitions basic!** I can't stress this one enough. Watch a television program or movie. The action "jumps" from one scene or person to the next. Fancy transitions that involve exotic "wipes," dissolves, or cross fades take too long for the average viewer and make your video ponderous.

Composition

In movie shooting, several factors restrict your composition, and impose requirements you just don't always have in still photography (although other rules of good composition do apply). Here are some of the key differences to keep in mind when composing movie frames:

- **Horizontal compositions only.** Some subjects, such as basketball players and tall buildings, just lend themselves to vertical compositions. But movies are generally shot and shown in horizontal format only. (Unless you're capturing a clip with your smartphone; I see many vertically oriented YouTube videos.) So, if you're shooting a conventional video and interviewing a local basketball star, you can end up with a worst-case situation like the one shown in Figure 10.4. If you want to show how tall your subject is, it's often impractical to move back far enough to show him full-length. You really can't capture a vertical composition. Tricks like getting down on the floor and shooting up at your subject can exaggerate the perspective but aren't a perfect solution.

- **Wasted space at the sides.** Moving in to frame the basketball player as outlined by the yellow box in Figure 10.4 means that you're still forced to leave a lot of empty space on either side. (Of course, you can fill that space with other people and/or interesting stuff, but that defeats your intent of concentrating on your main subject.) So, when faced with some types of subjects in a horizontal frame, you can be creative, or move in *really* tight. For example, if I was willing to give up the "height" aspect of my composition, I could have framed the shot as shown by the green box in the figure and wasted less of the image area at either side.

- **Seamless (or seamed) transitions.** Unless you're telling a picture story with a photo essay, still pictures often stand alone. But with movies, each of your compositions must relate to the shot that preceded it, and the one that follows. It can be jarring to jump from a long shot to a tight close-up unless the director—you—is very creative. Another common error is the "jump cut" in which successive shots vary only slightly in camera angle, making it appear that the main subject has "jumped" from one place to another. (Although everyone from French New Wave director Jean-Luc Goddard to Guy Ritchie—Madonna's ex—have used jump cuts effectively in their films.) The rule of thumb is to vary the camera angle by at least 30 degrees between shots to make it appear to be seamless. Unless you prefer that your images flaunt convention and appear to be "seamy."

Figure 10.4
Movie shooting requires you to fit all your subjects into a horizontally oriented frame.

■ **The time dimension.** Unlike still photography, with motion pictures there's a lot more emphasis on using a series of images to build on each other to tell a story. Static shots where the camera is mounted on a tripod and everything is shot from the same distance are a recipe for dull videos. Watch a television program sometime and notice how often camera shots change distances and directions. Viewers are used to this variety and have come to expect it. Professional video productions are often done with multiple cameras shooting from different angles and positions. But many professional productions are shot with just one camera, and with careful planning you can do just fine with your a7R III camera.

Here's a look at the different types of commonly used compositional tools:

■ **Establishing shot.** Much like it sounds, this type of composition, as shown at top left in Figure 10.5, establishes the scene and tells the viewer where the action is taking place. Let's say you're shooting a video of your offspring's move to college; the establishing shot could be a wide shot of the campus with a sign welcoming you to the school in the foreground. Another example would be for a child's birthday party; the establishing shot could be the front of the house decorated with birthday signs and streamers or a shot of the dining room table decked out with party favors and a candle-covered birthday cake. In this case, I wanted to show the studio where the video was shot.

■ **Medium shot.** This shot is composed from about waist to head room (some space above the subject's head). It's useful for providing variety from a series of close-ups and also makes for a useful first look at a speaker. (See Figure 10.5, top right.)

■ **Close-up.** The close-up, usually described as "from shirt pocket to head room," provides a good composition for someone talking directly to the camera. Although it's common to have your talking head centered in the shot, that's not a requirement. In the middle left image in Figure 10.5, the subject was offset to the right. This would allow other images, especially graphics or titles, to be superimposed in the frame in a "real" (professional) production. But the compositional technique can be used with a7R III videos, too, even if special effects are not going to be added.

Figure 10.5 Establishing shot (upper left); Medium shot (upper right); Close-up (middle left); Extreme close-up (middle right); Two shot (lower left); Over-the-shoulder shot (lower right).

- **Extreme close-up.** When I went through broadcast training, this shot was described as the "big talking face" shot and we were actively discouraged from employing it. Styles and tastes change over the years and now the big talking face is much more commonly used (maybe people are better looking these days?) and so this view may be appropriate. Just remember, the a7R III is capable of shooting in high-definition video and you may be playing the video on a high-def TV; be careful that you use this composition on a face that can stand up to high definition. (See middle right, Figure 10.5.)

- **"Two" shot.** A two shot shows a pair of subjects in one frame. They can be side by side or one subject in the foreground and one in the background. This does not have to be a head-to-ground composition. Subjects can be standing or seated. A "three shot" is the same principle except that three people are in the frame. (See Figure 10.5, lower left.)

- **Over-the-shoulder shot.** Long a composition of interview programs, the "over-the-shoulder shot" uses the rear of one person's head and shoulder to serve as a frame for the other person. This puts the viewer's perspective as that of the person facing away from the camera. (See Figure 10.5, lower right.)

Lighting for Video

Much like in still photography, how you handle light pretty much can make or break your videography. Lighting for video can be more complicated than lighting for still photography, since both subject and camera movement are often part of the process.

Lighting for video presents several concerns. First off, you want enough illumination to create a useable video. Beyond that, you want to use light to help tell your story or increase drama. Let's take a better look at both.

Illumination

You can significantly improve the quality of your video by increasing the light falling in the scene. This is true indoors or out, by the way. While it may seem like sunlight is more than enough, it depends on how much contrast you're dealing with. If your subject is in shadow (which can help him from squinting) or wearing a ball cap, a video light can help make him look a lot better.

Lighting choices for amateur videographers are a lot better these days than they were a decade or two ago. An inexpensive incandescent video light, which will easily fit in a camera bag, can be found for $15 or $20. You can even get a good-quality LED video light for less than $100. Work lights sold at many home improvement stores can also serve as video lights since you can set the camera's white balance to correct for any color casts. You'll need to mount these lights on a tripod or other support, or, perhaps, to a bracket that fastens to the tripod socket on the bottom of the camera.

Much of the challenge depends upon whether you're just trying to add some fill light on your subject versus trying to boost the light on an entire scene. A small video light will do just fine for the former. It won't handle the latter. Fortunately, the versatility of the a7R III comes in quite handy here. Since the camera shoots video in Auto ISO mode, it can compensate for lower lighting levels and still produce a decent image. For best results though, better lighting is necessary.

Creative Lighting

While ramping up the light intensity will produce better technical quality in your video, it won't necessarily improve the artistic quality of it. Whether we're outdoors or indoors, we're used to seeing light come from above. Videographers need to consider how they position their lights to provide even illumination while up high enough to angle shadows down low and out of sight of the camera.

When considering lighting for video, there are several factors. One is the quality of the light. It can either be hard (direct) light or soft (diffused) light. Hard light is good for showing detail, but it can also be very harsh and unforgiving. "Softening" the light, but diffusing it somehow, can reduce the intensity of the light but make for a kinder, gentler light as well.

While mixing light sources isn't always a good idea, one approach is to combine window light with supplemental lighting. Position your subject with the window to one side and bring in either a supplemental light or a reflector to the other side for reasonably even lighting.

Lighting Styles

Some lighting styles are more heavily used than others. Some forms are used for special effects, while others are designed to be invisible. At its most basic, lighting just illuminates the scene, but when used properly it can also create drama. Let's look at some types of lighting styles:

- **Three-point lighting.** This is a basic lighting setup for one person. A main light illuminates the strong side of a person's face, while a fill light lights up the other side. A third light is then positioned above and behind the subject to light the back of the head and shoulders. (See Figure 10.6, left.)

- **Flat lighting.** Use this type of lighting to provide illumination and nothing more. It calls for a variety of lights and diffusers set to raise the light level in a space enough for good video reproduction, but not to create a particular mood or emphasize a particular scene or individual. With flat lighting, you're trying to create even lighting levels throughout the video space and minimize any shadows. Generally, the lights are placed up high and angled downward (or possibly pointed straight up to bounce off of a white ceiling). (See Figure 10.6, right.)

- **"Ghoul lighting."** This is the style of lighting used for old horror movies. The idea is to position the light down low, pointed upward. It's such an unnatural style of lighting that it makes its targets seem weird and ghoulish.

Figure 10.6 With three-point lighting (left) and flat lighting (right).

■ **Outdoor lighting.** While shooting outdoors may seem easier because the sun provides more light, it also presents its own problems. As a general rule of thumb, keep the sun behind you when you're shooting video outdoors, except when shooting faces (anything from a medium shot and closer) since the viewer won't want to see a squinting subject. When shooting another human this way, put the sun behind her and use a video light to balance light levels between the foreground and background. If the sun is simply too bright, position the subject in the shade and use the video light for your main illumination. Using reflectors (white board panels or aluminum foil-covered cardboard panels are cheap options) can also help balance light effectively.

Audio

When it comes to making a successful video, audio quality is one of those things that separates the professionals from the amateurs. We're used to watching top-quality productions on television and in the movies, yet the average person has no idea how much effort goes in to producing what seems to be "natural" sound. Much of the sound you hear in such productions is actually recorded on carefully controlled sound stages and "sweetened" with a variety of sound effects and other recordings of "natural" sound.

Your a7R III has a pair of stereo microphones on its top surface, able to capture Dolby Digital Audio. You can plug an external microphone into the mic jack on the left side of the camera, or work with a microphone designed specifically for Sony cameras, such as the (roughly $130) Sony ECM-XYST1M mic. If you stick with the built-in microphones, you must be extra careful to optimize the sound captured by those fixed sound-grabbers. You will find an Audio Recording entry in the Camera Settings II-2 menu (it just turns sound on or off), along with an Audio Recording Level and Audio Level display entry. In the Camera Settings II-3 menu, you'll find an Audio Out Timing entry (to compensate for a delay when viewing live video through the a7R III's HDMI port), and a Wind Noise Reduction on/off entry. The latter is a low-cut filter feature that can further reduce wind noise; however, this processing feature also affects other sounds, making a wind screen on the microphone itself far more useful. Your camera options were explained in Chapter 4.

Tips for Better Audio

Since recording high-quality audio is such a challenge, it's a good idea to do everything possible to maximize recording quality:

- **Turn off any sound makers you can.** Little things like fans and air handling units aren't obvious to the human ear but will be picked up by the microphone. Turn off any machinery or devices that you can plus make sure cell phones are set to silent mode. Also, do what you can to minimize sounds such as wind, radio, television, or people talking in the background.

- **Make sure to record some "natural" sound.** If you're shooting video at an event of some kind, make sure you get some background sound that you can add to your audio as desired in postproduction.

- **Consider recording audio separately.** Lip-syncing is probably beyond most of the people you're going to be shooting, but there's nothing that says you can't record narration separately and add it later. It's relatively easy if you learn how to use simple software video-editing programs like iMovie (for the Macintosh) or Windows Movie Maker (for Windows PCs). Any time the speaker is off-camera, you can work with separately recorded narration rather than recording the speaker on-camera. This can produce much cleaner sound.

Lens Craft

I'll cover the use of lenses with the a7R III in more detail in Chapter 12, but a discussion of lens selection when shooting movies may be useful at this point. In the video world, not all lenses are created equal. The two most important considerations are depth-of-field, or the beneficial lack thereof, and zooming. I'll address each of these separately.

Depth-of-Field and Video

Have you wondered why professional videographers have gone nuts over still cameras that can also shoot video? The producers of *Saturday Night Live* could afford to have Alex Buono, their director of photography, use the niftiest, most-expensive high-resolution video cameras to shoot the opening sequences of the program. Instead, Buono opted for a pair of digital SLR cameras. One thing that makes digital still cameras so attractive for video is that they have relatively large sensors. That provides two benefits compared to cameras with a smaller sensor. In addition to improved low-light performance, the large chip allows for unusually shallow depth-of-field (a limited range of acceptable sharpness) for blurring the background; this effect is difficult or impossible to match with most professional video cameras since they use smaller sensors.

As you'll learn in Chapter 12, a larger sensor calls for the use of longer focal lengths to produce the same field of view, so, in effect, a larger sensor allows for making images with reduced depth-of-field. And *that's* what makes cameras like the a7R III attractive from a creative standpoint. Shallow depth-of-field makes it easier to blur a cluttered background to keep the viewers' eyes riveted on the primary subject. Your camera, with its larger sensor, has a distinct advantage over consumer camcorders in this regard, and even does a much better job than professional video cameras.

Zooming and Video

When shooting still photos, a zoom is a zoom is a zoom. The key considerations for a zoom lens used only for still photography are the maximum aperture available at each focal length ("How *fast* is this lens?"), the zoom range ("How far can I zoom in or out?"), and its sharpness at any given f/stop ("Do I lose sharpness when I shoot wide open?").

When recording video, the priorities may change, and there are two additional parameters to consider. The first two I listed, lens speed and zoom range, have roughly the same importance in both still and video photography. Zoom range gains a bit of importance in videography, because you can always/usually move closer to shoot a still photograph, but when you're zooming during a shot most of us don't have that option (or the funds to buy/rent a dolly to smoothly move the camera during capture). But, oddly enough, overall sharpness may have slightly less importance under certain conditions when shooting video. That's because the image changes in some way many times per second (30/60 times per second), so any given frame doesn't hang around long enough for our eyes to pick out every single detail. You want a sharp image, of course, but your standards don't need to be quite as high when shooting video.

- **Zoom lens maximum aperture.** The "speed" of the lens matters in several ways. A zoom with a relatively wide maximum aperture (small f/number) lets you shoot in lower light levels with fewer exposure problems. A wide aperture like f/1.8 also enables you to minimize depth-of-field for selective focus. Keep in mind that with most zooms, the maximum aperture gets smaller as you zoom to longer focal lengths. A variable-aperture f/3.5 to 5.6 lens like the power zoom kit lens, offers a fairly wide f/3.5 maximum aperture at its shortest focal length but only f/5.6 worth of light capturing ability at the long end. Zooms with a wide and constant (not variable) maximum aperture such as f/2.8 are available, but they are larger, heavier, and more expensive.

- **Power zoom.** An ideal movie zoom should have a power zoom feature, and that's available with Sony lenses with the PZ designation. PZ lenses offer smooth, silent zooming that's ideal for video shooting. Mechanical zooming with other lenses during capture can produce jerky images, even with vibration reduction turned on. As I mentioned earlier, you can mimic power zoom using the a7R III's digital zoom feature.

- **Zoom range.** Use of zoom during actual capture should not be an everyday thing, unless you're shooting a kung-fu movie. However, there are effective uses for a zoom shot, particularly if it's a "long" one from wide angle to telephoto. The Sony 18-200mm zoom, which has a relatively quiet autofocus motor and built-in stabilizer, can be used in this way, with mechanical zooming, of course. Most of the time, you'll use the zoom range to adjust the perspective of the camera *between* shots, and a longer zoom range can mean less trotting back and forth to adjust the field of view. Zoom range also comes into play when you're working with selective focus (longer focal lengths produce shallower depth-of-field) or want to expand or compress the apparent distance between foreground and background subjects. A longer range gives you more flexibility.

- **Linearity.** Interchangeable lenses may have some drawbacks, as many photographers who have been using the video features of their digital SLRs have discovered. That's because lenses with mechanical zooming are rarely linear unless they were specifically designed for shooting movies. Rotating the zoom ring manually at a constant speed doesn't always produce a smooth zoom. There may be "jumps" as the elements of the lens shift around during the zoom. Keep that in mind if you plan to zoom during a shot and are using a non-linear lens. In practice, those include virtually all the lenses at your disposal, aside from power zoom lenses, a special E-mount cine lens, or a cine lens in an entirely different mount that you can use with your a7R III with an optional third-party adapter.

11

Advanced Video Features

As I've noted several times in this book, the a7R III boasts professional-level video features not found in most consumer- or even some pro-oriented digital still cameras. Many of those looking for the best Sony camera for video may prefer a dedicated camcorder, like the Sony VG30 Handycam (about $2,700), which uses E-mount lenses, or the 4K-capable Sony AX1 Professional Handycam ($4,500), which has a fixed 20X zoom lens. Even so, the a7R III is no slacker when it comes to capturing clips that can be assembled into polished video productions.

This chapter will introduce you to some of the most important concepts you'll need to learn as you continue your educational journey toward professional cinematography. Some of this will seem a little technical to those who are just learning about video, so if you're not going to be venturing into serious movie making soon, you might want to skim through this chapter simply to gain some background. As I mentioned when I talked about the a7R III's backside illuminated sensor, I don't normally venture this deeply into tech territory in my books, but the a7R III isn't an ordinary camera!

More on Sensors and Crop Factors

In Chapter 10, I described some of the reasons why the large sensor size of a full-frame still camera provides video shooters with some selective focus advantages when compared to the much smaller sensor found on many professional video cameras in the past. I'll be explaining the concept of the *crop factor* in detail in Chapter 12. Both aspects are important in the video world, but with a few variations caused by the differences in how video is captured and used.

Sensor Size

Sensor size is important because smaller sensors use lenses with shorter focal lengths to fill their frames, and the shorter the focal length, the larger the depth-of-field. That's why point-and-shoot cameras (or smartphones), with their minuscule sensors can produce acceptably sharp images for subjects located a few inches from the lens out to infinity. Conversely, because a normal lens on an APS-C camera is in the 38mm range, and on a full-frame camera is roughly 55mm, a full-frame camera like the a7R III has less depth-of-field for the same field of view.

Selective focus is a definite creative plus for videographers. We've all seen shots in which focus initially emphasizes some foreground object that's sharply rendered, and then the camera operator pulls focus out to a more distant subject, which suddenly appears in great detail. Larger sensors make such techniques easier, which is why current video cameras are often segregated into *small sensor* and *large sensor* categories. The Sony VG30 Handycam I mentioned earlier has a large APS-C sensor, measuring 23.5mm × 15.6mm, while the Sony AX1 Professional Handycam has a smaller $1/2.3$-inch sensor. (Video cameras dating back to the dawn of television have used the diameter of the video tube as a measurement.)

Figure 11.1 shows the relative size of the 4K and/or full HD capture area of some typical sensor sizes, starting with the a7R III's full-frame sensors at upper left, the "small" sensor of typical pro cameras and the $1/2.3$-inch sensor of Sony's least expensive pro camera at right, and an APS-C sensor and the RED Raven "large" sensor shown at the bottom. Note that the 4K/Full HD Area region shown in the figure applies *only* when the a7R III is *not* set to APS-C/Super 35 mode. Your camera is capable of shooting 4K video using both full-frame *and* cropped sensor modes (the latter producing a 1.5X field of view crop, just as in still photography.) I'll explain this difference next.

Figure 11.1

Relative video capture areas for example sensor sizes.

Crop Factor

The *crop factor* is important because with any given lens, the field of view will vary depending on how much of that lens's coverage area is used to capture video. (If you're unfamiliar with crop factors, skip ahead to Chapter 12 and read about them.) Still photos can be shot in both vertical or horizontal orientations, and most often using the 3:2 aspect ratio used outside the Micro Four Thirds (4:3) world. So, the crop factor for stills is calculated by comparing the diagonal measurement of the frame with the diagonal of the traditional 35mm frame.

For video, clips are normally captured with the camera in a horizontal orientation (at least, outside the realm of the smartphone), and the proportions or aspect ratio of the video frame can vary, with 16:9 being the standard for standard HD, full HD, and 4K (Ultra HD) video (and beyond).

The 16:9 proportions work out to roughly 1.78:1, which is close enough to the 1.85:1 widescreen cinema aspect ratio that it's easy to show movies captured in either aspect ratio on displays compatible with either. Given the 16:9 standard, it's common to represent the resolution of a video image by its horizontal measurement and scanning method: that is, 720p, 1080p, and 4K (actually 3840 pixels with your Sony a7R III camera; 4096 pixels with some other 4K devices) for progressive scan (p) video.

Your full-frame sensor provides a 1X crop factor for video when shooting Standard HD (720p), Full HD (1080p), or 4K (3840p). Sensors with smaller areas produce various crop factors, based, not on the sensor's diagonal measurement, but the relative *width* of the sensor area, compared to the full frame. Super 35 is a popular format for video and is available with your a7R III. By comparing the widths of the sensor area, we can arrive at a crop factor of roughly 1.5X when shooting in APS-C/Super 35mm mode with the a7R III. (See Figure 11.2.)

Figure 11.2
Full-frame and Super 35/APS-C crops of the Sony sensor.

35mm Full-Frame 4K/Full HD

Super 35mm 4K/Full HD

There are subtle differences between shooting video in full frame versus Super 35/APS-C modes. Both capture more pixels than needed, but process them differently, using pixel binning and over-sampling, respectively. These two processes are *different,* regardless of what you may have heard, even though they are often incorrectly used interchangeably:

- **Full-frame mode.** Video shot in full-frame mode grabs pixels across the full width of the sensor, combining them using a process called *pixel binning,* which takes clumps of red, green, and blue pixels and merges them with others of the same color to create a larger "pixel" at a reduced resolution, resulting in faster capture with reduced noise. The remaining pixels are then *demosaiced,* which interprets the colors of adjacent pixels to produce a full color image even though each physical pixel actually is sensitive to only one of the three primary colors.

- **Super 35/APS-C mode.** In this mode, the a7R III captures pixels within the smaller APS-C-sized area of the sensor, which results in the 1.5X field-of-view crop. However, it *oversamples,* grabbing more pixels than required for the final video frame. That large number of pixels is demosaiced *first,* and *then* downsized to the required size. Because oversampling happens *after* the RGB pixels have been analyzed and demosaiced, the process allows for better capture of details for a sharper final image.

In practice, the image quality difference is not great, but still can be important when capturing ultra-high-definition 4K video. You'll probably want to shoot in full-frame mode to avoid the crop factor under most circumstances, and switch to Super 35/APS-C mode when you actually need the 1.5X field-of-view crop or must have the sharpest possible image.

But should you be shooting full high-definition movies, or ultra-high-definition (4K) video? If your memory card (which should be a 64GB or larger SDXC card) or external recorder like the Atomos Shogun, can handle the data rates, 4K is alluring, even if your movies will never be viewed in anything other than 1080p format. All that extra detail is hard to resist.

Video gurus who have studied the Sony cameras have concluded that the a7R III's Super 35 4K video provides the most detailed movies with the best dynamic range and noise characteristics. As I described earlier, each pixel within the Super 35 image area is captured, producing more information than is required for even a 4K video frame, and then downscaled. Paradoxically, this oversampling means that Super 35 4K has better detail than 4K video produced from the a7R III's full-frame 42 MP sensor.

Conversely, when using 1080p instead of 4K, the full-frame video typically has more detail than 1080p shot the using Super 35/APS-C setting. If full HD shooting is your intent, you're better off reserving Super 35/APS-C format for those times when you want to take advantage of the 1.5X crop factor to increase the reach/magnification of your lenses, say, for wildlife photography or sports. In all cases, though, 4K video in either full-frame or Super 35/APS-C mode is superior to what you get using 1080p alone. Your video will still be better if shot in 4K and then downscaled to 1080p. The choice is yours.

Other Important Parameters

But wait, as they say, there's more! The last sections of this chapter will explain some of the other technical details of shooting video, providing enough detail, I hope, to get you reading more complex tomes that cover this information in depth.

Frame Guides

Frame guides are a useful way of visualizing the area that will be captured within a larger visible display. In ancient times, interchangeable-lens rangefinder film cameras that used an optical viewfinder would have bright frame outlines appear, often automatically when a particular lens was mounted on the camera, and sometimes through the use of an attachment that fit over the built-in viewfinder. In the digital age, frame guides have been popular with digital cameras that use an optical viewfinder, providing a masked off display to preview the actual image area that will be captured in crop or video modes. Cameras with electronic displays, like the a7R III, don't necessarily need frame guides, because the capture area can be enlarged and masked off electronically to show only the actual image area.

Even so, frame guides are a popular tool for videographers, because they allow viewing the area outside the actual frame that will be captured (the "look-around area") so you can monitor moving subjects before they enter the frame. In professional productions, it's useful to look at the region outside the captured frame to detect when boom microphones, careless crew members, or other objects threaten to intrude on the frame.

The a7R III cameras offer a variety of frame guides that can be turned on or off in the Camera Settings II menu, including grid lines, aspect ratios, frame center markings, and "safety" areas. These markers appear *only* on the EVF or LCD monitor, and not in the captured video itself (see Figure 11.3 for example placement).

Figure 11.3
Video guide markers.

Center   Safety Zone   Guide Frame

4:3 Marker   13:9 Marker

Here are your options:

- **Marker Display.** This Camera Settings II-3 menu entry works in conjunction with the Marker Settings option (described next), and simply turns settings on or off.

- **Marker Settings.** This menu entry allows you to specify Center, Aspect Ratio, Safety Zone, or Guide Frame. Each can be specified individually, and turned on or off independently, so you can display any, all, or none.

  - **Center.** This crosshair can be used to determine whether your subject is placed in the exact center of the screen.

  - **Aspect Ratio.** Use these guides to frame your image so the important subject matter is contained within a desired aspect ratio, or to frame the image for later cropping to that aspect ratio. You can select among 4:3, 13:9, 14:9, 15:9, 1.66:1, 1.85:1, or 2.35:1. These conform to various movie formats in common use. (*Star Wars*, for example, was filmed in CinemaScope, with a 2.35:1 aspect ratio.)

  - **Safety Zone.** It's common to shoot movies knowing in advance that they will be cropped down eventually for display in a slightly different format. The director simply makes sure that the important parts of the frame are included in the "safety zone" that will never be cropped out. For example, you wouldn't want to put two characters who are talking to each other at opposite ends of the entire frame but would instead locate them in the safety zone so both would be visible. Your camera's safety zone display can be set for 80 percent or 90 percent of the frame to represent the area that will always be shown when the movie is viewed on a standard HDTV.

  - **Guide Frame.** This grid is used to help you determine whether horizontal and vertical lines are skewed and can also be used as a Rule of Thirds guide for composition.

Time Codes and User Bits

The Time Code (TC) and User Bit (UB) settings are information that can be embedded and used to sync clips and sound when editing movies. Advanced video shooters find SMPTE- (Society of Motion Picture and Television Engineers) compatible time codes embedded in the video files to be an invaluable reference during editing. To oversimplify a bit, the time system provides precise *hour:minute:second:frame* markers that allow identifying and synchronizing frames and audio. The time code system includes a provision for "dropping" frames to ensure that the fractional frame rate of captured video (remember that a 24 fps setting actually yields 23.976 frames per second while 30 fps capture gives you 29.97 actual "frames" per second) can be matched up with actual time spans.

Using time codes and user bits is a college-level film school class on its own, but I'm going to provide a quick overview to get your started. If you're at the stage where you're using time codes, you don't need this primer, anyway. However, the a7R III's TC/UB Settings entry, which Sony has hidden away in the Setup 3 menu, includes the following options:

- **TC Preset.** Sets the time code. If you'll be shooting 60i/50i, you can choose time codes from 00:00:00:00 (hours, minutes, seconds, frame) to 23:59:59:29 or 23:59:59:24, respectively. With 24p, you can set multiples of four from 0 to 23 frames. If you own the RMT-VP1K remote commander, the time code can be reset to zero using a button on the controller.

- **UB Preset.** Sets the user bit, which is a marker you can insert in your video, say to designate a scene or take. There are four digits in each user bit (for example, 01:02:03:04), and the digits are each hexadecimal in nature, so you could create a code like C0 FF EE if you were feeling facetious.

- **TC Format.** Sets the recording method for the time code. You can choose from DF (drop-frame) or NDF (non-drop-frame) formats. Drop frames are a way of compensating for the discrepancy between the nominal number of frames per second and the actual number (for example, 30 fps yields 29.97 actual frames per second, and 60 fps gives you 59.95 frames per second). In drop-frame format, the camera will skip some time code numbers at intervals to eliminate the discrepancy. The first two frame numbers are removed every minute except for every tenth minute (think of it as a leap year). You may notice a difference of several seconds per hour when using the non-drop-frame option.

- **TC Run.** Sets the count-up format for the time code. You can choose Rec Run, in which the time code counts up only when you are actually capturing video; or Free Run (also known as Time of Day), which allows the time code to run up even between shooting clips. The latter is useful when you want to synchronize clips between multiple cameras that are shooting the same event. When using Free Run, even if the cameras record at different times, you'll be able to match the video that was captured at the exact same moment during editing.

- **TC Make.** Sets the recording format for the time code on the recording medium. Choose Preset to record a new time code, or Regenerate to read the previous time code setting and record the new time code consecutively. When Regenerate is selected, the time code advances no matter what TC Run setting has been selected.

- **UB Time Rec.** Sets whether or not to record the time as a user bit.

Picture Profiles

If you've been taking photos for a while, you're probably familiar with all the fixes and tweaks you can do with your still images within image editors like Photoshop. It's relatively easy to adjust color tones, contrast, sharpness, and other parameters prior to displaying or printing your photo. Movies are a little trickier, because any given video typically consists of *thousands* of individual photos, captured at 24 frames per second (or faster), with the possibility that each and every frame within a particular sequence might need fixes or creative adjustments.

Shooting video does not preclude doing post-processing during editing. Indeed, many videographers deliberately shoot relatively low-contrast video in order to capture the largest dynamic range possible, and then fine-tune the rendition later using their editing software. Picture Profiles let you do that—and also allow you to adjust your camera so that the video you capture is *pre-fine-tuned* in order to reduce or eliminate the amount of post-processing you do later.

The a7R III camera is furnished with ten "canned" picture profiles, which you can think of as Creative Styles for movies. The parameters included in these profiles can be further adjusted by you to better suit the "look" you are striving for in your videos. You can connect your camera to a TV or monitor using the HDMI Out connector and an HDMI cable, view the image produced by the camera on the larger screen, and then make adjustments to the picture profile. I described the process in how-to form briefly in Chapter 3.

Needless to say, creating and using Picture Profiles is a highly technical aspect of video making, at least in terms of the amount of knowledge you need to have to correctly judge what changing one of the parameters will do to your video. I hope to get you started with a quick description of what those parameters do, so you'll have a starting point when you start to explore them.

Gamma, Gamma Ding Dong

The ten Picture Profile presets in the Camera Settings I-12 menu already have their own default values, each adjusted for a particular type of shooting, using various gamma and color tone settings. Thanks to our evolutionary heritage, humans don't see differences in tones in a linear manner. An absolutely smooth progression of pixels from absolute black to pure white (with 0 representing black and 256 representing white) would not look like a continuous gradient to our eyes. We'd be unable to detect differences in shadows and highlights that have the same change in tonal values as midtones. So, everything from computer monitors to printers use a correction factor (gamma) to cancel out the differences in the way we see tones.

This correction takes the form of a curve, called a *gamma curve.* If you remember your geometry, the x and y axes on a graph are used to define the shape of a curve, and in the case of gamma curves, the values use logarithmic units (ack!) to define the slope. That's where the terms S-Log2, S-Log3, HLG and other mind-numbing jargon comes from. The whole shebang is needed to reconcile the ability of sensors to capture, video systems to display, and printers to output a range of tones in a linear way with the actual tones we perceive non-linearly. Gamma correction and gamma compression are used to help make sure that what we get is what we see. While gamma correction between computer platforms (that is, between Macs and PCs) may be different, the actual gamma values defined by video standards like NTSC and PAL are fixed and well-known. Picture Profiles allow you to configure your camera to capture video using a desired amount of gamma and color tone correction.

S-Log2/S-Log3/HLG

S-Log2 is a log gamma curve that is used when the video will be processed after shooting and captures a much larger range of tones (as many as 14 stops!) than standard gamma curves. Indeed, the tones captured using S-Log2 can't be displayed in all their glory on a standard TV or monitor, which are generally adjusted for the broadcast television BT-709 standard. Instead, the unprocessed video will look darker and lower in contrast because all those tonal values have been squeezed into the BT-709 (also called REC-709) range.

Video signals normally encompass brightness levels from 0 percent to 109 percent (you read that right: modern video cameras can record detail in highlights that are actually brighter than was possible when the video age began; the old scale was retained, reminiscent of Nigel Tufnel's 11 setting on his amp). However, even the 109 percent provides too much of a limitation; cameras can capture detail in highlights that are even brighter than *that*. So, a log gamma curve (in this case one called S-Log2) is used to *compress* all that image detail to fit into the space allowed for conventional video signals. Post-processing in a video editor allows working with all that information and produces a finished video that contains the filmmaker's selection of tonal values in a form that can be displayed comfortably. The full dynamic range can be used to produce the finished movie. You might find that useful when exposing for highlights while avoiding blowing out the sky, or for capturing detail in shadows without losing mid tones and highlights.

The Picture Profile 7 (PP7) is already set up for S-Log2 and should be your choice if you want to work with that curve. I've oversimplified things a bit, because there are many other great things you can do with S-Log2, such as overexposing or "pushing" your video to reduce noise (but at the risk of losing some detail in brighter skin tones), and then output (called "grading") to produce an optimized final image. Picture Profiles 8 and 9 (PP8 and PP9) are set up for S-Log3, which is a gamma curve optimized to look more like what you would have gotten if you shot film. Both also assume your video will be processed for your final production. HLG/HLG1–HLG3 gamma curves are provided for various high-dynamic range formats.

I know this chapter doesn't tell you everything you need to know to take the next step in movie making with your a7R III camera, but my intent was to introduce you to enough of your Sony's capabilities to spur additional exploration of this exciting creative arena.

VIEWING FIX

Movies captured using gamma profiles appear to be very low in contrast until processed using software on your computer. Because Picture Profiles extend the dynamic range of recorded video, the clips normally appear very low in contrast during review in the camera. The Gamma Display Assist entry in the Setup 1 menu allows you to adjust playback when viewing images captured using Picture Profiles, so that the appearance on the a7R III's EVF and LCD appears more natural, which is useful if you use live view to evaluate your captures. The display is not changed if you're viewing through a device plugged into the HDMI port, and you'll still need to process the video in your video-editing software. You can turn Gamma Display Assist off, allow the camera to select an appropriate adjustment automatically, or manually set the assist feature to use the gamma you are using. Your choices include S-Log2 and S-Log3, and two HLG (Hybrid Log Gamma) settings, which are used for delivery of video to high dynamic range TVs that are currently the rage. These are a bit esoteric for the average a7R III user who isn't heavily into professional-quality video capture.

More on 4K Video

It's probably a great time for you to start working with 4K video, especially since 8K video is already on the way. In practice, shooting 4K is not much different than shooting full HD or standard HD. The only changes you might make involve your realization that as long as you are capturing higher-quality video, you might as well upgrade your technique (and, perhaps, your auxiliary equipment).

While 4K video still seems new and exotic, given the usual pace of technology, it's very likely that your next HDTV will have 4K capabilities (if your current set does not), and cable/satellite/streaming systems as well as Blu-Ray discs will all make the leap sooner than any of us expect.

Shooting in 4K is still in its infancy: few of us own 4K high-definition televisions that allow playing back 4K content at its full resolution. However, the number of 4K-capable TVs is growing all the time, and there are some definite benefits to shooting ultra-high resolution now, even before the ability to take advantage of the format is widespread. Simply speaking, if you shoot 4K and then convert it to conventional full HD, your video will generally be much higher in quality than if you originated in 1920 × 1080 resolution. All you need is editing software like Adobe Premiere Pro, Final Cut Pro, or Corel Video Studio that can work with and edit your 4K clips.

The key thing to know is that your a7R III can record 4K video internally, export 4K video to an external recorder, or to *both* simultaneously. If you want to record *only* to the memory card, you don't need to do anything special other than select XAVCS 4K under the File Format entry and your desired frame/bit rate under Record Setting (both in the Camera Settings II-1 menu).

Figure 12.2
This image illustrates the field of view provided by a full-frame camera like the Sony a7R III (1X) with a 200mm lens, as well as the field of view you'd get when using a camera with the smaller sensor (1.5X crop) like the Sony a77 II.

is cropped. Of course, the term *crop factor* has a drawback: it implies that a 24mm × 36mm frame is "full" and anything else is "less than full."

I get e-mails all the time from Hasselblad and Mamiya medium-format photographers who point out that they, too, own "full-frame" cameras that employ oversized 36mm × 48mm and larger sensors. By their logical reckoning, the 24mm × 36mm sensors found in full-frame cameras like the Sony a7R III are "cropped."

The Crop Factor and the a7R III

So, what should the crop factor mean to you? Here's a checklist of things you should consider:

■ **Lens compatibility.** Lenses designed for APS-C cameras may not cover the entire 24mm × 36mm full frame of the a7R III, although some zoom lenses may have a large enough image circle at some focal lengths. With most APS-C lenses you will experience vignetting (darkening) in the corners and reduced sharpness along the edges of the image. For full-frame photography, these lenses will usually be less than satisfactory.

■ **Crop mode.** As described in Chapter 4, you'll find the APS-C/Super 35mm crop mode in the Custom Settings menu. It has three settings:

• **On.** The a7R III *always* shoots in cropped mode, regardless of which lens is mounted on the camera. Both full-frame and APS-C lenses will produce images with a cropped field of view. You might use this setting to give your lenses some extra "reach" for sports or wildlife photography.

• **Auto.** If the camera detects that an APS-C lens is mounted, it will switch to crop mode. Not all lenses will be automatically detected, so you may have to use the On setting instead to manually select crop mode.

• **Off.** The camera *never* switches to crop mode. Even APS-C lenses will be used in full-frame mode. If you have a lens that *almost* covers the full frame at certain zoom settings, you can use this option and crop out the offending dark corners in your image editor.

- **Reduced resolution.** In crop mode, your images will have reduced resolution, producing 18MP shots with the a7R III. You'll find that, unless you're shooting photos for snapshots or to post on web pages, 10MP is not particularly useful, but the a7R III's 18MP images are more than enough.

- **Shoot now, crop later?** Some point out that you can always shoot everything in full-frame mode and crop your images, perhaps with greater flexibility, in an image editor. While that's true, it's not necessarily the best route. In crop mode, the a7R III enlarges the cropped image to fill the EVF and LCD monitor, and it's more intuitive to frame and compose your images already cropped. Sports photographers and photojournalists who fire off 1,000 shots at an event won't be eager to go through their digital files and manually crop images. It's easier to crop as you shoot.

SteadyShot and You

Even the highest resolution lenses and sensors can do nothing to correct image sharpness lost due to movement. And while higher shutter speeds can counter most subject movement, when it's the *camera* that's causing blur due to vibration, other approaches have to be taken. Your a7R III has improved technology that can help avoid blur caused by shutter movement and bounce, but when the entire camera and lens are vibrating, that's where *image stabilization* (IS) comes into play.

Image stabilization/vibration reduction can take many forms, and Sony has expertise in all of them. Electronic IS is used in video cameras and involves shifting pixels around from frame to frame so that pixels that are not moving remain in the same position, and portions of the image that *are* moving don't stray from their proper path. Optical image stabilization, which Sony calls Optical SteadyShot (OSS), is built into many FE-mount lenses and involves lens elements that shift in response to camera movement, as detected by motion sensors included in the optics. Then, Sony introduced a new (at least for its mirrorless lineup) wrinkle: in-body, anti-shake technology called SteadyShot Inside (SSI), which adjusts the position of the sensor carriage itself along five different axes to counteract movement. If you're using an OSS lens with your a7R III camera, you actually have access to two different, complementary image stabilization systems.

The results can be spectacular. Sony claims a 4.5-stop improvement from its in-body SteadyShot technology. That is, a photograph taken at 1/30th second should have the same sharpness (at least in terms of resistance to camera shake) as one shot at 1/750th second. I've found this to be true. Figure 12.3 shows two shots of pelicans taken a few minutes apart with a 100-400mm Minolta A-mount zoom lens (using the Sony EA-LA4 adapter) at 400mm and 1/125th second hand-held. This older lens has no image stabilization built-in, so the shot at top was taken using only the camera's in-body IS. For the bottom photo, SteadyShot was turned off.

Figure 12.3 When hand-holding a lens at 400mm (top) and panning slightly to follow the pelican's movement, I was able to get a blur-free photo at 1/125th second. With SteadyShot deactivated, camera movement produced noticeable blurring (bottom).

No amount of SteadyShot can eliminate blur from moving subjects, but you should find yourself less tied to a tripod when using longer lenses, or when working with wide-angle lenses under dim lighting conditions than in the past. If you're taking photos in venues where flash or tripods are forbidden, you'll find the a7R III's image stabilization tandem invaluable. Because lens-based and in-body image stabilization work together, it's appropriate to discuss their use in this lens-oriented chapter.

How It Works

As I mentioned, stabilization uses gyroscope-like motion sensors to detect camera motion, which can occur along one of five different axes, as in Figure 12.4, which uses the previous a7R II for illustrative purposes. Shifts in the *x* and *y* directions are likely to occur when shooting macro images hand-held but can take place any time. *Roll* happens when you rotate the camera along the axis passing through the center of the front of the lens, say, to align the horizon while shooting a landscape. There may be a tendency to continue to "correct" for the horizon as you shoot, producing vibration along the roll axis. Roll is especially noticeable in video clips, because it's easy to see straight lines changing their orientation during a shot.

Pitch movements happen when the camera shake is such that the lens moves up or down, often because the lens itself is a front-heavy telephoto lens. The magnification of the tele only serves to exaggerate the changes in pitch. Telephotos are also a major contributor to *yaw* vibrations, in which the camera pivots slightly as if you were shooting a panorama—even when you're *not*. All five of these types of movement can be countered through image stabilization.

OSS does best in nullifying changes in pitch and yaw. SSI in the body can correct for all five types of movement. If both OSS and SSI are active at the same time, the a7R III uses the two in tandem, allowing the lens to correct for pitch and yaw, while the in-body IS compensates for x, y, and roll movements. That makes a lot of sense, because in correcting for x, y, and roll, the camera is able to keep the sensor in the exact same plane to preserve precise focus and simply move the sensor carriage

Figure 12.4
The five axes of in-body SteadyShot stabilization.

up, down, or slightly rotated to nullify the movement. If your lens does *not* have OSS, the SSI technology handles all the image stabilization tasks, in effect bringing IS to *every* lens you mount on the camera. That includes all E-mount lenses, as well as A-mount lenses attached with an EA-LA3 or EA-LA4 adapter (more on those later), and even "foreign" lenses like Canon EF optics using an appropriate adapter.

However, not all non-stabilized lenses benefit in identical ways from Sony's stabilization technology. For best results, the SSI system needs to know both focal length and focus distance to provide optimum stabilization. That's an advantage of OSS: stabilization built into the lens always knows exactly what focal length setting and focus distance is being used. For SSI, the same information has to be supplied to the smarts inside the camera body, using the SteadyShot Settings entry on the Camera Settings menu.

The lens may be one that can communicate this information to the camera. Focal length and distance data is also used with Sony's advanced distance integration (ADI) technology for flash exposure, as described in Chapter 13. Focal length information is needed to correct for pitch and yaw, while x and y compensation need to know the focal distance. (Roll correction needs neither type of data and can do its thing just from what SteadyShot sees happening on the sensor.)

However, when all the data is available, the full array of the a7R III's IS capabilities can be used to correct on all five axes. If the lens *cannot* communicate this information, the focal length can still be specified using the SteadyShot Settings entry in the Camera Settings menu, as described in Chapter 3. Simply change the SteadyShot Adjustment option to Manual, then use the SteadyShot Focal Length sub-entry to specify the focal length of the lens or the zoom position you're going to use from the range 8mm to 1000mm.

Unless you're working with a non-zoom lens, going this route can be clumsy, but at least it works. When I am shooting sports with my 100-400mm Minolta lens, I set the focal length to 400mm, and get appropriate IS the majority of the time. Manually entering the focal length doesn't provide the second half of the required data—the focus distance. But with only the focal length data to work with, the IS can calculate the amount of compensation to provide to correct for pitch and yaw, and it doesn't *need* that data to fix roll. When using your non-compatible and foreign lenses, and lenses from third-party vendors like Rokinon/Samyang, you must forgo corrections along the x and y axes, but that deficit can be lived with, I've found.

One interesting variation comes when using an autofocus-compatible Metabones Canon adapter or Commlite Nikon adapter with lenses that *do* have built-in image stabilization. Sony recommends turning off the lens's image stabilization/vibration reduction using the switch on the lens, because, even with an autofocus/autoexposure-compatible adapter, the foreign lens has no way of working harmoniously with the in-body stabilization (and vice versa). The result would be having *both* the lens and the a7R III trying to correct for pitch and yaw simultaneously, and possibly overcompensating.

Here's a quick summary of some things you should keep in mind:

- **Compatible lenses.** All FE lenses and most Sony E-mount lenses should be compatible, and you can leave SteadyShot turned on. The a7R III will identify the lens and choose how to apply the in-lens and in-body stabilization. For best results, turn off SteadyShot when the camera is mounted on a tripod.

- **SteadyShot doesn't stop action.** Unfortunately, no stabilization is a panacea to replace the action-stopping capabilities of a faster shutter speed. If you need to use 1/1,000th second to freeze a high jumper in mid-air, neither type of image stabilization achieves the desired effect at a longer shutter speed.

- **Stabilization might slow you down.** The process of adjusting the lens and/or sensor to counter camera shake takes time, just as autofocus does, so you might find that SteadyShot adds to the lag between when you press the shutter and when the picture is actually taken. In a situation where you want to capture a fleeting instant that can happen suddenly, image stabilization might not be your best choice.

- **Give SteadyShot a helping hand.** When you simply do not want to carry a tripod all day and you'll be relying on the OSS system, brace the camera or your elbows on something solid, like the roof of a car or a piece of furniture. Remember that an inexpensive monopod can be quite compact when not extended; many camera bags include straps that allow you to attach this accessory. Use a monopod for extra camera-shake compensation. Brace the accessory against a rock, a bridge abutment, or a fence and you might be able to get blur-free photos at surprisingly long shutter speeds. When you're heading out into the field to photograph wild animals or flowers and want to use longer exposures and think a tripod isn't practical, at least consider packing a monopod.

Choosing a Lens

Since the introduction of the original a7R and a7, Sony has been introducing new full-frame FE lenses for the system at an admirable pace, including the Sony FE 24-105mm f/4 G OSS lens offered as a kit lens for the a7R III. So, while I'm going to provide a quick listing of some of the lenses currently available for the a7R III series, it will necessarily be somewhat incomplete. After all, I expect additional lenses to be introduced as this book goes into production and, with luck, during the life of the book itself.

I'm going to cover only full-frame lenses in this chapter. If you read through my explanation of the crop factor, you know that APS-C lenses can also be used with a7R III, which still gives you an 18MP image in crop mode. But, as I noted, there are pros and cons to that approach, and the number of APS-C lenses available is vast, so I'm not going to list those options here.

In addition, most of my books rarely discuss third-party offerings, whether it's lenses, flash units, or accessories. There are so many of them, and the product churn can quickly make any recommendation obsolete. And, besides, for the most part the original vendor, such as Sony, provides the superior product. The situation is slightly different in the case of Sony's full-frame mirrorless cameras. In addition to Sony's own product line, produced internally from the company's own designs or with the cooperation of Zeiss, there are some excellent third-party optics you really should consider.

Some of these are from Zeiss and some are from third parties looking to fill the vacuum caused by the initial dearth of full-fledged FE lenses, and more recently encouraged by the popularity of Sony's full-frame lineup. Samyang, Lensbaby, Venus Optics Laowa, Mitagon, Handevision, and others have all jumped into the Sony arena. Even *more* possibilities derive from the a7R III's capability of using "foreign" lenses with tolerable—or better—autofocus and autoexposure features. As I noted in the introduction to this chapter, you can use a zillion A-mount lenses with the EA-LA3 and EA-LA4 adapters, Canon EF lenses and Nikon F-mount optics with an appropriate auto adapter from Metabones, Commlite, or other vendors, and adapters for virtually every other possible lens mount if you're willing to forgo autofocus and some other features.

I'll break down my overviews by vendor and provide you with my own recommendations where appropriate.

Sony FE Lenses

While the Sony-designated E-mount FE lenses should meet the needs of most photographers, you'll also find several premium-grade (and expensive) products with the Carl Zeiss ZA designation. The Carl Zeiss models all boast rugged metal construction for great durability, the very effective T* multi-layer anti-reflective coating for flare control, and one or more large high-tech optical elements for effective correction of optical aberrations. I'm going to list my favorite E-mount options for a7-series owners who want the very best.

The Affordable Trinity

First up, the trinity of (reasonably) affordable must-have lenses. These three lenses all have built-in optical image stabilization that can work in tandem with the a7R III's in-body SteadyShot. All have a constant f/4 maximum aperture that doesn't change as you zoom and are reasonably affordable (as far as premium optics go) at $1,200–$1,500 each. (See Figure 12.5.)

- **Sony FE 16-35mm f/4 ZA OSS lens.** This is the lens you need for your architectural, land-scape, and indoor photography in tight quarters. It covers an almost perfect range of focal lengths, from an ultra-wide 16mm to the street/urban photographer's favorite 35mm field of view. Some might prefer Sony's 12-24mm zoom instead (which wouldn't overlap with the 24-70mm lens described next), but I find the extra 11mm useful. I don't have to swap lenses when I need to zoom in a little tighter. One wonderful thing about this optic is that it has *curved* aperture blades, producing smooth circular defocused highlights for great *bokeh*. At around $1,250, you can afford this lens, and if you shoot a lot of wide-angle images, you can't afford *not* to have it.

Figure 12.5
Sony's three key FE lenses, left to right: 16-35mm f/4, 24-70mm f/4, and 70-200mm f/4.

- **Sony Vario-Tessar T* FE 24-70mm f/4 ZA OSS lens.** This lens includes my personal least-used focal length range. I tend to see my subjects either with a wide-angle view, often with an apparent perspective distortion aspect, or with a telephoto/selective focus approach. Another Zeiss-branded product, it has excellent balance with the a7R III, making it useful as a walk-around lens for travel photography, full-length and three-quarters portraits, and indoor sports like basketball and volleyball. Unfortunately, it won't be the sharpest optical knife in your toolkit, despite the Zeiss label. I find it perfectly acceptable when stopped down two or three stops from maximum aperture, but for $1,100, I expected more. You might explore the sub-$400 Sony FE 28-70mm f/3.5-5.6 OSS kit lens. It's abominably slow (f/5.6) at the 70mm zoom position, but you might find that saving $700 while filling out your trinity alleviates the pain.

- **Sony FE 70-200mm f/4 G OSS lens.** Compared to 70-200mm f/4 lenses designed for other full-frame cameras, this $1,400, 3-pound, 10.4 × 5.4 × 5.3–inch lens is almost petite, but it's quite a beast mounted on the tiny a7R III. It's well balanced and these cameras do have the new beefed-up mounting bayonet, but you really should consider using the swiveling tripod collar, either when mounting on a tripod/monopod or as a support when hand-holding. It's a Sony premium G lens (the G stands for "Gold") and its optical performance won't disappoint.

The Elite Three

In response to professionals and others who prefer fast, super-sharp lenses with a larger maximum aperture, Sony has begun introducing what it calls its G-Master (GM) lineup; three of them span the same focal length range as the "affordable trinity." Others available now (or expected in the future), such as the Sony FE 85mm f/1.4 GM and Sony FE 100mm f/2.8 SFT GM OSS, offer additional focal lengths.

Sony's top-of-the-line trio include:

■ **Sony FE 16-35mm f/2.8 GM.** Like all G-Masters, this lens is dust and moisture-resistant, has extra-low dispersion elements, and a price to match its high quality: in this case about $2,200. It focuses as close as 11 inches and uses 82mm filters. The downside? It's a larger lens than its f/4 cousin, and at 1.5 pounds is almost six ounces heavier.

■ **Sony FE 24-70mm f/2.8 GM.** Also priced at $2,200, this lens is massive compared to its f/4 sibling, at almost 32 ounces weighing more than twice as much. It focuses down to 1.25 feet, uses 82mm filters, and is a superb lens with this focal length range.

■ **Sony FE 70-200mm f/2.8 GM.** The costliest lens in the elite trinity, this one is priced at $2,600—but your cost for filters will be reduced if you already own the popular 77mm size this lens takes. It has 11 rounded aperture blades for great bokeh (the blur of the out-of-focus areas), weighs a hefty 3.26 pounds, and focuses down to about three feet for intimate telephoto close-ups.

These are my choices among the other Sony FE lenses. They include walk-around lenses, some fast primes for photojournalism and other available-light applications, and even a stellar macro.

■ **Sony FE 24-105mm f/4 G OSS.** This is the perfect walk-around lens for me. It focuses down to 16 inches, uses my full arsenal of 77mm filters, and has Optical Steady Shot. While not petite, I find its 4.5-inch length and 24 ounce weight not burdensome to carry around. As a G lens it has great image quality. It was in short supply and back-ordered for months after the a7R III was introduced, but if you can find one, at $1,300 it's a bargain.

■ **Sony FE 12-24mm f/4 G.** This $1,600 lens might be the walk-around lens for landscape, architectural, and, maybe, street photographers who love (or need) the wide-angle look. As I mentioned earlier, it has the added advantage of no focal length overlap with either Sony 24-70mm zoom. Roughly the same size as the 24-105mm lens, it weighs 20 ounces, but lacks image stabilization (which is less important with wide-angle lenses with most shutter speeds). I'd use this lens if the combination of the Sony 16-35mm zoom and Voigtlander 10mm f/5.6 manual focus lens didn't give me all the wide-angle flexibility I need.

■ **Sony FE 100mm f/2.8 STF GM OSS.** What do you get for $1,500? This G-Master is one of two near-ideal portrait/short telephoto lenses that Sony offers. The f/2.8 maximum aperture makes it easy to defocus the backgrounds, and the STF (Smooth Trans Focus) technology uses something called an apodization filter to produce achingly smooth bokeh with nice, round out-of-focus highlights. ("Apodization" is technical mumbo-jumbo that Sony applies to its use of a radially graduated neutral-density filter that, clear in the center and darker at its edges, in effect, counters the fade-out of those blurry round disks we call "bokeh," for a more pleasing effect.) Reduced flare for greater contrast, fast autofocus, OSS, and focus as close as 1.9 feet (you can switch focus ranges from 2.8 feet to infinity or 1.9–3.3 feet) make this a formidable lens for portraiture and other subjects.

■ **Sony FE 85mm f/1.4 GM.** This is Sony's other awesome G-master portrait lens, priced at $1,800. It's good for head-and-shoulders work, too, and a focal length shorter than the 100mm f/2.8 makes it easier to shoot full-length, couples, and group portraits. It has wonderful bokeh, weighs about 29 ounces, and can focus as close as 20 inches. I like this lens's large maximum aperture for concert and performance photography, other subjects under low light, and subjects I want to isolate with selective focus. Videographers will like the ability to de-click the actual physical lens aperture ring (most lenses these days do not have one at all) so exposure can be changed smoothly while a sequence is captured.

■ **Sony FE 100-400mm f/4.5-5.6 GM OSS.** Yet another very welcome G-Master lens, this one covers an ideal focal length range for sports and wildlife photographers, especially since it has OSS and superb weather-sealing. The price, at $2,500, is not even exorbitant considering its likely market and what you get. (Prime and zoom lenses in the 400mm and longer range can easily top $5,000 to $10,000.) It's a little over three pounds in weight, but that's normal in the long-tele-zoom territory.

■ **Sony FE 55mm/1.8 ZA lens.** So, why get excited about a "normal" lens with an f/1.8 maximum aperture and a $900 price tag? After all, both Nikon and Canon offer full-frame 50mm f/1.8 prime lenses for $200 or less. In this case, your ten Benjamins buys you one of the sharpest lenses ever made, with exquisite resolution at every f/stop—including wide open. Given that perspective, this lens is actually a bargain. You'll love using it for head-and-shoulders or 3/4-length portraits using selective focus at f/1.8. It's said to rival super-costly lenses, like the 55mm f/1.4 Zeiss Otus, which has a $4,000 price tag. You owe it to yourself to get this lens.

■ **Sony FE 24-240mm f/3.5-6.3 OSS lens.** On first glance, a 10X zoom lens stretching from a true wide-angle 24mm field of view to the edge of super telephoto range at 240mm sounds very tempting. With a second look, this optic's $900 price adds to the appeal. The reality check comes only when you realize that mating this hefty (1.72 pound), somewhat slow lens (f/6.3 at maximum zoom) to the compact a7R III counters the best reason for toting around a tiny full-frame mirrorless camera. If you truly want to walk around with only a single lens and can justify the bulk, this optic does fill the bill. It would also be an efficient choice for photography that might call for extreme wide-angle views and telephoto reach in rapid succession. Given its modest price tag, you can expect this lens will be a jack-of-all-trades and master of none. I'd rather carry a medium-sized camera bag and fill it with the trio of lenses described in the previous section, even at a cost premium of $3,000.

■ **Sony FE 28-135mm f/4 G PZ OSS lens.** The specs alone might lead you to believe this is a faster, heavier (5 pounds) walk-around lens with a more restricted zoom range. You'd be wrong. This $2,500 monster is especially designed for pro-level 4K video productions, and if heavy-duty movie making isn't on your agenda, you probably don't want or need this lens. Video shooters, though, will delight in its near-silent precision variable 8-speed power zoom, and responsive manual control rings for zoom (with direction reversal for smooth zooms), focus pulling, and aperture.

■ **Sony FE 28mm f/2.0 lens.** Here's a lens that comes with its own bag of tricks. It's a compact prime lens with a fast f/2.0 aperture, so you can shoot in low light and even gain a modicum of selective focus with its (relatively) shallow depth-of-field wide open. Despite its $450 price, it boasts an advanced optical design with ED (extra-low dispersion) glass elements that improve contrast and reduce troublesome chromatic and spherical aberrations. (You'll find descriptions of lens aberrations later in this chapter.) If that's not enough, you can attach either of two adapter optics to the front. There is a wide-angle version ($250), which converts it to a 21mm f/2.8 wide angle that focuses down to eight inches, and a 16mm fisheye attachment ($300) that I personally find more interesting and fun. But then, I own eight different fisheye lenses, so I'm susceptible.

■ **Sony Distagon T* FE 35mm f/1.4 ZA lens.** This Zeiss lens is a photojournalist's dream, with a wide-angle focal length that lets you get up close and personal with your subject, and a fast f/1.4 aperture suitable for low light and selective focus. The Zeiss T* (T-star) coating suppresses contrast loss from internal reflections among the lens elements. It's great for video, too, as the aperture ring can be de-clicked with a switch. The only drawback is the price: $1,600, which is a lot to pay for a lens that doesn't give you a range of different focal lengths to work with. However, the shooters this lens is designed for will confirm that it's worth it.

■ **Sony Sonnar T* FE 35mm f/2.8 ZA lens.** This tiny lens is a perfect match for the compact a7R III. At a mere eight ounces and measuring 2.42 × 1.44 inches, it makes a great walk-around lens for stealthy photographers. The image quality is great, but you'd expect that from a Zeiss lens that, at $800, is not bargain-basement cheap.

■ **Sony FE 90mm f/2.8 Macro G OSS.** While Sony will continue to make additional macro lenses available for the a7R III, this affordable (in the Sony FE realm, anything in the $1,000 range is considered affordable) $1,100 lens is an excellent choice. Its 90mm focal length gives you a decent amount of distance between the camera and your close-up subject, even at its minimum focusing distance of 11 inches. With internal focusing such that only the internal elements move, the lens doesn't get longer as you focus, avoiding a common problem. You can add a set of auto extension tubes to get even closer. I use Fotodiox Pro 10mm and 16mm tubes. Those tubes are primarily plastic and not especially rugged but are serviceable for light-duty use.

■ **Sony FE 400mm f/2.8 GM OSS.** This stupendous lens, announced in October 2017, was spotted by slavering Sony photographers at the Winter Olympics in February 2018, and was promised for delivery to ordinary humans before the year was out. Those ordinary humans almost certainly will need at least $10,000 to buy one, but this optica will be a most-desired lens for a7R III and a9 users in the sports photography realm, as well as among wildlife photographers and well-heeled enthusiasts with sufficient storage space in their Porsches.

A-Mount Lenses

If you're coming to the Sony mirrorless world from the SLT/A-mount arena, you may already own some Sony or Minolta lenses that can work very well with your a7R III. And even if you *don't* have any A-mount lenses now, you may want to investigate purchasing some. In some cases, they are as good as—or better—than the current roster of FE lenses. I know one professional photographer who skipped both FE mid-range zooms (the 24-70mm Zeiss and 28-70mm Sony kit lens) entirely, because he already owned the superb Sony Zeiss 24-70mm f/2.8 ZA SSM I Vario Sonar T* lens, which he used with his Sony a99. Of course, at $2,100, you'd only want to buy one if you were *very* serious about working with those particular focal lengths. You'd also need to sink another $200–$350 into a Sony A-Mount to E-Mount adapter, which I'll describe later in this chapter.

However, a viable option for everyone is to buy gently *used* A-mount lenses from reliable sources, such as KEH Camera (www.keh.com). I've purchased more than a dozen lenses from them over the last few years, including the ever-popular "beercan," the Minolta AF Zoom 70-210mm f/4, an ancient optic prized for its tank-like solid build, commendable sharpness, constant maximum aperture, and smooth bokeh. Of course, my favorite is my Minolta AF 100-400mm f/4.5-6.7 APO Tele-Zoom lens. (See Figure 12.6.) It's not my sharpest lens, but I would never have been able to afford a 400mm autofocus lens otherwise.

I'm not sure where KEH gets 30-year-old lenses that are like new, but their selection is huge and the prices are a fraction of what you'd pay for new A-mount optics. Keep in mind that when it took over Konica Minolta's camera/lens technology, Sony simply rebranded quite a few of the most popular lenses, so you may find a 50mm f/1.4 Minolta lens that's identical to the Sony 50mm f/1.4 lens at a much lower price.

Figure 12.6 A Minolta 100-400mm lens mounted using the Sony EA-LA4 adapter.

The only drawback to the most affordably priced A-mount lenses is that they probably use Minolta's original screw-drive autofocus technology. To use them on your a7R III, you'll need the Sony LA-EA4 adapter, which has its own SLT (single-lens translucent) phase-detect autofocus system, similar to that used in the Sony a99.

It's highly preferable to use A-mount lenses with built-in autofocus motors of the SSM or SAM variety. These lenses work with the less expensive Sony LA-EA3 adapter and let you use the a7R III's own hybrid phase detect/contrast detect AF system, which is typically both faster and more accurate. (Such lenses are easy to spot: they incorporate the SSM, SSM II, SAM, or SAM II designations in their official names.) SSM stands for SuperSonic motor, which uses a ring-type ultrasonic driver that is fast and virtually silent and is found on upper-end lenses. SAM stands for Smooth Autofocus Motor, an alternate system built into some lower-end Sony optics introduced since 2009.

I won't recommend specific additional A-mount lenses here, as the selection is so vast and varied. Just keep these provisos in mind:

■ **Both full-frame and APS-C.** The older Minolta lenses you'll find were designed for full-frame film cameras, but Sony has introduced both full-frame and APS-C lenses for A-mount. You can usually identify Sony APS-C A-mount lenses by the designation DT in the lens name; if DT is not included, it is a full-frame lens. Third-party lens manufacturers such as Tokina, Sigma, Vivitar, and Tamron also offer a mixture of both types. Research your lenses before you buy.

■ **Motor/No Motor.** It's easy to discern Sony A-mount lenses with internal motors, as the specification is included in their name. However, specs of the offerings of third-party vendors are not always obvious. Somewhere in their catalog descriptions they will usually specify whether a particular lens includes an internal motor, and they'll also reveal whether a lens is intended for full-frame or APS-C models.

Zeiss Loxia Lenses

While the Zeiss FE lenses produced and sold by Sony all feature autofocus, Zeiss also independently sells its own optics, including the Loxia lineup designed specifically for Sony full-frame E-mount cameras.

Zeiss lenses are all premium optics, and, as I write this, the super-premium Zeiss Otus lineup (priced at $4,000 and up) is not available in Sony E-mount. Nor can you buy the new Milvus full-frame lenses to fit your A7R III, and, just in case you're wondering, the Zeiss Touit lenses in E-mount are designed for APS-C sensors only.

However, these Loxia lenses are among the best we can get, with, so far, four available, all manual focus. Not including autofocus helps keep the price down on these otherwise premium-quality super-sharp lenses. Keep in mind that your a7R III has a wealth of manual-focus-friendly features, including focus peaking and focus magnification, all described elsewhere in this book.

Here are some excellent Zeiss Loxia lenses:

- **Zeiss Loxia 85mm f/2.4 lens.** Its maker describes this $1,400 lens as portable, inconspicuous, and powerful and urges you to use it for portrait, street, and landscape photography. It is remarkably sharp from edge to edge. Like all the Loxia lenses, the manual aperture ring can be de-clicked, using a supplied tool, for use when constantly varying apertures are desired when shooting video.

- **Zeiss Loxia 50mm f/2 Planar T* lens.** If you've been involved with photography for any length of time, you'll recognize the Zeiss Planar name, first applied to a symmetrical lens design as far back as 1896. This fast manual focus lens does a good job of correcting for chromatic aberration and distortion and is one of the best lenses you can buy for roughly $1,000.

- **Zeiss Loxia 35mm f/2 Biogon T* lens.** Another name out of the past, Biogon lenses have historically been some of the best wide-angle optics you can buy, and this fast 35mm f/2 lens has been optimized for use with digital cameras (that is, illumination emerges from the back of the lens at a less steep angle, as explained in Chapter 2). Your $1,300 buys you a well-corrected lens suitable for street photography, architecture, landscapes, and other subjects.

- **Zeiss Loxia 21mm f/2.8 T* lens.** This final lens in the trio was the last introduced, in December 2015 for $1,500. It's an extra-compact lens using the famed Distagon design, which overcomes some of the drawbacks of many wide angles to provide consistent sharpness from edge to edge, with little light falloff and excellent correction for chromatic aberrations.

Zeiss Batis Lenses

Here we have four reasonably priced autofocus lenses from Zeiss, which help fill out holes in Sony's full-frame E-mount lineup. If you're looking for a futuristic touch, they each feature an illuminated OLED (organic LED) display that dynamically shows focus distance and depth-of-field. In the good old days, prime (non-zoom) lenses had etched or painted color-coded depth-of-field markers on the lens barrel, but those largely disappeared when zoom lenses became dominant. Now depth-of-field can be displayed on your lens in a more useful form. As I write this, the four available Batis lenses are as follows:

- **Zeiss Batis 135mm f/2.8 lens.** For $1,500 you get a Zeiss Sonar-design lens with OSS, fast autofocus, and impressive image quality. Some may think this lens verges on being too long for head-and-shoulders portraits, but it's a versatile lens for many types of sports, especially since it has great anti-flare and ghosting properties that are useful when shooting into sunlight.

- **Zeiss Batis 85mm f/1.8 lens.** This is a $999 medium-telephoto autofocus lens that's ideal for portraits, and a primo choice for low-light photography and selective focus. It's the first Zeiss lens that has optical image stabilization (the equivalent of Sony's trademarked OSS), giving you hybrid IS when used with the a7R III's in-body SteadyShot Inside.

- **Zeiss Batis 25mm f/2.0 lens.** There's a bit of overlap in potential use between this autofocus lens and Sony's own 28mm f/2.0 optic. This one is more expensive at less than $1,200, sharper, and isn't compatible with Sony's wide-angle/fisheye adapters.

- **Zeiss Batis 18mm f/2.8 lens.** Featuring the famed Zeiss Distagon wide-angle design, this $1,500 optic focuses down to about 10 inches, which is useful if you like wide-angle (apparent) perspective distortion effects. (It's *apparent* rather than *real*, because the distortion is due to the placement of the subject matter within the field of view, not any defect in the lens itself.) At 12 ounces, it's not heavy and makes a good walk-around lens for those who want a prime lens with a wide field of view.

Other Third-Party Lenses

Because the a7R III has relatively short back-focus distances (the gap between the lens mount bayonet and sensor), it's fairly easy for third parties to adapt their existing full-frame lenses to fit your camera. There are some interesting lenses available. Among them:

- **Mitakon.** This company makes an ultra-fast 85mm f/1.2 manual focus lens ($800), and a hyperfast 50mm f/0.95 lens ($850) in Sony E-mount, with the latter having the distinction of being the world's fastest full-frame E-mount lens. The company also offers a 20mm f/2 super macro at a bargain $199 that can focus down to less than one inch!

- **Voigtlander.** Probably the oldest name in camera gear, dating back to its founding in Vienna in 1756 (well before the invention of photography itself). It produces some interesting lenses, including their 10mm 5.6 Heliar ($1,100), 12mm f/5.6 Heliar ($1,000), 15mm f/4.5 Super Wide Heliar ($800), 435mm f/1.4 Nokton ($800), 40mm f/1.2 Nokton ($1,100), 60mm f/2 Macro APO-Lanthar ($1,000). My 10mm *rectilinear* (non-fisheye) Heliar is one of my most-used lenses.

- **Samyang/Rokinon.** This company's manual focus 12mm f/2.8 fisheye resides in my fisheye collection, and I often alternate its use with my 15mm f/2.8 Sigma fisheye. I use them in manual focus mode with adapters, but Samyang/Rokinon also sells lenses in E-mount (sometimes under the Bower brand name). They include a 24mm f/1.4, 35mm f/1.4, 50mm f/1.4, 85mm f/1.4, 135mm f/2, and a 100mm f/2.8 macro lens that produce 1:1 (life-size) magnification at a minimum focusing distance of 12 inches. They are starting to issue autofocus lenses in Sony FE mount, including an affordable FE 35mm f/2.8 for a mere $300 and a 14mm f/2.8 for $630.

- **Tamron/Sigma.** Tamron, which is partially owned by Sony, appears to be venturing into Sony E-mount autofocus territory. Their first FE offering is the Tamron 28-75mm f/2.8 Di III RXD, which is lighter and smaller than Sony's own 24-70mm f/2.8 G-Master. With the price Tamron has announced, with luck, it will be both sharp and affordable. Sigma is also increasingly venturing into FE territory, with a 105mm f/1.4 ART lens rumored to be coming by the time this book is published. As Sony full-frame cameras gain in popularity, continue to look for additional lenses from these major manufacturers.

Using the LA-EA Series Adapters

Sony makes four A-mount to E-mount adapters, which allow using Sony/Minolta A-mount lenses on an Alpha E-mount camera such as the a7R III. Why four different adapters? All four, the LA-EA1, LA-EA2, LA-EA3, and LA-EA4, allow connecting an A-mount lens to an NEX/Alpha-series camera. The two odd-numbered adapters use *only* contrast detect autofocus with lenses that have built-in AF motors and are compatible with them. The two even-numbered adapters have built-in SLT-like phase detection AF systems for fast focusing with lenses that use the original screw-drive AF system. The LA-EA1 and LA-EA2 are designed for APS-C cameras, while the LA-EA3 and LA-EA4 shown in Figure 12.7 are intended for full-frame models like the a7R III. Table 12.1 should clear things up a bit.

Figure 12.7
The LA-EA3 (left) and LA-EA4 (right) adapters allow using A-mount lenses on the a7R III.

Table 12.1 LA-EA Series Adapters

Adapter	Autofocus	Format
LA-EA1	Contrast detect with lenses that have built-in SSR or SAM AF motors. Lenses using a screw-drive motor in the camera body will not autofocus.	APS-C
LA-EA2	Phase detect using Translucent Mirror technology.	APS-C
LA-EA3	Contrast detect with lenses that have built-in SSM or SAM AF motors. Lenses using a screw-drive motor in the camera body will not autofocus.	Full Frame and APS-C
LA-EA4	Phase detect using Translucent Mirror technology.	Full Frame and APS-C

Figure 12.8
The design of the LA-EA4 adapter looks like this.

The LA-EA3 adapter or LA-EA4 adapter are both satisfactory, depending on the type of autofocus used in your A-mount lenses. I own both, because I have a mixture of SSM, SAM, and screw-drive lenses.

The LA-EA2 and LA-EA4 are clever because both involve, basically, building a version of Sony's Translucent Mirror Technology, found in the SLT cameras, into an adapter, as you can see in the exploded diagram shown in Figure 12.8. (In actual use, the lens must be physically mounted to the adapter.)

Other Lens Options

Because of the popularity of the camera line, third-party vendors have rushed to produce lenses for these models. As I mentioned earlier, because the a7-series' "flange to sensor" distance is relatively short, there's room to use various types of adapters between camera and lens and still allow focusing all the way to infinity. There are already a huge number of adapters that allow mounting just about any lens you can think of on the a7R III cameras, if you're willing to accept manual focus and, usually, a ring on the adapter that's used to stop down the "adopted" lens to the aperture used to take the photo. You can find these from Novoflex (www.novoflex.com), Metabones (www.metabones.com), Fotodiox (www.fotodiox.com), Rainbow Imaging (www.rainbowimaging.biz), Cowboy Studio (www.cowboystudio.com), and others.

Some adapters of certain types and brands sell for as little as $20–$30. With many of them you should not expect autofocus even if you're using an AF lens from some other system; as well, many of the cameras' high-tech features do not operate. However, you can usually retain automatic exposure by setting the a7R III to Aperture Priority, stopping down to the f/stop you prefer, and firing away. Figure 12.9, left, shows a Nikon-to-E-Mount adapter I bought from Fotodiox.

The ultra-high-grade Novoflex and Metabones adapters for using lenses of other brands sell for much higher prices. I found only two that are said to maintain autofocus with a lens of an entirely different brand. The Metabones Canon EF-to-Sony Smart Adapter (Mark IV) and their similar Speed Booster model ($400 and $600, respectively) maintain autofocus, autoexposure, and the Canon lens's image stabilizer feature when used with a camera. The "Speed Booster" part of the name comes from the adapter's ability to magically add one f/stop to the maximum aperture of the lens (thanks to the adapter's internal optics), transforming an f/4 lens into an f/2.8 speed demon.

The Metabones Smart Adapter has been especially popular, thanks to the ability to use AF-C with Canon's EF or EF-S lenses and your camera's hybrid phase detect/contrast detect autofocus system. Reports are that autofocus with these lenses is equal to or superior to that of the same lenses when mounted on their native Canon camera bodies. The Canon lenses' in-lens IS also works, but you may want to disable it and rely solely on the a7R III's own SteadyShot capabilities. The Metabones Smart Adapter is well made, with brass components, and costs a hefty $399, but if you are switching over from a Canon system, the ability to use your existing lenses is priceless.

Figure 12.9
It's possible to mount lenses of entirely different brands on your a7R III with a manual adapter, but many camera functions are then disengaged (left). Adapters with full automation are available for mounting Canon lenses as well as Nikon autofocus lenses on your a7R III (right).

Commlite and other vendors have begun offering adapters that preserve full autofocus/autoexpo-sure/image stabilization features for Nikon AF-S and AF-D lenses. The AF-S lenses have their own built-in autofocus motors; the AF-D lenses must be focused using a motor built into the lens adapter.

My absolute favorite lens bargain is the 35mm f/1.7 Fujian (no relation to Fuji) optic, which I pur-chased brand new for a total of $28, with the E-mount adapter included in the price. It's actually a tiny CCTV (closed-circuit television) lens in C-mount (a type of lens mount used for cine cameras). It's manual focus and manual f/stop, of course (and it works in Aperture Priority mode); it's a toy lens, or something like a super-cheap Lensbaby, or a great experimental lens for fooling around. It covers the full APS-C frame (more or less; expect a bit of vignetting in the corners at some f/stops), so you'll have to use it in APS-C crop mode. It is not incredibly sharp wide open and exhibits a weird kind of "bokeh" (out-of-focus rendition of highlights) that produces fantasy-like images. The only drawback (or additional drawback, if you will), is that you may have to hunt some to find one; the manufacturer doesn't sell directly in the USA. I located mine on Amazon.com.

Once you own the C-mount-to-E-mount adapter, you can use any of the host of other similar CCTV lenses on your a7R III. Also relatively cheap, but not necessarily of equal quality, are a 25mm f/1.4, 35mm f/1.7, and 50mm f/1.4 lens (shown in Figure 12.10), as well as a Tamron 8mm f/1.4, and other lenses that I haven't tried and probably won't cover even the APS-C image area, but are worth borrowing to try out if you have a friend who does CCTV.

Figure 12.10
These CCTV lenses make great "toys" for your a7R III.

Fine-Tuning the Focus of Your A-Mount Lenses

In Chapter 3, I introduced you to the a7R III's AF Micro Adjustment feature in the Custom Settings menu, which can be manipulated *only* when you're using a Sony or a Minolta Maxxum/Dynax A-mount lens with the EA-LA2 or EA-LA4 adapters. It is not available when using the LA-EA1 or LA-EA3 adapters. (The micro adjustment may work with an A-mount lens of another brand, but Sony warns that the results may be inaccurate.) Millions of A-mount lenses have been sold over the years, and the adapter is not terribly expensive, so I will assume that many readers will eventually want to consider the fine-tuning feature.

If you do not currently have such lenses or the adapter, you cannot us AF Micro Adjustment (you can turn the feature on or off, but you cannot enter any adjustment factor). But if you do own the relevant equipment, you might find that a particular lens is not focusing properly. If the lens happens to focus a bit ahead or a bit behind the desired area (like the eyes in a portrait), and if it does that consistently, you can use the adjustment feature.

Why is the focus "off" for some lenses in the first place? There are lots of factors, including the age of the lens (an older lens may focus slightly differently), temperature effects on certain types of glass, humidity, and tolerances built into a lens's design that all add up to a slight misadjustment, even though the components themselves are, strictly speaking, within specs. A very slight variation in your lens's mount can cause focus to vary slightly. With any luck (if you can call it that) a lens that doesn't focus exactly right will at least be consistent. If a lens always focuses a bit behind the subject, the symptom is *back focus*. If it focuses in front of the subject, it's called *front focus.*

You're almost always better off sending such a lens in to Sony to have them make it right. But that's not always possible. Perhaps you need your lens recalibrated right now, or you purchased a used lens that is long out of warranty. If you want to do it yourself, the first thing to do is determine whether or not your lens has a back focus or front focus problem.

For a quick-and-dirty diagnosis (*not* a calibration; you'll use a different target for that), lay down a piece of graph paper on a flat surface, and place an object on the line at the middle, which will represent the point of focus (we hope). Then, shoot the target at an angle using your lens's widest aperture (smallest available f/number) and the autofocus mode you want to test. Mount the camera on a tripod so you can get accurate, repeatable results.

If your camera/lens combination doesn't suffer from front or back focus, the point of sharpest focus will be the center line of the chart, as you can see in Figure 12.11. If you do have a problem, one of the other lines will be sharply focused instead. Should you discover that your lens consistently front focuses or back focuses, it needs to be recalibrated. Unfortunately, it's only possible to calibrate a lens for a single focusing distance. So, if you use a particular lens (such as a macro lens) for close-focusing, calibrate for that. If you use a lens primarily for middle distances, calibrate for that. Close-to-middle distances are most likely to cause focus problems, anyway, because as you get closer to infinity, small changes in focus are less likely to have an effect.

Figure 12.11 Correct focus (top), front focus (middle), and back focus (bottom).

Lens Tune-Up

The AF Micro Adj setting in the Custom Settings menu is the key tool you can use to fine-tune your A-mount lens used with the LA-EA2 or LA-EA4 adapter. Of course, this assumes you are using an A-mount lens and the adapter. You'll find the process easier to understand if you first run through this quick overview of the menu options:

- **AF Adjustment Setting. Set:** This option enables AF fine-tuning for all the lenses you've registered using this menu entry. If you discover you don't care for the calibrations you make in certain situations (say, it works better for the lens you have mounted at middle distances but is less successful at correcting close-up focus errors), you can deactivate the feature as you require. You should set this to On when you're doing the actual fine-tuning. Adjustment values range from –20 to +20. **Off:** Disables autofocus micro adjustment.

- **Amount.** You can specify values of plus or minus 20 for each of the lenses you've registered. When you mount a registered lens, the degree of adjustment is shown here. If the lens has not been registered, then +/–0 is shown. If "–" is displayed, you've already registered the maximum number of lenses—up to 30 different lenses can be registered with each camera.

- **Clear.** Erases *all* user-entered adjustment values for the lenses you've registered. When you select the entry, a message will appear. Select OK and then press the center button of the control wheel to confirm.

Evaluate Current Focus

The first step is to capture a baseline image that represents how the lens you want to fine-tune autofocuses at a particular distance. You'll often see advice for photographing a test chart with millimeter markings from an angle, and the suggestion that you autofocus on a particular point on the chart. Supposedly, the markings that actually *are* in focus will help you recalibrate your lens. The problem with this approach is that the information you get from photographing a test chart at an angle doesn't actually tell you what to do to make a precise correction. So, your lens back focuses three millimeters behind the target area on the chart. So what? Does that mean you change the Saved Value by –3 clicks? Or –15 clicks? Angled targets are a "shortcut" that don't save you time.

Instead, you'll want to photograph a target that represents what you're actually trying to achieve: a plane of focus locked in by your lens that represents the actual plane of focus of your subject. For that, you'll need a flat target, mounted precisely perpendicular to the sensor plane of the camera. Then, you can take a photo, see if the plane of focus is correct, and if not, dial in a bit of fine-tuning in the AF Fine Tuning menu, and shoot again. Lather, rinse, and repeat until the target is sharply focused.

You can use the focus target shown in Figure 12.12, or you can use a chart of your own, as long as it has contrasty areas that will be easily seen by the autofocus system, and without very small details that are likely to confuse the AF. Download your own copy of my chart from www.dslrguides.com/FocusChart.pdf. (The URL is *case sensitive*.) Then print out a copy on the

Figure 12.12 Use this focus test chart or create one of your own.

largest paper your printer can handle. (I don't recommend just displaying the file on your monitor and focusing on that; it's unlikely you'll have the monitor screen lined up perfectly perpendicular to the camera sensor.) Then, follow these steps:

1. **Position the camera.** Place your camera on a sturdy tripod with a remote release attached, positioned at roughly eye-level at a distance from a wall that represents the distance you want to test for. Keep in mind that autofocus problems can be different at varying distances and lens focal lengths, and that you can enter only *one* correction value for a particular lens. So, choose a distance (close-up or mid range) and zoom setting with your shooting habits in mind.

2. **Set the autofocus mode.** Choose the autofocus mode you want to test.

3. **Level the camera (in an ideal world).** If the wall happens to be perfectly perpendicular, you can use a bubble level, plumb bob, or other device of your choice to ensure that the camera is level to match. Many tripods and tripod heads have bubble levels built in. Avoid using the center column, if you can. When the camera is properly oriented, lock the legs and tripod head tightly.

4. **Level the camera (in the real world).** If your wall is not perfectly perpendicular, use this old trick. Tape a mirror to the wall, and then adjust the camera on the tripod so that when you look through the viewfinder at the mirror, you see directly into the reflection of the lens. Then, lock the tripod and remove the mirror.

5. **Mount the test chart.** Tape the test chart on the wall so it is centered in your camera's viewfinder.

6. **Photograph the test chart using AF.** Allow the camera to autofocus and take a test photo using the remote release to avoid shaking or moving the camera.

7. **Make an adjustment and re-photograph.** Navigate to the Custom Settings menu and choose AF Micro Adj. Make sure the feature has been turned on, then press down to Amount and make a fine-tuning adjustment, plus or minus, and photograph the target again.

8. **Lather, rinse, repeat.** Repeat steps 6 and 7 several times to create several different adjustments to check.

9. **Evaluate the image(s).** If you have the camera connected to your computer with a USB cable or through a Wi-Fi connection, so much the better. You can view the image(s) after transfer to your computer. Otherwise, *carefully* open the camera card door and slip the memory card out and copy the images to your computer.

10. **Evaluate focus.** Which image is sharpest? That's the setting you need to use for this lens. If your initial range doesn't provide the correction you need, repeat the steps between –20 and +20 until you find the best fine-tuning. Once you've made an adjustment, the –7 will automatically apply the AF fine-tuning each time that lens is mounted on the camera, as long as the function is turned on.

MAXED OUT

If you've reached the maximum number of lenses (which is unlikely—who owns 30 lenses?), mount a lens you no longer want to compensate for, and reset its adjustment value to +/–0. Or you can reset the values of all your lenses using the Clear function and start over.

What Lenses Can Do for You

A sane approach to expanding your lens collection is to consider what each of your options can do for you and then choose the type of lens that will really boost your creative opportunities. Here's a guide to the sort of capabilities you can gain by adding a lens (using an adapter, if necessary) to your repertoire.

- **Wider perspective.** A 24-70mm or 28-70mm lens can serve you well for moderate wide-angle to medium telephoto shots. Now you find your back is up against a wall and you *can't* take a step backward to take in more subject matter. Perhaps you're standing on the boulevard adjacent to the impressive domed walls of the Mirogoj Cemetery in Zagreb, Croatia, and you want to show the expanse of the walls, as I did for the photo at top in Figure 12.13, made with the Sony/Zeiss 16-35mm f/4 zoom lens. Or, you might find yourself just behind the baseline at a high school basketball game and want an interesting shot with a little perspective distortion tossed in the mix. If you often want to make images with a super-wide field of view, a wider lens is in your future.

- **Bring objects closer.** A long focal length brings distant subjects closer to you, allows you to produce images with very shallow depth-of-field, and avoids the perspective distortion that wide-angle lenses provide. If you find the traffic on the street intrusive, as I did in Zagreb, you can zoom in to eliminate the distraction, as in Figure 12.13, center. A lens like the Sony/Zeiss 24-70mm f/4 can be your best friend.

  Or, perhaps you want to zoom in on one of the domes. As I write this, the longest focal length in an FE lens zooms from 200 to 600mm. If you own such a lens, it's easy to blur the background because the maximum remains f/4 at long focal lengths. With the right adapter, you can also use a much longer super telephoto lens on your a7R III, as I did for Figure 12.13, bottom, using my own Minolta 100-400mm lens.

- **Bring your camera closer.** Sony's 90mm FE macro lens is great, but you can also use an adapter and work with other close-up lenses if you don't want to purchase the E-mount 30mm f/3.5 macro lens. Sony has two excellent A-mount macro lenses that would be fine for use with an adapter; you might own one of these or may be able to borrow one: the 50mm f/2.8 and the 100mm f/2.8 macro lens.

  Even if the autofocus speed you get isn't fast enough for you, the need to manually focus an A-mount macro lens is not a tremendous hardship. Most serious photographers use manual

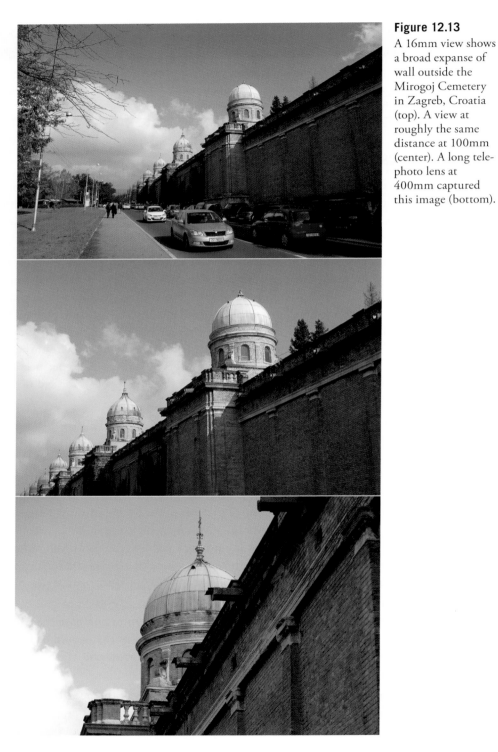

Figure 12.13
A 16mm view shows a broad expanse of wall outside the Mirogoj Cemetery in Zagreb, Croatia (top). A view at roughly the same distance at 100mm (center). A long telephoto lens at 400mm captured this image (bottom).

focus in extreme close-up photography for the most convenient method of controlling the exact subject element that will be in sharpest focus. The A-mount 100mm f/2.8 macro lens ($800) is preferable to the shorter macro lenses in nature photography because you do not need to move extremely close to a skittish subject for high magnification. And you can get a frame-filling photo of a tiny blossom without trampling all the other plants in its vicinity.

■ **Look sharp.** Many lenses, particularly the higher-priced Sony and Zeiss optics, are prized for their sharpness and overall image quality. Your run-of-the-mill lens is likely to be plenty sharp for most applications at the optimum aperture (usually f/8 or f/11), but the very best optics, such as the Zeiss 55mm f/1.8, are definitely superior. You can expect to get excellent sharpness in much of the image area at the maximum aperture, high sharpness even in the corners by one stop down, more consistent sharpness at various focal lengths with a zoom, and better correction for various types of distortions (discussed shortly).

■ **More speed.** Your basic lens might have the perfect focal length and sharpness for sports photography, but the maximum aperture may be small at telephoto focal lengths, such as f/5.6 or f/6.3 at the far end. That won't cut it for night baseball or football games, since you'll need to use an extremely high ISO (where image quality suffers) to be able to shoot at a fast shutter speed to freeze the action. Even outdoor sports shooting on overcast days can call for a high ISO if you're using a slow zoom lens (with small maximum apertures).

That makes the FE-mount lenses with a very wide aperture (small f/number) such as the 24mm f/2 optic a prime choice (so to speak) for low-light photography when you can get close to the action; that's often possible at an amateur basketball or volleyball game. But, you might be happier with an adapter and an A-mount lens, such as the Carl Zeiss Sonnar T* 135mm f/1.8 lens (if money is no object; it costs $1,800). But there are lower-cost fast lens options, such as the 50mm f/1.4 lens ($400), which might be suitable for indoor sports in a gym and whenever you must shoot in dark locations, in a castle or cathedral or theater, for example.

Categories of Lenses

Lenses can be categorized by their intended purpose—general photography, macro photography, and so forth—or by their focal length. The range of available focal lengths is usually divided into three main groups: wide-angle, normal, and telephoto. Prime lenses fall neatly into one of these classifications. Zooms can overlap designations, with a significant number falling into the catchall wide-to-telephoto zoom range. This section provides more information about focal length ranges, and how they are used.

Any lens with a focal length of 10mm to 20mm is said to be an *ultra-wide-angle lens*; from about 20mm to 40mm is said to be a *wide-angle lens. Normal lenses* have a focal length roughly equivalent to the diagonal of the film or sensor, in millimeters, and so fall into the range of about 45mm to 60mm on a full-frame camera like your a7R III. *Telephoto lenses* usually fall into the 75mm and longer focal lengths, while those with a focal length much beyond 300mm are referred to as *super telephotos.*

Using Wide-Angle Lenses

To use wide-angle prime lenses and wide zooms, you need to understand how they affect your photography. Here's a quick summary of the things you need to know.

- **More depth-of-field (apparently).** Practically speaking, wide-angle lenses seem to produce more extensive depth-of-field at a particular subject distance and aperture. However, the range of acceptable sharpness actually depends on magnification: the size of the subject in the frame. With a wide-angle lens, you usually include a full scene in an image; any single subject is not magnified very much, so the depth-of-field will be quite extensive. When using a telephoto lens however, you tend to fill the frame with a single subject (using high magnification), so the background is more likely to be blurred. (I'll discuss this in more detail in the sidebar below.)

  You'll find a wide-angle lens helpful when you want to maximize the range of acceptable sharpness in a landscape, for example. On the other hand, it's very difficult to isolate your subject (against a blurred background) using selective focus unless you move extremely close. Telephoto lenses are better for this purpose and as a bonus, they also include fewer extraneous elements of the scene because of their narrower field of view.

- **Stepping back.** Wide-angle lenses have the effect of making it seem that you are standing farther from your subject than you really are. They're helpful when you don't want to back up—or can't because of impediments—to include an entire group of people in your photo, for example.

- **Wider field of view.** While making your subject seem farther away, as implied above, a wide-angle lens also provides a more expansive field of view, including more of the scene in your photos.

- **More foreground.** As background objects appear further back than they do to the naked eye, more of the foreground is brought into view by a wide-angle lens. That gives you extra emphasis on the area that's closest to the camera. Photograph your home with a 50mm focal length, for example, and the front yard probably looks fairly conventional in your photo. Switch to a wider lens, such as the 16mm setting of the 16-35mm f/4 zoom, and you'll discover that your lawn now makes up much more of the photo. So, wide-angle lenses are great when you want to emphasize that lake in the foreground, but problematic when your intended subject is located farther in the distance.

- **Super-sized subjects.** The tendency of a wide-angle lens to emphasize objects in the foreground while de-emphasizing objects in the background can lead to a kind of size distortion that may be more objectionable for some types of subjects than others. Shoot a bed of flowers up close with a 16mm or shorter focal length, and you might like the distorted effect of the nearby blossoms looming in the photo. Take a shot of a family member with the same lens from the same distance, and you're likely to get some complaints about that gigantic nose in the foreground.

■ **Perspective distortion.** This type of distortion occurs when you tilt the camera so the plane of the sensor is no longer perpendicular to the vertical plane of your subject. As a result, some parts of the subject are now closer to the sensor than they were before, while other parts are farther away. This is what makes buildings, flagpoles, or NBA players appear to be leaning over backward (like the building shown in Figure 12.14). While this kind of apparent distortion is actually caused by tilting the camera/lens upward (not by a defect in the lens), it can happen with any lens, but it's most apparent when a wide angle is used.

Figure 12.14
Tilting the camera produces this "falling back" look in architectural photos.

- **Steady cam.** You'll find that it is easier to get photos without blur from camera shake when you hand-hold a wide-angle lens at slower shutter speeds than it is with a telephoto lens. And, thanks to SteadyShot stabilization, you can take sharp photos at surprisingly long shutter speeds at a long focal length without using a tripod. That's because the reduced magnification of the wide-angle lens or wide-zoom setting doesn't emphasize camera shake like a telephoto lens does.

- **Interesting angles.** Many of the factors already listed combine to produce more interesting angles when shooting with wide-angle lenses. Raising or lowering a telephoto lens a few feet probably will have little effect on the appearance of a distant subject that fills the frame. The same change in elevation can produce a dramatic effect if you're using a short focal length and are close to your subject.

DOF IN DEPTH

The depth-of-field advantage of wide-angle lenses disappears when you enlarge your picture. Believe it or not, a wide-angle image enlarged and cropped to provide the same subject size as a telephoto shot will have the same depth-of-field. Try it: take a wide-angle photo of a friend from a fair distance. Then, use a longer (telephoto) zoom setting from the same shooting position to take the same picture; naturally, your friend will appear to be larger in the second because of the greater telephoto magnification.

Download the two photos to your computer. While viewing the wide-angle shot, magnify it with the zoom or magnify tool so your friend is as large as in the telephoto image. You'll find that the wide-angle photo will have the same depth-of-field as the telephoto image; for example, the background will be equally blurred.

Avoiding Potential Wide-Angle Problems

Wide-angle lenses have a few quirks that you'll want to keep in mind when shooting so you can avoid falling into some common traps. Here's a checklist of tips for avoiding common problems:

- **Symptom: converging lines.** Unless you want to use wildly diverging lines as a creative effect, it's a good idea to keep horizontal and vertical lines in landscapes, architecture, and other subjects carefully aligned with the sides, top, and bottom of the frame. To prevent undesired perspective distortion, you must take care not to tilt the camera. If your subject is very tall, like a building, you may need to shoot from an elevated position (like a high level in a parking garage) so you won't need to tilt the lens upward. And if your subject is short, like a small child, get down to a lower level so you can get the shot without tilting the lens downward.

■ **Symptom: color fringes around objects.** Lenses often produce photos that are plagued with fringes of color around backlit objects, produced by *chromatic aberration.* This common lens flaw comes in two forms: *longitudinal/axial*, in which all the colors of light don't focus in the same plane, and *lateral/transverse*, in which the colors are shifted to one side. Axial chromatic aberration can be reduced by stopping down the lens (to f/8 or f/11, for example), but transverse chromatic aberration cannot.

Better-quality lenses reduce both types of imaging defect; it's common for reviews to point out these failings, so you can choose the best performing lenses that your budget allows. The Lens Compensation feature in the Custom Settings menu can help reduce this problem. Leave it set for Auto to get the chromatic aberration reduction processing that the camera can provide.

■ **Symptom: lines that bow outward.** Some wide-angle lenses cause straight lines to bow outward, an effect called barrel distortion; you'll see the strongest effect at the edges. Most fisheye (or *curvilinear*) lenses produce this effect as a feature of the lens; it's much more obvious than with any other type of lens. (See Figure 12.15.) The mild barrel distortion you get with a conventional lens is rarely obvious except in some types of architectural photography. If you find it objectionable, you'll need to use a well-corrected lens.

Manufacturers like Sony do their best to minimize or eliminate it (producing a *rectilinear* lens), often using *aspherical* lens elements (which are not cross-sections of a sphere). You can also minimize barrel distortion simply by framing your photo with some extra space all around, so the edges where the bowing outward is most obvious can be cropped out of the picture. The Lens Correction feature can help reduce this problem, too. Leave it set to Auto to allow the processor to minimize the slight barrel distortion that can occur with the more affordable lenses.

■ **Symptom: light and dark areas when using a polarizing filter.** You should be aware that polarizers work best when the camera is pointed 90 degrees away from the sun and have the least effect when the camera is oriented 180 degrees from the sun. This is only half the story, however. With lenses like the 16-35mm f/4 zoom, the range is extensive enough to cause problems.

Think about it: if you use the widest setting of such a zoom and point it at a part of a scene that's at the proper 90-degree angle from the sun, the areas of the scene that are at the edges of the frame will be oriented at much wider angles from the sun. Only the center of the image area will be at exactly 90 degrees. When the filter is used to darken a blue sky, the sky will be very dark near the center of your photo. Naturally, the polarizing effect will be much milder at the edges so the sky in those areas will be much lighter in tone (less polarized). The solution is to avoid using a polarizing filter in situations where you'll be including the sky with lenses that have an actual focal length of less than about 28mm.

Figure 12.15
Many wide-angle lenses cause lines to bow outward toward the edges of the image. That's often not noticeable unless you use a fisheye lens; the effect is considered to be interesting and desirable.

Using Telephoto and Tele-Zoom Lenses

Telephoto lenses also can have a dramatic effect on your photography. Here are the most important things you need to know. In the next section, I'll concentrate on telephoto considerations that can be problematic—and how to avoid those problems.

- **Selective focus.** Long lenses have reduced depth-of-field, a shallow range of acceptably sharp focus, especially at wide apertures (small f/numbers); this is useful for selective focus to isolate your subject. You can set the widest aperture to create shallow depth-of-field or close it down (to a small f/number) to allow more of the scene to appear to be in acceptably sharp focus. The flip side of the coin is that even at f/16, a 300mm and longer lens will not provide much depth-of-field, especially when the subject is large in the frame (magnified). Like fire, the depth-of-field aspects of a telephoto lens can be friend or foe.

- **Getting closer.** Telephoto lenses allow you to fill the frame with wildlife, sports action, and candid subjects. No one wants to get a reputation as a surreptitious or "sneaky" photographer (except for paparazzi), but when applied to candids in an open and honest way, a long lens can help you capture memorable moments while retaining enough distance to stay out of the way of events as they transpire.

- **Reduced foreground/increased compression.** Telephoto lenses have the opposite effect of wide angles: they reduce the importance of things in the foreground by squeezing everything together. This so-called *compressed perspective* makes objects in the scene appear to be closer than they are to the naked eye. You can use this effect as a creative tool. You've seen the effect hundreds of times in movies and on television, where the protagonist is shown running in and out of traffic that appears to be much closer to the hero (or heroine) than it really is.

■ **Accentuates camera shakiness.** Telephoto focal lengths hit you with a double whammy in terms of camera/photographer shake. The lenses themselves are bulkier, more difficult to hold steady, and may even produce a barely perceptible seesaw rocking effect when you support them with one hand halfway down the lens barrel. As they magnify the subject, they amplify the effect of any camera shake. It's no wonder that image stabilization like Optical SteadyShot (OSS) is especially popular among those using longer lenses, and why Sony includes this feature in the 18-200mm zooms (and many of the long A-mount lenses).

■ **Interesting angles require creativity.** Telephoto lenses require more imagination in selecting interesting angles, because the "angle" you do get on your subjects is so narrow. Moving from side to side or a bit higher or lower can make a dramatic difference in a wide-angle shot, but raising or lowering a telephoto lens a few feet probably will have little effect on the appearance of the distant subjects you're shooting.

Avoiding Telephoto Lens Problems

Many of the "problems" that telephoto lenses pose are really just challenges and not that difficult to overcome. Here is a list of the seven most common picture maladies and suggested solutions.

■ **Symptom: flat faces in portraits.** Head-and-shoulders portraits of humans tend to be more flattering when a focal length of 50mm to 85mm is used with a full-frame camera. Longer focal lengths compress the distance between features like the nose and ears, making the face look wider and flat. (Conversely, a wide-angle lens will make the nose look huge and ears tiny if you move close enough for a head-and-shoulders portrait.) So, avoid using a focal length much longer than about 60mm with your a7R III unless you're forced to shoot from a greater distance. (Use a wide-angle lens only when shooting three-quarters/full-length portraits, or group shots.)

■ **Symptom: blur due to camera shake.** Because a long focal length amplifies the effects of camera shake, make sure the SteadyShot stabilization is not turned off (with a menu item). Then, if possible, use a faster shutter speed; that may mean that you'll need to set a higher ISO to be able to do so. Of course, a firm support like a solid tripod is the most effective tool for eliminating camera shake, especially if you trip the shutter with a remote commander accessory or the self-timer to avoid the risk of jarring the camera. Of course, only the fast shutter speed option will be useful to prevent blur caused by *subject* motion; SteadyShot or a tripod won't help you freeze a race car in mid-lap.

■ **Symptom: color fringes.** Chromatic aberration is the most pernicious optical problem found in telephoto lenses. There are others, including spherical aberration, astigmatism, coma, curvature of field, and similarly scary-sounding phenomena. The best solution for any of these is to use a better lens that offers the proper degree of correction for aberrations or stop down the lens (to f/8 or f/11) to minimize the problem. But that's not always possible. Your second-best choice may be to correct the fringing in your favorite RAW conversion tool or image editor. Photoshop's Lens Correction filter offers sliders that minimize both red/cyan and blue/yellow fringing. A feature such as this (also available with some other software) can be useful in situations where the a7R III's Lens Compensation feature doesn't fully correct for chromatic aberration.

- **Symptom: lines that curve inward.** Pincushion distortion is common in photos taken with many telephoto lenses; lines, especially those near the edges of the frame, bow inward like the pincushion your grandma might have used. You can take photos of a brick wall at various focal lengths with your zoom lens to find out where the pincushion distortion is the most obvious; that will probably be at or near the longest focal length. Like chromatic aberration, it can be partially corrected using tools like Photoshop's Lens Correction filter (or a similar utility in some other software).

- **Symptom: low contrast from haze or fog.** When you're photographing distant objects, a long lens shoots through a lot more atmosphere, which generally is muddied up with extra haze and fog. The dust or moisture droplets in the atmosphere can reduce contrast and mute colors. Some feel that a skylight or UV filter can help, but this practice is mostly a holdover from the film days. Digital sensors are not sensitive enough to UV light for a UV filter to have much effect. A polarizer might help a bit, but only in certain circumstances. I don't consider this to be a huge problem because it's easy to boost contrast and color saturation in Picture Styles (a menu item) or later in image-editing software.

- **Symptom: low contrast from flare.** Lenses are often furnished with lens hoods for a good reason: to minimize the amount of stray light that will strike the front element causing flare or a ghost image of the diaphragm containing the aperture. A hood is effective when the light is at your side, but it has no value when you're shooting toward the sun. On the other hand, you'll often be shooting with the light striking the lens from an angle. In this situation, the lens hood is only partially effective, so minimize flare by using your hand or cap to cast a shadow over the front element of the lens. (Just be careful not to let your hand or cap intrude into the image area.)

- **Symptom: dark flash photos.** Edge-to-edge flash coverage isn't as problematic with telephoto lenses as it is with wide angles. (The built-in flash simply cannot provide light that covers the entire field of view that's recorded by a lens shorter than 16mm.) The shooting distance is the problem with longer lenses. A 210mm focal length might allow you to make a distant subject appear close to the camera, but the flash isn't fooled. You'll need extra power for distant flash shots, making a large accessory flash unit a valuable accessory.

If you do not have a powerful flash unit and cannot get closer to the subject (like Lady Gaga strutting her stuff on a dark stage), try setting the camera's ISO level to 3200. This increases the sensitivity of the sensor so less light is required to make a bright photo; of course, the photo is likely to be grainy because of digital noise. If that does not solve the problem, you will need to set an even higher ISO, but then you'll get even more obvious digital noise in your photo.

13

Working with Flash

Photography is a form of visual art that uses light to shape the finished product. The photographer may have little or no control over the subject (other than posing human subjects) but can often adjust both viewing angle *and* the nature of the light source to create a particular compelling image. The direction and intensity of the light sources create the shapes and textures that we see. The distribution and proportions determine the contrast and tonal values: whether the image is stark or high key or muted and low in contrast. The colors of the light (because even "white" light has a color balance that the sensor can detect), and how much of those colors the subject reflects or absorbs, paint the hues visible in the image.

As a Sony photographer, you must learn to be a painter and sculptor of light if you want to move from *taking* a picture to *making* a photograph. Most of the time, you'll be working with available or ambient light, perhaps with reflectors or other modifiers, or even some additional continuous light sources, such as incandescent or fluorescent lamps. But at times you'll want to turn to one of the most versatile sources of illumination you have available, the brief, but brilliant snippets of light we call *electronic flash*. This chapter will show you the differences between working with continuous illumination and working with flash and explain how to use the flash capabilities of the Sony a7R III.

Why Flash?

Flash sometimes gets a bad rap, but that's usually prompted by photographers who make poor use of the capabilities electronic flash offers. In some respects, working with continuous lighting instead is easier and more predictable. Conventional lighting is exactly what you might think: uninterrupted illumination that is available all the time during a shooting session. Daylight, moonlight, and the artificial lighting encountered both indoors and outdoors count as continuous light sources (although all of them can be "interrupted" by passing clouds, solar eclipses, a blown fuse, or simply by switching off a lamp). Indoor continuous illumination includes both the lights that are there already (such as incandescent lamps or overhead fluorescent lights indoors) and fixtures you supply yourself, including photoflood lamps or reflectors used to bounce existing light onto your subject.

On the face of things, electronic flash may be uncomfortably *different* from what we are used to, and sometimes considered difficult to use. In practice, you can use flash in all the same ways you use continuous lighting to shape your images, and, in some cases, take advantage of its special properties, such as its action-freezing short duration. Electronic flash is notable because it can be much more intense than continuous lighting, lasts only a brief moment, and can be much more portable than supplementary incandescent sources. It's a light source you can carry with you and use anywhere.

Of course, your Sony a7R III does not have a built-in flash of any sort. There are several reasons for that. The company wanted to make the a7-series cameras exceptionally compact, and a built-in flash would have added bulk. In addition, even though Sony upgraded the size and power of the a7R III's NP-FZ100 battery, the features of the camera alone do a good job of consuming all that extra juice during a shooting session. With a camera like the a7R III, a pop-up flash (which most advanced photographers would likely use only as fill or to trigger off-camera units wirelessly) would provide an unacceptable amount of extra drain. So, any electronic flash used with these cameras is necessarily an external flash with its own power supply, which happily solves the power drain situation while reducing red-eye and other effects of on-camera flash.

Before moving on to discussing flash in detail, here's a quick comparison of the pros and cons of continuous illumination versus flash:

- **Lighting preview—Pro: continuous lighting.** With continuous lighting, such as incandescent lamps or daylight, you always know exactly what kind of lighting effect you're going to get. If you're using multiple lights, you can visualize how they will interact with each other. With electronic flash, the general effect you're going to see may be a mystery until you've built some experience.

- **Lighting preview—Con: electronic flash.** Compact portable flash units often do not provide a "modeling light" function, although studio flash typically do.

- **Exposure calculation—Pro: continuous lighting.** Your camera has no problem calculating accurate exposure for continuous lighting, because the lighting remains constant and can be measured through built-in light meters that interpret the light reaching the sensor. The amount of light available just before the exposure will, in almost all cases, be the same amount of light present when the shutter mechanism is opened to take the shot. The Spot metering mode can be used to measure brightness in the bright areas of the scene and the dark areas; if you have a bit of expertise in this technique, you'll know whether it would be useful to bounce some light into the shadow areas using a reflector panel accessory.

■ **Exposure calculation—Con: electronic flash.** A flash unit provides no illumination until it actually fires so the exact exposure can't be measured by the a7R III's exposure sensor before you take a photo. Instead, the light must be measured by metering the intensity of a *pre-flash* triggered an instant before the main flash, as it is reflected back to the camera and through the lens.

■ **Evenness of illumination—Pro/con: continuous lighting.** Of continuous light sources, daylight, in particular, provides illumination that tends to fill an image completely, lighting up the foreground, background, and your subject almost equally. A sunlit scene may have shadow areas too, of course, so you might need to use reflectors or fill-in light sources to even out the illumination. Barring objects that block large sections of your image from daylight, the light is spread fairly evenly. Indoors, however, continuous lighting is much less likely to be evenly distributed. The average living room, for example, has hot spots and dark corners. But on the plus side, you can *see* this uneven illumination and compensate with additional lamps.

■ **Evenness of illumination—Con: electronic flash.** Electronic flash units, like the continuous light provided by lamps, don't have the advantage of being located 93 million miles from the subject as the sun is. Because of this factor, they suffer from the effects of their proximity.

The *inverse square law*, first applied to both gravity and light by Sir Isaac Newton, dictates that as a light source's distance increases from the subject, the amount of light reaching the subject falls off proportionately to the square of the distance. In plain English, that means that a flash or lamp that's 12 feet away from a subject provides only one-quarter as much illumination as a source that's 6 feet away (rather than half as much). (See Figure 13.1.) This translates into relatively shallow "depth-of-light."

■ **Action stopping—Pro: electronic flash.** When it comes to the ability to freeze moving objects in their tracks, the advantage goes to electronic flash. The brief duration of the emitted light serves as a very fast "shutter speed" when the flash is the main or only source of illumination for the photo. In other words, this effect is possible when shooting in a dark area without much, if any, lighting provided by ambient sources but assumes that the subject is not beyond the range of the flash.

In flash photography, your camera's shutter speed (called *sync speed* in flash photography) is set to 1/250th second, but when flash is the primary light source, the *effective* exposure time will be the 1/1,000th to 1/50,000th second or less; this is the actual duration of the flash illumination. As you can see in Figure 13.2, it's possible to freeze motion with flash of very short duration. The only fly in the ointment is that, if the ambient light is strong enough, it may produce a secondary "ghost" exposure, as I'll explain later in this chapter.

■ **Action stopping—Con: continuous lighting.** Action stopping with continuous light sources is completely dependent on the shutter speed you've dialed in on the camera. And the speeds available are dependent on the amount of light available and your camera's ISO sensitivity setting. Outdoors in daylight, there will probably be enough sunlight to let you shoot at 1/2,000th second and f/6.3 with a non-grainy ISO of 400. That's a fairly useful combination of settings if you're not using a super-telephoto with a small maximum aperture.

But indoors, the reduced illumination quickly has you pushing your a7R III to its limits. For example, if you're shooting indoor sports in a dark arena, there probably won't be enough available light to allow you to use a 1/2,000th second shutter speed unless you use a lens with an extremely wide aperture, such as f/1.8, with, say, the Sony Sonnar T* FE 55mm f/1.8 ZA. You can also specify a very high ISO setting, and accept that image quality may suffer. (In truth, the gym where I shoot indoor basketball allows me to do so at 1/500th second at f/4 using ISO 1600.) In many indoor sports situations, you may find yourself limited to a shutter speed of 1/500th second or slower.

- **Flexibility—Pro: electronic flash.** The action-freezing power of electronic flash, at least for nearby subjects in a dark location, allows you to work without a tripod; that provides extra flexibility and speed when choosing angles and positions.

- **Flexibility—Con: continuous lighting.** Because incandescent and fluorescent lamps are not as bright as electronic flash, the slower shutter speeds required (see "Action stopping," above) mean that you may have to use a tripod more often, especially when shooting portraits. The incandescent variety of continuous lighting gets hot, especially in the studio, and the side effects range from discomfort (for your human models) to disintegration (if you happen to be shooting perishable foods like ice cream).

Figure 13.1
A light source that is twice as far away provides only one-quarter as much illumination.

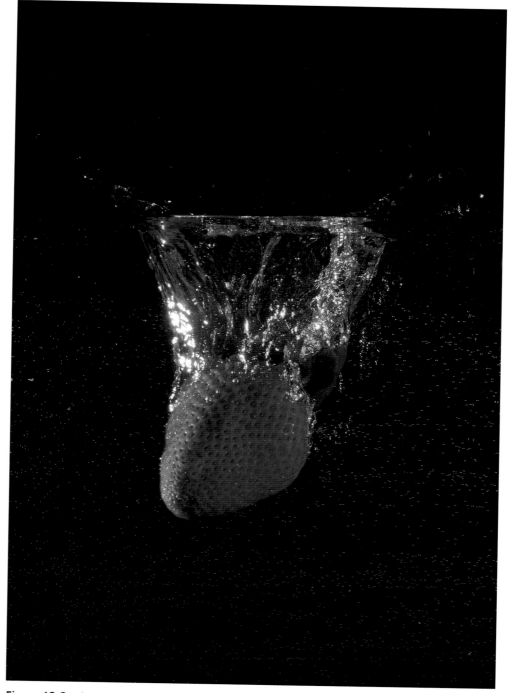

Figure 13.2 Electronic flash can freeze almost any motion because of its extremely short duration.

Electronic Flash Basics

Until you delve into the situation deeply enough, it might appear that serious photographers have a love/hate relationship with electronic flash. You'll often hear that flash photos are less natural looking, and that on-camera flash in most cameras should never be used as the primary source of illumination because it provides a harsh, garish look. Some photographers strongly praise available ("continuous") lighting while denouncing electronic flash.

That bias is against *bad* flash photography. Indeed, flash—often with light-modifier accessories—has become the studio light source of choice for many pro photographers. That's understandable, because the light is more intense (and its intensity can be dialed up or down by the photographer), freezes action, frees you from using a tripod (unless you want to use one to lock down a composition), and has a snappy, consistent light quality that matches daylight. (While color balance changes as the flash duration shortens, some Sony flash units can communicate to the camera the exact white balance provided for that shot.) And even conservative photographers will concede that electronic flash has some important uses as an adjunct to existing light, particularly to fill in dark shadows.

How Electronic Flash Works

The electronic flash you use will be connected to the camera by slipping it onto the hot shoe or linked by a cable connected to an adapter mounted on the shoe. In all cases, the flash is triggered at the instant of exposure, during a period when the sensor is fully exposed by the shutter.

The a7R III has electronic shutter options, which I'll describe later, and a conventional vertically traveling physical shutter that consists of two curtains. The front curtain opens and moves to the opposite side of the frame, at which point the shutter is completely open. The flash can be triggered at this point (so-called *front-curtain sync,* which is the default mode), making the flash exposure. Then, after a delay that can vary from 30 seconds to 1/250th second, a second, *rear curtain* begins moving across the sensor plane, covering up the sensor again. If the flash is triggered just before the rear curtain starts to close, then the optional *rear-curtain sync* is used. In both cases, though, a shutter speed of 1/250th second is (ordinarily) the *maximum* that can be used to take a photo, because that's the speed at which both the front and rear curtains are tucked out of the way, leaving the entire full frame exposed to capture the flash burst.

Figure 13.3 illustrates how this works, with a fanciful illustration of a generic shutter (your a7R III's shutter does *not* look like this). As an exposure is made using the conventional (non-electronic) shutter, the curtains move as follows:

1. Both curtains open. With a mirrorless camera like the a7R III, the sensor remains completely exposed, so that the image that's being captured can be viewed on the electronic viewfinder and LCD monitor.

2. Front curtain closes. As the exposure begins, the front curtain rises to cover the sensor.

Figure 13.3 A focal plane shutter has two curtains, the lower, or front curtain, and an upper, or rear curtain.

3. **Prior image is dumped.** When the sensor is completely covered, the preview image is dumped, resetting the pixels so that the exposure can begin.

4. **Front curtain begins to descend.** As the front curtain drops, the sensor is gradually exposed to light, and the *ambient* exposure (using the available light in the scene) begins.

5. **Front curtain continues to descend.** More of the sensor is uncovered, and the ambient exposure continues.

6. **Both curtains open.** With the sensor fully exposed, the electronic flash's brief burst can fill the frame.

  • If this burst takes place as soon as the curtains are fully open, then *front-curtain sync*, which is the default, has been used. Following the flash, the sensor continues to be exposed for the length of the exposure, which can range from 1/250th second to 30 seconds (or longer, with a Bulb exposure).

  • The burst can also take place *at the very end* of the exposure, just before the rear curtain starts to descend. This is called *rear-curtain sync*.

  • When the exposure is finished, the rear curtain descends and the captured image is conveyed off the sensor to the camera's internal buffer, and thence to your memory card. The rear curtain then ascends to the top of the frame, exposing the sensor again and a preview image for the next picture appears in the EVF and LCD monitor.

Keep in mind that the a7R III *always* defaults to front-curtain sync unless you explicitly select another sync mode using the Fn button or Flash Mode entry in the Camera Settings I-11 menu.

And Now for Something Completely Different...

If you've absorbed that, things are about to get *really* interesting. The a7R III has special modes available from the Custom Settings II-4 menu, in which either the physical front curtain or both the physical front curtain *and* the rear curtain are simulated electronically. Only one of the two modes can be used with flash. Here's the difference:

- **e-Front Curtain Shutter.** Recall that the sensor of a mirrorless camera is always exposed and feeding its image to the EVF and LCD monitor; in order to capture an image within a specified period of time, the sensor needs to *stop* collecting the image so the exposure can begin. In normal operation, as described above, when you press the shutter release down all the way, the shutter closes and the camera dumps the image you were previewing, resetting the pixels and leaving the sensor blank and ready to capture an exposure. When the e-Front Curtain Shutter is enabled, the physical front shutter doesn't close: the image is dumped *electronically*, and then the sensor immediately begins capturing an image. The physical rear curtain shutter then closes at the end of the exposure.

  The advantages of the electronic front curtain are that the camera can respond more quickly with less shutter lag, there is no possibility of vibration caused by the physical shutter bouncing at the end of its travel (this was a significant problem with the original a7 series), and an electronic front curtain shutter is quieter. As the a7 series is mirrorless, these cameras are already quieter than dSLR models, which have a mirror flapping about before and after the exposure.

  However, an electronic front curtain shutter can exhibit problems with certain lenses and very fast shutter speeds. In such cases, when you are using an unusually wide aperture, such as f/1.8, some areas of the photo may exhibit a secondary (ghost) image. The aperture of an affected lens requires the diaphragm's "leaves" to travel a greater distance, and there may simply not be enough time. An overexposure may result. If you encounter that problem, turn the e-curtain option off; otherwise, you can do as I do and leave it on all the time.

- **Electronic shutter.** The a7R III has an all-electronic shutter that can be activated by selecting Silent Shooting in the Custom Settings menu. In that case, both the physical front and rear curtains are replaced by electronic equivalents. Exposure is started and stopped electronically, with no curtains at all. Silent Shooting is indeed silent; I've had other photographers watching me snap away in that mode ask me whether I was really taking pictures at all. It is an excellent mode for religious ceremonies and other events where even the quiet click of the e-Front Curtain might be intrusive.

  As I described in Chapter 10, silent shooting's rolling shutter captures the image line by line (as opposed to a global shutter that grabs the image in one fell swoop) and is subject to the same unwanted side effects found in video cameras, including wobble/Jell-O effect in hand-held shots, diagonal skewing, smear, and other defects. But the most important complication, in terms of the subject of this chapter, is that the electronic shutter cannot be used with flash at all. If you have a flash mounted and powered up and press the shutter release, it won't go off when the electronic shutter is active. Indeed, the Flash Mode options in the Camera Settings I-11 menu are grayed out and unavailable.

Avoiding Sync-Speed Problems

Using a shutter speed faster than the maximum sync speed can cause problems. Triggering the electronic flash *only* when the shutter is completely open makes a lot of sense if you think about what's going on. To obtain shutter speeds faster than 1/250th second, the a7R III exposes only part of the sensor at one time, by starting the rear curtain on its journey before the front curtain has completely opened. That effectively provides a briefer exposure as the slit of the shutter passes over the surface of the sensor. If the flash were to fire during the time when the front and rear curtains partially obscured the sensor, only the slit that was actually open would be exposed.

You'd end up with only a narrow band, representing the portion of the sensor that was exposed when the picture was taken. For shutter speeds *faster* than the top sync speed, the rear curtain begins moving *before* the front curtain reaches the bottom of the frame. As a result, a moving slit, the distance between the front and rear curtains, exposes one portion of the sensor at a time as it moves from the top to the bottom. Figure 13.4 shows three views of our typical (but imaginary) physical focal plane shutter. At left is pictured the closed shutter; in the middle version you can see the front curtain has moved about 1/4 of the distance down from the top; and in the right-hand version, the rear curtain has started to "chase" the front curtain across the frame toward the bottom.

If the flash is triggered while this slit is moving, only the exposed portion of the sensor will receive any illumination. You end up with a photo like the one shown in Figure 13.5. Note that a band across the bottom of the image is black. That's a shadow of the rear shutter curtain, which had started to move when the flash was triggered. Sharp-eyed readers will wonder why the black band is at the *bottom* of the frame rather than at the top, where the rear curtain begins its journey. The answer is simple: your lens flips the image upside down and forms it on the sensor in a reversed position. You never notice that, because the camera is smart enough to show you the pixels that make up your photo in their proper orientation during picture review. But this image flip is why, if your sensor gets dirty and you detect a spot of dust in the upper half of a test photo, if cleaning manually, you need to look for the speck in the *bottom* half of the sensor.

Figure 13.4 A typical exposure being made using the conventional physical shutter.

Figure 13.5
If a shutter speed faster than 1/250th second is used with flash, you can end up photographing only a portion of the image.

I generally end up with sync speed problems only when shooting in the studio, using studio flash units rather than my Sony dedicated unit. That's because if you're using either type of "smart" flash, the camera knows that a strobe is attached, and remedies any unintentional goof in shutter speed settings. If you happen to set the a7R III's shutter to a faster speed in S or M mode, the camera will automatically adjust the shutter speed down to the maximum sync speed as soon as you attach and turn on an external flash (or prevent you from choosing a faster speed if the flash is powered up). In A or P, where the a7R III selects the shutter speed, it will never choose a shutter speed higher than 1/250th second when using flash.

But when using a non-dedicated flash, such as a studio unit plugged into an adapter attached to the accessory shoe, the camera has no way of knowing that a flash is connected, so shutter speeds faster than 1/250th second can be set inadvertently.

Note that the a7R III can use a feature called *high-speed sync* that allows shutter speeds faster than the maximum sync speed with certain external dedicated Sony flash units. When using high-speed sync, the flash fires a continuous series of bursts at reduced power for the entire duration of the exposure, so that the illumination is able to expose the sensor as the slit moves.

HS sync is set using the controls that adjust the compatible external flash units, which include the HVL-F60M/RM, HVL-F58AM, HVL-F56AM, HVL-45RM, HVL-F43AM/HVL-F43M, HVL-F32M, and HVL-F36AM. (Note that all flashes ending in AM use the older Minolta-style foot and cannot be mounted on the a7R III without an inexpensive Sony ADP-MAA adapter.) High-speed sync cannot be used when working with multiple flash units. When active, the message H appears on the LCD panel on the back of the flash. You'll find complete instructions accompanying those flash units.

Ghost Images

The difference might not seem like much, but whether you use front-curtain sync (the default setting) or rear-curtain sync (an optional setting) can make a significant difference to your photograph *if the ambient light in your scene also contributes to the image.* At faster shutter speeds, particularly 1/250th second, there isn't much time for the ambient light to register, unless it is very bright. It's likely that the electronic flash will provide almost all the illumination, so front-curtain sync or rear-curtain sync isn't very important.

However, at slower shutter speeds, or with very bright ambient light levels, there is a significant difference, particularly if your subject is moving, or the camera isn't steady. In any of those situations, the ambient light will register as a second image accompanying the flash exposure, and if there is movement (camera or subject), that additional image will not be in the same place as the flash exposure. It will show as a ghost image and, if the movement is significant enough, as a blurred ghost image trailing in front of or behind your subject in the direction of the movement.

As I mentioned earlier, when you're using front-curtain sync, the flash goes off the instant the shutter opens, producing an image of the subject on the sensor. That happens whether you're using the mechanical shutter or the optional electronic Front Curtain option from the Custom Settings II-4 menu. Then, the shutter remains open for an additional period (which, as I've noted, can be from 30 seconds to 1/250th second). If your subject is moving, say, toward the right side of the frame, the ghost image produced by the ambient light will produce a blur on the right side of the original subject image, making it look as if your sharp (flash-produced) image is chasing the ghost. For those of us who grew up with lightning-fast superheroes who always left a ghost trail *behind them,* that looks unnatural (see Figure 13.6).

So, Sony provides rear- (second-) curtain sync to remedy the situation. In that mode, the shutter opens, as before. The shutter remains open for its designated duration, and the ghost image forms. If your subject moves from the left side of the frame to the right side, the ghost will move from left to right, too. *Then,* about 1.5 milliseconds before the rear shutter curtain closes, the flash is triggered, producing a nice, sharp flash image *ahead* of the ghost image.

EVERY WHICH WAY, INCLUDING UP

Note that although I describe the ghost effect in terms of subject matter that is moving left to right in a horizontally oriented composition, it can occur in any orientation, and with the subject moving in *any* direction. (Try photographing a falling rock, if you can, and you'll see the same effect.) Nor are the ghost images affected by the fact that modern shutters travel vertically rather than horizontally. Secondary images are caused between the time the front curtain fully opens, and the rear curtain begins to close. The direction of travel of the shutter curtains, or the direction of your subject, does not matter.

Figure 13.6

Front-curtain sync produces an image that trails in front of the flash exposure (left), whereas rear-curtain sync creates a more "natural looking" trail behind the flash image (right).

Slow Sync

Another flash synchronization option is *slow sync*, which is actually an exposure option that tells the a7R III to use slower shutter speeds when possible, to allow you to capture a scene by both flash and ambient illumination. To activate Slow Sync, press the Fn button, navigate to the flash options, and choose Slow Sync. Or, make the same selection from the Flash Mode entry in the Camera Settings II-11 menu.

Then, the exposure system will try to use longer shutter speeds with the flash, so that an initial exposure is made with the flash unit, and a secondary exposure of subjects in the background will be produced by the slower shutter speed. This will let you shoot a portrait of a person at night and, much of the time, avoid a dark background. Your portrait subject will be illuminated by the flash, and the background by the ambient light. It's a good idea to have the camera mounted on a tripod or some other support or have SteadyShot switched on to avoid having this secondary exposure produce ghost images due to camera movement during the exposure. (See Figure 13.7.)

Because Slow Sync is a type of exposure control, it does not work in Manual mode or Shutter Priority mode (because the a7R III doesn't choose the shutter speed in those modes). It is not disabled in those modes: you can still select it using the Camera Settings menu or Function menu, but your shutter speed will not be changed.

Figure 13.7

Without slow sync, ambient light may not be sufficient to balance with the flash exposure (left). When slow sync is activated, longer shutter speeds are selected, allowing the ambient light to register, too (right).

Determining Exposure

Calculating the proper exposure for an electronic flash photograph is a bit more complicated than determining the settings by continuous light. The right exposure isn't simply a function of how far away your subject is, even though the inverse square law I mentioned does have an effect: the farther away the subject is, the less light is available for the exposure. The a7R III can calculate distance if you're using lenses with a *distance encoder chip,* which detects the position of the focusing mechanism as focus is locked in just prior to exposure. The component transmits this information to the camera, which can use it to determine the distance to the subject, and, therefore, much flash output is required to illuminate the scene. This Advanced Distance Integration (ADI) delivers high-precision flash metering that is unaffected by the reflectance of subjects or backgrounds.

But, of course, flash exposure isn't based on distance alone. Various objects reflect more or less light at the same distance so, obviously, the camera needs to measure the amount of light reflected back and through the lens. Yet, as the flash itself isn't available for measuring until it's triggered, the a7R III has nothing to measure.

The solution is to fire the flash twice. The initial shot is a pre-flash that can be analyzed, then followed by a main flash that's given exactly the calculated intensity needed to provide a correct exposure. As a result, the primary flash may be longer for distant objects and shorter for closer subjects, depending on the required intensity for exposure. This through-the-lens evaluative flash exposure system uses distance information, and it operates whenever you have attached a Sony dedicated flash unit to the a7R III, and a lens that provides the necessary distance integration information.

Flash Modes

There are several flash modes available in the Camera Settings menu:

- **Flash Off.** The flash never fires; this may be useful in museums, concerts, or religious ceremonies where electronic flash would prove disruptive. This option is not available in P, A, S, or M mode; if you do not want flash to fire, turn it off.

- **Auto Flash.** The flash fires as required, depending on lighting conditions. Not available in P, A, S, or M mode because flash *always* fires in these modes if it's attached and powered up.

- **Fill-Flash.** When this option is set, the flash will always fire when set to P, A, S, or M modes, using one of the two Auto modes or in SCN modes where flash is not disabled. The camera balances the available illumination with flash to provide a balanced lighting effect. (See Figure 13.8.)

- **Slow Sync.** The camera combines flash with slow shutter speeds; the nearby subject can be illuminated by flash, but during the longer shutter speed, there's enough time for the darker surroundings (lit by ambient light) to record on the sensor.

- **Rear Sync.** Fires the flash at the *end* of the exposure time, after the ambient light exposure has been made, producing more satisfying photos of moving subjects when using a long exposure; light trails will be behind the "ghost" image, as illustrated earlier in Figure 13.6, right.

- **Wireless.** This is available from a separate entry in the Camera Settings II-11 menu. (On and Off are your options.) Wireless allows an optional external flash or flash trigger mounted on the camera's multi-interface shoe to activate one or more external flash units that support wireless off-camera flash; there's no need for any cable connection between the camera and the remote flash unit. I'll explain the Sony wireless system later in this chapter.

Figure 13.8 The owl (left) was in shadow. Fill flash (right) brightened up the bird, while adding a little catch light to its eye.

Flash Exposure Compensation

This is a feature discussed previously in Chapter 3. It's important to keep in mind how the camera's exposure compensation system works when you're using electronic flash. To activate exposure compensation for flash, visit the Flash Comp. item in the Camera Settings menu or use the Function menu, and set the amount of plus or minus compensation you want. This function is not available when using Intelligent Auto mode. When you find that your flash photos are too dark even after you have set the highest amount of compensation, then the flash simply cannot provide more power; you must move closer to the subject, or use a wider aperture, or set a higher ISO, or take all of these steps. Note too that when a subject is extremely close to the camera, even a −3 setting may not prevent an excessively bright image. You'll probably have to *reduce* your ISO setting in that case.

Flash exposure compensation affects only the amount of light emitted by the flash. If you want to adjust the brightness of the ambient light exposure, you would also need to use the conventional exposure compensation feature. In fact, you can use both features at the same time, to get a brighter subject and a darker background, or vice versa. Let's say you're taking a photo of a friend posing against a light-toned background such as a white cabana on a beach. A plus exposure compensation setting (perhaps +1 when using multi-segment metering) will ensure that the cabana won't be underexposed while a −1/3 or −2/3 flash exposure compensation will ensure that shadows on your friend's face will be lightened by a very gentle burst of flash. This is an advanced technique that requires some experimentation but can be valuable when used with some expertise.

Figure 13.9
Set flash exposure compensation.

Red Eye Reduction

When using semi-automatic or manual exposure modes, red-eye reduction is available if Red Eye Reduction is On in the Camera Settings II-11 menu (as described in Chapter 4). The flash will fire a burst before the photo is actually taken as you depress the shutter release button. That will theoretically cause your subjects' irises to contract (if they are looking toward the camera), thereby reducing the red-eye effect in your photograph.

Using an External Electronic Flash

As I write this, Sony offers six accessory electronic flash units that are compatible with the a7R III's new-style multi-interface shoe: the HVL-F60M, its radio-wireless-capable sibling the HVL-F60RM, as well as the HVL-45RM, HVL-F43M, HVL-F32M, and HVL-F20M. These external units can be mounted on the camera, connected to the camera's multi-interface shoe with a cable (I'll detail how later), or (except for the HVL-F20M) used off-camera with wireless connectivity when triggered by another external flash used as a controller/master. Each can also function as the controller/master mounted on an a7-series camera to trigger other flash units wirelessly.

In addition, there are earlier Sony flash units designed for the older Minolta/Sony proprietary hot shoe. They can be used with the a7-series cameras if you purchase an inexpensive adapter, such as the Sony ADP-MAA (about $25). Or, you can skip the adapter and use wireless-compatible legacy flash units off-camera in wireless mode, triggered by an on-camera master/controller. Although they are discontinued, I'll describe some of these earlier flash units because you may already own one or can find one used at a price that's hard to resist. I don't recommend the legacy flash/adapter approach, because older units operate using a more limited communication protocol, which I'll describe later. But because some of you may have an older flash or can pick one up used at a decent price, it doesn't make sense to pretend that these discontinued models don't exist, because they still can work with your a7R III, especially as remote/slave units.

LET'S BE FRANK...

Although one of my jobs is to show you how to get the best from your wise decision to purchase a Sony camera, I'm not a cheerleader for the company. It's done a great job in responding to customer requests for features and upgraded gear, but Sony is still playing catch-up in the flash arena. It's been especially slow in providing affordable radio control flash options (as I'll note later in the chapter). The introduction of the HVL-F60RM in February 2018 adds options, but at $600, many may find it expensive.

The sheer volume of third-party options for gear makes it impossible to cover all of them in detail. So, I have generally devoted the available space to Sony products in this book, with the exception of a discussion of additional lens options. In terms of full-featured TTL-compatible third-party electronic flash units for your a7R III, there are a number of excellent products you should check out. Godox, in particular, makes good Sony-friendly flash which are marketed under the Godox name as well as rebranded for other vendors.

Guide Numbers, Hot Shoes, and More

Before I describe the flash units themselves, there are a few aspects you need to understand in order to compare electronic flash. If you're a veteran Sony (or Minolta) shooter, you can skim over this section, or skip it entirely. Those new to photography or the Sony realm should find this information useful.

Guide Numbers

The first thing you need to learn when comparing flash units is that Sony incorporates the Guide Number (GN) of each flash in the product name. So, what's a Guide Number? The GN designation derives from the good old days prior to automatic flash units and through-the-lens flash metering, when flash exposures had to be calculated mathematically. Those days are very long ago, indeed, as Honeywell introduced Auto/Strobonar flash units way back in the 1960s.

Guide numbers are a standard way of specifying the power of a flash when used in manual, non-autoexposure mode. Divide the guide number by the distance to determine the correct f/stop to use at full power. With a GN of 197 at ISO 100, you would use an aperture of around f/19.7 for a subject that's 10 feet from the camera (197 divided by 10), or around f/9.5 for a subject at a distance of 20 feet. Because most countries in the world use metric measurements, guide numbers are given using values for both meters and feet. Thus, Sony's HVL-F60M/RM unit has a guide number of 60/197 in meters/feet, and the 60 GN is incorporated into the unit's product name.

The Guide Number data is most useful for comparing the relative power of several flash units that you're considering. According to the Inverse Square Law, a flash unit with a GN of 200 (in feet) puts out four times the amount of light as one with a GN of about 100. If your accessory flash has a zoom head, which can change coverage to match the focal length setting of your lens, the GN will vary according to the zoom setting, as wider zoom settings spread the same light over a broader area than a telephoto zoom setting.

Hot Shoes

Starting in 1988, Minolta phased in a proprietary hot shoe, the so-called *iISO* shoe, which was supposedly more rugged and secure than the original ISO 518 shoe, based on a design that dates back to 1913, when it was used to attach viewfinders to a camera (electronic flash hadn't been invented yet). No other vendors, including Canon and Nikon, embraced Minolta's design and continued to use the industry standard shoe. The ISO 518 standard doesn't specify any electronic connections between camera and flash, other than the "dumb" triggering circuit, so when sophisticated electronic flash units with TTL metering and other capabilities were developed, each vendor created their own hot shoe version with the necessary electrical contacts for their cameras and flash units. The chief consequence for non-Minolta/Sony shooters was that you could mount dedicated flash units from one brand onto the ISO 518 shoe of another vendor's camera, and trigger that flash in manual, non-TTL mode.

When Sony purchased Konica Minolta's camera technology it began redesigning legacy features, and the old iISO hot shoe came under scrutiny. In 2012, Sony introduced a 21+3–pin hot shoe which it dubbed the *multi-interface shoe*, which resembles a standard ISO 518 hot shoe with its "dumb" contacts. However, tucked away at the front of the shoe are additional electrical contacts that allow intelligent TTL flash metering communication between the camera and flash, and much more. For example, a whole series of stereo microphones from Sony and others, designed to plug into the multi-interface shoe, are available. As I noted earlier, you can purchase adapters that allow you to connect older iISO flash to the a7R III, or to attach new model flash units to a camera that has the original iISO hot shoe.

Cable Connections

In some cases, you can get your external flash off the camera without using a wireless connection by linking an HVL-F60M/RM and a7R III with a physical cable. The gear needed for the hook-up can be costly, so I don't recommend it, but if you want to go that route, here's the way to go. Purchase the Sony FA-CS1M multi-interface shoe adapter (about $40). It slides into the a7-series camera's multi-interface shoe and has a four-pin TTL socket on the front. Connect that socket to a matching four-pin outlet located on the underside of the HVL-F60M/RM, beneath a protective terminal cap, using a 4.9-foot FA-MC1AM cable ($60). If you need more length, the FA-EC1AM extension cable ($50) adds another 4.9 feet to your connection. The HVL-F43M does not have the four-pin socket and connecting it to a cable requires some additional adapters, so you're better off not going that way.

HVL-F60M/RM Flash Units

Sony now has *two* top-of-the-line flash units, the HVL-F60M, which uses optical triggering only, and the HVL-F60RM, which is compatible with both optical and radio control. The F60M version is currently listed at $550, but the price will probably come down a tad now that its $600 radio-friendly sibling has been introduced. Other than optical/radio control, the two units are functionally identical (except for the location of the LED video light on the F60RM. The F60M model is shown in Figure 13.10. The duo are the most powerful units the company offers, with an ISO 100 guide number (GN) of 60 in meters or 197 in feet at ISO 100. As I noted earlier, the GN does not indicate actual flash range but it's useful when comparing several flash units in terms of their general power output.

Figure 13.10 The Sony HVL-F60M is the top-of-the-line external flash unit and includes a bonus LED light for video.

Like all Sony multi-interface shoe flash units except the HVL-F20M, the F60M/F60RM automatically adjust the zoom head to vary the angle of coverage to suit the lens focal length in use. You can zoom the head manually instead, if you prefer. A built-in slide-out diffuser panel boosts wide-angle coverage so it's suitable for photos taken at short focal lengths. There's also a slide-out "bounce card" that can reflect some light forward even when bouncing the flash off the ceiling, to fill in shadows or add a catch light in the eyes of your portrait subjects. This dust- and moisture-resistant 21-ounce unit uses four AA batteries but can also be connected to the older FA-EB1AM external battery adapter, which has room for 6 AA batteries for increased capacity and faster recycling.

You may find the FA-EB1AM available at reduced prices, as it was recently replaced by the FA-EB1 ($250). The new pack is compatible with both the F60M and F60RM units, and capable of accepting *either* four or eight AA batteries in replaceable magazines, for up to 660 flashes with speedy recycle times of 0.6 seconds. When connected to the flash, it becomes the unit's primary power source.

ANOTHER GOODIE

Along with the F60RM flash and FA-EB1 battery pack, Sony has introduced the FA-RG1 Multi Interface Shoe Rain Guard, which prevents water from seeping into the electrical contacts of the camera.

Regardless of power source, the F60M/RM automatically communicates white balance information to your camera, allowing the a7R III to adjust WB to match the flash output. It also offers a dedicated video light that can be useful for a bit of extra illumination if the subject is close to the camera. When you point the flash head upward, the trio of LED video illuminator lamps are revealed.

You can use this large unit as a main flash or allow it to be triggered wirelessly by another compatible flash unit. A pre-flash burst of light from the triggering master/controller unit causes a remote flash unit to fire. When using flash wirelessly, Sony recommends rotating the unit so that the flashtube is pointed to the location where light should be directed, while the front (light sensor) of the flash is pointed toward the camera. In wireless mode, you can control up to three groups of flashes, and specify the output levels for each group, giving you an easy way to control the lighting ratios of multiple flash units.

This flash unit can provide a simulated modeling light effect at two flashes per second or at a more useful (but more power-consuming) 40 flashes per second for 4 seconds for 160 continuous mini-bursts. In wireless off-camera flash, the HVL-60M/RM can function as the main (on-camera) flash in wireless mode or it can be the remote flash, triggered wirelessly by another compatible flash unit, as discussed earlier.

HIGH-SPEED SYNC

Those who are frustrated by an inability to use a shutter speed faster than 1/250th second will love the High-Speed Sync (HSS) mode that allows for flash at 1/500th to 1/4,000th second! (HSS is also available with the HVL-F43M, HVL-F32M, and the discontinued HVL-58AM and HVL-F36AM.) This is ideal when you want to use a very wide aperture for selective focus with a nearby subject with flash; HSS at a fast shutter speed such as 1/1,000th second is one way to avoid overexposure. The Mode button on the back of the flash is used to choose either TTL or Manual flash exposure. You can then use the Menu button and plus/minus keys to activate HSS mode; HSS appears in the unit's data panel as confirmation of the mode.

Keep in mind that flash output is much lower in High-Speed Sync than in conventional flash photography. That's because less than the full duration of the flash is used to expose each portion of the image as it is exposed by the slit passing in front of the sensor. As a result, the effective flash (distance) range is much shorter.

In addition, HSS will not work when using multiple flash units or when the flash unit is set for left/right/up bounce flash or when the wide-angle diffuser is being used. (If you're pointing the flash downward, say, at a close-up subject, HSS can be used.)

HVL-F45RM Flash Unit

If you want an on-camera flash capable of triggering external flash units optically *and* by radio control and are intimidated by the price of the HVL-F60RM, this flash is an affordable ($350) option. It also can be triggered wirelessly by an optical master, by another HVL-F45RM or an HVL-F60RM mounted on the a7R III, or by the Sony FA-WRC1M Wireless Radio Commander mounted on the camera. When using radio control, it uses 14 channels to communicate with up to 15 flash units in five groups. It has a guide number of 45/148 (meters/feet) at ISO 100, and a fast 2.5-second recycle time. Its zoom head adjusts for the field of view from 24mm to 105mm (perfect for the a7R III's kit lens) and has an LED video light.

HVL-F43M Flash Unit

This less pricey ($328) electronic flash (shown in Figure 13.11) shares many of the advanced features of the HVL-F60M/RM but has a lower guide number of 43/138 (meters/feet). Features shared with the high-end unit include HSS, automatic white balance adjustment, and automatic zoom with the same coverage of focal lengths and the slide-out diffuser, as well as a built-in bounce card. Its quick-shift function allows you to direct the flash upward or to the side by rotating the head. This unit also can be used in wireless mode as a master/controller or remote/slave, and it also offers the quick-shift bounce feature. The HVL-F43M is a tad lighter (at 12 ounces) than its bigger sibling and runs on four AAs. This flash replaces the similar HVL-F43AM unit, which uses the older iISO hot shoe.

HVL-F36AM Flash Unit

Although discontinued, you can easily find this versatile flash available online or in used condition. It uses the old iISO hot shoe, so you'll need an adapter. The guide number for this lower-cost Sony flash unit is (surprise!) 36/118 (meters/feet). Although (relatively) compact at 9 ounces, you still get some big-flash features, such as wireless operation, auto zoom, and high-speed sync capabilities. Bounce flash flexibility is reduced a little, with no swiveling from side to side and only a vertical adjustment of up to 90 degrees.

HVL-F32M Flash Unit

The $250 HVL-F32M is Sony's lowest-cost wireless-compatible electronic flash unit. (See Figure 13.12.) It features a high-speed synchronization mode, wireless control, and automatic white balance compensation. In wireless mode, it can be used only on Channel 1 (as I'll describe shortly) but can function as both a master/controller and remote/slave. The flash is powered by a pair of AA batteries and it is resistant to both dust and moisture. Those who love to use bounce flash will like the built-in bounce sheet and retractable wide-angle panel that spreads the light to cover the equivalent of a 16mm lens.

Figure 13.11 The Sony HVL-F43M.

Figure 13.12 The Sony HVL-F32M.

HVL-F20M Flash Unit

The least-expensive Sony flash (see Figure 13.13) is the HVL-F20M ($130), designed to appeal to the budget conscious, especially those who need just a bit of a boost for fill flash, or want a small unit (just 3.2 ounces) on their camera. It has a guide number of 20 at ISO 100, and features simplified operation. For example, there's a switch on the side of the unit providing Indoor and Outdoor settings (the indoor setting tilts the flash upward to provide bounce light; with the outdoor setting, the flash fires directly at your subject). This flash can serve as a master/controller on the a7R III to trigger off-camera flash units wirelessly but cannot be used as a remote/slave flash. There are special modes for wide-angle shooting (use the built-in diffuser to spread the flash's coverage to that of a lens with a very wide field of view or choose the Tele position to narrow the flash coverage to that of a 50mm or longer lens for illuminating more distant subjects). While it's handy for fill flash, owners of an a7-series camera will probably want a more powerful unit as their main electronic flash.

Figure 13.13 The HVL-F20M flash unit is compact and inexpensive.

BATTERY TIP

You may not use your flash very often, but when you do, you want it to operate properly. The problem with infrequent flash use is that conventional nickel-metal hydride batteries lose their charge over time, so if your flash unit is sitting in your bag for a long time between uses, you may not even be aware that your rechargeable batteries are pooped out. Non-rechargeable alkaline cells are not a solution: they generally provide less power for your flash and replacing them can be costly. The Energizer Lithium Ultimate AA batteries last up to three times longer, but they sell for about $10 for four.

I've had excellent luck with a new kind of battery developed by Panasonic called *eneloop* cells. They retain their charge for long periods of time—as much as 75 percent of a full charge over a three-year period (let's hope you don't go that long between uses of your flash). They're not much more expensive than ordinary rechargeables and can be revitalized up to 1,500 times. They're available in capacities of 1500 mAh to 2500 mAh. I use the economical models with 1900 mAh capacity.

Setting Ratios

Once you've set up one or more flash for the RMT group, and more or more for the RMT2 group, you can adjust the ratio used between them.

Ratios with the HVL-F43M

Just follow these steps when using the HVL-F43M as the controller or remote/slave. Remember that all flashes in all remote groups must be set to the same channel, as described previously:

1. The easiest way to set ratios is to mount the controller/master and remote/slave units on the camera in turn. With each flash mounted on the camera set to Wireless Flash as described earlier, press the Mode button on the flash to display WL.

2. Press the Fn button, then press the left/right directional buttons until CTRL and RATIO are *both* blinking.

3. Press the Fn button again. The line at upper right will display:

   CTRL RMT RMT1

   1 : 1 : 1

4. Use the left/right directional buttons to move the highlighting to CTRL. When CTRL is highlighted, you can press the up/down buttons to choose the relative power of that flash, compared to the others, from 1, 2, 4, 8, 16, or - - (the latter disables the flash). For example, a setting of 16:1:4 would specify that the flash mounted on the camera has 1/16th the power of the RMT group, while the RMT2 group would have 1/4 the power of the RMT group. Selecting - - disables that flash or group. You might want to do that so that the on-camera flash doesn't contribute to the exposure, even though it will still fire a pre-flash to trigger the remote/slave units (see Figure 13.14).

5. Press the TTL/M button to display TTL.

6. Repeat for each flash.

Ratios with the HVL-F60M/RM

Just follow these steps when using the HVL-F60M/RM as the controller or remote/slave. Again, all flashes in all remote groups must be set to the same channel, as described previously:

1. You can mount each flash on the camera and set the ratios. Press the Mode button to produce the Mode screen and select WL CTRL.

2. Press the Fn button to access the Quick Navi screen and use the control wheel to highlight WL CTRL. Press the control wheel center button to access the dedicated settings screen.

3. Use the control wheel to highlight RATIO. Press the center button to access your choices, Ratio: Off (the controller flash does not contribute to the exposure), TTL Ratio, and Manual Ratio. You can highlight TTL Ratio and use the control wheel to choose ON.

Figure 13.14 Set ratios on the HVL-F43M.

Figure 13.15 Set ratios on the HVL-F60M/RM.

4. Press the center button to return to the indicator screen.

5. Press the Fn button to display the Quick Navi screen and choose the Wireless Lighting Ratio control indicator located at middle left of the screen. Press the control wheel center button, then use the control wheel to change the lighting ratio of each group. Rotate the control wheel to choose the relative power of each flash, compared to the others, from 1, 2, 4, 8, 16, or - -. The - - setting disables that group. (See Figure 13.15.)

6. Press the center button when finished.

Radio Control

Your Sony electronic flash communicate with each other using optical control, via the pre-flashes emitted before the actual exposure takes place. That type of linking requires line-of-sight communication between master and remote units and works only over limited distances. Early in 2016 Sony introduced its wireless radio commander/receiver duo, which gives you a much greater range, many more channels to work with, and more control. Unfortunately, Sony's radio control solution is expensive, making it impractical for all but the most avid (and well-heeled) shooters. I expect it will be more popular among professionals who can justify the expense, and those, such as photojournalists, who need the flexibility of a larger number of channels to avoid conflicts with other photographers covering the same event.

To properly equip yourself, you'll need:

- **Commander.** You'll need one HVL-F60RM flash, HVL-F45RM flash, or FA-WRC1M wireless radio commander ($349) for every camera you want to equip with radio control. The radio-compatible flash or commander reside in the hot shoe of the a7R III and are used to trigger the off-camera electronic flash.

- **Flash units.** You must have at least one Sony flash from those listed above for the wireless commander to trigger. Ideally, you'll have several to allow you to configure multi-light setups, so plan on spending $250 to $600 for each remote flash.

- **Receivers.** As I write this, only the HVL-F60RM and HVL-F45RM can be triggered by radio controls. So, if you're using any other wireless-compatible (optical only) flash, it must be connected to a FA-WRR1 wireless radio receiver ($149). The flash units are *not* sensitive to radio controls on their own.

- **Light stands or an assistant.** The wireless commander generally resides on the multi-interface shoe of your camera, so you'll need light stands to accept each receiver, which has its own hot shoe your flash is attached to. Alternatively, you can enlist the aid of an assistant to hold the receiver/flash in proper position.

- **VMC-MM1 Multi Terminal cable (optional).** This $28 cable allows you to connect another one of those $149 wireless receivers to a second (or third…) *camera* so the auxiliary cameras fire in unison with the flash and main camera. This very cool feature will appeal to sports and news photographers covering events.

Each commander transmitter can support up to 15 receivers in any combination of flash units and slave cameras, with your choice of 14 different channels (reducing those conflicts at the next presidential convention you cover in 2020). All the devices on a particular channel can be divided up among as many as five different groups, so you could conceivably have a dozen or more flash units spread among all those groups to provide very sophisticated lighting effects, over a range of more than 98 feet (30 meters).

But wait! There's more. The HVL-F60RM, HVL-F45RM, and FA-WRC1M wireless radio commanders give you Manual, TTL, and Group control of flashes, and power adjustment from full power (1/1) to 1/256th power in 1/3-stop increments. The 3.3-ounce commander and 3-ounce receiver each run on two AA batteries. While I don't expect to see many a7R III owners springing for this system, it's nice for ambitious photographers to know that these capabilities are there for them to grow into. Eventually, Sony will introduce additional radio-capable flash units and commanders, probably at more affordable prices.

14

Troubleshooting and Prevention

One of the nice things about modern mirrorless cameras like the Sony a7R III is that they have fewer mechanical moving parts to fail, so they are less likely to "wear out." No film transport mechanism, no wind lever or motor drive, and no complicated mechanical linkages from camera to lens to physically stop down the lens aperture. Instead, tiny, reliable motors are built into each lens (and you lose the use of only that lens should something fail).

Of course, the camera also has a moving physical shutter (which augments the electronic shutter "curtains"). It can fail, but the shutter is built rugged enough that you can expect it to last several hundred thousand shutter cycles or more. Unless you're shooting sports in continuous mode day in and day out, the shutter on your Sony a7R III is likely to last as long as you expect to use the camera.

The only other things on the camera that move are switches, dials, buttons, and the doors that open to allow you to remove and insert the memory card and battery. I'm not fond of the removable battery door mechanism, which I have to use each time I mount the battery grip to my camera, but it hasn't failed me yet. Unless you're extraordinarily clumsy or unlucky or give your camera a good whack while it is in use, there's not a lot that can go wrong mechanically with your Sony a7R III.

On the other hand, one of the chief drawbacks of modern electronic cameras is that they are modern *electronic* cameras. Your Sony a7R III is fully dependent on two different batteries, the main NP-FZ100 that powers most functions, and a smaller inaccessible battery within the camera's innards that stores setup and settings information. Without them, the camera can't be used. There are numerous other electrical and electronic connections in the camera (many connected to those mechanical switches and dials), and components like the color LCD that can potentially fail or suffer damage. The camera also relies on its "operating system," or *firmware*, which can be plagued by bugs that cause unexpected behavior. Luckily, electronic components are generally more reliable and trouble-free, especially when compared to their mechanical counterparts from the pre-electronic film camera days.

Digital cameras have problems unique to their breed, too; the most troublesome being the need to clean the sensor of dust and grime periodically. This chapter will show you how to diagnose problems, fix some common ills, and, importantly, learn how to avoid some of them in the future.

Upgrading Your Firmware

As I said, the firmware in your Sony a7R III is the camera's operating system, which handles everything from menu display (including fonts, colors, and the actual entries themselves), what languages are available, and even support for specific devices and features. Upgrading the firmware to a new version makes it possible to add new features while fixing some of the bugs that sneak in.

Official firmware for your Sony a7R III is given a version number that you can view by turning the power on, pressing the MENU button, and navigating to Version in the Setup menu. The first number in the string represents the major release number, while the second and third represent less significant upgrades and minor tweaks, respectively. Theoretically, a camera should have a firmware version number of 1.0 when it is introduced, but vendors have been known to do some minor fixes during testing and unveil a camera with a 1.1 firmware designation. If a given model is available long enough, it can evolve into significant upgrades, such as the current 2.0 or higher designations.

Firmware upgrades are used for both cameras and certain lenses (each listed separately in the Version entry), most frequently to fix bugs in the software, and much less frequently to add or enhance features. The exact changes made to the firmware are generally spelled out in the firmware release announcement. You can examine the remedies provided and decide if a given firmware patch is important to you. If not, you can usually safely wait a while before going through the bother of upgrading your firmware—at least long enough for the early adopters to report whether the bug fixes have introduced new bugs of their own. Each new firmware release incorporates the changes from previous releases, so if you skip a minor upgrade you should have no problems.

WARNING

Don't open the memory card door or turn off the camera while your old firmware is being overwritten. You *should* have sufficient power for the camera while upgrading, because Sony requires you to connect the camera to your computer using a USB cable, and that cable conveys power from the host computer as well as information.

Upgrading your firmware is ridiculously easy. As I write this, the only firmware update was Version 1.01, announced in December 2017. The following is a fictitious example that may not coincide exactly with the procedure you will use, as Sony changes the process from time to time. Simply follow these steps:

1. **Search for firmware.** Visit the Sony support site for your area, such as esupport.sony.com and navigate to the Drivers and Software page for your camera. It will vary by country, but you can quickly click the Drivers and Software link, enter model information about your camera, select your operating system, such as Windows 10 64 Bit, and eventually arrive at the Firmware download page.

2. **Download firmware.** You'll see a message like the following when you reach the download page. Click the Download button.

   UPDATE: ILCE-7RM3 System Software Update.

   Release Date 10/19/2019

   Version 2.00

   File Size 236.80MB

   [Download]

3. **Check USB Connection status.** Make sure the USB Connection entry in the Setup 4 menu is set to Mass Storage. Then turn off your camera.

4. **Connect camera to your computer.** Link to a USB port on your Internet-connected computer using the USB cable that came with your camera for use when recharging the battery. Then turn on the camera.

5. **Open firmware file.** It will have a name like Update_ILCE7RM3V200.exe (for Windows) or Update_ILCE7RM3V200.dng (for Macs). The version number will vary, depending on the particular release it is.

6. **Follow the instructions** shown on the update utility, pictured in Figure 14.1.

7. **Turn off camera.** When finished, you can turn off the camera. It will have the new firmware installed the next time you power up.

Protecting Your LCD

The color LCD monitor on the back of your Sony a7R III almost seems like a target for banging, scratching, and other abuse. Fortunately, it's quite rugged, and a few errant knocks are unlikely to shatter the protective cover over the LCD, and scratches won't easily mar its surface. However, if you want to be on the safe side, there are a number of protective products you can purchase to keep your LCD safe.

Figure 14.1 The firmware update utility.

Sony itself offers the PCK-LG1 (about $30) semi-hard protective sheet. It's not too costly and includes an anti-fingerprint coating to reduce smudges. Like other such protectors, it fastens securely to the LCD monitor with a residue-free adhesive and can be easily removed by threading a piece of dental floss between the sheet and screen. I prefer the ultra-thin (0.3mm) glass GGS screens available on Amazon and from a variety of other sources for anywhere from around $10 to $20 for the deluxe "Larmour" version, which use a strong silicon adhesive for gapless mounting. You can also use simple plastic overlay sheets, or "skins" made for smartphones, cut to fit your LCD.

Troubleshooting Memory Cards

Sometimes good memory cards go bad. Sometimes good photographers can treat their memory cards badly. It's possible that a memory card that works fine in one camera won't be recognized when inserted into another. In the worst case, you can have a card full of important photos and find that the card seems to be corrupted and you can't access any of them. Don't panic! If these scenarios sound horrific to you, there are lots of things you can do to prevent them from happening, and a variety of remedies available if they do occur. You'll want to take some time—before disaster strikes—to consider your options.

All Your Eggs in One Basket?

The "Don't put all your eggs in one basket" myth is one of the most contentious in photography, second only to the "protective" filter myth. Most of us have had a memory card fail and have lost—or have thought we lost—some photos that we'd rather have kept. That certainly underlines the importance of backing up our pictures to other media at regular intervals, even while traveling. But whether multiple smaller cards offers an additional degree of protection is a separate issue.

Given the 42.4MB images my a7R III produces, as I noted at the beginning of this book, I prefer the 64GB Sony G-series SDXC cards and will purchase 128GB cards when the prices come down a little. The debate about whether it's better to use one large memory card or several smaller ones has been going on since even before there were memory cards!

I can remember when computer users wondered whether it was smarter to install a pair of 200 megabyte (not *gigabyte*) hard drives in their computer, or if they should go for one of those new-fangled 500MB models. By the same token, a few years ago the conventional wisdom insisted that you ought to use 128MB memory cards rather than the huge 512MB versions. Today, most of the arguments involve 32B cards vs. 64GB cards, with the implication that smaller cards are "better" in this regard. Conventional wisdom is often more conventional than wise.

For professional users, this does make sense. I have professional wedding photographer friends who chortle at the folly of using large memory cards (I've actually witnessed the chortling), and they have special reasons for their preference. Of course, in addition to multiple cards, they use second shooters, copy photos on-site from a full memory card to a laptop, and employ other techniques in order to avoid having to ask the bride and groom whether it would be possible to restage a wedding. When your living depends on never losing *any* pictures, different rules apply.

But most of us have no cause to fear using mature memory storage technologies. Resorting to lots of small cards instead of fewer large ones may actually increase the chances of losing some. While I don't want to be a pioneer in working with 512GB memory cards (and have no need to do so), but I'm perfectly comfortable with my 64GB and larger cards for the following reasons:

- **Memory cards don't magically wait until they are full before they fail.** You will not automatically lose 64GB worth of photos, rather than 32GB if a memory card implodes. If you typically shoot 16GB worth of images on a typical day before you have the chance to back them up to your computer or laptop, then that's the most you are at risk for under average circumstances. Whether you're using a 16GB, 32GB 64GB, or 128GB card, the amount of images you shoot in a *typical* session prior to backup will be the number you actually may lose. The only time I actually fill up my 128GB memory cards is when I am traveling, and in those instances, I have already backed up each day's shooting to multiple additional media. Most of the time, all a larger memory card does is give you greater flexibility when you want to shoot *more* in one session and don't want or don't have time to swap cards.

Many photojournalists and sports photographers change cards when they are 80 percent full to avoid missing a crucial shot. Instead of interrupting your shoot to swap out a 16GB card that becomes full, you can go ahead and shoot 17 or 18GB on your 32GB card and change media during lulls in the festivities. In truth, the biggest danger comes from waiting too long—say several days—to back up your images. We all know photographers who have New Years Eve, July 4, and Thanksgiving images on a single card, and who *never* backup their photos.

- **64GB cards aren't twice as likely to fail as 32GB cards,** although many seem to feel that's so. Indeed, I've heard the same advice to use "safer" 256MB cards, 2 GB cards, or 4GB cards virtually up the line as capacities have increased. Once a fabrication technology is mature, the reliability of particular sizes is the same across the board. Any easy way to tell is to compare the per-gigabyte costs for the card. Once a particular card is less than twice the cost of a card with half the capacity, you can bet the technology is solid.

- **Using multiple smaller cards may increase your odds of losing photos.** Memory cards do fail, but that most often happens from user error. The first 128GB card I bought, a Sony model, failed within a few months, because I put it in my wallet for "safekeeping" and accidentally folded it nearly in half. It's also common for photographers to lose cards, put them through a wash and dry cycle, or perform other atrocities unrelated to the reliability of the card itself.

  Yes, if you use smaller cards you may lose half as many photos, but you might also find that more cards equates to a higher risk of losing one or damaging one through stupidity. I find it's better to use the minimum number of photo "baskets" and then make sure nothing happens to that basket. If all your images are important, the fact that you've lost 100 of them rather than 200 pictures isn't very comforting.

- **When your family goes on vacation, do you split up family members to travel in several smaller cars?** After all, in a terrible collision, with multiple cars you might lose only a *couple* of your kinfolk rather than all of them. Keep in mind that your family is much more important to you than your photos, and the odds of being in a traffic accident is much *greater* than encountering a faulty memory card. Humans are susceptible to the cognitive fallacy "neglect of probability." I've taken hundreds of thousands of pictures and lost two memory cards, and I know three other photographers who've had memory card problems. On the other hand, I've driven hundreds of thousands of miles and been in four traffic accidents and know a dozen people who have had auto mishaps. Should my family be riding around in different cars while I stick to 16GB memory cards?

- **The typical memory card is rated for a Mean Time Between Failures of 1,000,000 hours of use.** That's constant use 24/7 for more than 100 years! According to the manufacturers, they are good for 10,000 insertions in your camera, and should be able to retain their data (and that's without an external power source) for something on the order of 11 years. Of course, with the millions of cards in use, there are bound to be a few lemons here or there.

So, what can you do? Here are some options for preventing loss of valuable images:

- **Internal backup.** Your a7R III has dual memory card slots, so when your photos are particularly important use the Backup feature to write copies to both cards simultaneously. Or, if you're on vacation, copy a day's shots onto another card when you get back to your hotel room.

- **External backup.** It's easy to physically transfer your images to a laptop, smart device, or other backup storage, particularly when you're on vacation. When I'm traveling, I take a tiny MacBook Air and at least two 1TB portable drives and copy my pictures to them frequently. (See Figure 14.2.) Ideally, one of your backups should be offsite, and that's difficult while traveling. However, offsite can be a DVD you burn and mail home, or a storage site in the cloud.

- **Transmit your images.** Another option is to transmit your images frequently over a network to your laptop or smart device. Or upload them to a cloud drive, such as iCloud, Google Drive, OneDrive, or DropBox. Many cameras have that option.

- **Interleaving.** You can also interleave your shots. Perhaps you don't shoot weddings, but you do go on vacation from time to time. Take 100 or so pictures on one card. Then, replace it with a different card and shoot another 100. Repeat these steps with diligence (you'd have to be determined to go through this degree of inconvenience), and, if you use four or more memory cards (of whatever capacity), you'll find your pictures from each location scattered among the different media. If you lose or damage one (which, alas, may be more likely because of the use of those multiple cards), you'll still have *some* pictures from all the various stops on your trip on the other cards. That's more work than I like to do, especially when it comes to sorting out the pictures back at home, but it's an option.

- **Be smart.** If you're having problems, the first thing you should do is stop using that memory card. Don't take any more pictures. Don't do anything with the card until you've figured out what's wrong. Your second line of defense (your first line is to be sufficiently careful with your cards that you avoid problems in the first place) is to do no harm that hasn't already been done. If necessary, decide on a course of action (such as using a data recovery service or software) before you risk damaging the data on your card further. If you take a picture of your business card as the first photo in a session, should the memory card be lost, your odds of having it returned to you are increased.

Figure 14.2
Back up your images when traveling.

What Can Go Wrong?

There are lots of things that can go wrong with your memory card, but the ones that aren't caused by human stupidity are statistically very rare. Yes, a memory card's internal bit bin or controller can suddenly fail due to a manufacturing error or some inexplicable event caused by old age. However, if your memory card works for the first week or two that you own it, it should work forever. There's really not a lot that can wear out.

Given the reliability of solid-state memory, compared to magnetic memory, though, it's more likely that your memory problems will stem from something that you do. Memory cards are small and easy to misplace if you're not careful. For that reason, it's a good idea to keep them in their original cases or a "card safe" offered by Gepe (www.gepecardsafe.com), Pelican (www.pelican.com), and others. Always placing your memory card in a case can provide protection from the second-most common mishap that befalls memory cards: the common household laundry. If you slip a memory card in a pocket, rather than a case or your camera bag, often enough, sooner or later it's going to end up in the washing machine and probably the clothes dryer, too. There are plenty of reports of relieved digital camera owners who've laundered their memory cards and found they still worked fine, but it's not uncommon for such mistreatment to do some damage.

Memory cards can also be stomped on, accidentally bent, dropped into the ocean, chewed by pets, and otherwise rendered unusable in myriad ways. It's also possible to force a card into your Sony a7R III's memory card slot incorrectly if you're diligent enough. Or, if the card is formatted in your computer with a memory card reader, your Sony a7R III may fail to recognize it. Occasionally, I've found that a memory card used in one camera would fail if used in a different camera (until I reformatted it in Windows, and then again in the camera). Every once in a while, a card goes completely bad and—seemingly—can't be salvaged.

Another way to lose images is to do commonplace things with your memory card at an inopportune time. If you remove the card from the Sony a7R III while the camera is writing images to the card, you'll lose any photos in the buffer and may damage the file structure of the card, making it difficult or impossible to retrieve the other pictures you've taken. The same thing can happen if you remove the memory card from your computer's card reader while the computer is writing to the card (say, to erase files you've already moved to your computer). You can avoid this by *not* using your computer to erase files on a memory card but, instead, always reformatting the card in your Sony a7R III before you use it again.

What Can You Do?

Pay attention: As I mentioned, if you experience problems with a card, stop using that card immediately. Don't do anything else with the card until you've figured out what's wrong.

Now that you've calmed down, the first thing to check is whether you've actually inserted a card in the camera. If you've set the camera in the Shooting menu so that Shoot w/o Card has been turned on, it's entirely possible (although not particularly plausible) that you've been snapping away with no memory card to store the pictures to, which can lead to massive disappointment later on. Of course, the No Memory Card message appears on the LCD when the camera is powered up, and it is superimposed on the review image after every shot, but maybe you're inattentive, or aren't using picture review. You can avoid all this by turning the Shoot w/o Card feature off and leaving it off.

Things get more exciting when the card itself is put in jeopardy. If you lose a card, there's not a lot you can do other than take a picture of a similar card and print up some Have You Seen This Lost Flash Memory? flyers to post on utility poles all around town.

If all you care about is reusing the card, and have resigned yourself to losing the pictures, try reformatting the card in your camera. You may find that reformatting removes the corrupted data and restores your card to health. Sometimes I've had success reformatting a card in my computer using a memory card reader (this is normally a no-no because your operating system doesn't understand the needs of your Sony a7R III), and *then* reformatting again in the camera.

If your memory card is not behaving properly, and you *do* want to recover your images, things get a little more complicated. If your pictures are very valuable, either to you or to others (for example, a wedding), you can always turn to professional data recovery firms. Be prepared to pay hundreds of dollars to get your pictures back, but these pros often do an amazing job. You wouldn't want them working on your memory card on behalf of the police if you'd tried to erase some incriminating pictures. There are many firms of this type, and I've never used them myself, so I can't offer a recommendation. Use a Google search to turn up a ton of them. I use a software program called RescuePro, which came free with one of my SanDisk memory cards.

A more reasonable approach is to try special data recovery software you can install on your computer and use to attempt to resurrect your "lost" images yourself. They may not actually be gone completely. Perhaps your memory card's "table of contents" is jumbled, or only a few pictures are damaged in such a way that your camera and computer can't read some or any of the pictures on the card. Some of the available software was written specifically to reconstruct lost pictures, while other utilities are more general-purpose applications that can be used with any media, including floppy disks and hard disk drives. They have names like OnTrack, Photo Rescue 2, Digital Image Recovery, MediaRecover, Image Recall, and the aptly named Recover My Photos.

DIMINISHING RETURNS

Usually, once you've recovered any images on a memory card, reformatted it, and returned it to service, it will function reliably for the rest of its useful life. However, if you find a particular card going bad more than once, you'll almost certainly want to stop using it forever. See if you can get it replaced by the manufacturer, if you can, but, in the case of memory card failures, the third time is never the charm.

Cleaning Your Sensor

There's no avoiding dust. No matter how careful you are, some of it is going to settle on your camera and on the mounts of your lenses, eventually making its way inside your camera to settle in the mirror chamber. As you take photos, the physical shutter movement causes the dust to become airborne and eventually come to rest atop your sensor. There, dust and particles can show up in every single picture you take at a small enough aperture to bring the foreign matter into sharp focus. No matter how careful you are and how cleanly you work, eventually you will get some of this dust on your camera's sensor.

Fortunately, one of the Sony a7R III's most useful features is the automatic sensor cleaning system that reduces or eliminates the need to clean your camera's sensor manually. Sony has applied anti-static coatings to the sensor and other portions of the camera body interior to counter charge build-ups that attract dust. The sensor carriage vibrates ultrasonically to shake loose any dust. You can activate sensor cleaning at any time.

Dust the FAQs, Ma'am

Here are some of the most frequently asked questions about sensor dust issues.

Q. I see a bright spot in the same place in all of my photos. Is that sensor dust?

A. You've probably got either a "hot" pixel or one that is permanently "stuck" due to a defect in the sensor. A hot pixel is one that shows up as a bright spot only during long exposures as the sensor warms. A pixel stuck in the "on" position always appears in the image. Both show up as bright red, green, or blue pixels, usually surrounded by a small cluster of other improperly illuminated pixels, caused by the camera's interpolating the hot or stuck pixel into its surroundings, as shown in Figure 14.3. A stuck pixel can also be permanently dark. Either kind is likely to show up when they contrast with plain, evenly colored areas of your image.

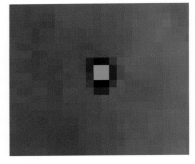

Figure 14.3 A stuck pixel is surrounded by improperly interpolated pixels created by the Sony a7R III's demosaicing algorithm.

Bad pixels can also show up on your camera's color LCD panel, but, unless they are abundant, the wisest course is to just ignore them.

Q. I see an irregular out-of-focus blob in the same place in my photos. Is that sensor dust?

A. Yes. Sensor contaminants can take the form of tiny spots, larger blobs, or even curvy lines if they are caused by minuscule fibers that have settled on the sensor. They'll appear out of focus because they aren't actually on the sensor surface but, rather, a fraction of a millimeter above it on the filter that covers the sensor. The smaller the f/stop used, the more in-focus the dust becomes. At large apertures, it may not be visible at all.

Q. I never see any dust on my sensor. What's all the fuss about?

A. Those who never have dust problems with their Sony a7R III fall into one of four categories: those for whom the camera's automatic dust removal features are working well; those who seldom change their lenses and have clean working habits that minimize the amount of dust that invades their cameras in the first place; those who simply don't notice the dust (often because they don't shoot many macro photos or other pictures using the small f/stops that makes dust evident in their images); and those who are very, very lucky.

Identifying and Dealing with Dust

Sensor dust is less of a problem than it might be because it shows up only under certain circumstances. Indeed, you might have dust on your sensor right now and not be aware if it. The dust doesn't actually settle on the sensor itself, but, rather, on a protective filter a very tiny distance above the sensor, subjecting it to the phenomenon of *depth-of-focus*. Depth-of-focus is the distance the focal plane can be moved and still render an object in sharp focus. At f/2.8 to f/5.6 or even smaller, sensor dust, particularly if small, is likely to be outside the range of depth-of-focus and blur into an unnoticeable dot.

However, if you're shooting at f/16 to f/22 or smaller, those dust motes suddenly pop into focus. Dust spots can easily show up in your images if you're shooting large, empty areas that are light colored. Dust motes are most likely to show up in the sky, as in Figure 14.4, or in white

Figure 14.4
Only the dust spots in the sky are apparent in this shot.

backgrounds of your seamless product shots and are less likely to be a problem in images that contain lots of dark areas and detail.

To see if you have dust on your sensor, take a few test shots of a plain, blank surface (such as a piece of paper or a cloudless sky) at small f/stops, such as f/22, and a few wide open. Open Photoshop, copy several shots into a single document in separate layers, then flip back and forth between layers to see if any spots you see are present in all layers. You may have to boost contrast and sharpness to make the dust easier to spot.

Avoiding Dust

Of course, the easiest way to protect your sensor from dust is to prevent it from settling on the sensor in the first place. Some lenses come with rubberized seals around the lens mounts that help keep dust from infiltrating, but you'll find that dust will still find a way to get inside. Here are my tips for eliminating the problem before it begins.

- **Clean environment.** Avoid working in dusty areas if you can do so. Hah! Serious photographers will take this one with a grain of salt, because it usually makes sense to go where the pictures are. Only a few of us are so paranoid about sensor dust (considering that it is so easily removed) that we'll avoid moderately grimy locations just to protect something that is, when you get down to it, just a tool. If you find a great picture opportunity at a raging fire, during a sandstorm, or while surrounded by dust clouds, you might hesitate to take the picture, but, with a little caution (don't remove your lens in these situations and clean the camera afterward!) you can still shoot. However, it still makes sense to store your camera in a clean environment. One place cameras and lenses pick up a lot of dust is inside a camera bag. Clean your bag from time to time, and you can avoid problems.

- **Clean lenses.** There are a few paranoid types that avoid swapping lenses in order to minimize the chance of dust getting inside their cameras. It makes more sense just to use a blower or brush to dust off the rear lens mount of the replacement lens first, so you won't be introducing dust into your camera simply by attaching a new, dusty lens. Do this before you remove the lens from your camera, and then avoid stirring up dust before making the exchange.

- **Work fast.** Minimize the time your camera is lens-less and exposed to dust. That means having your replacement lens ready and dusted off, and a place to set down the old lens as soon as it is removed, so you can quickly attach the new lens.

- **Let gravity help you.** Face the camera downward when the lens is detached so any dust in the mirror box will tend to fall away from the sensor. Turn your back to any breezes, indoor forced air vents, fans, or other sources of dust to minimize infiltration.

- **Protect the lens you just removed.** Once you've attached the new lens, quickly put the end cap on the one you just removed to reduce the dust that might fall on it.

■ **Clean out the vestibule.** From time to time, remove the lens while in a relatively dust-free environment and use a blower bulb like the ones shown in Figure 14.5 (*not* compressed air or a vacuum hose) to clean out the mirror box area. A blower bulb is generally safer than a can of compressed air, or a strong positive/negative airflow, which can tend to drive dust further into nooks and crannies.

■ **Be prepared.** If you're embarking on an important shooting session, it's a good idea to clean your sensor *now*, rather than come home with hundreds or thousands of images with dust spots caused by flecks that were sitting on your sensor before you even started. Before I left on my recent trip to Spain, I put both cameras I was taking through a rigid cleaning regimen, figuring they could remain dust-free for a measly 10 days. I even left my bulky blower bulb at home. It was a big mistake, but my intentions were good.

■ **Clone out existing spots in your image editor.** Photoshop and other editors have a clone tool or healing brush you can use to copy pixels from surrounding areas over the dust spot or dead pixel. This process can be tedious, especially if you have lots of dust spots and/or lots of images to be corrected. The advantage is that this sort of manual fix-it probably will do the least damage to the rest of your photo. Only the cloned pixels will be affected.

■ **Use filtration in your image editor.** A semi-smart filter like Photoshop's Dust & Scratches filter can remove dust and other artifacts by selectively blurring areas that the plug-in decides represent dust spots. This method can work well if you have many dust spots, because you won't need to patch them manually. However, any automated method like this has the possibility of blurring areas of your image that you didn't intend to soften.

Figure 14.5
Use a robust air bulb for cleaning your sensor.

Sensor Cleaning

Those new to the concept of sensor dust actually hesitate before deciding to clean their camera themselves. Isn't it a better idea to pack up your Sony a7R III and send it to a service center so their crack technical staff can do the job for you? Or, at the very least, shouldn't you let the friendly folks at your local camera store do it?

Of course, if you choose to let someone else clean your sensor, they will be using methods that are more or less identical to the techniques you would use yourself. None of these techniques are difficult, and the only difference between their cleaning and your cleaning is that they might have done it dozens or hundreds of times. If you're careful, you can do just as good a job.

Of course, vendors like Sony may not tell you this, but it's not because they don't trust you. It's not that difficult for a real goofball to mess up his camera by hurrying or taking a shortcut. Perhaps the person uses the "Bulb" method of holding the shutter open and a finger slips, allowing the shutter curtain to close on top of a sensor cleaning brush. Or, someone tries to clean the sensor using masking tape, and ends up with goo all over its surface. If Sony recommended *any* method that's mildly risky, someone would do it wrong, and then the company would face lawsuits from those who'd contend they did it exactly in the way the vendor suggested, so the ruined camera is not their fault.

You can see that vendors like Sony tend to be conservative in their recommendations, and, in doing so, make it seem as if sensor cleaning is more daunting and dangerous than it really is. Some vendors recommend only dust-off cleaning, through the use of reasonably gentle blasts of air, while condemning more serious scrubbing with swabs and cleaning fluids. However, these cleaning kits for the exact types of cleaning they recommended against are for sale in Japan only, where, apparently, your average photographer is more dexterous than those of us in the rest of the world. These kits are similar to those used by official repair staff to clean your sensor if you decide to send your camera in for a dust-up.

There are three basic kinds of cleaning processes that can be used to remove dusty and sticky stuff that settles on your dSLR's sensor. All of these must be performed with the shutter locked open. I'll describe these methods and provide instructions for locking the shutter later in this section.

- **Air cleaning.** This process involves squirting blasts of air inside your camera with the shutter locked open. This works well for dust that's not clinging stubbornly to your sensor.
- **Brush cleaning.** A soft, very fine brush is passed across the surface of the sensor's filter, dislodging mildly persistent dust particles and sweeping them off the imager.
- **Liquid cleaning.** A soft swab dipped in a cleaning solution such as ethanol is used to wipe the sensor filter, removing more obstinate particles.

Air Cleaning

Your first attempts at cleaning your sensor should always involve gentle blasts of air. Many times, you'll be able to dislodge dust spots, which will fall off the sensor and, with luck, out of the interior. Attempt one of the other methods only when you've already tried air cleaning and it didn't remove all the dust.

Here are some tips for doing air cleaning:

- **Use a clean, powerful air bulb.** Your best bet is bulb cleaners designed for the job, like the Giottos Rocket. Smaller bulbs, like those air bulbs with a brush attached sometimes sold for lens cleaning or weak nasal aspirators, may not provide sufficient air or a strong enough blast to do much good.

- **Hold the Sony a7R III pointed downward.** Then look up into the cavity behind the lens mount as you squirt your air blasts, increasing the odds that gravity will help pull the expelled dust downward, away from the sensor. You may have to use some imagination in positioning yourself. (See Figure 14.6.)

- **Never use air canisters.** The propellant inside these cans can permanently coat your sensor if you tilt the can while spraying. It's not worth taking a chance.

- **Avoid air compressors.** Super-strong blasts of air are likely to force dust under the sensor filter.

Figure 14.6 Point the camera downward.

Brush Cleaning

If your dust is a little more stubborn and can't be dislodged by air alone, you may want to try a brush, charged with static electricity, that can pick off dust spots by electrical attraction. One good, but expensive, option is the Sensor Brush sold at www.visibledust.com. You need a 24mm version, like the one shown in Figure 14.7, that can be stroked across the short dimension of your Sony a7R III's sensor.

Ordinary artist's brushes are much too coarse and stiff and have fibers that are tangled or can come loose and settle on your sensor. A good sensor brush's fibers are resilient and described as "thinner than a human hair." Moreover, the brush has a wooden handle that reduces the risk of static sparks.

Brush cleaning is done with a dry brush by gently swiping the surface of the sensor filter with the tip. The dust particles are attracted to the brush particles and cling to them. You should clean the brush with compressed air before and after each use and store it in an appropriate air-tight container between applications to keep it clean and dust-free. Although these special brushes are expensive, one should last you a long time.

Figure 14.7 A proper brush is required for dusting off your sensor.

Figure 14.8 The motor in the Arctic Butterfly flutters the brush tips for a few minutes to charge them for picking up dust (left). Then, turn off the power and flick the tip above the surface of the sensor (right).

I like the Arctic Butterfly, shown in Figure 14.8. You activate the built-in motor that spins the brush at high speed to charge it with static electricity. Then, shut the motor off and pass the charged brush *above* the sensor surface so that dust will leap off the sensor and onto the brush.

Liquid Cleaning

Unfortunately, you'll often encounter really stubborn dust spots that can't be removed with a blast of air or flick of a brush. These spots may be combined with some grease or a liquid that causes them to stick to the sensor filter's surface. In such cases, liquid cleaning with a swab may be necessary. During my first clumsy attempts to clean my own sensor, I accidentally got my blower bulb tip too close to the sensor, and some sort of deposit from the tip of the bulb ended up on the sensor. I panicked until I discovered that liquid cleaning did a good job of removing whatever it was that took up residence on my sensor.

You can make your own swabs out of pieces of plastic (some use fast-food restaurant knives, with the tip cut at an angle to the proper size) covered with a soft cloth or Pec-Pad, as shown in Figures 14.9 and 14.10. However, if you've got the bucks to spend, you can't go wrong with good-quality commercial sensor cleaning swabs, such as those sold by Photographic Solutions, Inc. (www.photosol.com).

You want a sturdy swab that won't bend or break so you can apply gentle pressure to the swab as you wipe the sensor surface. Use the swab with methanol (as pure as you can get it, particularly medical grade; other ingredients can leave a residue), or the Eclipse solution also sold by Photographic Solutions. Eclipse is actually quite a bit purer than even medical-grade methanol. A couple drops

Figure 14.9 You can make your own sensor swab from a plastic knife that's been truncated.

Figure 14.10 Carefully wrap a Pec-Pad around the swab.

of solution should be enough, unless you have a spot that's extremely difficult to remove. In that case, you may need to use extra solution on the swab to help "soak" the dirt off.

Once you overcome your nervousness at touching the protective cover of your Sony a7R III's sensor, the process is easy. You'll wipe continuously with the swab in one direction, then flip it over and wipe in the other direction. You need to completely wipe the entire surface; otherwise, you may end up depositing the dust you collect at the far end of your stroke. Wipe; don't rub.

If you want a close-up look at your sensor to make sure the dust has been removed, you can pay $50–$100 for a special sensor "microscope" with an illuminator. Or, you can do like I do and work with a plain old Carson MiniBrite PO-55 illuminated 5X magnifier, as seen in Figure 14.11. It has a built-in LED and, held a few inches from the lens mount with the lens removed from your Sony a7R III, provides a sharp, close-up view of the sensor, with enough contrast to reveal any dust that remains. You can read more about this great device at http://dslrguides.com/carson.

Figure 14.11
An illuminated magnifier like this Carson MiniBrite PO-55 can be used as a 'scope to view your sensor.

Index